Imagining Methodism
in Eighteenth-Century Britain

Imagining Methodism in Eighteenth-Century Britain

❋ Enthusiasm, Belief & the Borders of the Self ❋

MISTY G. ANDERSON

THE JOHNS HOPKINS UNIVERSITY PRESS
Baltimore

© 2012 The Johns Hopkins University Press
All rights reserved. Published 2012
Printed in the United States of America on acid-free paper
9 8 7 6 5 4 3 2 1

The Johns Hopkins University Press
2715 North Charles Street
Baltimore, Maryland 21218-4363
www.press.jhu.edu

Library of Congress Cataloging-in-Publication Data

Anderson, Misty G., 1967–
   Imagining Methodism in eighteenth-century Britain : enthusiasm, belief, and the borders of the self / Misty G. Anderson.
     p. cm.
   Includes bibliographical references and index.
   ISBN-13: 978-1-4214-0480-6 (hdbk. : acid-free paper)
   ISBN-13: 978-1-4214-0528-5 (electronic)
   ISBN-10: 1-4214-0480-X (hdbk. : acid-free paper)
   ISBN-10: 1-4214-0528-8 (electronic)
   1. English literature—18th century—History and criticism. 2. Religion in literature. 3. Methodism in literature. 4. Great Britain—Intellectual life—18th century. I. Title.
   PR448.R45A53   2012
   820.9′38287—dc23   2011034744

A catalog record for this book is available from the British Library.

Special discounts are available for bulk purchases of this book. For more information, please contact Special Sales at 410-516-6936 or specialsales@press.jhu.edu.

The Johns Hopkins University Press uses environmentally friendly book materials, including recycled text paper that is composed of at least 30 percent post-consumer waste, whenever possible.

For Trevor, Andy, and John

Contents

	Acknowledgments	ix
	Introduction. Longing to Believe: Methodism and Modernity	1
1	Historicizing Methodism	34
2	The New Man: Desire, Transformation, and the Methodist Body	70
3	Words Made Flesh: *Fanny Hill* and the Language of Passion	100
4	Actors and Ghosts: Methodism in the Theater of the Real	130
5	"My Lord, My Love": The Performance of Public Intimacy and the Methodist Hymn	171
6	A Usable Past: Reconciliation in *Humphry Clinker* and *The Spiritual Quixote*	200
	Afterword. 1778 and Beyond	232
	Notes	239
	Bibliography	257
	Index	273

Acknowledgments

Many individuals and institutions have made this book possible, and it is a pleasure to thank some of them here. The University of Tennessee's Hodges Better English Fund, the College of Arts and Sciences's Professional Development Awards, department heads John Zomchick and Chuck Maland, Dean Carolyn Hodges, Provost Susan Martin, and Dean Bruce Burstein supported the research leave during which much of the work for this project was completed. Their unflagging support has been a great boon to this project and an inspiration to me. The Beinecke Library's John D. and Rose H. Jackson Fellowship and the Lewis Walpole Library's Visiting Research Fellowship provided invaluable opportunities for archival research and precious writing time. Alan Rutenberg from the UT Office of Research was a great help in applying for fellowships and helping me think about this book for multiple audiences. Matthew McAdam at the Johns Hopkins University Press and his entire staff have been wonderful. I am grateful to Matt for his faith in this project and for finding thoughtful readers for the manuscript. Kara Reiter and Helen Myers brought keen eyes and expertise that helped to bring the book into its present form.

Much of this book was written and researched while at Yale, where many friends and colleagues made my stay a delight. Ala Ayers, Barbara Benedict, Jill Campbell, James Caudle, Julia Fawcett, Todd Gilman, Dan Gustafson, Hilary Menges, Claude Rawson, Joe Roach, and Nicole Wright welcomed me into the English Department, the Yale libraries, and the regional eighteenth-century studies working group. Gordon Turnbull, General Editor of the Yale Boswell Editions, deserves special thanks for Methodist-spotting, a timely reading of chapter 4, and a hilarious series of lunches. At the Yale Divinity School, Patrick Evans, Jan Fournier, Siobhán Garrigan, Bill and Maria Goettler, Martin Jean, Dale Peterson, Anna Ramirez, Markus Rathey, Shelly Stackhouse, Paul Stuehrenberg, and Tom Troeger embraced me as part of that wonderful community, offered their expertise, and made me feel at home as I rambled around their library. The librarians and archivists at the Lewis Walpole Library were and are splendid. I owe special thanks to Maggie Powell for supporting my time there and accommodating my schedule over the course of many visits. Ellen Cordes, Todd Falkowski, Paul Grant-Costa, Brian Parker, Cynthia Roman, and Sue Walker provided fantastic research assistance throughout this project. They are cherished colleagues, friends, and marvelous croquet players. Cindy Roman in particular kept an eye out for new prints and gave me the opportunity to curate the "Sacred Satire" show at the Walpole, with her expertise always at my back. At the Beinecke, Kathryn James, Leah Jehan, and Naomi Saito were unfailingly helpful.

Many audiences and respondents have been kind enough to give feedback, ask great questions, and share my enthusiasm for enthusiasts; they have been integral to the development of this project. Colleagues at the University of Michigan, the University of Arkansas, Conway, and the Eighteenth-Century Studies Group at the Newberry Library invited me to speak about the material in chapter 2, "The New Man: Desire, Transformation, and the Methodist Body," at various stages in its development. Their challenging questions and thoughtful comments made it much stronger. Special thanks to David Porter and Valerie Traub for inviting me to Michigan; to Mary Ruth Marrotte for the chance to give the Nolte-Behrens Lecture; and to Lisa Freeman, John Shanahan, and Helen Thompson for the invitation to lead a seminar at the Newberry. Colleagues in Yale's Eighteenth-Nineteenth-Century Working Group and Vanderbilt's Robert Penn Warren Humanities Center invited me to speak, and the conversations that ensued, in particular those with Ala Ayers and Humberto Garcia, provided very helpful critiques of chapter 4, "Actors and Ghosts: Methodism in the Theater of the Real," as it evolved and helped me to integrate its moving parts. Respondents at meetings of the American Society for Eighteenth-Century Studies, the Southeastern Society for Eighteenth-Century Studies, and the Johnson Society of the Central Region have given me additional food for thought and impressed me with their insights about other parts of the project. At the most recent JSOCR, Alex Dick, Tina Lupton, Deirdre Lynch, and Sean Silver asked questions that energized me for the final review of the manuscript, a great gift indeed.

My students, current and former, who contributed to this project through lively class discussions and their own work include Lauren Holt-Matthews, Caitlin Kelly, Misty Krueger, Mary Mechler, Neil Norman, Micah Rickerson, Teresa Saxton, and Jeremy Wear. Working with Justin Crisp on critical theory and theology was and is a particular delight. As part of that community of amazing students, Shelby Johnson and Julia Stamper also offered valuable research assistance in the final stages of the project. My colleagues at the University of Tennessee, including Amy Billone, Katy Chiles, Gerard Cohen-Vrignaud, Dawn Coleman, Stan Garner, David Goslee, Martin Griffin, Tom Haddox, Nancy Henry, Heather Hirschfeld, Laura Howes, Ben Lee, Roy Liuzza, Lisi Schoenbach, Urmila Seshagiri, and Anthony Welch continue to make it a great place to write and teach.

Colleagues who read portions of this project and helped me clarify them include Paula Backscheider, Lori Branch, Margaret Doody, Amy Elias, Lisa Freeman, Ronald Paulson, David Porter, Mark Schoenfield, Jennifer Snead, Helen Thompson, Frank Tirro, Valerie Traub, Gordon Turnbull, Howard Weinbrot, James Winn, and John Zomchick. My admiration for their brilliance and my thanks for their generous help is ongoing. A very early version of chapter 3 appeared as "Mr. Barvile's Enthusiasm: Habit, Discipline, and Methodism in the Eighteenth-Century British Imagination" in *Launching Fanny Hill: Critical Essays*, ed. Patricia Fowler and Alan Jackson, 2003. A preliminary version of chapter 4 also appeared as "'Our Purpose is the Same': Whitefield, Foote, and the Crisis of Methodist Theatricality" in *Studies in Eighteenth-Century Culture* 34 (2005). My thanks to all the readers, anonymous and known, for their helpful suggestions on these pieces. They helped me to begin to conceive of this book and provided important early guidance to its argument.

In addition to those already named, I am blessed to have friends and colleagues within the world of eighteenth-century studies (and a few from adjacent neighborhoods) who possess generous intelligence, incredible collective learning, and good cheer. They include Martha Bowden, Brian Corman, Jack DeRochi, Jay Dickson, Dan Ennis, Lynn Festa, Melinda Finburg, Robert Folkenflik, Patsy Fowler, Emily Friedman, Marilyn Gaull, Blake Gerard, Jody Greene, Catherine Ingrassia, Joe Johnson, George Justice, Paul Kelleher, Matt Kinservik, Jonathan Kramnick, Devoney Looser, Jack Lynch, Jean Marsden, Madeline Marshall, Heather McPherson, Danny O'Quinn, John Richetti, Laura Rosenthal, Laura Runge, Mark Schoenfield, Judy Slagle, John Stevenson, Rivka Swenson, John Vance, and Jodi Wyatt. I am honored to call them colleagues. They make the scholarly conversation of conferences one of the great pleasures of being in this profession.

So many friends supported me, fed me, and kept me happy during the writing of this project, but a few deserve special mention. Fiona Scott-Morton and Stephen, Sophie, Ellie, and Rory Latham embraced my family during our time in New Haven, and the happy memory of many a dinner and Burns Night at their home will be with us forever. Delfin Bautista, Peter and Sarah Crumlish, Anibal Gonzalez, Justin Haaheim, Jason Hernandez, Gordon Hinshalwood, Stephanie Johnson, Priscilla Melendez, and the students and teachers at St. Thomas's Day School made our time at YDS and in Connecticut nothing short of marvelous. Lisa Burke, Mary Chan, Chris Chase, Amy Figg, Anne Harley, Amy Hiestand, Karen Hough, Trevor Jefferson, Elizabeth Letcher, Steve Misenheimer, Ward Misenheimer, Sandi Ostraski, Claudia Overstrom, Leigh Anna Reichenbach, Gina Roccanova, Elizabeth Solomon, and Abby Tate have been on this journey with me for a very long time, and to each of them I owe debts of gratitude that are impossible to repay. Frank and Charlene Tirro, Gale and Charles Anderson, Kelli Anderson-Corwin, and Chris Anderson have never failed to raise my spirits and hopes about what I do and why I do it. During the writing of *Imagining Methodism in Eighteenth-Century Britain*, Andy and Trevor Tirro have provided laughter, balance, distraction, and joy, without which the book and certainly I would not have been the same. For many years now, John Tirro has been my partner on a grand adventure that has taken me into new territory and back to sweet homecomings I never could have foreseen. In ways obvious and not at all obvious, his care, conversation, and passion have shaped this project.

Imagining Methodism
in Eighteenth-Century Britain

INTRODUCTION

Longing to Believe
Methodism and Modernity

Charlotte Grandison, writing to her friend Harriet Byron in *Sir Charles Grandison*, observes the recent religious conversion of the flighty Mrs. O'Hara:

> By the way, do you know that Mrs. O'Hara is turned *Methodist?* True as you are alive. And she labours hard to convert her husband. Thank God she is any thing that is serious! Those people have really great merit with me in *her* conversion—I am sorry that our own clergy are not as zealously in earnest as they. They have really, my dear, if we may believe aunt Eleanor, given a face of religion to subterranean colliers, tinners, and the most profligate of men, who hardly ever before heard either of the word or thing. But *I* am not turning *Methodist*, Harriet. No, you will not suspect me.[1]

Charlotte's mixed reaction exemplifies a familiar split in early accounts of Methodism, the eighteenth-century religious movement that eventually became a denomination, led by John Wesley, Charles Wesley, and George Whitefield. On the one hand, Methodism represented an expression of personal religious transformation, including charity, literacy, self-discipline, and other practices which overlapped with eighteenth-century discourses of civic engagement and self-improvement. On the other, this religious zeal is something of which Charlotte should not be suspected, a dangerous "turning" that would leave her less reasonable, less Charlotte. Charlotte's paradoxical admiration for and skepticism about Methodism, in which class is made to speak to the anxieties about a self open to radical change, captures a live debate in eighteenth-century Britain about what it meant to be modern. Eighteenth-century novels, newspapers, afterpieces, cartoons, and broadsides caricatured Methodism as the conceptual boundary of the reasonable, modern British self. But lurking in the background of these portraits is a fascination with the Methodist conversion, its instantaneous warming of the heart as a moment of divine contact, and its capacity to remake the self. Methodism emphasized a Pauline, kenotic, self-emptying Christian "I," the self who is not autonomous, who is "not I but Christ in me." This orthodox theological concept had new consequences for a self defined by its capacity for consciousness, cognitive continuity, and self-possession. Methodism's simultaneous modernity and mysticism seemed to unravel the skein of the eighteenth-century conscious self just as it was being woven.

David Hempton, Mark Noll, Henry Rack, Phyllis Mack, W. B. Ward, Richard Heitzenrater, and others have provided excellent histories of the movement that read Methodism as a global force as well as a particular formation within British culture.[2] My contribution to this conversation is not to establish another version of what Methodism was but to attend to the question of how it functioned in the British imagination. I use the term Methodism to name a cultural category read by eighteenth-century Britons who defined themselves against it rather than the denomination that evolved from it with the understanding that these different uses are not fully separable. The label Methodism referred to real people, though popular representations buried those real people under layers of comic costume. On the one hand, this is the modus operandi of topical satire and farce. But it is also an attempt to parse the Methodist project of conversion, belief, and community in more material, rational terms as sex, theater, or populism, an attempt that itself becomes a kind of hysterical symptom, a project of unmasking that also revels in what it cannot resolve about the attractions of Methodism: the transsexual escapades of Mary/George Hamilton; the sadomasochistic sex of Mr. Barvile; Foote's bracketed impersonation of Whitefield; the Methodist associations of the Cock Lane ghost; the Methodist hymn in mass performance; and the social reintegration of the quixotic Methodist in Graves and Smollett. Albert Lyles and T. B. Shepherd catalogued the satiric and literary responses to

Methodism, providing indispensable bibliographies of eighteenth-century responses to the movement.[3] This study seeks to understand how these tales of Methodist excess tell a story about the vulnerable, contingent, credulous, responsive self that sees the "heart religion" of Methodism as both a threat to and the fascinating possibility of release from the tyranny of the "I."

The often uncharitable portraits of Methodism in the popular press reveal a culture that reads its sense of the boundaries of the modern self in and into Methodism. In attending to these representations of Methodism, not because they are true but because they are telling, I show that Methodism served imaginatively as a space of intimacy, desire, and even ecstasy for the modern British self even as, and indeed because, it served as a boundary for that self. This study is thus not so much about the lives of Methodists as it is about the imagined life of the Methodist as modernity's homegrown, mystic-evangelical other. Popular treatments of Methodism in its first phase, from 1736 to 1778, used Methodists as figures who fail to be modern selves. These representations chart the problematic relationships among belief, consciousness, and modernity. This book traces a rough chronological arc of the representations of Methodism as it goes from a new, highly suspect movement within the Anglican church to a denomination that has just begun to settle into institutional solidity. In the course of this timeframe, British culture finds ways to come to terms with this first expression of modern evangelicalism. Methodism became a flashpoint for eighteenth-century conceptions of modernity because it captured both the anxiety about whether a self could be autonomous and cognitively coherent, and the longing for intimate connection with the other in a material world of cognitive isolation.

Methodism's emphasis on the warming of the heart, a felt experience of contact with God, subverted the material terms of Lockean consciousness by bringing to bear on it a mysticism that was at once both antimodern and sensuously immediate. Wesley called this movement both "experimental religion," which gestured to the ways Methodism was engaged with modern epistemology, and yet also "primitive Christianity," which implied ancient ties to the early church and suggested an antimodern bent. Both were apt descriptions in their own ways. Methodists used modern media, a discourse of self-improvement, an emphasis on reason, and Lockean theories of mind to define their "experimental religion" as a modern mode of religious expression. But they also declared themselves primitive participants in a mystical experience of divine presence, and in so doing became a collective scapegoat for anxieties about the relationship of the modern self to history. Here was a new movement that, like the old whipping post of Roman Catholicism, threatened to breed antimodern and thus anti-British selves, but that did so out of the materials of modern epistemology. Horace Walpole seized on this dimension of their evangelical message and accused them of creeping "Papism" that would become a threat to the "future improvement" of the arts (*Anecdotes of Painting in England* 4: ix). Walpole's accusation puts the temporality of Methodism's "primitive Christianity" up against a national narrative of progress; to paraphrase Christopher Hitchens's petulant title, he suggests that Methodism is the kind of religion that "ruins everything," particularly the project of modernity. The charitable accomplishments and nonviolent progress of the movement were overshadowed by its antimodern insistence on a cognitively permeable, "primitive" self. Yet Methodism was undeniably part of the cultural present, formed in the crucible of enlightenment culture and philosophy and intertwined with its epistemologies of the self.

The underlying danger posed by Methodism was the event of Methodist conversion, an experience in time that challenged the agency and autonomy of the modern self as a secular and autonomous enterprise. The Methodist conversion event proposed an irruption of divine presence into historical time and into an individual consciousness that threatened both to reveal the self and yet, in the process, to change it. Much like the surge of miracle claims in seventeenth- and eighteenth-century Protestant England that Jane Shaw analyzes in *Miracles in Enlightenment England*, Methodism's appeal illuminates the ways that religion was reshaped, enlivened, and circulated through the crucible of eighteenth-century British thought, even as it was discursively situated as part of an "irrational," mystical, and primitive past that was a threat to the modern self.[4] Through a populist, religious adaptation of Lockean consciousness that, paradoxically, emphasized the vulnerability of this self in its own secular terms, Methodism brought the discussion about modern Lockean psychology to general audiences and encouraged them to talk, think, and write about both their evangelical transformation and their experience of their inward state. In this they embodied a modern model of consciousness, supported by its own print culture and an evangelical version of the public sphere. But the Methodist "warming of the heart," the conversion experience, underscored the fragile temporality of what Locke called the "identity of consciousness." Conversion was a moment of utter authenticity in which the self was, paradoxically, destroyed. Methodists and their critics agreed, at some level, on this constitutive tension.

Methodism claimed both to break down and to "regenerate" modern people. George Lavington, Bishop of Exeter, declaimed against their persuasive methods "considering how *inconsiderate and injudicious*, how *unlearned and unstable*, a large Portion of Mankind is" (Lavington, *Enthusiasm* 2: 1). Lavington implicitly posits a rational self against Methodism, but he frets that the "unstable" majority of the population are ready, even predisposed, to embrace the ecstatic Methodist event of conversion, which made the Lockean self, "a conscious thinking thing," seem fragile indeed (Locke 341). Charlotte's playful yet nervous "you will not suspect me" is an admission that it could even happen to witty, modern Charlotte, and that she feels she must define herself against this possibility. Conversion pressed the question not just on the Lockean question of whether Socrates (or Charlotte) sleeping and Socrates waking were the same man, but whether Socrates (or Charlotte) would be the same in light of something like "the new birth," and what such a transformation might mean for a modern nation of self-possessing, autonomous, and forensic subjects.[5]

The success of Methodism, in spite of dismissals from Walpole, Richardson, Fielding, Jefferson, and a host of others, tells a story about the way that Methodism spoke to the modern self, a story generously documented in Phyllis Mack's *Heart Religion in the British Enlightenment*. Methodism was both effective and troubling because it was so close to Anglican religious and philosophical orthodoxies. John Wesley claimed he died a minister of the Church of England and initially discouraged his followers from leaving their home parishes, yet the movement was in competition with the Anglican church for members and resources. Methodism's legacy is complex, extending to practices like working-class literacy, hymn singing, urban charities, field preaching, and small group structures. Theologically, it worked from within Anglican discourse to place the contingent, open-ended idea of the modern self in dialogue with a mystical, intensely somatic moment of divine intervention, and situated this dialectic within the language of modern consciousness, a term which itself comes from religious debates about "conscience" that provide the basis for a more cognitively and psychologized "consciousness" (McKeon, *Secret History* 35). The nervous joking about Methodism barely masks an interwoven fear and hope about the discourse of felt spirituality: the fear that Methodism would overwhelm individual consciousness, and the hope that it could break through the alienation and solitude and close the gap between what Charles Taylor calls "experience and its construal," the space between sensation and reflection through which the self constitutes itself as a consciousness (Taylor, *Secular Age* 11). This model of experience competed both with strictly materialist accounts of consciousness, *pace* Descartes and La Mettrie, as well as with accounts of the "forming power" of aesthetic experience in Shaftesbury, Hutcheson, and Addison, in which sublimity emerges as a category to mediate the experience of God as an experience of order, nature, or beauty. The constitutive tensions between the particular evangelical experientialism named in the Methodist "warming of the heart" in relation to philosophical materialism on the one hand, and aesthetics on the other, tell us something about the ways that the idea of the modern British self used the idea of Methodism to chart its boundaries and serve as the repository for its most intimate longings for connection.

Methodism's paradoxical place as both a flourishing modern religious phenomenon and as an antimodern backlash movement is scripted into the way critics and historians have told the story of modernity. In the version represented in the work of Peter Gay, the eighteenth century sees the banishment of religion by Enlightenment, the cradle of secular modernity; as John Sheehan summarized this school of thought, "modern is modern, in a sense, to the degree that it is secular" (1066). But recent "postsecular" critical methodologies, including the work of Charles Taylor, Hent de Vries, and Jürgen Habermas, argue for a skepticism about "a straightforward narrative of progress from the religious to the secular" that has been dominant in accounts of modern history and that, if reconsidered, challenges some of the long-held assumptions within eighteenth-century studies about the meaning of its modernity.[6] Their skepticism about skepticism (qua the arc of history) illuminates how Methodism, the largest new religious movement in the period and at the heart of modern evangelicalism, might be intrinsic to our understanding of eighteenth-century culture and its active negotiation of religion in "a secular age," which redefines rather than destroys modern belief.[7] Methodism unfolded in the midst of the age of reason, which, because it began to imagine secularism as a viable worldview, gave birth to religion in the modern sense of the word. How eighteenth-century Britons experienced this category of religion, how they contested it, and how it shaped the imagined boundaries of the modern self are the questions that frame this inquiry.

The Methods of Modern Selves

Though Methodism was named in part for its rationalized "method" of managing one's time and devotional life as well as Wesley's "reasonable enthusiasm" and his methodological triumvirate of "Scripture, reason, and experience," it was above all a religion of feeling, as G. J. Barker-Benfield, Felicity Nussbaum, and

Phyllis Mack have all noted.[8] Ann Taves places Methodism at the center of "theologies of experience" that redefined religion in the eighteenth century as primarily an internal experience of the self's relation to God (47). For Wesley, God does not exist because we can "think" God, but because we can "feel" God, an experience that entails a loss of cognitive control but also the possibility of divine intimacy from within the modern world. Methodism represented the possibility of a Pauline rending of the veil of the self to reach the other in the midst of the age of reason. The price of autonomy for the modern secular self was a constant critical distance on its own mental produce, ever skeptical and questioning lest it be misled by bad information or cognitive error. Methodism, by adapting Peter Browne's 1728 revision of Locke in *The Procedure, Extent, and Limits of Human Understanding*, which allowed for spiritual sensations, provided some relief from the impossible burdens of being a conscious, cognitively wary, isolated self, and from the loneliness of modern theories of mind, while at the same time using its rubrics and procedures. The attractions of this sensational religious intimacy are confirmed in the tremendous growth of the movement, which was neither Dissenting nor Roman Catholic, but instead an Anglican, Oxford-born movement.

But a self that "feels God" and conceives of its own agency intersubjectively as doing the will of God is a breached or failed consciousness in the language of modern liberalism. Such a self has given way to enthusiasm or "revelation" by the definitions Locke established, a "failure" that both Fielding and Lavington represented as feminizing. As Ruth Salvaggio has argued, the figuration of chaos or irrationality as feminine in eighteenth-century discourse is part of a rhetorical strategy that props up the priority of a masculine set of values in the emerging scripts of modern gender, among them autonomy, rationality, and invulnerability, which have political and imaginative traction.[9] If eighteenth-century conceptions of mental states are tied up in "a peculiar capacity for meaning and agency," as Jonathan Kramnick has suggested, then is a Methodist, whose critical distance and agency are compromised by the experience of divine presence, a modern self?[10] Methodism amplified the sense of feminine malleability and emotional responsiveness from the novel and from conduct literature, as described by Armstrong and others, and relaunched it within Christian metaphysics. That the movement appealed to so many women, some of whom became Methodist teachers and preachers, both reaffirms the gendered association that has dominated Methodist history and, as Mack has shown, reflects the activism, writing practices, and communities of actual women who were a part of the movement

(*Heart Religion* 26). The association between Methodism and women has a material historical basis, but the idea of the hysterical, feminized Methodist self is a function of a narrative about the eighteenth century and religion that is magnified in the satires. In them, we can see how Methodism, like the emerging discourse of femininity, provided an imaginative dumping ground for anxieties about the limits of self-knowledge and autonomy.

Methodism hailed and cultivated this feeling, penetrable self, an appeal exemplified in the sermons of George Whitefield. Whitefield did not merely talk about the effects of conscience; in his thirty-first sermon, "On the Care of the Soul," he personified the relentless procedure of conscience by rhetorically invading the mental space of his listeners:

> Does not conscience follow you to your beds, even if denied the opportunity of meeting you in your closets, and, though with an unwelcome voice, there warn you, "that your soul is neglected, and will quickly be lost." Does it not follow you to your shops and your fields, when you are busiest there? Nay, I will add, does it not sometimes follow you to the feast, to the club, to the dance, and perhaps, amidst all resistance, to the theatre too? Does it not sometimes mingle your sweetest draughts with wormwood, and your gayest scenes with horror? (WORKS 5: 466)

Whitefield traces the pattern of an invasive, nagging conscience with his own invasive appeal, asking a series of direct, catechetical, diagnostic questions that ask the hearer to engage with his message at a personal rather than propositional level as he "appeals to your conscience" directly. Whitefield was also apt to use materials directly at hand to jolt his listeners out of abstractions and into direct engagement. Thomas Somerville notes that on August 12 of 1758, after a fire had raged in Edinburgh's Carruber's Close for ten hours, Whitefield mounted his makeshift pulpit at the Orphan Hospital in the evening, warning:

> "All of you," said he, "were witnesses of yonder scene." After a solemn pause he then proceeded to describe, in interesting and affecting detail, the more diversified and wider field of destruction which was to be witnessed by his audience hereafter, when the globe itself should be burnt up; recalling the feelings and impressions still fresh in the minds of all of them, as faint presages and anticipations of the awe and horror which they must expect to feel in that great and terrible day of the Lord. (SOMERVILLE 73)

The materialized "word made flesh" of these mostly extemporaneous sermons (the record of which was provided by listeners like Somerville and Joseph Gurney, who transcribed or recollected them) was not the stable world of print but a live, persuasive event made to speak to the occasion. In the midst of what Ong described as the shift from orality to literacy, Whitefield deployed an intensely visual, oratorical language of immediacy.[11] It situates the addressee within a sacred present through the event of the fire; like a clerical Garrick, Whitefield wants his listeners to see ghosts, fires, and miraculous feasts along with him. Whitefield's preaching encouraged listeners to invest in the illustration as a real object, translating it as the material manifestation of divine rupture within modern time.

By comparison, Benjamin Hoadly's seventh sermon, "Concerning Impartial Inquiry in Religion," which is as typical of his style as these two examples of Whitefield are of his, has no such rhetorical directness and, instead, emphasizes a reasoned, distanced approach to the question of belief as a dangerous threat to reason. Hoadly cautions against "Credulity" on the part of "Reasonable Creatures" who are apt to be persuaded by

> every Pretender with a Zeal equal to that which he shews for the person who brings the justest Credentials ... the Result of such a Man's pretended *Enquiries*, is not what can be called *Faith*; which is a *Virtue*, as it is worked by due Means, and as it is the Consequence of our attending to proper Evidence: but rather *Superstition*, prompted either by *Fear*, or *Folly*, to take all *Pretenses* equally for *Truth*; all *Uncommon things* equally for *Miracles* wrought by God; all *Appearances* equally for *Realities*. This is such a Submission of *Reason* and *Understanding*, below the Dignity of Human Nature, as They only want to be exercised, who have nothing to shew that can bear an *Enquiry*, or stand the Test of an *Impartial Examiner*.
>
> (HOADLY 143–44)

Hoadly's appeal, which all but names Whitefield and Wesley as the zealous "pretenders," is in the name of preserving the reasonable self from the dangers of belief. The "pretended Enquiries" of the zealot (a stab at both Wesley's tracts on miracles and Whitefield's emotional, direct style) are misapprehensions of disenchanted reality, like the fire at Carruber's Close, for "Miracles wrought by God." Hoadly's sermon speaks of both a discourse of secularism that demands "proper evidence" separated out from appearances and pretenses, and a counterdiscourse of felt spirituality that connects the self to the phenomenal world. Whitefield's sermon compels his listeners to "make the trial" of their consciences to save their eternal souls and so is directed at the individual "you" who responds inwardly with emotion, conviction, and belief. In Hoadly, the danger is the loss of the reasonable self to enthusiasm, and his appeal is accordingly directed to an impartial, logical listener who needs to rise to the plane of evidences, proofs and "Matters of Fact" rather than sink "below the Dignity of Human Nature" by submitting "Reason and Understanding" in a moment of credulity (153). Hoadly, as an apologist for a Latitudinarian faith that comes from scientific procedures of evidence and experiment (the "Test of an Impartial Examiner"), brackets the power of the more immediate Methodist version of "experimental religion" as a challenge to the modern self.

Methodist hymns echoed the message of felt immediacy that Whitefield performed in his sermons in their Eucharistic theology, referring to the "still warm" sacrifice and the blood flowing "now." This position was in strong contrast to more Latitudinarian dispositions toward communion as memorial in the work of Samuel Clarke, Gilbert Burnet (son of the bishop who attended Rochester's deathbed), and Hoadly; as such, it is testament to the ongoing doctrinal contest within the eighteenth-century Anglican church. Regina Schwartz has recently argued that the explosion of sacramental language in seventeenth-century English poetry is evidence that the changing conditions of belief in the modern project prompted a return to sacramental language and symbolism:

> At the very dawn of secularism, Eucharistic mystery persisted and was woven into allegedly secular discourses. Poetry grasped for it through language; the nation grasped for it through symbolizing community; love longed for it through mutual devotion; materialism clung to it through vitalism. (15)

Richard Rambuss, in a very different argument about this same sacramental language, argues that the seventeenth-century lyric proffers "a spirituality that paradoxically bespeaks embodiment" in queer terms (2). Methodism continued the metaphysicals' fascination with the Eucharist, the body, and a rhetoric of somatic immediacy, adapting Crashaw and Herbert for their eighteenth-century hymnals. In both the original seventeenth-century poems and the Wesleyan versifications, these lyrics, along with Methodist sermons, cry out for contact from a range of gendered positions, for an overwhelming somatic experience that exceeds aesthetic pleasure or rational account.

The eighteenth-century record of images, representations, and literary versions of Methodism shows not the story of the waning of religion but of an energetic, at times fierce cultural conversation between modern expressions of felt religious belief and modern versions of secular belief in human reason. Methodism as it was conceived of in popular culture seemed to form a conceptual limit for the modern self: Could modern selves have transforming encounters with God? Was such an experience in the realm of orthodoxy or insanity? What did such a change say about the nature of identity, individual and communal? At stake was how self-contained, how rational, and how secular the definition of the modern self should be, but the answers were not uniform. This contest played out variously in Locke's "On Enthusiasm," Hume's "On Miracles" (which he represented as the phallic thrust of his *Treatise of Human Nature* when he told his friend Henry Home he was "castrating" it by cutting it out), the Bangorian controversy over the Eucharist, popular mystics like Fenelón, and the relationship of evangelical Christianity to the literature of sensibility.[12] The mystic, sensual, and performative elements of Christianity that Locke and Hume bracketed off from modernity flourished in Methodism, with its charismatic preachers, its eucharistic theology, and its immediate "warming of the heart."[13] The popularity of Methodism in the eighteenth century and the persistence, even resurgence, of religious belief in the twenty-first century have undermined the historical proposition that religious belief wanes in modernity. That we can trace both this thesis and the implicit definition of modern on which it relies to the eighteenth century implicates ongoing critical investments in what that modernity means.

Historian Jonathan Sheehan has called for an approach to the eighteenth century that does not depend on secularization as "shorthand for the inevitable (intentional or not, serious or ironic) slide of the pre-modern religious past into the modern secular future" but that could instead yield "an account of how religion was made modern, how it was reconstructed in such a way as to incorporate it into the fabric of modernity" (Sheehan 1076–77). The cultural reception of eighteenth-century Methodism can help us better understand the fraught process through which religion was made modern and continued to encode, as Terry Eagleton puts it, "needs and longings which will not simply evaporate at the touch of tough-minded analysis," amid anxieties and even panic about what such needs and longings meant for the modern self (90). Simon During, expressing his skepticism both about the concept of "spiritual hunger" and the Hegelian bent of Charles Taylor's *A Secular Age*, makes a bid for the space of the "mundane" in modernity as a third category, beyond secular and religious (116). My argument is not that secular and religious capture the complete horizon of possibility in the project of modernity, but that their opposition achieves a cultural dominance that defines the era. The case of Methodism supports McKeon's observation that religious expression and experience in the modern world may have been concentrated and intensified by the process of disaggregating church and state authority after the Reformation. But Methodism was not a private matter; Methodism's use of media, its outdoor meetings, its popular music, as well as its efforts to relieve urban poverty are examples of what John Wesley meant when he claimed in the preface to *Hymns and Sacred Poems* (1739) that "the gospel of Christ knows no religion, but social; no holiness, but social holiness" (Wesley and Wesley viii). Placing Methodism as a significant aspect of eighteenth-century British culture challenges a simple historical narrative of progressive secularization and the privatization of religious belief that is tantamount to religion's slow disappearance from the public sphere. "The people called Methodists" became part of the conversation about modern British identity, both as a response to perceived secularization but also as part of a complex modern experience of spirituality that unfolded through the psychological language of inwardness, sensation, and self-transformation and that cut across private and public domains of experience.

Each of these key terms in my study, "secular," "modern," and "self" is freighted with assumptions about history and identity, and each demands further definition. My use of the term self, as opposed to subjectivity, is part of an effort to conceive of the cultural function of Methodism in historical terms that capture the experiences of autonomy and vulnerability that were part of the developing discourses of individual consciousness. Locke defines the term "self" as "that conscious thinking thing, (whatever Substance, made up of whether Spiritual, or Material, Simple, or Compounded, it matters not) which is sensible, or conscious of Pleasure and Pain, capable of Happiness or Misery, and so is concern'd for it *self*, as far as that consciousness extends" (Locke 341). Locke's self emphasizes conscious continuity, or "identity of consciousness," in the midst of its sensibility of new experiences of pleasure, pain, and other sensations that will also constitute it, sensations that could include the problematic Methodist "warming of the heart." Subjectivity, as useful as the term has been in arguments about the social construction of identity, does not suit the task of understanding the crisis that Methodism seemed to provoke in part because, as Dror Wahrman, Jonathan Kramnick, Lisa Freeman, and others have noted, subjectivity proposes identity categories in advance of an individual's experience of them.[14]

The theoretical mismatch of subjectivity with eighteenth-century accounts of mind and self resides in the way that subjectivity downplays the more individual, sensual process of formation in Lockean and later Scottish Enlightenment epistemologies of the self. The historical risk of subjectivity as a critical keyword is a presentism that implicitly presupposes a modern self "as a latent bud waiting patiently for the sun rays of modernity to wake it to life" (Wahrman xii). Governed by the logic of the "emergent," it seeks confirmation for present formulations of self (and implicitly, their ideological presuppositions) in the story of the past and thus tends to ignore or devalue other possible formations of human experience. Within eighteenth-century culture, Wahrman argues that Methodism seems to invert the logic of self as a movement that moved, "not in parallel with other [identity] categories we have seen, from a collective, group identity to an internalized, individual one, but the other way around" (280). Methodism does not fit Wahrman's dominant formulation of modern identity because, by his own account, it was grounded in the practices of a distinctly experimental, individualist account of the self that was then fostered by practices, disciplines, and forms of community after the fact. The Methodist was a self in process, but the process began with internal changes (in the Wesleyan vocabulary, repentance, faith, justification, assurance, the new birth, and sanctification), moments of internal awareness or experience of the self in relation to God that were the gateway to a sense of participation within the movement.[15] Because Methodist discourse appealed first to inner states, self as a term captures the psychological stakes of Methodism for eighteenth-century British culture better than identity and more historically than subjectivity.

The next two terms, modern and secular, as well as their conjugates, require a more historical account of their critical function, which I provide in the next section. Like Asad, Sheehan, and Wahrman, I use the term modern to name an ideology that unfolded in time rather than a specific period in time. Twentieth-century accounts of eighteenth- and nineteenth-century Western culture have invoked a concept of religious antimodernity as a foil in the narrative of modernity's rise, implying its fundamental secularity. Secularism, as a post-Reformation historical phenomenon, has a similarly complex and ideologically fraught legacy. Charles Taylor puts forward three possible definitions of secularism: (1) the separation of church and state authority, which makes religion a more private matter; (2) the ascendance of science and reason over faith; and (3) the changed conditions of belief in the historical shift "from a society in which it was virtually impossible not to believe in God, to one in which faith, even for the staunchest human believer, is one human possibility among others" (*A Secular Age* 3). I share Taylor's frustration with the first two definitions, which provide partial (both in the sense of incomplete and tendentious) descriptions of what we might name by secularism. The first definition has historical and political descriptive power, but the privatization of religion does not fully explain the continued role of public expressions of religious faith. The second definition seems overly indebted to a Kantian reformulation of the eighteenth century. It stages a binary contest between science and religion that depends on questionable assumptions about what religion is and what it proposes to explain, as well as what Eagleton has called elsewhere an "extraordinarily Pollyannaish view of human progress."[16] Taylor's third definition, an alternative way of thinking about the conditions of belief that shape one's lived experience, incorporates elements of the first two definitions without demanding a titanic historical contest in which one emerges victorious. Taylor's argument uses the concept of "fullness," the individual experience of peace, wholeness, or deeper meaning, to leverage the priority of self-sufficient reason and to provide a way to think about how religion and belief both persisted and flourished in eighteenth-century Britain as the "whole context in which we experience and search for fullness" undergoes the substantial, epistemic shift he calls "the coming of a secular age" (14). If belief in God "is no longer axiomatic" in the way it may have been in 1500, it was at the same time newly defined by the possibility of unbelief, an unbelief with its own concomitant doubts and hopes for deeper meaning (3).

The Temporality of Secularization

The case of Methodism raises a question about the narrative demands implicit in the story of what it means to be modern. Being aware of being "modern" is something we share with what Wahrman calls "the foreign country of the eighteenth-century past," just as we share the sense that modernity is still to come, what Derrida called the yet-to-be fulfilled "invincible promise" of the project of Enlightenment.[17] Thinking about modernity in these provisional terms reminds us to be wary of the looking-glass effect of eighteenth-century culture and remember that "their" modernity is not our modernity, even if the two are in dialogue, and that modernity is more an ideology than an historical territory, even as it underwrites "the triumphalist history of the secular" (Asad, *Formations* 25). This vision of modernity as an integrated and historical project of disenchantment that would bring "direct access to reality, a stripping away of myth, magic, and the sacred" harbors its own hopes of revelation and redemption (Asad 13). Henry Tilney invokes such a vision (and Austen tweaks him for it) when he chastises Catherine Moreland for her suspicions of evil doings at Northanger Abbey: "Remember the country and the age in which we live. Remember that we are

English, that we are Christians" (Austen 203). Being modern, English, and Christian are part of the same seamless identity that precludes Catherine's fears as an assault on the disenchanted, optimistic rationality of "the age in which we live." Tilney imagines a Christianity that is supposed to guarantee one's modernity by being opposed to feelings and, ironically, beliefs, which become the gothic domain of irrational and magical thinking. The keyword function Asad assigns to "disenchantment," which is similar to its conceptual function in Horkheimer and Adorno's landmark *Dialectic of Enlightenment,* focuses the issue on a critical reading process, the removal of myth that will reveal a secular reality in its place, which the English gothic performed even as it tantalized with images of enchantment and mystery. This narrative instantiates a set of reading practices that must uncover truths that will both conform to and confirm the temporality of modernity; old myths give way to new realities. Though it is a vision that appears to separate the terms religious and secular by defining them against one another, it must actually produce their difference out of a more mixed experience. The terms secular and religious are themselves a product of changing understandings about the nature of the state's power, the concept of the individual, and a narrative of history as developmental, in which people "*aim* at modernity and expect others . . . to do so too" (Asad, *Formations* 13).

Questions about how we read religion in historical time (Is it part of a waning past? Is it the persistence of the past? Is it a new formation?) are written into the eighteenth-century discussion of Methodism as well as into histories of the eighteenth century. While no serious student of the period would propose that on a particular Tuesday in 1701, all but a few of England's citizens awoke to find themselves rational and free of mysticism, it is nonetheless notable how many histories of the period (from within it and subsequent to it) are invested in an account of progressive secularization as the narrative of modernity.[18] In the narrative of secularization as historical progress, politics becomes, in the words of Deborah Valenze, "the enlightened heir to religion, finally enabling the less powerful to shake off the control of the hegemonic classes."[19] The reading strategy translates the content of any religious event, statement, or representation into a cultural past or as a misrecognized desire for liberation in the present. Religious revival becomes a misplaced experience of social unrest; religious fervor is misrecognized eroticism; and hopes of heaven are deferrals of political revolution. Transposing spiritual searching into "more fundamental, often unconscious human needs" that must be decoded is a form of symptomatic reading that informs eighteenth-century critical discourse as well as subsequent methodologies

(Mack, *Heart Religion* 9). It is worth considering the way that this approach translates the materials of history in advance into always-already secular categories that demand the end of religious faith as such. The script also makes religious belief the enemy of political revolution, and thus, ironically, renders salvific the critical reading process of overcoming the ideological vision of the past that religion represents. Revolution itself, in a paradoxical transfer of valence, takes on a religious aura; revolution carries the messianic hope of social salvation and the peaceable kingdom of a political heaven on earth. As Kristeva has put it, "a synonym of dignity, revolt is our mysticism" (4).

By appropriating religious narratives of revelation and redemption for the project of history itself, this narrative of secular modernity makes it difficult to parse the overlapping experiences of belief and faith that were part of eighteenth-century history and philosophy of mind.[20] Charles Taylor, William Bouwsma, Webb Keane, Janet Jakobsen, Ann Pellegrini, Jürgen Habermas, and John Caputo, among others, have raised questions about the limits of the secularization thesis that proposes a progressive disenchantment of human experience and, by implication, disenchantment as progress.[21] In that narrative, Methodism has tended to take the fall for some of the failures and disappointments of British modernity. It has, in different arguments, been used to explain the absence of a British worker's revolution, sexual repression, colonialism, and populist anti-intellectualism. Time and again, mainstream British histories have described Methodism as a movement that tried to look backward in a time of progress, pushing the train of modernity back on its tracks into a religious antimodernity. This narrative has proven methodologically and ideologically durable until only recently.

Thomas Jefferson helped to write the script that identifies Methodism with the past or as a retrograde movement when he confidently predicted in 1822 to his friend Dr. Thomas Cooper that American religion was headed to Unitarianism because it was inevitable that the nation would move beyond Christianity and its irrational investments: "this will, ere long, be the religion of the majority from the north to the south" and a remedy to the "fever of fanaticism . . . chiefly among the women" who "pour forth the effusions of their love to Jesus, in terms as amatory and carnal, as their modesty would permit them to use."[22] Jefferson's prediction did not come true; Methodism far outstripped the appeal of Unitarianism in the nineteenth century to become the largest denomination in America (Hempton, *Methodism* 8). But more to the point, Jefferson's prediction, like the secularizing imperative that guides some of the most luminous histories of the period, reads religious beliefs, especially those touching on embodiment, as the fetishistic remnant of a primitive, unenlightened past that will be naturally written out by historical progress itself.[23] The vaguely Latitudinarian point is implicit in history writing after Gibbon; religious belief is a form of false consciousness awaiting the remedy of a demystifying materialism, whether historical or scientific.[24] In this story, religion survives in the new world order only as a trace of the source of natural law that provides some ethical infrastructure for the sprawling, mobile project of modernity. Methodism did not fit Jefferson's narrative, but, as it turned out, neither would American religious history.

E. P. Thompson, Élie Halévy, Max Weber, and Christopher Hill have read Methodism as an explanation for glitches in the progress narrative, much like the eighteenth-century satires tended to do. Materialist historians since Halévy have argued that Methodism's self-discipline and political conservatism stemmed the revolutionary energies of the English working class at the end of the eighteenth century. The religion qua revolution thesis in the work of Halévy, Thompson, and Weber claims that Methodist evangelicalism transformed what should have been the extension of the political impulses within seventeenth-century Dissent into religious complicity with industrial capitalism. By using Methodism to explain class formation, however, they share what David Hempton has called a "lack of congruence between intention and result," sidestepping eighteenth-century Methodist attitudes toward the spiritual danger of private property, the importance of charity and communal obligation, and the priority of spiritual practice and worship over work in favor of the nineteenth-century economic implications of Methodism's emphasis on diligence, self-discipline, and thrift ("Evangelicalism" 31).

Halévy's story of eighteenth-century anxieties about Methodism and work has been paved over by the more familiar Weberian thesis, which attempts to explain the emotional structure of modern economic subjectivity. The emotional profile of Methodism in Weber is of the managed rather than enthusiastic self. His 1904–5 *The Protestant Ethic and the Spirit of Capitalism* finds the language of restraint, delayed satisfaction, and calling everywhere in seventeenth- and eighteenth-century Protestantism, making a powerful case that Calvinism and the doctrine of predestination contributed to the infrastructure of early capitalist behavior. But Wesleyan Methodism defined itself against Calvinism, and critics of both the Wesleyan and Connexion variants saw Methodists as enemies to industry. In dozens of satires, the problem with Methodists is that they don't work. Cobblers leave their shops (the joke apparently is about moving from work on one kind of "sole" to another), women abandon their housekeeping, and young men leave behind family obligations to attend worship, watch nights, and love feasts. In the epilogue to *The Mournful Nuptials* (1739/1744) the closing verse laments that "For them the shuttle's left by lazy weavers;/ And butchers drop their marrow-bones and cleavers" (Cooke n.p.). In "A Letter to Mr. Foote, Occasioned by Christian and Critical Remarks . . ." (1760), an unhappy upholsterer complains his wife has stopped making dinner and his foreman only sings hymns. This author includes a note to the effect that there are many more examples, but they are "too well known" to bear repeating.[25] Again and again, the Methodist convert disrupts public and private economies, which are each left to the care of the more worldly and very frustrated spouse, often the husband who loses the wife's labor.

In these stories, the Methodist, male or female, abandons work for spiritual pursuits, exemplifying a "religious fanaticism . . . pernicious to society" and destructive of "all industry and commerce" of which Adam Smith complained in *A Theory of Moral Sentiments*.[26] In the ballad with the satiric print *Dr. Squintum's Exultation, or The Reformation*, zealous Methodists tip over the carts and wares of merchants, inspired by Squintum's antinomian message:

> We may do what we please, quoth the Carpenter bold
> We may take up the Young & imprison the Old:
> On Sunday's we'll kick all the fruit about Street,
> And punish the Butchers for selling their Meat.

Contrary to Weber's and Thompson's theses about Methodism enabling a culture of endless work, these figures disrupt work in the name of liturgical time. These selves express the poles of spiritual passivity and the desire for self-improvement, which subtend their actions and constitute a threatening version of class mobility. In satires, they become a vision of social disorder in the name of an evangelical mission of holy reform, with a particular focus on Sunday trading. *Modern Reformers* (ca. 1763) is yet another work disruption by Methodists who are unhappy about vendors selling their wares on Sunday.[27] A Wilkes figure, lifted from Hogarth's 1763 *John Wilkes, Esq.*, leers in the foreground, while a Whitefield figure preaches in the background. The cross-eyed appearance of both Wilkes and Whitefield provided the superficial connection, but the underlying concern was that both were charismatic peddlers of libertinism at odds with good social order and commerce. In this and other images of Methodists disrupting work, Methodists are a threat to the world of goods and exchanges.

Modern Reformers, anon. ca. 1763.
Courtesy the Lewis Walpole
Library, Yale University

The story that Methodism worked hand in glove with modern capitalism crystallizes in Weber's selective and second-hand quotation of Wesley in *The Protestant Ethic and the Spirit of Capitalism*. Weber picks up on Wesley's observation that "religion must necessarily produce both industry and frugality," hence riches, but quotes from Southey's biography of Wesley (not from Wesley directly) and then overlooks the argument against capitalism in Wesley's claim:

> Wherever riches have increased, the essence of religion has decreased in the same proportion. Therefore I do not see how it is possible in the nature of things for any revival of religion to continue long. For religion must necessarily produce both industry and frugality, and these cannot but produce riches. But as riches increase, so will pride, anger, and love of the world in all its branches. . . . We ought not to prevent people from being diligent and frugal; we must exhort all Christians to gain all they can, and to save all they can; that is, in effect, to grow rich. What way, then, can we take, that our money may not sink us to the nethermost hell? There is one way, and there is no other under heaven. If those who *gain* all they can, and *save* all they can, will likewise *give* all they can, then the more they gain the more they will grow in grace, and the more treasure they will lay up in heaven. (QTD. IN SOUTHEY 516–17)

Wesley's position reported by Southey was that the modern ethos of acquisition was an empty enterprise, and that wealth needed to be redistributed through charitable giving. In this passage, Southey is complaining about Wesley's disregard for capital and capitalism. He calls Wesley's position "inconsistent with the existing order of society" and worries "how injurious, if such opinions were reduced to practice, they would prove to general industry" (517). Southey identifies in Wesleyan Methodism a refusal to coordinate the discourses of philosophical and economic materialism, making it a religious enemy of the modern order. Weber's hard twist on Southey's version of Wesley's quotation, in which he adds italics and truncates the point, thus obscures two key points from this passage: Wesley is expressing his fear that capitalist wealth would destroy Methodism, and Southey is then pitting Wesley against capitalism for proposing to redistribute that wealth.

Southey's concern about Wesley's economic philosophy squares with his thoughts on the dangerous and appropriate uses of wealth elsewhere in his work. Wesley's often-quoted charge in "The Use of Money" was to "Having, First, gained all you can, and, Secondly saved all you can, Then 'give all you can.'" His explication of this charge, however, does not sit comfortably with capitalism, as it excludes any gain that harms self, spirit, or neighbor, including, as Sondra

Wheeler explains, "several practices we would likely consider part of healthy competition or the efficient operation of the market and regard as inseparable from capitalism . . . not only predatory lending practices, price gouging, and profiting from another's hardship, but also routine competitive practices" (Wheeler 48). Wesley's actions substantiated his commitment at a personal level. He gave away all but about £30 a year from the thousands he earned from book sales, and he lamented that those who are "continually employed" in business are caught up in an unreasonable hoarding that will not satisfy them (*Works* 11: 61). Wesley took on acquisitive desire, the culture of endless work, the creation of cravings for products, luxuries, and the general "desire of novelty" that is the engine of a consumer culture. For him, these were sins woven into the structure of the emerging capitalist society that he challenged in "On Riches," quoting Prior's "Alma" and Pope's "Epistle to Bathurst" (scoffing at the rich man for "the embroidery plaistered on his tail") along the way to illustrate his point (*Abingdon Works* 3: 524). Wheeler calls Wesley an analyst of "the psychology of desire" who "provides a kind of phenomenology of the captivity of influence" (Wheeler 49). Without question, the Methodist was to be disciplined, aware of time in ways that comported with the modern development of wage labor, but that discipline was for the sake of activities outside the world of wage labor, and it does some violence to Wesley's message to read this disposition directly into Weber's thesis about Puritanism.[28]

These historical theses about modernity invoke Puritanism generally to describe Methodism, even though the term is an awkward fit for much of the movement, granting the trace of Susanna Wesley's (rejected) Puritan upbringing on her well-known sons. As the daughter of one of the most influential of the post-Restoration Puritan ministers, Samuel Annesley, she was raised a Dissenter but broke from her father's church at thirteen to become an Anglican. Puritan practices, including a rigorous domestic devotional life, theological argument, and childhood literacy, shaped the Wesleys, but the theologically Wesleyan position, drawn from Lutheran Pietism, celebrated "free grace," not the doctrine of election or even the economic logic of redemption. This difference was the substance of the split between John Wesley and George Whitefield and evident in satires that talk about Methodism's excesses not as hypocrisy but as an expression of license that was part of the movement. The presence of both the Arminian and Calvinist strands of Methodism creates a range of satiric complaints against them, including, inevitably, that they are confused, but the common eighteenth-century complaint that Methodists abandon labor for a spiritual life runs contrary to the Weberian iron cage. Their chief economic metaphor comes from a gift economy, not a capitalist one, matching the public perception that Methodism was threatening to a culture of work. This perspective might qualify Methodism as "antimodern," but not in the terms that Weber suggests.

E. P. Thompson uses Halévy's and Weber's theses to forward the notion that Methodism redirected the revolutionary energy of the English working class in the eighteenth century, thwarting the British claim to a Bastille Day. The evangelical revival, in Thompson's account, co-opted the frustration of the working classes, which otherwise would have fomented political revolt, into religious devotion that only made them more docile workers in industrial capitalism. Part of the limit of Thompson's account of Methodism in *The Making of the English Working Class*, in the tradition of John Forster, Southey, and other early nineteenth-century observers, is that his primary examples are drawn from Methodism's early Victorian second wave. Looking past Wesley and Whitefield, he paints a movement indistinguishable from the politically reactionary Jabez Bunting, who rose to prominence in the early nineteenth century, and from Dr. Andrew Ure, whose *Philosophy of Manufactures* (1835) described the perfect factory full of laborers whose virtue and self-discipline were secured through "the transforming power" of the cross.[29] The Methodism he describes may be the offspring of the eighteenth-century movement, but it is not the movement itself. Even for the improvisational Whitefield, hellfire was overshadowed by sermons of near-erotic divine love. Thompson admits in a footnote that "nor is this work-discipline in any sense limited to Methodism" (358), but the drive to find in Methodism the "method" of capitalism emphasized nineteenth-century Calvinist sermons from a late-blooming fringe of the fire and brimstone school at the expense of Wesley's more polished Ciceronian style and his theological focus on free grace.[30]

Thompson's influence in critical discourses of gender, sex, domesticity, education, and subjectivity in eighteenth-century studies justifies some scrutiny of the story he tells about Methodism, a story that separated out Methodism from the general thrust of modernity.[31] But even where his argument does not fit the facts, Thompson, as Hempton observes, "was on to something in his attempt to get at the apparent extremism of Methodist piety," an emotional power that wove together sex and the sacred, desire and discipline, and primitive and modern in combinations as appealing to some as they were disturbing to others (Hempton, *Methodism* 64). Thompson's claim that Methodism's conversion narratives involved the violent remaking of personalities could also be applied to other forms of conduct literature and the novel. In this sense, his partial account of Methodism foregrounds the ways that Methodism's discourse of transformation comports with popular projects for education and self-improvement. Early Methodist narratives are shaped by the desire for an overwhelming experience of intensity that confounds modern categories of material and immaterial, of primitive and modern. The moment of divine contact that shapes the self in the Methodist narrative also names the kernel that both demands and resists another interpretation in a modern, secular narrative.

Recent cultural studies of the eighteenth century, such as McKeon's *The Secret History of Domesticity*, offer a more nuanced view of the development of eighteenth-century British interiority and privacy in relation to religion through political, literary, and philosophical texts. McKeon's account of secularization in the history of domesticity builds on Conal Condren's argument in *The Language of Politics in Seventeenth-Century England*. He describes secularization as "not the mechanical separation of religion from politics and science but the religion of Protestantism itself" (McKeon 34). He argues that the Protestant reformation, using the epistemological tools of inquiry, disembeds religion from its previous location in the cultural matrix:

> which altered it from the universal precondition of human existence to the personal and private experience of the individual, [and] also defined it as the last refuge of embedded belief precisely because its metaphysics could not withstand the cold but normative scrutiny of empirical epistemology. The long-term result was the modern emergence not only of secularity but also of religion itself in the modern sense of the term (34).

This formulation of "modern religion" is both compelling and problematic. On the one hand, it gives an historical framework to Methodist "heart religion" and its eighteenth-century flowering within a cultural discourse of individualism that McKeon describes and substantiates at length. McKeon notes that religion as a domain was arguably intensified and concentrated as it was separated out from the universal condition to the personal experience of the individual, a shift that Methodism reflects. But the privatization of religion implies a corresponding secularization of the public sphere, which does not match the experience of print, oratory, and eighteenth-century Methodism. As Jennifer Snead has observed of early evangelical magazine and print culture, participation in the public sphere was neither necessarily secular nor directed to an imagined "public of abstracted, impartial reader-participants."[32] The proposition we call the public sphere is composed of "publics and counterpublics" that mix secular and religious voices. Methodism made canny use of the public sphere, particularly the world of print, in a mass-media effort to get its spiritually and emotionally intense message of "inward religion" out, and in so doing complicated the terms of these modern conceptual separations.

McKeon's formulation also invokes a familiarly monolithic Protestantism that obscures varieties of religious experience within Anglican and Dissenting traditions, particularly the sacramentalism of the early Methodists and their highly public, outdoor meetings. Their sacramental theology, adapted from both high Anglican and Lutheran traditions, was a version of consubstantiation, as opposed to the symbolic reading of more Latitudinarian Anglican theology. Positing Protestantism as a unified category of identity flattens out the terrain between high Anglicans and Ranters, making it harder to understand the content of religious debates in the eighteenth century, particularly those surrounding Methodism. McKeon further frames his account of the "Protestant separation" as a question of "how religious discourse contributed to the economic elaboration of a public virtue separable from the state and grounded not in disinterestedness but in the satisfaction of private interests" (33). But the ideology that he sees elaborated by the portmanteau category of modern Protestantism is already economic and complicit in capitalism, and he concurs that Weber's thesis is an "answer to the question how religious faith and economic interest, the Protestant ethic and the spirit of capitalism, came to be allied in the early modern period" (McKeon, *Secret History* 36). The interiority of modern religion thus becomes collusion with the notion of private property and self-interest, which is at odds with the communal experiments and economic ethos of early Methodism. As in Weber's argument, the slippage between the categories of Protestant, Calvinist, and Puritan makes the doctrines of election and predestination the characteristics of all Protestant theology, rather than the specific language of Calvinism, against which Wesleyan Methodism defined itself, and which was the substantive issue in the split between Whitefield and the Wesleys.

McKeon's distinction between traditional and modern knowledge in terms of their degrees of distance from the object of knowledge is a key heuristic in tracking the "devolution of absolutism" that illustrates Methodism's interstitial relation to this formulation of modernity. At stake in his formulation is the possibility of a distinction between believing (aligned with traditional knowledge) and knowing (the domain of modern knowledge). Believing and knowing become part of a temporal argument about cognitive progress that Methodism, as a "modern" movement, complicates. Traditional knowledge, McKeon argues, is tacit in the sense that it is embedded in cultural practice and that it discourages the separating out of knowledge for self-conscious examination.

> "Modern" knowledge is, on the contrary, an explicit and self-conscious awareness, characterized not by the way it saturates social practice but by the way it satisfies canons of epistemology, which impose on knowledge the test of self-justifying self-sufficiency. Disembedded from the matrix of experience it seeks to explain, modern knowledge is defined precisely by its explanatory ambition to separate itself from its object of knowledge sufficiently to fulfill the epistemological demand that what is known must be divided from the process by which it is known. (xix)

Methodist practice exemplifies the first part of McKeon's proposition. The devotional and confessional practices, as Phyllis Mack has shown, reveal an extraordinary degree of emotional self-consciousness on the part of people actively participating "in the cultural discourse about the nature of feeling and sensibility" (5). Wesley's call to "consider" the situation of the self called on his readers to turn their critical gaze inward, to feel and to think about feeling. Methodism, particularly in the Wesleyan tradition, meant weighing evidence, following arguments, and relying on personal observation, all of which we might term modern protocols of knowledge.

But Methodism failed spectacularly to submit to the demand for cognitive objectivity, grounding its claims in the nonobjective yet somatic experience of "the love of God shed abroad in my heart" that John Wesley described to his brother Samuel in a letter of October 30, 1728. Whitefield regularly made this appeal to a mystical, unverifiable change a part of his direct address to his congregations: "Has God by his blessed Spirit wrought such a change in your hearts?" (Whitefield, *Works* 5: 346). Wesley was aware of that situation when he opined in *Advice* that Methodists will give offense by their name and their principles:

> To *Men of Form*, by insisting so frequently and strongly on the *inward Power* of Religion: To *Moral Men* (so called) by declaring the absolute Necessity of *Faith*, in order to Acceptance with GOD: To Men of *Reason* you will give Offence, by talking of Inspiration and receiving the Holy Ghost. (ABINGDON WORKS 9: 127)

By claiming inward knowledge of divine power, through faith, Methodists refused to agree that "what is known must be divided from the process by which it is known" and, in the process, pointed to the impossibility of such a complete separation. That impossibility lurks grammatically in McKeon's text, which has to elide the self and disembody "knowledge" as an agent, itself disembedded from experience and with ambitions of its own. Conversely, the Methodist notion of "spiritual senses" and intimate, externally unverifiable points of contact with God that were their own self-verifying propositions mitigated against this separation, which itself philosophically recedes into an imaginary pure objectivity. The modern reader McKeon describes must separate out the process from the self, which is divided from itself in the very act of knowing anything. Methodism addressed this split in the self with the proposition of embedded spiritual knowledge, which came from "spiritual senses," and became the largest Western eighteenth-century religious movement by doing so. The affective immediacy of Methodism's conversion experience, coupled with its forms of sociability, bridged the gap in the cognitively divided modern self by using Locke's "modern" method to assert that one could have a "primitive," unmediated experience of God that was its own proof. In this sense, the movement took up Hume's proposition that "reason is and ought to be only the slave of the passions," though perhaps not in terms that would have pleased Hume.

These various cultural histories of eighteenth-century Britain tell a story about Christian belief that survives into modernity at one of two ideological extremes: as a disembodied, deistic Protestantism that fuels modern capitalism, or as Roman Catholicism, recalcitrantly lodged in an historical past.[33] Neither of those extremes describe the embodied language of Christian belief in Methodist writing, preaching, or hymnody (or in high Anglican devotional discourse) and its popular success in the eighteenth century, contested as it was. Part of the difficulty lies in the inadequacy of the bare categories Protestant and Catholic to the complex debates within seventeenth- and eighteenth-century Anglican circles and in Methodism's Eucharistic emphasis on the body of Christ. But this story about modern religion is also a function of late nineteenth- and early twentieth-century critical assumptions that have provided the interpretive lens for a modernity that is material, demystified, and defined through its procedures of demystification. What the historical narrative of secularization as progressive does reflect is the way that, as Charles Taylor put it, modern religion was "narrowed to moralism" in modernity's own accounts of itself, though not in the whole of religious experience (Taylor, *A Secular Age* 225). The descriptive merit of this story lies in its summary of the best-known apologetic strain of Anglicanism in Tindal, Toland, and Sprat, bent on avoiding the doctrinal conflicts of the seventeenth century and "tale of a tub" minutiae, and anxious to reconcile religion to an optimistic belief that, as Tillotson put it, "the glory of God and our Happiness cannot reasonably be supposed to cross and contradict one another" (Tillotson 195). Tillotson also wrote *A Discourse Against Transubstantiation* (1684), one of many such treatises that shaped eighteenth-century Anglican views on the Eucharist as memorial and, by contrast, regarded mystical or spiritualist understandings of it as "papist" and a threat to the modern project of the British nation. But this largely Latitudinarian story about eighteenth-century religion elides the more mystic and spiritual strains of eighteenth-century religious life in England. In it, Hoadly, Warburton, and Tillotson speak for the moment, while mystics and spiritualist figures such as William Law, Fenelon, Mme. de Guyon, and Methodists collectively play the antimoderns or disappear.

Methodism's success is a reminder that issues of presence beyond quantifiable meaning, of what, in the words of Gumbrecht, "meaning cannot convey," had broad purchase in the eighteenth-century British imagination. The imaginative investments in this expression of a modern spiritual longing cut across aesthetic and religious terrain, a longing that brings together the cultural fascination with Pamela's letters and the Wesleyan "warming of the heart." Picking up on this script of secularization and revolution at a cultural level, twentieth-century literary criticism became something of an echo chamber for the claim that the eighteenth century marks the rise of a secular literary aesthetic, art for art's sake. The case of hymns, consumed both as poetry and as devotional lyric, complicates this proposition, but so does the more general point that the biggest sellers of the day were religious materials—books, tracts, sermons, hymnals, and treatises, the greatest portion of them Methodist—as Isabel Rivers has demonstrated.[34] Jennifer Snead, in a useful overview of eighteenth-century literary arguments, shows how the incompatibility of religion and literature (and their readers) in Ian Watt's account of the rise of the novel presumes the validity of the secularization thesis to establish the ascendance and development of formal realism ("Religion" 709).[35] One feature of this account that has been prominent in novel criticism is the use of the "imaginary Puritan" as the template for modern secular subjectivity. By making the Puritan "imaginary," this critical perspective tends automatically to secularize devotional claims of characters like Robinson Crusoe, who becomes always-already *homo economicus*, or to read the devotional lyric of the seventeenth century as only expressions of sexual desire. This reading strategy makes expressions of religious belief as such into a misrecognition of other social or material impulses, which are the real historical content to be explored in literary reading and writing. This narrative forces the segregation of literary writing as implicitly secular from an obviously distinct category of religious or devotional writing, which obscures the mixed experience of being an eighteenth-century reader and the active production of these terms in the period.

Methodism in the British Imagination

The first chapter of this study walks briefly through the history of Methodism. From the beginning, the story was satiric. The name "Methodist" originated as a taunt for the members of the Oxford Holy Club led by John and Charles Wesley in the 1730s, becoming a familiar yet broad label by the 1750s and reaching well beyond the circle of the Wesleys' and George Whitefield's direct influence. Wesley captured the sense of ironic distance that many so-called Methodists had on their own name in the phrase "called *Methodist*," which appears with italics in several sermons and tracts, including the widely reprinted *Advice to the People call'd Methodists*. Wesley reminds his readers in *The Character of a Methodist* that it was "not a Name which they take to themselves, but One fixt upon them, by Way of Reproach" (*Abingdon Works* 9: 32). The negative construction and fundamental uncertainty about what exactly Methodism was made it a canvas for fears about a modern *sensus communis* gone awry, part of what John Mee has called the "monstrous alter-ego of eighteenth-century civility," as well as for the thinly cloaked fascination with the experiences of divine presence in the modern world that Methodists described (Mee 24). The range of voices mocking the movement in this period, included well-known satirists such as Fielding, Foote, Pottinger, and Smollett, but also Frances Burney, whose demure, eponymous heroine Evelina laughs at Samuel Foote's bawdy anti-Methodist farce *The Minor*; these voices invoke Methodism as a negative boundary for the modern self.

Methodism depended on Lockean arguments about consciousness to articulate the terms of "experimental Christianity" but the result challenged the coherence of the Lockean self at a cognitive as well as forensic level. Methodism's "experimental Christianity" provided a troubling counter-public to the *sensus communis*. Methodists insisted that their experimental religion had a place in the public conversation about the modern self through massive outdoor meetings, its extensive print media, and contemporary music that spoke an embodied language of "heart religion." But the Methodist event of conversion detonated powerfully in an era self-conscious about its own modernity and wrestling with the definition of the modern self. Their messages shared space in the public sphere along with literary texts promising their own experience of inspiration and meaning. The debate that unfolded was over whether Methodist inspiration was too dangerous for the modern self, and what kind of writing, speech, or performance was too immediate and might change the self too much, a debate that shaped the articulation of the categories of modern literature and modern critical reading practices.

Chapters 2 and 3 of this study reflect on the old practice of sexualized satire as it relates to the new Methodist movement. The connection between sexual perversity and religious fervor was common in anti-Catholic and anti-Puritan literature, including Rabelais's *Gargantua* and *Pantagruel*, tales of Reynard the Fox, Boccaccio's *Decameron*, Butler's *Hudibras*, and *Venus in the Cloister*. As Peter Wagner has observed, eighteenth-century anticlerical themes illustrate the broader point that satire is limited to "exaggeration, myth, and stereotype, which do not allow much variation of a given theme" (Wagner 72). Historically, most satires of religious hypocrites show the holy person in question masking sexual intentions with a pious act. This type of hypocrisy informs Rabelais's portrait of the Monk and the Abbey of Thélème, wafts about Chaucer's carnal pilgrims, and frames Moliére's *Tartuffe*. Restoration and early eighteenth-century British stage comedy added its own chapter with parodic Puritans and Quakers in plays like Howard's *The Committee*, Shadwell's *The Fair Quaker of Deal*, and Behn's *Sir Patient Fancy*. Closest in approach to anti-Methodist satires are the images of Quakers, like Centlivre's Obadiah Prim in *A Bold Stroke for a Wife* (1718) who quakes with the holy spirit but then begs the housemaid Mary to show him "a little, little bit of her delicious bubby" when they are alone (2.2: 74).

In the most general sense, then, the accusations of sexual impropriety leveled against Methodists were unoriginal and built on the battle-tested strategies for mocking religious figures that were well-worn by the time Chaucer engages with them. The twist in midcentury portraits of Methodists is that they are not so much hypocrites with secrets to be discovered, but unstable selves open to radical re-formation.[36] Eighteenth-century satirists tended to treat the Methodist conversion of the modern self like a sexuality, a set of practices at the intersection of body and social script, building on the conventions of clerical satire but bending them to new concerns about the relationship of sexual desire to identity and agency. As Jonathan Kramnick has observed, sex troubles human willing, perception, and desire, all of which subtend human agency in the modern world, a particular concern for Rochester, Behn, and later Jane Barker, in the wake of Hobbsian and Lucrecian materialism. Methodism functioned analogically as a category through which to think through the paradoxes of agency and involuntary feeling; of identity and transformation; and of determinism and free will that cycle through eighteenth-century narratives of sex and self. Fielding's "female husband" Mary/George Hamilton and Cleland's Mr. Barvile are examples of sexy enthusiasts who are disconcertingly "born again" through their overwhelming desires and inclined to convert others.

Sex also provides a provisionally secular answer to the formerly theological question of the soul. Sex, as the acts and practices that are at the intersection of an emerging sex/gender system, promises to tell the deeper truth of the self. But insofar as sex becomes the truth of the self in modernity as Foucault claimed, it does so by borrowing its language from religious discourses. James Grantham Turner's and Bradford Mudge's reappropriations of the Biblical "the word made flesh" to describe pornography in the long eighteenth century illustrate how the embodied language of the heart made strange bedfellows of the modern libertine and evangelical projects. Methodism shares with libertinism a somatic intensity that returns to the body amid an experience of modern alienation from the body. Julia Kristeva observes in *Intimate Revolt*, "Christian mysticism unknowingly allowed the possibility of a dramatic formulation of intimacy in spite of the efforts of rationalist spirituality to dismantle the symbolism of the body and condemn it" (Kristeva 48). Recognizing the relationship between embodiment and Christian mysticism helps us navigate the eighteenth century's tendency to lump together Quakers, Methodists, and Roman Catholics as a set of perverse, sensual heretics defined against "reasonable Christianity." The confusion of Methodists for Roman Catholics in particular, whether satiric or sincere, signals that the discourse of embodied Christianity, located in the incarnation of Christ, becomes a different kind of scandal in the eighteenth century. Methodism described its spirituality and high Christology (primarily in its emphasis on the Eucharist and on a conversion experience) as a challenge to deism, freethinking, atheism, and agnosticism, a challenge which was grounded in the embodied divinity of Christ and untranslatable into discourses of rationality, ethics, or even representation. In the theological terms of consubstantiation, which both Calvinist and Wesleyan Methodists embraced, it was an event that continued to unfold, not an idea subject to rational or historical mastery.

Chapters 4 and 5 examine the nature and implications of Methodist performativity crystallized in two of their signature practices, animated preaching and hymn singing. The size of the crowds gathered for field preaching and hymn singing was in itself spectacular. Even their earliest congregations were larger than those that could be held by any British theater. Their print volume was also astounding; Methodist journals, autobiographies, hymnals, and eventually magazines poured off the presses. The mainstay of their print ventures, sermons and hymnbooks, translated the performative core of the Methodist experience into cheap, widely available text. Whitefield and both Wesley brothers were highly charismatic preachers, which drew a mix of admiration and judgment from figures such as Goldsmith and Johnson. Though Goldsmith mocks Methodists who "preach best with a skinfull" in Tony Lumpkin's ballad in *She Stoops to Conquer*, he also offers a backhanded compliment to Whitefield in the *Lady's Magazine*, suggesting that he could serve "as a model to some of our young divines" who could add his "earnest manner of delivery" to a more commonsensical Anglicanism (Goldsmith 3: 154). And Johnson, who judged gesticulation and theatricality in sermons as a potentially ridiculous appeal "to the ignorant and rude," nonetheless grants in *The Idler* no. 90 that he "would not deter those who are employed in preaching to common congregations from any practice which they might find persuasive" for the sake of converting sinners (S. Johnson 281). Both Goldsmith and Johnson regarded Methodist theatricality as a useful supplement to devotion, even if they considered Methodism an outlier set of practices, situating it, as Paul Goring has put it, on the borders of politeness.

The air of theatricality lingered especially about Whitefield both as a secular explanation of his power and as a description of the admittedly theatrical situation of his public persona, but the issue went well beyond the charisma of Whitefield and Wesley to name a deeper concern about the stability of the Methodist self and the question of whether any self could be said to have a consistent, self-identical core. Lockean psychology underscored this problem of locating selfhood in the dialectic of sensation and reflection, which Fielding's "An Essay on the Knowledge of the Characters of Men" tried and failed to stabilize as an inward identity that could be revealed in actions, facial expressions, and appetite or drive. Fielding, caught in the semantic trap of character as both fixed identity and the impress on the face of a malleable coin, shows how, as Lisa Freeman explains it, "the concept of character raised the frightening possibility either that there was no true 'inside' or that if there were, we have no 'real' access to it" (27). Methodist sermons, which made a performative appeal for belief in the moment, and Methodist hymns, which invoked a collective "I" through emotional lyric and music, pushed and pulled on the boundaries of self through performed experiences of mystical presence. The experiences of the listeners and hymn singers provided part of the spectacle to supplement the theatricality of the Methodist meeting, a species of "theater of the real," which included the risk of being reshaped by this message. Hogarth, Foote, and Fielding all took shots at Methodists as performers, but their fascination with what actually happens in the Methodist "theater of the real" drew them further into questions about the elusive nature of the self. The movement threw the question of the self into relief against its own conversion practices, which seemed poised to take advantage of this instability and pushed the rational, self-possessing individual off the path of modernity.

Chapter 6 focuses on two novels and their extended engagements with the question of how Methodism might supplement rather than challenge modern British identity. Smollett's *Humphry Clinker* (1771) and Richard Graves's *The Spiritual Quixote* (1773) present softer, kinder portraits of Methodism that translate the satiric vigor of earlier attacks into a comic meditation on community. Smollett's final novel is propelled by a secular circuit ride that follows father and redeeming son on a comic fairy-tale journey from alienation to family. As Smollett exchanges the Lucretian and Calvinist world of fatalistic givens for the happier and purposeful accidents of sympathy, he finds common cause, like it or not, with Wesleyan Methodism's communitarian drive and its optimistic vision of religious sociability's reforming touch. Clinker's Methodism is part of a necessary transformation of the Bramble family's traditional blood relations, patriarchalism, and personal differences into affinities and affections that can provide the emotional infrastructure of the emerging nation of Britons. As the conservative strain of *Humphry Clinker* reveals, this affective supplement can prop up the new economic order, allowing Matt Bramble to reinvent patriarchy and preserve traditional hierarchies as an expression of modern class difference. Graves's *The Spiritual Quixote* is a surprisingly kind portrait of Methodist itinerancy considering that most of Graves's own congregation was stolen away by a lay-Methodist preacher in the 1750s. *The Spiritual Quixote's* Wildgoose, who experiments with Methodism only to come back and resume his post as master of his country estate in the Cotswolds, walks the reader through a series of conversations across the British countryside that weave communities together in unexpected ways.

Methodism's method for converting selves through its democratic theater of the real becomes useful comic glue in these novels. W. R. Ward argues that Wesley's shift away from his early mystical influences (Guyon, Fenelon, and Law) encouraged this more sociable integration of the movement into British society over time as he charged the movement to "proclaim the glad tidings of salvation ready to be revealed, not only to those of your own household . . . to neighbor, and beyond" (qtd. in W. R. Ward 135). The material efforts of Methodists, their rhetoric of conversion, and the sociability of heart religion mediate the loneliness of the modern self in these novels and forge bonds of community in the far-flung territory of Great Britain. Their affective responsiveness, their foibles, and most of all their sociability are usable supplements to the notion of normative British identity that informs the novels. As acknowledged quixotes, Clinker's and Wildgoose's authority is undermined in advance by the literary structure that tells us how to read them. These comic but loveable Methodists turn out not to be revolutionaries at all but renewers of the old order through the language of heart religion, lending Methodism's affective sociability to British identity.

CHAPTER ONE

Historicizing Methodism

I n spite of the voluminous written record left by Wesley as well as an outpouring of journals, hymns, letters, and newspaper reports, early Methodism is strangely hard to define. As Methodist historian David Hempton has observed, "the more one looks for an essence of Methodism, the more one is convinced there is no essence, apart from inspired innovation based on biblical ideas" (*Methodism and Politics* 29). Albert Lyles goes so far as to say that by the 1750s "the term 'Methodist' was no longer an identifying term for a particular group but was an inclusive name, if not for all of those who took religion seriously, at least for all of those who were obviously evangelical" (24). John Wesley refused to define the "Character of a Methodist" in his essay of that same name beyond a belief in inspired scripture and the divinity of Christ: "But as to all opinions which do not strike at the root of Christianity, we think and let think" (*Abingdon Works* 9: 34). Wesley's lack of specificity about the movement was, on the one hand, of a piece with the broad trend of eighteenth-century theology toward toleration, but it also indicates the ways that Methodism was a floating anxiety. Samuel Richardson worried privately in a letter to George Cheyne that he had been "too much of a Methodist" about Pamela's piety, deploying the term as a boundary for tasteful religious feeling, much as Horace Walpole would in his negative definition of good sense and good breeding (Carroll 46–47). The exaggerated pictures of emotional, illiterate, antinomian Methodists in the eighteenth century show, as Albert Lyles put it, "Methodism mocked," which puts on display the anxieties that Methodism was called on to name.

Methodism's cultural role was further complicated because it only made its official break with the Church of England late in the century, which kept the threat to British Anglican identity (for their critics, at least) infuriatingly close to home. Methodism was a challenge to the priority of the national church from within it, which was already seeming more like a denomination competing with other denominations in a democratized ecclesial landscape (Barker-Benfield 71). Methodists were technically Anglicans for most of the century and wanted to provide a corrective from within the church to what John Wesley, George Whitefield, and others saw as a dangerous trend to deism, represented in the Latitudinarianism of the previous generation in Tillotson and Whichcote, and in their own moment by Lavington, Hoadly, Warburton, and Middleton Conyers. The movement did not require or even encourage its constituents to break with their local parish churches, and it remained entwined with the Church of England into the 1770s, when John Wesley was being readmitted to Anglican pulpits as a visiting preacher. Charles Wesley, who rejected itinerancy, affirmed his identity as a minister of the Church of England and kept an Anglican pulpit in Bristol until his death.[1] John Wesley insisted in *The Character of a Methodist* in 1742 that he and his followers "do vehemently refuse to be distinguished from other Men, by any but the Common Principles of Christianity" (*Abingdon Works* 9: 41). Methodism bedeviled the simple distinction between Anglican and Dissenter and, in a theological sense, between Protestant and Catholic, given their sacramental rather than memorial conception of the Eucharist and their emphasis on "primitive" Christianity in a world of "progressive" deists.

Methodist historian Henry Rack summarized the blend of Anglican, Lockean, libertine, Piestist, and scientific thought that shaped early Methodism in his epithet for John Wesley: "reasonable enthusiast." The phenomenon of eighteenth-century British Methodism was formed in the dialectic of "method," a reasoned empirical approach to self-making and spiritual improvement, and the "enthusiasm" of the mystical experience of being *en-theos*, possessed by a god and thus not oneself.[2] Their interstitial doctrinal existence made the movement a Rorschach test for post-Interregnum boundaries of the self with regard to religion and modernity. Rack's descriptor locates Wesley and, by extension, Methodism, in the crosshairs of the irresolvable eighteenth-century debate between free will and determinism; is the Methodist an autonomous agent who freely chooses, or an overwhelmed self who is ultimately unaccountable for his or her actions?[3] This question is at the heart of what Mack calls the "series of conundrums" in early Methodism that pit self-abnegation against agency and thus call for "a more complex definition of agency than the liberal model of individual autonomy used by most secular historians" (*Heart Religion* 26, 9). Methodists announced their malleability in both their formulation of the psychic release of becoming a "new man," which figures religion as *jouissance* rather than law, and in their "disciplines" and practices. Methodism's methods were exemplified by the small-group confessional practices of the bands (small meeting groups emphasizing spiritual accountability and confession), the rules for membership in Methodist societies (larger regional groups of believers), and John Wesley's prolific one-man advice literature industry. These methods stabilized and gave shape to the individual Methodist, but they also underscored the provisional nature of the modern self, vulnerable to an overwhelming, transformational experience of otherness in the "warming of the heart." In Wesley's adaptation and popularization of Locke, which exposed the relationship between belief and sensation at the heart of modern epistemologies of the self, the self looks less autonomous than the story of modern liberalism has suggested.

In his use of Lockean methodology, which runs throughout his tracts and sermons, Wesley didn't just revise Locke, he pointed to a conundrum in Locke's materialism that David Chalmers has more recently dubbed "the hard problem of consciousness," the question of the relationship between phenomena and experience, which required a leap of faith.[4] A Lockean conception of knowledge, in both its "secular" primary mode and in the Wesleyan adaptation of spiritual senses, depends on the event of sensation. In this event, an individual consciousness believes the senses when it accepts the data and reflects on it to produce ideas. Here is the paradox of the Lockean proposal, which the farcical and satiric images of Methodists inadvertently underscore: a secular account of knowledge presents sensation and reflection as rational, even mechanical, but it is nonetheless predicated on an act of faith in sensation itself. Berkeley seized on this moment and its potential for skepticism, but he exacerbated the philosophical problem by trying to contain all experience within the mind of God. Some belief, some act of faith is a part of any attempt at communication or interpretation, as is some doubt and anxiety about our own capacity for credulity. The performance of this moment as event, the act of faith, and the ways that it consequently reshapes the self are what the satires and other uncharitable representations of Methodists target. But the very critics who painted Methodists as failed moderns, people who substitute belief for knowledge, find themselves confronted with the act of faith implicit in all forms of communication. Their attempts to undermine Methodism's legitimacy return to the problem of faith, and to the need to believe in some first premises in order to constitute ourselves as selves, which includes the capacity for communication with others, even if that belief is staked on the self's ability to reason.

The movement's focus on "heart religion" pulls in the direction of a democratic, even anarchic experience of feeling that was a concern for Hutchenson, Shaftesbury, Hume, and others who tried to manage it in part by establishing a notion of good poetic enthusiasm in contrast to a more populist and uncritical emotional excess (Mee 45). The spectre of enthusiasm, a term often used interchangeably with Methodism, shaped the cultural conversation about good reading and the function of secular art. Samuel Foote, for instance, contrasted what he saw as bad religious enthusiasm with good (secular) aesthetic enthusiasm, "that glow of fancy, that ethereal fire" that transports both artist and viewer, exemplified for him by Hogarth (*Letter from Mr. Foote* 70). Close to Burke's articulation of the sublime, Foote frames his point in terms of the artist who must manage his or her own experience of an intense loss of conscious control in the production of art. Bad enthusiasm subjects the modern self to the "Dictates of an inflamed Imagination" as experienced by nonartists, an "ethereal fire" that deludes the individual into a primitive belief that he or she is inspired, when true enthusiasm belongs to the artistic genius who can regulate it, the proof of which is artistic production (19). But Foote's comparatively secular definition of the aesthetic depends on tropes from classical mythology that are themselves religious and mystified, like the term enthusiasm. He speaks in *The Minor* of the "Promethean torch" that illuminates good painting, and he refers to Delphic oracles and the Feast of Bacchus to describe Whitefield's theatrical presence. Foote grants the availability of some mystic experience that is in dialogue with an ancient, even primitive past, but the debate is over who should present it, the aesthete who loses the self in the sublime or the "enthusiast" who loses the self in the religious experience.

"Methodism"

Amid claims for a moralized version of Christianity from the pulpits of Butler, Hoadly, and Warburton, Methodists roared to the forefront of eighteenth-century religious life with their psychically and spiritually intense "warming of the heart." Methodism grew from a handful of pious Oxford students in the 1730s to nearly 26,000 declared members by 1767 and over twenty-five million by the late nineteenth century (Wolffe 25). The numbers who came to hear Methodist preaching, who happened upon an outdoor sermon and felt moved by it, or who had some contact with their printed sermons, tracts, or journals, were significantly larger. That we should speak of eighteenth-century "Methodism" with some ironic distance, however, is written into the story of the movement's name, which originates in mockery. Its use in the eighteenth century began as a taunt for the members of the Oxford "Holy Club," a group whose devotional and carefully structured days laid the groundwork for the Methodist movement. The name referred to the regularized method of followers who, in the words of historian T. B. Shepherd, began "to cut themselves off from worldly pleasures, to eat little, to rise early, to fill every moment of the day with work or with 'good works'" (15). The first known use of the term in English as a religious designation, however, predates Wesley by nearly a hundred years. As early as 1639 the term designated a vague religious identity ("plain, pack-staff methodists") as well as followers of Daniel Williams who were called "new Methodists in the great point of justification" (qtd. in R. Watson 16). Wesley accepted the taunt as the name for the burgeoning movement in the late 1730s, though the term remained an imprecise conceptual foil to the reasonable modern self. Methodism as it was conceived popularly was always already something to mock, yet also something to fear, an illustration of a modern self unmoored. Frances Brooke's flirtatious Anne Wilmot explains in *The History of Lady Julia Mandeville* that the Methodist, like the "Bel-Esprit," is a character "in which one might take a thousand little innocent freedoms," a figure who might say anything, and about whom one could make any remark (41). As late as 1771, Smollett uses the term in *Humphry Clinker* to refer both to Whitefield's and Wesley's disciples (including Clinker, Tabitha, and Win Jenkins) and to the Scotch Seeders, whom he also calls "methodists." It could be applied to anyone perceived as excessively religious or overzealous, a name for an Anglican interested in using contemporary hymns in worship, a prison or social reformer, or as a reference to Wesley, Whitefield, and their followers. Evangelicals like James Boswell's grandmother Lady

Betty Bruce Boswell, who used the language of calling and wrote that "all God's people are effectually called of God in time ... to embrace the offer of Christ," might have been identified as a Methodist if she had used this language just a few years later.[5] What exactly a Methodist was, then, was a matter of some debate; for their enemies, it could mean anything.

Wesley himself made the point on several occasions that the name "Methodist" means nothing; it is simply an empty signifier to which Wesley's enemies have attached prejudicial meanings that are the source of cheap laughs and thoughtless dismissals. Wesley complained in his *Extract of the Revd. Mr. John Wesley's Journal, From August 12, 1738 to Nov. 1, 1739* that it was used to cut off any discussion of the validity of the movement: "if any man dare to open his mouth in my favour, it needs only to be replied, 'I suppose you are a Methodist, too,' and all he has said is to pass for nothing" (*Abingdon Works* 19: 2). John and Charles Wesley made canny use of the rhetorical dynamics of the name "Methodist," as Heitzenrater, quoting from Charles Wesley's journals, explains:

> In December 1738, when "Methodists" were prohibited from preaching in St. Antholin's Church, London, Charles (Wesley) had responded to the Clerk's question, "Do you call yourself a Methodist?" by saying "I do not; the world may call me what they please." He was allowed to preach. (HEITZENRATER 104)

In his defense of Methodism against the attacks of George Lavington's 1749 *The Enthusiasm of Methodists and Papists Compared*, Wesley claims their name serves as an open invitation to their enemies to mock them:

> To hinder the Light of those whom GOD had thus charged, from shining before Men, he gave them all in general a Nick-name: He called them Methodists. And this Name, as insignificant as it was in itself, effectually answered his Intention. For by this Means, that light was soon obscured by Prejudice, which could not be withstood by Scripture or Reason. By the odious and ridiculous Ideas affixt to that Name, they were condemned in the Gross, without ever being heard. So that now any Scribler, with a middling Share of low Wit, not incumber'd with Good-nature or Modesty, may raise a Laugh on those whom he cannot confute, and run them down whom he dares not look in the Face. (OXFORD WORKS 11: 375)

Wesley suggests that the name is part of a plot to keep Great Britain and Ireland "covered with Vice" as they had been before the movement began. Lavington's attack associated Methodism with Roman Catholicism, which had additional political and cultural bite in the wake of post-1745 concerns about Jacobitism.

Whitefield deploys a similar strategy of nominal distance from the term in *A Brief Account . . . of a Late Trial at the Assize held at Gloucester, March 3, 1743*, while making his case against rioters who mobbed various Methodist meetings, with the implicit approval of local officials: "Both the Constable and Justices were applied to, but refused to act; and seemed rather to countenance the Mobbing, hoping thereby *Methodism* (as they called it) would be put a Stop to, at least at *Hampton*" (6). The policing function of the term became physical and violent in the case of widespread mob violence against the Methodists from the 1740s to the 1770s. More generally, the provisional sense of Methodist as something they were "called" and then, eventually, claimed as their own constituted their identity as a dialectic of internal definition and external reading.

Insofar as it was a set of defined practices, Methodism was, as David Hempton has put it, "a religious association coming to fruition in the age of associations" (*Methodism* 52). The name "Holy" or "Holiness" Club connected the Oxford Methodists to the male-identified clubs of the early eighteenth century, both the libertine clubs like the Hell-Fire Club and the more sociable and literary clubs like the Kit-Kat Club. But the question of who was in this club and, indeed, whether anyone was, became a pivot point in the early definition of the movement. The 1760 author of "A Letter to Mr. Foote" includes as an appendix "A serious address to the Methodists themselves" beginning with the question of how to address them: "Good people? No;—I fear this will give Offence to those, whose superlative Merit, it seems, consists in the Superlativeness of their Sins" (24).[6] The author then goes through other possible greetings:

> Courteous Readers!—But what if they cannot read, as, I am well assured, most of them cannot? . . . Dearly beloved Bretheren!—No:—This is so like the Exhortation of the common Liturgy, that I am persuaded, suppose they can read, they would go no farther. . . . My dear Bretheren! But I abhor Deceit as well as Flattery. . . . Gentlemen and Ladies! What? They would say, Do you laugh at us to our Faces? For tho' there may be some, perhaps, among them of the gentle Craft; yet, I hope, there are few of the gentle Class; . . . Ye mad Enthusiasts? . . . Ye Methodists? . . . I must defer my Address, till I can please myself with a proper Appellation for such Heterogeneous Mortals. (26–28)

The letter sports with the idea that Methodists are outsiders (commoners, anti-Anglican, barely literate, illiterate, and potentially mad), but the final appellation, "Heterogeneous Mortals," concludes that the constituency is mixed and difficult to define.

In *Advice to the People Called Methodist* (1745), Wesley stresses the newness of Methodism as a category of identity based on practices, non-normative beliefs, and perceptible patterns of self-presentation. He goes on to speak of the novelty of their name, their principles, and their existence:

> You are a new people: Your name is new, (at least, as used in a religious sense) . . . Your principles are new, in this respect, that there is no other set of people among us (and, possibly, not in the Christian world) who hold them all in the same degree and connexion. . . . Your strictness of life, taking the whole of it together, may likewise be accounted new. (ABINGDON WORKS 9: 125)

Methodists were, by Wesley's and other definitions, an emerging eighteenth-century species of Christianity responding to their historical moment as reformers in a more secular age, which was nonetheless the condition of their existence. But even as Methodism was being described as something new, its connections with the past situated the movement as a primitive, even antimodern phenomenon. Along with their claims to be "a new people," John Wesley and George Whitefield leaned into the temporal questions Methodism raised by reusing the seventeenth-century evangelical phrase "primitive Christianity," which they gleaned from Wycliffe and the Carolingians, religious reform movements that wanted to lay claim to an orthodoxy prior to the hegemonic voices of their own time.[7]

In *Advice*, John Wesley explained to his followers that the term Methodist is provisional and pejorative, an idea that depends on a connection to an ancient or disturbing past:

> *Do not imagine you can avoid giving Offense:* Your very *Name* renders this impossible. Perhaps not one in a hundred of those who use the Term *Methodist*, have any Idea what it means. To ninety-nine of them it is still Heathen *Greek*. Only they think it means something very bad, either a Papist, an Heretick, an Underminer of the Church, or some unheard of Monster; and in all Probability, the farther it goes, it must gather up more and more Evil. (ABINGDON WORKS 9: 127)

Wesley's comment that Methodism is "Heathen Greek" is a reference to Methodicus, a first-century Greek physician who published a gynecological treatise, and to his followers, the "Methodists" who were derided by Galenists and Hippocratics, hence known to Cambridge and Oxford educated men as examples of bad doctors.[8] Wesley took the joke public in *The Character of a Methodist* when he explained that the name Methodist was given at Oxford "by Mr. John

Bingham . . . either in allusion to the ancient sect of physicians so called (from their teaching that almost all diseases might be cured by a specific *method* of diet and exercise) or from their observing a more regular *method* of study and behavior." (*Abingdon Works* 9: 32–33). The references to Greek "Methodists" connected the movement, literally and metaphorically, to quackery and discredited science. The theme of quackery returns often in satires of Methodists who promise false cures or whose spiritual remedies act on the body in sexual ways. The medical connection was likely exacerbated by John Wesley's success in dispensing medical as well as spiritual advice. His *Primitive Physic* was, as G. S. Rousseau demonstrated, one of the most widely read books in the eighteenth century.[9] *Primitive Physic*, which popularized ideas from George Cheyne, makes explicit in a more physical register a hope for an inaccessible simplicity in an age of complexity, something that structures successive ideologies of modernism, from neoclassicism to Marxism to psychoanalysis. The longing for a more basic and clearer set of answers rooted in the past but lost in the confusion of the present is produced by the context of a modernity conscious of too many options and possible ways of construing meaning. In this sense, "primitive" simplicity is a remedy for the modern condition.

The term "primitive" provides a particular contrast to the modernizing language and zeitgeist of the eighteenth century. Methodists themselves seemed very aware of the oppositional valence of their "primitive Christianity" against the "modern" eighteenth century. John Wesley tried to seize and redeploy the term "primitive" as a positive descriptor of Methodism's return to first-century Christian doctrines and practices. But to claim to be "primitive" swam against the tide of both the scientific mainstream and the Latitudinarian Anglicanism of Bishop Hoadly, Woolston, and Samuel Clarke, voices for a modern and rational rather than a mystical or enthusiastic "primitive" Christianity. The story fits what Webb Keane calls "the moral narrative of modernity . . . a story of human liberation from a host of false beliefs and fetishisms that undermine freedom" (Keane 5). The power of this narrative, which associates modernity with emancipation qua secularization, is implicated in some of the most prized enlightenment values: discourses of rights, tolerance, narratives of secular improvement, democratic civil cultures, and the belief that they are uniquely situated to render justice. In the name of enlightened tolerance, the irrational, embodied, or ethically troubling elements of religion, which in Christianity are expressed as miracles, a God who intervenes in human affairs, the divinity of Jesus, the status of the Eucharist, and the ethical crisis of the crucifixion, must be contained in more private discourses, where their "antimodern" irrationality cannot derail the modern project into either another civil war, a political merger with Roman Catholic nations, or unscientific mysticism. But, paradoxically, that same bracketing off of the sacred or mystic concentrates it and creates new patterns of feeling and experience that are shaped by a discourse of secularity.

This concentration of sacred or mystical experience in Methodist discourse was often read as a front for Roman Catholicism, which would drag the nation back into a "superstitious" past and place it under papal control. Horace Walpole claimed that the rigor of the Methodists "seems to soften and adopt the artifices of the catholics" and that they may soon "borrow the paraphernalia of enthusiasm now waning in Italy" to become a threat to the "future improvement" of the arts (*Anecdotes of Painting in England* 4: ix). Walpole's concern about Methodism brings together fears of foreign influence and temporal regression. Though Methodism was bred at Oxford from within the Church of England and not in Rome, Edinburgh, or Geneva, Roman Catholicism was a convenient, familiar category of religious otherness that reflected Methodism's high Christology, its emphasis on the Eucharist, and its openness to mysticism. Henry Stebbing, in *An Earnest and Affectionate Address to the People Called Methodists* (1745), fretted that Methodists leaned toward transubstantiation because

> in the Administration of the *Lord's Supper*, wherein the *Distribution* of the *Elements*, the Custom of some of them is to pronounce only the words *The Body of our Lord Jesus Christ* and *the Blood of our Lord Jesus Christ*; leaving out the Remainder of what the Rubric of our Liturgy expressly proscribes to be said by the minister. (35)

That remainder, "Take and eat this in remembrance that Christ dies for thee, and feed on him in thy heart by faith with Thanksgiving," emphasized the representational or memorial quality of the act over its sacramentalism. *The Book of Common Prayer* also included several pages of exclusions for those unprepared for communion due to insufficient penitence, self-examination, or lack of a "quiet conscience."[10] These caveats suggest the contrast to Anglican practice that the Methodist emphasis on communion made. Roman Catholicism still entailed real social, political, and economic alienation in eighteenth-century Britain; early Methodism, by comparison, explored a more sacramental Eucharistic discourse and affirmed the possibility of miracles within Protestant Anglican culture, arguably an even more problematic proposition.[11]

Methodism's emphasis on the crucifixion of Christ pushed back against the idea that religion could be reconfigured into sociable morality in the modern age. Wesley declaimed against "formal Christianity," or Christianity as simply "good sense, good nature, and good manners" in *An Earnest Appeal* (*Oxford Works* 11: 54) and in favor of a faith that brought present, not future, change and "a recovery of the divine nature" and the knowledge of the love of God in *A Farther Appeal* (*Oxford Works* 11: 106). Unlike a civic version of enlightened Christianity, which sought to derive moral principles from religion to which anyone might give their assent under the broadly ecumenical impulse of toleration, Methodists insisted on what Dietrich Bonhoeffer later called the scandal of the cross.[12] Sermons like "God's Love to Fallen Man" (59) and "Justification by Faith" (5) on the vulnerability and suffering of Christ and the blood sacrifice tied Methodist experimental religion to the event of the crucifixion. In tension with Marcal Gauchet's claim that at the end of the seventeenth century in the West, God retreats as an alien other from a now-disenchanted world, Wesley's and Whitefield's emphasis on "Christ crucified" was a message of God's entry and mystical re-entry into the world.

Deists and, to a lesser extent, Latitudinarians, had to set the questions of Christ's divinity and humanity aside in order to focus on the social utility of religious principles. The Latitudinarian arguments so influential in the Anglican pulpits of Bishop Gilbert Burnet and John Tillotson softened or sidestepped the ethically embarrassing issues of the crucifixion and original sin (images and themes that explode graphically in Methodist discourse). As Richard Nash has argued, Latitudinarianism moved mainstream Anglican discourse away from pointed doctrinal claims to allow for a broad range of interpretations of the Thirty-Nine Articles in the Anglican big tent.[13] For deists, religion could be a prop to our "moral sense" (Shaftesbury's term in *Inquiry concerning Virtue and Merit*), but its value needed to be defined extrinsically, as a source of public mores and ethics within a rational system, rather than intrinsically, as felt personal experience. Shaftesbury explains that he is willing to tolerate the particular content of religion as long as it is conducive to social and moral order, particularly among the lower classes. Religion, which is prone to the "Pannick" of enthusiasm, requires *"Publick Leading,"* though Shaftesbury confesses in his quotation from Terence that this is only because trying to get rid of religion would be like "putting effort into going mad by means of reason," a sentiment he prudently left untranslated.[14]

Shaftesbury went much further than other proponents of a rational religion, but his approach shared with Tillotson's and Warburton's a concern for the public utility over the private conviction of religion. Like Toland's "Christianity Not

Mysterious," Shaftesbury's approach to the question of virtue rendered felt faith at best unnecessary and at worst a schismatic threat to a public project that abstracted Anglican Christian principles in the service of rational social order. Famously, he advocated humor as a precaution against melancholy and enthusiasm, but less well known are his anxious reflections on Christ in his private notebooks. Lamenting that the Italian artists he loved (Raphael, da Vinci, Michelangelo) were "forced" to make their living painting Christ for churches, he called Christ a "Wretched model" and "a mere *Jew* or *Hebrew* (originally an ugly scabby people).... Lank clinging Hair, sniveling Face, Hypocritical Canting Countenance & at best Melancholy-Mad & enthusiastical in the common & lower way, not so well even as the Bacchinals & Bacchaates" (qtd. in Branch 120). As Lori Branch notes, Shaftesbury exposes "the interconnected logic of class prejudice, aesthetic taste, misogyny, anti-Semitism, and antireligious sentiment, culminating in and brought to bear on the person of Christ" who is "the unthinkable, disgusting 'Thing' in Shaftesbury's system: God in a body, vulnerable, crucified, effeminately penetrated, subject to all manner of violence" (120–21). The vulnerability of an embodied and suffering image of God, what Milbank and Žižek call the "monstrosity of Christ," at odds with the creator-God of Addison's hymns "Gratitude" and "The Spacious Firmament on High," becomes the focus of Methodist hymnody and theology, which embraces the vulnerable, embodied "Christ crucified" and the believer's own somatic response to that image.

The implication that Methodism's Eucharistic theology proved an alliance with Roman Catholics further defined modern Britishness as more deistic, and singled out their embodied Christian theology (orthodox as it was) as foreign failure to be properly British. The many trips that the Wesleys and Whitefield made to the southern American colonies fed rumors of the national threat Methodism might represent and the suspicion that its leaders had Catholic ties. In the anonymous 1739 *The Methodists*, Satan brags about spreading divisions among Protestants through Methodism to strengthen Rome. He transforms himself into Whitefield, who makes wives rob husbands, seduces young women by putting on "a formal Gown and Band," and fills his ranks with child followers. The chaos of Methodist fervor here turns out to be a diabolical and well-organized plan to weaken the "true" Church of England through Whitefield's crypto-Catholic sex appeal. Beyond the attempt to associate Methodism with an irrational, superstitious past, the connection alluded to the colonial activities of the Wesleys and Whitefield in Georgia, where Oglethorp had driven back a Spanish incursion at Savannah. Evangelicals like Methodists accused of Roman Catholicism in the colonies were a part of this nationalist colonial struggle over territory, while they also represented the possibility of an invading religious ideology, including "Jesuitical" confession, mysticism, emphasis on communion, and irregular worship practices. Concerns were significant enough that the trustees of the Georgia colony planted William Stevens as a spy in Methodist meetings to observe whether or not they were "concealed Papists." Though Stevens concluded they were not, William Norris, a visiting Anglican priest of Tillotsonian leanings and a missionary for the Society for Propagating the Gospel, believed that they were and raised the concern with the trustees, which may (along with a rumor that Wesley had an affair with an engaged woman) have contributed to the chilled climate Wesley encountered and his abrupt departure from Savannah in 1737.[15] Politically, Whitefield was a supporter of the crown and of British colonial activity in the Americas, as were the Wesley brothers. But the impression of Methodism as either cloaked Roman Catholicism or Dissent and, either way, a risky invasion of anti-British ideas, ran throughout the satires. The subsequent realities of its growth as an independent movement and de facto challenge to the Anglican establishment outweighed Wesley's personal politics.

Methodism's actual Moravian ties, which included an at times shockingly embodied focus on the crucified Christ, were prominent in the 1730s and 1740s, and tagged the movement as un-British. Both Wesley brothers encountered the Moravians, a group of Lutheran pietists, and learned German in part in order to translate their hymns. In turn, John Wesley helped teach English to David Nitschmann, the Moravian Bishop, and other Herrnhut Moravians in the Georgia colony (*Oxford Works* 1: 137). Wesley's first published journal makes clear the important influence of German Pietism in his early thought, which provided the theological core of his notions about salvation, somatic religious experience, and instantaneous conversion. Conversations with Peter Böhler shaped his thinking on salvation by faith, and he borrowed the concept of "the witness within yourself," or the assurance of salvation, from the Moravian Spangenberg, blending it with a more English Lockean account of sensation. Spangenburg instructed him in Georgia and introduced him to Count Nikolaus Zinzendorf, whose Herrnhut settlement he would later visit (*Oxford Works* 1: 146). Zinzendorf embraced the conversion experience and a mysticism that undercut strict denominationalism. He established an experimental religious community at his estate in Herrnhut, where men and women lived in separate dormitories, working and worshipping communally in an arrangement financed by Zinzendorf's private wealth. Wesley traveled there in the summer of 1738 and was struck by the spiritual exuberance of life at Herrnhut. He wrote to his mother that he was "received in a manner I was quite unacquainted with" by Zinzendorf and his followers, a reception he likens to Jesus taking the little children in his arms. He describes a utopian society of love and declares he could stay forever in such a place, exclaiming "See how these Christians love one another!"[16]

Wesley's attitude changed in 1740 after a theological falling out with the Moravians at Fetter Lane. He also felt pressure to define his movement against the Moravians and their theatrical displays of Christian joy and celebration, including extravagant birthday celebrations for Count Zinzendorf, reports of drunken revelry, and the sacred eroticism described by Andrew Frey in his 1753 tell-all *A True and Authentic Account of Andrew Frey*.[17] Wesley was at pains to distinguish Methodism from Moravianism in *The Principles of a Methodist Farther Explained* (1746); in a series of published letters to George Lavington, Bishop of Exeter, regarding Lavington's *The Enthusiasm of Methodists and Papists Compared* (1749); and in his published reply to Downes's *Methodism Examined and Exposed* (1759). Both Lavington and Downes had accused the Methodists of participating in eroticized Moravian practices and being under their influence. The presumption of the Methodist association with Moravians, including their belief that sexual intercourse was a sacramental activity, persisted into the 1770s, leaving the Methodists to defend themselves against charges of sacred eroticism.[18]

Methodism also detonated a network of explicitly political fears about religious revivalism. The Pentecostal tone of early Methodist meetings and the mix of foreign national tags raised concerns about a Cromwellian-style Puritanism that would overrun the public sphere and state, fueled by a more psychological "primitivism" of antimodern thinking within the private sphere. Bishop George Lavington, a lifelong enemy of the movement, saw it as a head-on challenge to class and church hierarchy, and thus an agent of chaos. Edmund Gibson references the Restoration as a before and after mark to describe a religious history in which Methodism is a dangerous, regressive force. The memory of "unbounded Licentiousness in holding Assemblies for Divine Worship" before the Restoration, a practice being revived by Methodists, should lead the government to be more watchful about the "confusion" that springs from unregulated worship. And after the Restoration, the best Christian writers, he says, have encouraged people to "moral Duties, and to cure them of that Madness and Enthusiasm into which they had been led by the Antinomian Doctrines and others of the like Tendency, during the Times of Anarchy and Confusion" (Gibson 13).

This temporal construction is meant as a clear warning: Methodists represent old dissent, and their enthusiasm will lead to political consequences, not a farfetched scenario in the wake of the Jacobite rebellions of 1715 and 1745 and renewed concerns about Roman Catholic influence in Britain. Though Methodism never became political in the way Gibson imagined, the temporal construction of Methodism as either old Dissent or Roman Catholicism suggested that Methodism would drag England back into an anarchic past.

Early Methodism included both the Calvinist-Whitefieldian Methodist Connexion, which preached predestination and election, and the Arminian-Wesleyan Methodists, who were organized around the more Lutheran principle of free grace. Some of the attacks on Methodist doctrinal confusion were, in a sense, legitimate responses to that internal split. The anonymous *The Progress of Methodism in Bristol, by an Impartial Hand* (1743), a representative example of the occasional doggerel aimed at Wesley and Whitefield ("these two extolling one another/Soon drew a Multitude together") lists the sources of the Methodist "Multitude":

> Those, who with their Shepherd's Crook,
> All sorts together seek to hook;
> The Church of England, what they can
> The Romanists, all to a Man,
> The Quaker, and the Antinomian,
> The Arian, and the Muggletonian,
> The Independent, and Arminian,
> Predestinarian, and Socinian,
> The Ana-Baptist, Presbyterian,
> And the unsteady Here and There-ian. (31)

The radical mixing that this satire sees in Methodism corresponds to what religious historian John Walsh calls the "cannibalizing" of the Anglican devotional cells that had sprung up by 1700, small religious societies of men and women that flourished quietly (Walsh 280). Many characteristics associated with the Methodists, particularly emotive worship and evening meetings, were features of seventeenth-century Dissenter movements such as the Quakers and Anabaptists, but the Methodist movement grew at remarkable rates and outpaced other new and recent denominations, using print communication effectively and adapting the small-group infrastructure from the Moravians and Anglican pietists to organize their followers.

Beyond the internal differences between their Calvinist and Arminian strains and the external perception of theological confusion, the branches of Methodism shared charismatic preaching, a somatic language of transformation, and the rhetoric of the spiritual event, which distinguished them from mainstream Anglican practices. Edmund Gibson, then Bishop of London, complained in 1740 that Methodists were led by "a few young Heads, without any Colour of a Divine Commission, [who] set up their own Schemes, as the great Standard of Christianity . . . (and) indulge their own Notions to such a Degree, as to perplex, unhinge, terrify and distract the Minds of Multitudes of People" (12). He proceeds to list in double-column form what he considers the expressions of the "Extraordinary Presences . . . Communications . . . and Directions" from God, primarily from Whitefield's *Journal*, that qualify Methodists as enthusiasts and threaten to mislead an impressionable public. Whitefield speaks of his soul being filled with God, having "felt much the Presence of God," and being called by God to specific actions throughout his journal so often that it is not difficult for Gibson to generate nearly four pages of examples. Gibson would have found many of the same constructions in Wesley's journals, in which he speaks of providential thaws that allow him to travel on missions and the felt presence of God returning to him again and again after his initial "warming of the heart."

Enthusiasm, the term for irrational beliefs and responses that means, at an etymological level, "possessed by a god," seemed to critics an obvious way to describe Methodists. "Enthusiasm," which enjoys such positive connotations in modern American English, was, in the eighteenth century, a term for religious feeling in excess of rational moral principles that divided the world into sane and insane people. Samuel Johnson's hermit in *Rasselas* summarizes the sentiment nicely in the compliment to the Hermit, who was "pious without enthusiasm." Such a self could divide "what is known . . . from the process by which it is known" by separating religious principles, piety, or morals from a more inward and experiential religious encounter, which should be regarded with suspicion because it could not be confirmed or corroborated by others (McKeon, *Secret History* xix). The label of enthusiasm followed the early Methodists, disparaging their claims to an immediate, somatic experience of divine presence as dangerous "false light," even though Methodists tried to defend themselves against this charge. Wesley cautioned against enthusiasm in *The Witness of the Spirit*, a sermon he first wrote in 1746 to rebut charges of enthusiasm leveled by Edmund Gibson (Bishop of London), Thomas Herring (Archbishop of York), and Richard Smalbroke (Bishop of Litchfield and Coventry) but also to declare for "a middle course" between enthusiasm and a materialism that precludes the possibility of having some experience through the "Spirit." He rewrote it substantially in 1767, affirming that the idea of "direct testimony of the Spirit" was possible, not just as an affirmation of the "consciousness of our own good works" but "confirmed by the experience of innumerable children of God" who had the experience of divine forgiveness and presence. Wesley states that the recurrence of these experiences and the "fruit of the Spirit" in those who claimed them provide evidence that Methodist reports of "direct testimony" were not delusion or enthusiasm.

Wesley spoke and wrote against enthusiasm often, warning his followers to "carefully avoid *enthusiasm*," but the term remained synonymous with the movement into the nineteenth century (*Abingdon Works* 9: 130). Enthusiasm could be used to condemn religious irregularity while evading the burden of any specific charge; attempts by Methodists to defend themselves against the charge tended to fall into stalemate. For every sermon by Trapp or Lavington against Methodist enthusiasm, there was a reply from Seagrave, Whitefield, or Wesley declaring that Methodists were not enthusiasts. Whitefield opined the damage done by the label of enthusiasm: "The *Methodists*, you know, are everywhere accounted Enthusiasts, in the worst Sense of the Word; but tho' they are accounted such, yet they wou'd not be Enthusiasts in Reality" (*Works* 4: 101). He goes on to explain that "real" Methodists are not enthusiasts because they do not expect to attain certain ends without using the proper means, and because they do not, as their opponents suggested, seek out persecution, as witnessed by their lawsuit against those who instigated the mob violence against Methodists in Gloucestershire. Understanding the term "enthusiasm" in the eighteenth century means understanding that its pejorative valence named a perceived irrationality that Methodists also rejected while also etymologically announcing the crisis of self that Methodism represented: being *en-theos*, possessed by a god and thus not a modern, contained self.

Enthusiasts in the previous century had made their religious beliefs grounds for political revolution, and fears that the same pattern would emerge from Methodism haunted the first generation of the movement, in spite of John Wesley's own conservative Tory politics. Visions of tens of thousands gathered to hear Methodist preaching in fields and on hillsides fed those fears, born of the immediate past case of Cromwellian Puritanism, in which religious fervor became directly political. The category of Dissent as a way to name non-Anglican Christian sects was a misnomer, since the early Methodists affirmed their Anglican identity, but it did name a political concern. Dissent, which had become an important strategy for regulating and institutionalizing religious differences, reaffirmed the priority of state religion even as it allowed for the possibility of nonstatist forms of Christianity as a matter of "conscience." Conscience in this religious sense was a way to found a claim for a difference from the state and state religion that invoked the first of Taylor's definitions of secularism, the separation of religious institutions and state power, but also tied it to individual feelings and considered judgments, which can be credible without being orthodox. Methodism is a visible example of the etymological relationship of conscience and consciousness that begin to take on distinct meanings in the eighteenth century.[19] The importance of conscience in the sixteenth and seventeenth centuries laid the groundwork for the concept of modern consciousness as the inward locus of the self, which was at the heart of Wesleyan pedagogy. Wesley called on Methodists to observe both the conversion event and the practices of self-making, and to grapple with this paradox. Wesley puts forth the intensely self-conscious quality of Methodism's existence in *Advice to the People Called Methodist* (1745) as his first advice axiom, which appears as a quotation within the text: "Consider, with deep and frequent attention, the peculiar circumstances wherein you stand" (*Abingdon Works* 9: 125). Wesley's call to "consider" the situation of the self turns the critical gaze inward to the dialectic of ecstatic self-resignation and rational self-making that Methodism championed. He uses the language of "inward and outward conformity . . . to the revealed will of God," encapsulating the dialectic of the inward experience of "inspiration or influence of the Holy Ghost" and the set of confessional, study, and worship practices Wesley outlined in *The Character of a Methodist* (1742), *The Principles of a Methodist* (1742), and the rules for the band societies (9: 123, 125). As an intra-Anglican movement that tested the principle of toleration from within the Church of England, Methodism depended on both the religio-political legacy of conscience and the psychological terms of modern consciousness.

Methodism and the Epistemology of the Modern Self

Wesley's use of the phrase "experimental religion" captures the ways that his message harnessed modern philosophy to Christianity, baptizing Lockean empiricism for evangelicalism. Wesley's acquaintance with Locke's thought goes back literally to the cradle. His mother Susanna Wesley was well-read in contemporary philosophy and theology, and her elaborate tutorial program for her nine children (male and female) included Pascal and Locke. She was deeply sympathetic to Pascal's account of the paradox of Christianity, "composed and tempered of the internal and external way. It raises the ignorant to spiritual acts and abases the intelligent by pressing the obligation to outward performances" (Wesley and Wallace 285). Interested in Locke's *Essay concerning Human Understanding* but quick to repudiate the potential skepticism of his materialism, she argues for a reconciled body and mind, a task her most famous son would embrace.[20] Rather than try to escape the materialism of Locke's account of consciousness as Bishop Berkeley did, by retreating into mind as the "mind of God" or depending on Malabranche's Platonism, John Wesley embraced the sensational, formative thrust of *Human Understanding*. His sensational model of spiritual knowledge follows Locke closely, adding to bodily sensation the premise that the soul has its own version of the eye, ear, and palate. In a scientific community with various ideas about sensation circulating from Lucretius's shaped atoms to Margaret Cavendish's model of a dual "rational and sensative" model of sensation (112) to Arnauld's notion of ideas that trigger nervous motion, Wesley's proposition of spiritual sensations is at once tame and revolutionary. As Helen Thompson has argued, Locke's *Essay concerning Human Understanding*, following Arnauld's *On True and False Ideas* (1683), "knits" a complex notion of the idea "to the physiology of perception" that rebuts the Platonism of contemporaries like Malabranche (231). It is of a piece with the experimental thrust in modern epistemology that seeks to account for how we know what we know, yet it is also a tear in the modern self, leaving it open to penetration through spiritual senses and radical remaking through an experience of God.

Wesley and Whitefield underscored the sense of a penetrable, vulnerable self in the feminine tropes and female subject positions they used to describe their involuntary, overwhelming experiences of God. In December of 1738, Wesley wrote about his own spiritual struggle as painful and likened it to childbirth:

> The love of God was shed abroad in my heart, and a flame kindled there, with pains so violent, yet so very ravishing, that my body was almost torn asunder. I loved. The Spirit cried strong in my heart. I sweated. I trembled. I fainted. I sung. . . . I thought my head was a fountain of water! I was dissolved in love.
>
> (OXFORD WORKS 19: 26)

Wesley then quotes from the Song of Solomon, exclaiming "My Beloved is mine, and I am his." He then details subsequent conversion experiences of his followers, including "a well-dressed, middle aged woman," colliers, and hundreds of attendees who called out, wept, and fell to the ground (*Oxford Works* 19: 32–51). The self in this Methodist dialectic of spiritual sensation and spiritual reflection, so often described as feminine, is distinct from a heroic version of the liberal subject, whose supposed inalienable rights and natural equality are belied by experiences of inequality and uneven distribution of power. The material practice of women teaching and sometimes preaching in the Methodist movement underscored the feminized availability of the Methodist self and the feminine pronouns used by Wesley and Whitefield in their sermon illustrations. Embodiment, femininity, and spiritual responsiveness were all fundamental components of the Methodist self.

Methodism's heady blend of naturalism and supernaturalism placed mystical writers such as Fenelón and Mme Guyon alongside Locke's *The Reasonableness of Christianity* in Wesley's *Christian Library* (1750). Wesley and other Methodists expressed an openness to the possibility of miracles or supernatural events, something Locke carefully qualifies as a possibility, provided is it "well attested" and not an error borne of "the Extravagancy of Enthusiasm" (Locke 667). His position was at odds with prominent philosophical explorations of religion, including Hobbes's *Ecclesiastical History from Moses to Luther* (Latin 1689, English 1722), John Trenchard's *The Natural History of Superstition* (1709), and John Toland's *Christianity Not Mysterious* (1696), all of which wanted to emphasize the political dangers of "inward light" and revelation. Shaftesbury, as Lori Branch has noted, went as far as to be revolted by his own interest in any such direct contact with the Divine: "Dost thou, like one of those Visionaryes, expect to see a Throne, a shining Light, a Court & Attendance? Is this thy Notion of *a Presence?* ... —Wretched Folly!" (qtd. in Branch 102). Wesley further pressed on modern temporality as strictly material when he embraced the language of miracles and the supernatural in his published tracts.[21] In *Advice to the People Called Methodists* (1745), he affirmed that Methodist principles included, among other things, acceptance "of a supernatural Evidence of Things not seen; of an inward Witness that we are the children of God, and of the inspiration of the Holy Ghost." (*Abingdon Works* 9: 125). Though he is loosely paraphrasing creedal Anglican phrases ("We believe ... all that is, seen and unseen," and "We believe in the Holy Spirit" are both statements in the Nicene Creed), his focus on these moments underlines the language of the miraculous at a time when many Anglican pulpits downplayed it. The Wesley family only half-joked about their household ghost, "Old Jeffries," a noisy spirit described in terms much like the

Cock Lane ghost, "scratching Fanny," who would be associated with Methodists in the 1760s. Hogarth read Methodism into a supernatural world of belief in witches and ghosts, placing his "Methodist Brain" on a copy of Glanvile on witches in *Credulity, Superstition, and Fanaticism* and reflecting the fear that Methodism was a reactionary stance, "primitive" beyond its claim to recapture the basic tenets of Christianity.

Wesley's interest in spiritual senses offered a correction from within Lockean epistemology to what he saw as a cultural trend toward "formal religion," which reduced Christianity to moral principles. Richard Brantley notes that the experiential idiom of Wesley's theology "*articulates* his understanding of empiricism" both in the sense of popularizing and of positioning it for his purposes (Brantley 23). Wesley's imaginary interlocutor in his 1743 *An Earnest Appeal to Men of Reason and Religion* is a deist who does not "believe the Christian system to be of God" and instead asserts natural religion as the rationality of the good (*Oxford Works* 11: 49). Working from the premise that the deist grants some notion of God, Wesley's proof for faith uses a Lockean argument about sensation that includes spiritual senses, which work just like physical ones:

> And seeing our ideas are not innate, but must all originally come from our senses, it is certainly necessary that you have senses capable of discerning objects of this kind—not those only which are called 'natural senses', which in this respect profit nothing . . . but *spiritual* senses, exercised to discern spiritual good and evil.
>
> (WORKS 11: 56)

His claim reworks Descartes's scholastic proof of God in the third *Meditation* in epistemological terms, but it requires that we grant the existence of spiritual senses alongside physical senses, an idea Wesley also encountered in Peter Browne's *The Procedure, Extent, and Limits of Human Understanding* (1728).

From within its open, penetrable model of consciousness, Methodism also posed a challenge to the forensic nature of the Lockean self. Justification by faith, which emphasized a salvific assurance rather than moral rectitude as the heart of religion, was at odds with a forensic self, whose "identity of Consciousness" can be literally put on trial. Wesley described "free grace" as a divine gift of salvation that is not a function of "good works or righteousness . . . endeavors" or even "good purposes or intentions" but something outside the law (*Abingdon Works* 3: 545). His point was based on Article XI of the Church of England's Thirty-Nine Articles ("we are justified by faith only") but elevated to new prominence by Wesley in sermons like "A Sermon on Salvation by Faith" (1738) and "Free Grace" (1739), works that defined the early direction of the movement. The pious Anglican response to this Methodist emphasis on free grace, exemplified in *A Letter from a Clergyman to One of His Parishoners, Who Was Inclined to Turn Methodist* (1753), was that their emphasis on justification by faith left the believer with no individual moral responsibilities or obligations since Christ alone had provided for the sinner's salvation.[22]

Theologically, Wesley's emphasis on faith and grace as well as his focus on the conversion experience grew from his interactions with the Moravians and Peter Böhler. Wesley embraced Böhler's emphasis on salvation by faith after his early failure to articulate a system of Christian discipline that would guarantee sanctification. Böhler had counseled a despairing Wesley in March of 1738 to "preach faith until you have it, and because you have it, you will preach faith" (*Oxford Works* 18: 228). The "you" of Böhler's exhortation is fundamentally fluid, hailed into being by the "act" of preaching, but nonetheless authentic. This "you" is performative rather than forensic, and in this is exempt from the demands of being a self-sufficient, autonomous self who must be realized before it can act. Böhler brought the young Wesley a Lutheran pietist perspective tinged with Christian mysticism as an antidote to a Calvinist Anglicanism that he increasingly experienced as legalism. Böhler encouraged Wesley to embrace atonement as a mystical reconciliation in which the believer participates, distinct from the more Puritan and Calvinist notions of legal covenant or the monetary language of paid debts, made possible by the crucifixion of Christ. This strain of Christian theology emphasizes the Pauline "justified by grace through faith" and the "warming of the heart" that overwhelms the economic metaphor of redemption. But theologically, this left the individual "unaccountable" in an age of civic accountability and modern laws addressing a rights-bearing subject. The value of good works appeared to decline as the importance of justification by faith rose. Critics like Gibson, Lavington, and Downes complained that Methodism's message of spiritual regeneration and free grace pulled up the sociable anchor of forensic identity and rejected the Judeo-Christian foundation of natural law. The concern that Methodists were antinomians, promulgating a message of lawlessness justified by grace, was the tip of an iceberg that went all the way down to the foundations of just how stable any self, in both mind and body, could be. The "no longer I" of evangelical Methodism was at odds with an imagined community of culpable, conscious, forensic Lockean subjects. Mrs. Cole, the Methodist madam of Samuel Foote's *The Minor*, who celebrates "the comforts of the new birth" while maintaining her brothel, travesties the elevation of private spiritual justification over the public, secularly accountable utility of religion as moral law. As Walpole joked, Methodists loved "big sinners" who could illustrate the reach of grace.

John Forster, an early nineteenth-century historian who wrote about the life of Samuel Foote, relays a story about Whitefield and a criminal named Gibson, perhaps Philip Gibson, tried in May 1751 for assault and robbery, who was to be hanged.[23] The setting is in theatrical dialogue with the story of Christ's crucifixion, underscoring the ethical dilemma of salvation by faith:

> [Whitefield] and his cartloads of followers had taken forcible possession of the stage at country fairs, and had scared whole villages from their customary mirth by invoking against it the doom and judgement. He stood by a worthless criminal, one Gibson, who after condemnation had embraced Methodism, and he told the thousands assembled to see him and another culprit hanged, that only by abandoning their mirth and stage-plays, and taking refuge from such temptations in the Tabernacle, could they ever hope to go to heaven as Gibson had done that day.
>
> (FORSTER 2: 370)

Gibson, a bathetic version of the believing thief crucified with Christ and a gallows convert, had of course abandoned no "mirth" or "stage plays" in order to "go to heaven" that day. The heart religion of Methodism and the doctrine of extreme grace offer him immediate salvation after a life of sin, just the sort of deathbed conversion that the author of *A Plain and Easy Road to Bliss* sarcastically called "a doctrine ... of huge comfort to those who cannot—or will not—or have not time to set about doing the commands of their master."[24] John Downes more pointedly asserts that the antinomian Methodists avow "that even the greater Crimes are no Crimes in the Saints:—that no Man's Conscience ought to trouble him for the Commission of any Sin" (17). Such attacks on Methodist hypocrisy and theatricality are both part of a long-standing tradition in clerical satire and a more local meditation on theater and modern subjectivity; if Locke could question the accountability of a drunken or sleepwalking man for his actions, what accountability did the Methodist convert have to society for past crimes? The scene of many of these conversions, the Methodist meeting and the heartfelt sermon, fueled objections that the experience was theatrical for both the convert and minister, more performance than substance. The charge of antinomianism read the crisis of agency in Methodist "regeneration" as a social problem. If grace is free, and if conversion is the work of a moment in the "warming of the heart," then the religion fails to offer an ethical framework or moral structure, and instead only provides emotion and license. This was the heart of the anti-Methodist charge of antinomianism.

The threat that Methodism represented to its enemies and critics, then, was not so much grounded in a specific theological position but in its disposition of openness that undermined the autonomous, cognitively confident, and legally accountable self. Phyllis Mack has observed that Methodism, much like the writing of early Quaker women, explored a spirituality of giving over, a breaching of the self rather than mastery over it. The kenotic mandate of Philippians to empty the self and "let the same mind be in you that was in Christ Jesus," which Wesley quotes in "The Character of a Methodist" (1742), was one of the many early doctrinal statements that helped to define the movement. In explaining what a Methodist was, Wesley defines such a person as not exclusively himself or herself:

> There is not a motion in his heart but is according to [God's] will.... *He thinks, speaks, and lives according to the* "method" *laid down in the revelation of Jesus Christ.* His soul is renewed after the image of God, "in righteousness and in all true holiness." And "having the mind that was in Christ" he "so walks as" Christ "also walked." (ABINGDON WORKS 9: 41)

Wesley's statements are orthodox by Anglican standards, and this representation of Christian piety is in one sense very familiar. Giving over the self to a higher, divine power is a component of many religions, and a clear part of the Christian tradition in particular, but it could be only partially reconciled to the psychological and political implications of Locke's thought. Locke's *Second Treatise of Civil Government* ties consciousness to the forensic subject, while *An Essay concerning Human Understanding* locates the self in rational cognitive processes; either way, Lockean philosophy wove together consciousness and control as the boundary of the modern self, while Methodist discourse asked for that self to reopen its boundaries. In Locke's account, the nervous system provides data that, in collaboration with the brain's native capacity for rational thought, produces a conscious self with relative consistency and autonomy. Conversely, the religious self, invaded by the divine other, can only be attributed to a "weakness of the nerves"; in a modern materialist epistemology, true religion, as E. Ann Taves observed, must be self-evident, reasonable, and orderly (Taves 29). Overwhelmed and yet actively laying aside its own sense of agency, the ecstatic self was at odds with a Lockean vision of a physiological account of consciousness in post-Cartesian terms, even though it grew and flourished from within those experiential terms.

The emphasis on event in Methodist theology described a Pauline rupture in the temporal experience of the believer that also made possible new forms of continuity and relationship to the past. Wesley and Whitefield identified strongly with Paul; the Pauline model of the instantaneous conversion and of the apostle who comes after the life of Christ provided a way for the early Methodist leaders to describe their sense of calling as both in and out of historical time. The heart religion that centers on the felt presence of God or God's grace challenges the law by providing a subjective standard truth, which Alain Badiou reads as the pattern of Western universalism beginning with Paul. Badiou is interested in the universalizing strategy he reads in Paul, who "brings forth the entirely human connection" between "the general idea of a rupture, an overturning, and that of a thought-practice that is this rupture's subjective materiality."[25] Though his argument is in many ways an extension of the deist eighteenth-century critiques of Christianity, his formulation of the "evental" terms of Pauline thought is illuminating for the study of early Methodism. The Pauline claim is at once experiential and unverifiable. Paul's temporal separation from the other apostles and from the events of the life of Christ are trumped by his individual experience of divine presence, which erupts through time and radically transforms Paul's sense of self, marked by his name change from Saul to Paul.

Whitefield and the Wesleys seized on the figure of Paul as a model for themselves. Whitefield, writing in his journals, imagines himself a new Paul the morning after his ordination (at the age of twenty-one):

> The next morning, waiting upon God in prayer to know what He would have me to do, these words, "Speak out, Paul," came with great power to my soul. Immediately my heart was enlarged. God spake to me by His Spirit, and I was no longer dumb. (*JOURNALS* 61)

The thrust of the event, like Paul's conversion on the road to Damascus, rejects legalism in favor of this subjective kernel of experience, a truth that is "evental, or of the order of what occurs," and hence singular (Badiou 14). Badiou reflects on this sense of evental time when he calls Paul the "poet-thinker of the event," a formulation that links the evangelical sense of inspiration with the literary sense of the term (2). Badiou teases out the consequences of this Pauline articulation of evental truth for the modern self, consequences that are thrust to the fore in the Methodist concept of conversion. First, it produces a new subjectivity, the "new man" of the "new birth" who is no longer identified by social class or other identity categories, who "does not preexist the event he declares (Christ's resurrection)" (14). Second, "evental" truth defines truth as subjective, which entails a radical critique of, in the case of Paul, both Jewish and Greek law and, in eighteenth-century terms, consolidates the charge that Methodists were antinomians. Third, it situates truth as "a process, and not an illumination," which keeps truth tied to the experiential terms of Methodist conversion in ways that echoed uneasily in the performativity of the Methodist meeting, where large groups experienced the event of salvation together (15). According to Badiou, this evental formulation creates "a necessary *distance* from the State" (15) in the modern subject which, in the case of Methodism, kept them on the borders of modern British selfhood, at once participating in its processes and threatening it from within.

The evangelical experience of "evental" truth included reflection and rational consideration, but it remained grounded in the event of the experience of "the love of God shed abroad in my heart" which John Wesley described to his brother Samuel in a letter of October 30, 1728. In theological terms, at least since the Jerusalem conference of 47 AD, the transformation described by the "warming of the heart" had been defined as salvation; but in Lockean terms, it is a relandscaping of the self that underscores the general malleability of modern consciousness. This "evental" sensibility was especially prominent in Whitefield's sermons, during which he was known to cry often and to bring his congregations to tears as well. In "Marks of a True Conversion," with a turn to his listeners typical of his sermon style, Whitefield asserts that "what Jesus said then, he says to you, to me, and to as many as sit under a preached Gospel":

> What say ye, my dear hearers? What say ye, my fellow-sinners? What say ye, my guilty brethren? Has God by his blessed Spirit wrought such a change in your hearts? (WHITEFIELD, WORKS 5: 346)

The evangelical sense of time is oriented around the event (the spoken word creates "a change in your hearts") that continues to unfold and that must be read anew by each believer as a transformative experience. The Wesleyan message of free grace and the immediacy of the conversion experience resituate the "event" as an experience of meaningfulness that is both an act of interpretation and an immediate form of knowledge prior to interpretation. Its "evental" immediacy unfolded in tension with literary and aesthetic models of secular inspiration and meaningfulness.

Aesthetics, Resonance, and Presence

The Methodist that emerges in the eighteenth-century British imagination illustrates the high-stakes contest over how critical the modern self needed to be, how literature was to play a part in delineating its boundaries, and how vexed the category inspiration would remain in modernity. The versions of Methodism that appear in the popular press and on stage, which exaggerated characteristics and practices associated with the movement, are also questions about what inspiration meant in the eighteenth century, and how far it could be effectively secularized through art. Methodist preachers and writers competed with satirists, novelists, and other literary voices in the print marketplace and in the theaters for audience share, blurring what were at best emergent distinctions between secular and sacred spheres of discourse. It is fitting that Joseph Trapp, the first Oxford Professor of Poetry, was also one of Methodism's first and loudest critics, cautioning against the enthusiastic belief that one could be "*divinely inspired;* or at least, that he has the *Spirit of God some* way or *other*;" a state of "inspiration" that belongs more properly to the poet (Trapp 39). Trapp's complaint denounces the populism of the movement, which exerted a cross-class appeal and also democratized the experience of inspiration. Is inspiration in the modern world a religious event, like the explosion of Methodist "heart religion," which shapes individuals directly, or is it proper to an aesthetic domain, something that happens in a creative act through which the artist mediates good taste, sensible feeling, and aesthetic pedagogy for individuals who are refined in the encounter with art? Trapp's definition of good inspiration as aesthetic or poetic (distinct from a dangerous, delusional, and populist religious mode of inspiration) uses Methodism as a trope for antimodern, antiaesthetic selves. By this definition, Methodism was a socially dangerous form of poor taste.[26]

Methodism's role in the increased rates of eighteenth-century literacy kept the movement tied to questions about taste and class that form eighteenth-century notions of the literary. While Methodist Sunday schools and boarding schools were part of the infrastructure of eighteenth-century literacy, the content and interpretive practices of "Methodist" reading marked an aesthetically suspect territory that reiterated social class positions. Orator Higgins, in *The Connoisseur*, no. 86 (September 18, 1755) explains to Mr. Town that he learned to read from popular, low sources: chalked graffiti obscenities, playbills, ballads, and the quack Dr. Rock's treatises. With this "public" education and these "rudiments of literature" that he saved from "the fury of pastry-cooks and trunk-makers" he learns the sublime notions of literature from "Wesley, Whitefield, and Zinzendorf," and becomes a Methodist preacher (until he loses his flock to another Methodist, a shoemaker turned preacher). Orator Higgins claims that he owes his improvements to both the Methodists and "the vociferous retailers of poetry," or ballad-sellers, and to the scraps of plays he overhears at the pit doors. Higgins's story, like many others, painted Methodists as failed moderns because they could not read with critical distance, judgment, and taste. But the exposé of his impolite literacy is comically material, coming from "pastry-cooks and trunk makers," and gathered up in pieces from a busy public sphere like the trampled paper of Grub Street in *The Dunciad*. The upshot is the suggestion that these words, chalk ballads, and scraps cannot be the vehicles for true inspiration. If, as Mee has suggested, enthusiasm in the eighteenth century was the "anti-self of enlightenment notions of civility," and was balanced against Shaftesburian notions of polite literary culture, taste, and self-regulation, the Methodist message was mixed, trafficking in definitions of inspiration that remained tied to a class-bound materiality and failed to meet the emerging standard for literature (23).

In contrast to this satiric vision of Methodism's material print practices, Wesley celebrated what he saw as edifying literature and drew up a plan of reading for his teachers full of Pope, Young, Rowe, Chaucer, and *Paradise Lost* (abridged), though he subsumed the aesthetic merit of literature to its spiritual function. His references to Pope, Matthew Prior, and Locke throughout one of his first public apologetics, *An Earnest Appeal to Men of Reason and Religion* (1743), are notably modern touches.[27] In it, he used Pope's *Eloisa to Abelard* to describe what he means by a "religion of love" and joy:

> Eternal sunshine of the spotless mind;
> Each prayer accepted, and each wish resigned; . . .
> Desires composed, affections ever even,
> Tears that delight, and sighs that waft to heaven.[28]

Wesley chooses from Pope's early work and the passionate strains of Eloisa's plea to be seized by heaven so that her desire for Abelard would be overcome by love of God: "Not touch'd, but rapt; not waken'd, but inspir'd!" In *Eloisa to Abelard*, passions swerve from the devotional to the erotic through the trope of "touch." Wesley, who pulls passages from Pope that sound more like Crashaw than the sharp-tongued author of *The Dunciad*, gives us an Eloisa who uses her passions in the cloister, where "Love finds an altar for forbidden fires" and sensations of erotic love are imperfectly refashioned into chaste spiritual devotion, to underscore the Methodist message of divine love. In spite of Wesley's explicit reference to the "spotless mind" of her devotion, it is Eloisa's erotic longing that detonates in the immediate experience of the Methodist encounter, which realizes the passion that literary writing represents at a mediated distance.

Methodist sermons, journals, altar calls, and band meetings took up what George Steiner calls the linguistic "wager" on divine presence that modern discourse locates in the work of art, a wager that "predicates the presence of a realness, of a 'substantiation' (the theological reach of the word is obvious) within language and form."[29] Whitefield in particular offered that "substantiation" in the here and now of his sermons and echoed it in his self-presentation. At a Boston revival, one listener described hearing a Whitefield sermon:

> To have seen him when he first commenced, one would have thought him anything but enthusiastic and glowing; but, as he proceeded, his heart warmed with his subject, and his manner became impetuous, till, forgetful of everything around him, he seemed to kneel at the throne of Jehovah and to beseech in agony for his fellow beings. (TYERMAN 1: 419)

Whitefield's improvisational preaching style made for an extraordinary level of intimacy, even in large crowds, but it also raised the stakes for his audiences, who were being hailed not as readers but as participants in an event. David Hempton notes that the most salient feature of Methodist sermons, across the lay and ordained spectrum, was the immediacy of their address to the individual hearer.[30] Whitefield used gripping, immediate illustrations as well as his own version of "pointing," the eighteenth-century acting technique of addressing key speeches to the audience directly, to captivating ends. One such example implicated the actor and comedian Edward (Ned) Shuter, who frequently came to hear Whitefield, and who was in attendance at the Tottenham Court Road chapel during a run of *The London Cuckholds*, in which he played Ramble. Whitefield, who knew Shuter,

> was giving full sally to his soul, and in his energetic address, was inviting sinners to the Saviour, he fixed himself full against Shuter, with an eye upon him, adding, to what he had previously said, "And thou, poor Ramble, who had long rambled from him, come you also. O end your rambling by coming to Jesus." Shuter was exceedingly struck and coming in to Mr. Whitefield, said, "I thought I should have fainted, how could you serve me so?" (WINTER 20)

The deliberate confusion of Shuter and Ramble allows Whitefield to work his pun, but it also opens the world of theater into the world at large. The problem posed by readers and believers alike in the media-intensive culture of eighteenth-century Britain is how much they will be changed by this experience of presence, how open the self can afford to be to the other. Literature mediates the experience through its "true fictions" and its aesthetic pedagogy of critical distance, but Methodism invited the individual to feel the warming of the heart directly. In this sense, however perversely, Cleland's *Memoirs of a Woman of Pleasure* (*Fanny Hill*) in its pornographic temporality of the present is as close kin to Methodist sermons and autobiographies, like George Whitefield's *A Short History*, as it is to its better known relative, *Pamela*. The Methodist word, filled with divine spirit, could bring about real effects, real changes, and claimed the language of presence over the language of rational critique.

Eighteenth-century print culture exploited the concept of immediacy in the epistolary novel, the "true history," travel literature, and other forms that encouraged readers to experience reading as believing through forms that appealed to a form of "faith at the very moment of 'letting you know'" (Saccamano 421). The structure of this evangelistic appeal, which characterizes novels like *Pamela* as well as Methodist sermons, invites the reader or listener into an immediate experience of "Truth, which every Man must feel, who lends his Ear to the inchanting Prattler," whose proof is its own emotional impact (Richardson xx). The expanding readership of many eighteenth-century forms of writing geared to new, young readers and working people brought pedagogical questions about the reading experience as an event. What was the effect of this kind of reading, and how strong were the impressions that it made? Richardson's first novel appeared first in its entirety in November of 1740, along with the first and second parts of Wesley's journal (June and November of 1740) and George Whitefield's confessional *A Short History of God's Dealings with the Rev. Mr. George Whitefield*, timing which underscored their shared rhetorical strategies and their appeal to an expanding reading public. Wesley shares in Pamela's practice of "writing to the moment" as Fielding called it in *Shamela*, making liberal use of dashes, exclamation points, and apostrophe, and sometimes literally writing his journals and sermons while on horseback, which lent a sense of immediacy and excitement to the reading process.[31] Methodism promised to take its listeners to the "real" beyond language and representation in an increasingly textual world.

The immediacy of so much eighteenth-century literature raises the problem of faith in aesthetic terms that go beyond the particular terms of the early novel. Derrida's critique of enlightenment, as Neil Saccamano has argued, highlights the "faith conditions of . . . communicative rationality," the act of faith entailed in every act of language, which is ultimately "irreducible ... it must appeal to faith as would a miracle ... [and] leaves no room for disenchantment" (Saccamano 413). These conditions of faith, Derrida argues, are masked by the demystifying style of "Enlightenment" that sets itself up against fanaticism and enthusiasm, or beliefs for which there is no public warrant, yet cannot confront its own mystified investments in self-founding reason. The exposé of enthusiasm in the name of a more rational public sphere, by this account, does not recognize the act of faith involved in language itself, which eighteenth-century literary forms underscored through "true stories," epistolary glimpses, and theatrical modes of performance that were so natural and realistic that audiences would be compelled to respond, particularly in the case of an actor like Garrick.[32] On the one hand, you do not need to believe in the presence of this "evidence" which provides its own somatic warrant. As Derrida puts it, "There is no need any more to believe; one can see, you are there before 'the thing itself'" (63). Epistolary novels like *Clarissa*, which give us the letters themselves (the fiction that the reader accepts as a condition of participation in the novel), make the reader feel that she or he is "touched" by the plight of another consciousness through an aesthetically mediated reading experience with moral consequences. Through the presentism of the epistolary novel, the eighteenth-century lyric (alive and well in the hymn), and Garrick's stylistic revolution of acting, the reader is also invited to "read to the moment," to participate in an aesthetic experience that is always on the verge of collapsing critical distance and acting too directly on the reader's emotions. Whitefield adopts a similar strategy when he distinguishes his preaching from literary text on the grounds of its urgency: "Pardon my plainness; if it were a fable or a tale, I would endeavour to amuse you with words, but I cannot do it where your souls are at stake" (*Works* 5: 472). The notion of a soul at stake underwrites his direct address, which is calculated to maneuver the listener into an internal dialogue that will fundamentally change the self.

Whitefield embodied the fears of Hume about the influence of eloquence over "the vulgar" public, swayed too easily by rhetorical or poetic devices (Potkay, *Eloquence* 70). Whitefield offered many examples to stoke concerns about the immediacy of his evangelistic appeal and the kind of reading practices it encouraged, like this from "Marks of a True Conversion":

> Though this is Saturday night, and ye are now preparing for the Sabbath, for what you know, you may yet never live to see the Sabbath. You have had awful proofs of this lately; a woman died but yesterday, a man died the day before, another was

killed by something that fell from a house, and it may be in twenty-four hours more, many of you may be carried into an unalterable state. Now then, for God's sake, for your own souls sake, if ye have a mind to dwell with God, and cannot bear the thought of dwelling in everlasting burning, before I go any further, silently put up one prayer, or say Amen to the prayer I would put in your mouths; "Lord, search me and try me, Lord, examine my heart, and let my conscience speak; O let me know whether I am converted or not!" What say ye, my dear hearers? What say ye, my fellow-sinners? What say ye, my guilty brethren? Has God by his blessed Spirit wrought such a change in your hearts? (WORKS 5: 346)

Whitefield's appeal, characteristic of his general extemporaneous style that was transcribed by faithful followers like David Crosley and Joseph Gurney, moves from immediate circumstances as divine signs (recent deaths in the community) to a press for an immediate change in the individual ("Oh let me know whether I am converted or not!"). Whitefield's mode of address is shockingly direct compared to Methodism's Anglican enemies such as George White, the climax of whose "An Englishman's rational proceedings in the Choice of Religion" (a 1741/2 sermon to his St. Giles parish) is "O that we could justify our Morals as well as our Religion!" (23) or George Lavington's 1745 sermon on the rebellion of that year, a series of rhetorical political questions about loyalty to the crown. Whitefield concludes his passionate sermon with the hope that an arrow "dipped in the blood of Christ, reach every unconverted sinner's heart!," a tactile image of the emotional and spiritual rupture he hopes to achieve within his listeners (*Works* 5: 351). How this kind of "mysterious power" might be used or abused in religious contexts concerned John Downes directly. In *Methodism Examined and Exposed* (1759), Downes opined of vulgar Methodist readers: "Their own vainer Imaginations . . . have deceived them more grossly than all the Poets and Philosophers in the world could do. . . . And that their Fancy may have a freer Scope, and a larger Field to rove in, they suppose that every Scripture Word hath a *Spiritual* as well as a *literal* sense, and that every true Believer hath the infallible Interpretation of it in his own Breast" (13). This kind of imaginative immediacy was, according to both Downes and Hume, dangerous enough in the case of literature, which Hume regarded as a weak alternative to philosophy, and even more troublesome in the public square.[33] As Rebecca Tierney-Bates has argued, Hume's worries about a mind that could be overwhelmed by powerful stories or performances "has something crucial in common with the productions of unruly fancy; Hume's anxiety about romance is an anxiety, in the end, about the extent to which he cannot separate himself and the productions of his own 'inflam'd Imaginations' from the dangers of fantastical, antisocial narratives."[34] Separating out literature from philosophy on the one hand and religious writing on the other was a way to try to keep from being overwhelmed by the effects of different voices and texts.

The separation of literary and religious texts and modes of reading is far from self-evident in eighteenth-century reflections on Methodism. *The Methodists* (1766) complains that the effects of the evangelist's appeal persuade the listener in "soft Moments" to believe their words beyond the bounds of reason and tradition:

> *Mad* with *Scripture*, void of Sense,
> And thoughtless; NOVELISTS commence
> Swerve from the Rules of *Mother Church*
> And leave her basely in the Lurch. (22)

The use of the term "novelist" situates the Methodists between two operant senses of the term. The primary emphasis is on their invention of new religious practices. Their "novel" ideas, like hymn singing in the worship service, outdoor and itinerant preaching, and more frequent administration of the sacrament, supposedly take traditional Anglicans away from the teaching of the Church of England. They also developed a "novel" language, a bricolage of modern terms and evangelical phrases from the past. George Lawton, in his study of Wesley's use of language, notes that "one of the paradoxes of the evangelical revival is that although Wesley was critical of the jargon of the sects, he, more than any other single person, helped to bring into being the distinctive terminology of Methodism."[35] But the joke turns on a connection between Methodists and literary writers. The prose novelists, in their hybridization of spiritual autobiography, travel narrative, romance, and personal letters, attempt a rhetorical formula for presence that hails the reader into an experiential moment. Just as the novel invites the reader into a cognitive and psychological intimacy, Methodists ask their readers and listeners to have a relationship to scripture and sermons that is too close. They seem to stand between these two definitions of novelist, promoting a language and a narrative that draws people into the Methodist fold and away from the "Mother Church."

The concern about the collapse of reading protocols, evident in Fielding, Trapp, and others, also speaks to a fascination with the possibility that art could make something happen. The outpourings of Quixotes in eighteenth-century literature are comic renditions of the problem. Methodism defined the dangers of misreading, particularly overly literal reading, against the civic and psychological restraint implicit in the aesthetic protocols of literary reading. In the second part of *The Enthusiasm of Methodists and Papists Compared*, George Lavington, Bishop of Exeter, complains:

> What Heart can stand out against their persuasive Eloquence, their *extravagantly fine Flights and Allusions?* Where is any thing so *sublime and elevated?* or sometimes what so *melting, tender and amorous, so soft and so sweet?* You will be in a *Rapture* by reading their *own Words.* — In the *Sublime,* "God gives them a *Text,* directs them to a *Method* on the *Pulpit-Stairs;* the *Lamb of God* opens their Mouth, and looseth their Tongue; and *Sister Williams,* who is near the *Lord,* opens her Mouth to confirm it:—So that all Opposers are struck dumb and confounded."
>
> (LAVINGTON, ENTHUSIASM 2: 4)

The irresistible force of the message that Lavington burlesques threatens to unleash a chaotic religious sublime that brings an overwhelming species of theatrical persuasion to the reading process, something no heart "can stand out against." Lavington sees the charismatic power of the movement's preachers as having tapped both "papist" enthusiasm (he compares them to St. Ignatius, St. Francis, and St. Anthony) as well as modern mass marketing and media. He says that where St. Anthony used a horn to gather his congregations, the Methodists "call People together ... by *Advertisements*" (3). They are, in a rhetorical and material sense, a poor man's public sphere. The Methodist as an unfit reader falls into an overly literal "primitive" and transforming religious encounter instead of engaging with the "good" enthusiasm of the great artist and the more temperate pedagogy of literary reading.

Wesley, in *A Word of Advice to Saints and Sinners* (1746), contrasted his experience of the emotional truth of religion to that of a "mere" story, in which "Christ is but a Fable, the Scriptures but a Story" (10). In his twenty-third sermon, entitled "Marks of a True Conversion," Whitefield made a similar point about wanting his own message to go beyond the forms of public communication:

> You know my way of preaching: I do not want to play the orator, I do not want to be counted a scholar; I want to speak so as I may reach poor people's hearts. What say ye, my dear hearers? Are ye sensible of your weakness? Do ye feel that ye are poor, miserable, blind, and naked by nature? (WORKS 5: 347)

In this characteristic aside, Whitefield hails his listeners into a relation of intimacy by appealing to their emotional self-awareness in an "I/you" address, which was often accompanied by tears, gesticulations, and the extemporaneous additions that are for the most part lost in the historical record. But he is also claiming to speak without aesthetic ornament, to reach his hearers directly, in a version of what Lisa Freeman has termed "antitheatrical theatricalism" (Freeman 49). Indeed, Methodists had a penchant for rhetorical nakedness, a declaration of textual immediacy that defied interpretation. Like Fanny Hill's claim "Truth! Stark naked Truth," Whitefield's exhortations to his followers called them to "follow naked the naked Christ," a phrase he also used to urge a friend to join him in becoming "a fool for Christ's sake" and "go hand in hand together, and follow naked a naked CHRIST."[36] Less flamboyantly, Wesley protests that the letter (attributed to William Law) which he prefixes to his published journal to vindicate the Oxford Methodists, is "without any addition, diminution, or amendment, it being only my concern here nakedly to 'declare the thing as it is'" (1: 122). Like the "bare truth" of Pamela's tale or the rhetorical zaniness of Sterne's direct references to his readers in *Tristram Shandy*, these gestures draw attention to the performance involved in any utterance. Wesley's ample use of exclamations, questions, and dashes demanded that the reader take notice of an event, a happening in which the reader should participate, a happening that Methodists in turn defined as beyond mere oration or rhetorical performance.

Methodism's impact on eighteenth-century English culture reveals active struggles about what kind of writing, speech, or art could "transport" and transform someone. With large groups of readers and a seemingly endless capacity for print, the question of how much a self should be changed by an encounter, either of private reading or public performance, took on greater urgency in the period. In a world of more literate people and an emerging concept of "literature" distinct from "true stories," reading with some critical distance was a necessary counterbalance to the "sensible" appeal of literary presence. To be improved and to be moved by a reading experience or a night at the theater posits a self who can anticipate a rational good (self-improvement) and who remains in control of the willed act of reading and interpreting. Methodism promised its own "method" for reforming the self, particularly the prostitutes, criminals, and the London poor who were the focus of its outreach, contemporary with and sometimes competing with the improving arguments of literary writing. But that transformation started with an explosive encounter that challenged the sociable boundaries of the "modern" self. The conversion event posits a loss of control on the part of the individual, who risks an indeterminate change from a mystical encounter that overwhelms the self. The prospect of both kinds of transformation, the more methodological and the more enthusiastic, proved to be topics of anxious fascination to both their congregations and their critics.

CHAPTER TWO

The New Man

Desire, Transformation, and the Methodist Body

The tabloid-ready sex crimes of "Mrs. Mary, otherwise Mr. George Hamilton" first appeared in Boddley's *Bath Journal* of November 8, 1746, and versions of her adventures spread quickly. The record shows that Hamilton passed herself off as an anatomical male to multiple wives, each of whom lived with Hamilton for periods ranging from two weeks to over three months. The case of Mary/George (and sometimes Charles) Hamilton had come before the Somerset General Quarter Sessions a few weeks earlier, where Mary/George Hamilton was accused of "certain vile and deceitful practices, not fit to be mentioned" and convicted under a clause of the Vagrant Act of 1744 for impersonation. Henry Fielding transformed the case into the crude and embellished picaresque tale, *The Female Husband*. *The Female Husband* is, in several senses, a mean little piece. It is a callous treatment of a real case that ended in the public whipping and probably the death of Hamilton. It is stylistically crude; Martin Battestin claims it is "the shoddiest work of fiction" Fielding ever penned (411). But it shows us the rough seams that connect discourses of sex and spirituality around the issue of evangelical conversion in the mid-eighteenth century. Fielding introduces a wily Methodist, Anne Johnson, "no novice in impurity, which, as she confess'd, she had learnt and often practiced at *Bristol* with her methodistical sisters," to provide a narrative that explains Hamilton's transformation, a narrative which the court accounts lack. Mary Hamilton is "susceptible enough of Enthusiasm, and ready to receive all those impressions which her friend the *Methodist* endeavoured to make on her mind" (31). While Fielding struggles to find terms, including pronouns, to describe the relationship between Anne and Mary, he does settle on a methodology that explains their relationship and Hamilton's subsequent transformation—Methodism. For Fielding, Methodism functions like a sexuality, explaining Hamilton's same-sex "conversion," shaping her subsequent cross-gender identity, and driving the picaresque narrative.

Methodism's highly somatic language of spiritual sensation, its same-sex devotional band meetings, and its populist appeal brought the erotic language of Christian mysticism from the monastery to the public sphere and deployed it within a Lockean model of self formed by experiences. The epistemological model of the Methodist self was shaped by overwhelming experiences of divine love and then "regenerated" by ongoing practices of confession, worship, and fellowship within the Methodist community. Methodists used the tradition of the divine marriage, mildly suggestive descriptions of "inward motions," and a focus on same-sex intimacy within the Methodist community to channel erotic desire into devotional practices, all of which mapped onto longstanding concerns about the relationship of religious intensity to sexual desire. Helmut Puff notes that anxieties about monastic sodomy and the dangers of "friendly conversation" led reformers, including Luther, to campaign against the "unmentionable sin" of sodomy, and same-sex activities between women in convents had long been a staple of clerical satire (Puff 170). But the historical relationship of religious and sexual discourses is not simply a matter of prohibition. In a more celebratory mode, Bernard of Clairvaux used the biblical Song of Songs in sermons, in particular the language of swelling breasts, to describe the mutual desire of Christ and the monks of his monastery, and Bernini's 1652 "The Ecstasy of St. Teresa," based on the autobiography of the Carmelite nun Teresa of Avilia, depicts her highly somatic religious experience, complete with sculptures of the Cornaro patriarchs looking on from a theater box. Patristic theology and Augustine in particular, as Graham Ward notes, emphasize the instability of the body of Christ as a liminal figure: alluring, transgressive, and abject.[1] Methodism redeployed these connection between religious fervor, gender instability, and same-sex eroticism in the midst of the eighteenth-century British conversation about sex, gender, and the modern self. Armstrong, Lanser, Haggerty, McKeon, and others have traced the emergence of a sex/gender system as well as the emergence of modern sexuality structured by the heterosexual/homosexual binary, which Methodism complicates.[2] The broad joke of the story, that Hamilton has become the "new man" of Methodism, reveals Fielding's fears about the indeterminacy of gender and the flexibility within the emerging sex gender system in the face of an evangelical discourse of spiritual *jouissance*.

The desires generated by spiritual sensations, parodied in the case of Hamilton, overwhelm first object choice and then gendered subject position in the passionate religious encounter that draws her into the fold of the "methodistical sisters." This Methodist self, similar to the modern eighteenth-century subject Nancy Armstrong posits, was first and foremost feminine in its receptivity and responsiveness. But because it existed to be transformed through "experimental religion," its gender identity was subject to revision. Fielding's cheeky voyeurism of Anne and Mary's initial encounter as "methodistical sisters" turns to panicked judgment when he observes that "it would not have been difficult for a less artful woman, in the most private hours, to turn the ardour of enthusiastic devotion into a different kind of flame," which, he suggests, is exactly what Anne does (31). Susceptible to Methodist "enthusiasm," Hamilton is transformed by a love that befuddles object choice, something the Rev. John Free also noted in his parody of Methodist religio-sexual language: "He sends his wanton Lambs a *thousand* Kisses:/ Pray! To the *Masters?*—Sir, or to the *Misses?*" (Free 40). Same-sex attraction and Methodism double one another in the heat of an "enthusiasm" that is always already sexual, and that overwhelms the emerging, seemingly fragile gendered scripts of object choice.[3] For readers like Fielding and Free, Methodism promoted exciting, somatic experiences of conversion that functioned as a queer technology of desire. Instead of standing in the place of religious law, Methodism, according to its critics, championed spiritual sensation and an "experimental religion" that multiplied desires instead of disciplining them.

Considering Fielding's mocking use of Methodism in historical context can help us better understand the epistemologies of the desiring self in the eighteenth century that are prior to our own understandings of sexuality and sexual desire. Susan Lanser, Sally O'Driscoll, and Theresa Braunchneider have all contributed to our understanding of *The Female Husband*'s place among the representational patterns of female homoeroticism in the eighteenth century: the sapphic picaresque, the passionless femme, gender as masquerade, and the relationship of cross-dressing and female homoeroticism.[4] The difficulty of trying to imagine desire prior to categories of identity while also situating narratives and historical cases in an unfolding history of sexuality is something with which all of these approaches grapple: Lanser situates Hamilton's story in a visible history of sapphic adventurers marked not by anatomical difference but by their mysterious desires that are not affixed to a more concrete difference; O'Driscoll wants to correct the thesis about the invisibility of female same-sex activity by turning to the construction of the "passionless femme" from antimasturbation literature; and Braunchneider attends to the specific cases of overlap between sexuality and gender as analytic categories to better understand the emerging connection between homoeroticism and cross-dressing. In each of these cases, the argument is framed as an intervention in the history of sexuality. But the risk of writing this history through the traces of behaviors, friendships, and forms of affiliation is, as David Halperin has suggested, a narrative of evolution that produces the "illusory convergence of a category like homosexuality" and recognizes all same-sex expressions of passion as part of that narrative (108). That Fielding turns to Methodism to explain both the genesis of Hamilton's queer desires and a category of identity to consolidate their meaning provides a historical pivot point beyond the consolidated modern rubrics of heterosexuality and homosexuality from which to think about the sexualized anxieties that haunted modern selves prior to developed notions of sexual identity. Unlike the identity categories "lesbian," "homosexual," or "transgender," Methodism is not an anachronistic term in discussions of eighteenth-century identity. Fielding, weaving together a host of inferences, declarations, and associations from Methodists and their enemies, uses the Methodist conversion narrative and its focus on the responsive individual to explain a series of same-sex relationships for which he has no clear identity category.

Making the "New Man"

Methodism's methodology of conversion proves to be a better fit than Fielding seems to have imagined and leads him into the conundrum of the modern self as both an ontological given and an epistemological production. Fielding launched the brief and bawdy *The Female Husband* by trying to naturalize heterosexual desire, only to discover that Hamilton's case unravels his defense as fast as he can construct it:

> That propense inclination which is for very wise purposes implanted in the one sex for the other, is not only necessary for the continuance of the human species; but

is, at the same time, when govern'd and directed by virtue and religion, productive not only of corporeal delight, but of the most rational felicity. But if once our carnal appetites are let loose, without those prudent and secure guides, there is no excess and disorder which they are not liable to commit, even while they pursue their natural satisfaction; and, which may seem still more strange, there is nothing monstrous and unnatural, which they are not capable of inventing, nothing so brutal and shocking which they have not actually committed.

(*FEMALE HUSBAND* 365)

His opening redundancy—"propense inclination"— is a revealing stylistic infelicity. Fielding, longing for what Castle dubbed a "theology of gender," declares that heterosexual desire is "implanted" as part of a providential plan that nonetheless intervenes in human affairs (69). But the "implanted" desire that provides the "propense inclination" is, by Fielding's own analysis, extrinsic to the self and in need of ongoing assistance from virtue and religion to survive. The fragile construct of desire implodes when the truly intrinsic "carnal appetites" are "let loose" by Methodism. Methodism as a discourse of transforming feeling seems to tap into the self prior to culture, providing a volatile point of access to a deeper interiority of Dionysian excess and passion that is both "natural" appetite and "unnatural," chaotic, and monstrous. Like Defoe in "A Relation of the Apparition of Mrs. Veal" or Jane Barker, attempting to account for Mrs. Bargrave, the "Unaccountable Wife" in *A Patchwork Screen for the Ladies* (1723), Fielding turns to vaguely supernatural forces to explain Hamilton's "unnatural" same-sex desire, which has been both liberated and produced by Methodism. In trying to account narratively for the origins of Hamilton's desire in Methodism, Fielding finds himself describing an interior matrix of desire that feeds the evangelical conversion and might destroy the fragile architecture of gender which, upon closer inspection, looks more prosthetic than natural.

Fielding had mocked Methodism before in *Miss Lucy in Town*, *Shamela*, and *Joseph Andrews*, and would do it again in *Tom Jones* and *Amelia*, tying it to both sexual excess and hypocrisy. In *Miss Lucy In Town*, Mrs. Haycock explains to Lord Bawble that the prostitute Jenny is not dead but "worse, if possible—she is—she is turned Methodist, and married to one of the brethren," which means she is not likely to return to the brothel because "they are powerful men, and put such good Things into women."[5] Shamela's mother sends her Whitefield sermons and a copy of "the Dealings," his early autobiography, and Parson Williams, her paramour, preaches a controversial Whitefield sermon, "Be not Righteous Overmuch," instructing his parishioners that good works are pointless, and in fact become sins, without faith and repentance, an exaggeration of the Methodist doctrinal emphasis on grace. This doctrine becomes the refuge of scoundrels like Bilfil in *Tom Jones* and the Methodist Cooper, who picks Booth's pocket at the opening of *Amelia*. Fielding's earlier work develops the somatic model of conversion that leads characters to passionate excess and antinomian self-justification under the banner of Methodism.

To create the backstory he needed for Hamilton's case, Fielding began with the court record and embellished it with narrative details that associate George/Mary with a Methodist past. But once Fielding gets started down this path, "queer" Methodists turn up everywhere. Hamilton, spurned by Anne Johnson for a male Methodist named "Rogers" (a name that returns ad nauseam in anti-Methodist writing) plans "to dress herself in men's clothes to embark for Ireland, and commence Methodist teacher," the term for lay preachers (33). Hamilton boards a ship to begin her sexual mission, bunking with a male Methodist who, still assuming she is a man, "thrust one of his hands into the other's bosom" in "the extacy of his enthusiasm" (33). The shipboard scene suggests that such improprieties might have been part of Whitefield's and Wesley's much-publicized missions to Georgia and South Carolina, during which they preached to and prayed with the crew. The record of Methodism's affective exuberance includes reports of same-sex kissing at revival meetings, Wesley championing a man named Blair in 1732, who was accused of sodomy during his Oxford days, and records of same-sex crushes and loves in letters, particularly one young man who seems to have been in love with Charles Wesley. Abelove notes several of these same-sex crushes, including one of a Mrs. Stonehewer on Hester Roe (later Rogers), one of the early female Methodist ministers, based on the record of Rogers's diary. Stonehewer manifested what Rogers called an "inordinate affection" for her, threatened suicide, and felt she was competing with Rogers's sister for her attentions.[6] At the level of public perception and of the intimate experience of followers, Methodism seems to have excited same-sex desire within the context of the spiritual intensity of their meetings. Methodism's "warming of the heart" appeared to be anterior to gender, overwhelming the heterosexual narrative with a heady model of desire but without a specific object, and muddling the sex/gender system and its working draft of modern sexuality.

Reports of the Bristol revivals, where Mary Hamilton's seducer Anne Johnson allegedly became acquainted with Methodism, also provide more Methodist context for Fielding's story. Records of the revivals claimed that thousands of people attending (many of them women) were thunderstruck, often working themselves into a state of "intoxication" and "falling into strange fits."[7] In July of 1739, Wesley reported seeing four people collapse at one of Whitefield's invitation sermons: "One of them lay without either sense or motion. A second trembled exceedingly. The third had strong convulsions all over his body but made no noise, unless by groans. The fourth, equally convulsed, called upon God with strong cries and tears" (*Oxford Works* 19: 79). Elizabeth Downs, in a letter to Charles Wesley dated April 13, 1742, reports her experience of hearing John Wesley preach at Bristol:

> I went att Evening to Expounding and soon after Mr John Wesley began I felt my heart Clipt as though an hand Graspt itt. The Greater he was in power the stronger I felt my pain. Att last itt Extorted strong Groans from me. I was not able to sitt but Laid my self on the floor. (RPD. IN BARRY AND MORGAN 87)

While Charles and John Wesley tried to distance themselves from such outbursts, they became a signature of the early meetings. These unruly bodies, as Paul Goring observes, could not be endorsed by polite spectators, but they could offer "positive attractions from within their alterity" as an expression of a culture of sympathy and feeling, even while serving as a negative example of excess and manipulation in their extremes (Goring 90). These responses were, on the one hand, authenticated by their own excesses; they were the sign of selves having experiences powerful enough to make them lose control. On the other hand, these events raised suspicions in their very regularity, which suggested a technology of desire that roused, manipulated, and even generated somatic responses.

Bristol also had a large Quaker population, which may have made it a more expressive community in response to Methodist preaching. Henry Rack has made the point that Bristol was identifiable as an "enthusiastic" city.[8] In his *Short Account of God's Dealings with the Rev. George Whitefield*, Whitefield describes Bristol as a site of inspiration where, as a teenager, he experienced "such unspeakable raptures, particularly once in St. John's Church, that I was carried beyond myself," years before the start of the Methodist revivals there (16). Bristol, associated with both Methodist and Quaker meetings, became identifiable as a place where religious feeling is sensual. The author of the satiric *The Progress of Methodism in Bristol* makes the cruder point that Wesley's houses of worship, "like his House in Town," are "Alike in both, for soft Amuses / Are proper Rooms for private Uses" (*Progress* lns. 297–98). Fielding also invents the detail that Hamilton is from the Isle of Man, a double joke on her ambiguous gender and the fact that the Isle of Man (or Isle of Wight) had a successful Methodist society composed entirely of women (Dyson 60–61). Hamilton is in a geographic territory where religion, instead of serving as a "prudent guide," unleashes in its followers something primitive and primal, associated with both women and bodily transformation. The jokes build on the association of Bristol with religious enthusiasm and are fueled by worries about whether the modern self is so malleable that it might be psychologically transformed or converted by a place like Bristol, which seems to breed Methodists.

The association of Methodism with women at both an imaginative and a historical level also seems to have informed Fielding's choice to make Hamilton a Methodist. Phyllis Mack's *Heart Religion in the British Enlightenment: Gender and Emotion in Early Methodism* provides valuable documentary evidence from the records left by these women, strengthening her earlier thesis that enthusiasm as a concept in the seventeenth and eighteenth centuries was attached to women.[9] Methodism celebrated the emerging terms of bourgeois femininity (tractability, receptivity, porous ego boundaries, and emotional sensitivity among them) as the ideal disposition of the self within "experimental" religion, rather than as an end unto themselves. Methodist historian David Hempton notes that before 1810, female domesticity was not modeled in Methodist publications; rather, "women were admired . . . for their religious experience, progress in holiness, and contribution to the religious and social mission of the church" (*Empire* 140). Early Methodism also included female leadership and, though Wesley resisted the idea, and some female preachers (known as "teachers"), such as Sarah Crosby and Mary Bosquanet, became well-known voices on the itinerant circuit. Women like Crosby, Bosquanet, Grace Murray, and the Countess of Huntingdon helped to shape the image of Methodism as a women's movement beyond the more visible leadership of the Wesley brothers and George Whitefield. Hempton went so far as to describe Methodism as "predominantly a women's movement" (*Empire* 5), and G. J. Barker-Benfield concurs that there were broad cultural associations of the movement with women. These associations began with the influence Susanna Wesley had on her sons John and Charles. It was through his mother that John Wesley first encountered Locke, had his first extended theological exchanges, and saw a woman preach so effectively that, when Samuel Wesley was away on business, she inadvertently stole the flock of the visiting curate with her evening teaching sessions at the Wesley home. Though Wesley tried to ban female preaching (prominent in the Quaker tradition, from which Wesley wanted to distinguish his followers), women were visible and influential in the early movement.

The rhetorical priority of a feminine self, which can be opened, changed, invaded, and reshaped by divine intervention, paradoxically extended gender boundaries to include their own dissolution. Hester Ann Roe (later Rogers), who cut her hair short and became a Methodist preacher, expressed this radical malleability in her journal: "I *will* lie in thy hands as passive clay" (qtd. in Mack 134). Female mystics in the Methodist movement, such as Mary Bosquanet (later Fletcher) and Mary Langston, used the image of dissolving into liquid to describe their experience of union with Christ. Bosquanet wrote of her soul as a stream of water, polluted but seeking to be cleansed by contact with God, while earlier, she adopted the language of Christian mystics to express her longing for Christ "as the bride in the Canticles."[10] These accounts of Methodist conversion circulated through Methodist meeting houses, informing Methodist rhetorics of the self before they became part of a print record. Many would eventually appear in John Wesley's *Arminian Magazine*, a print publication that built on the earlier practice of Methodist preachers reading letters from converted members in their meetings. *The Progress of Methodism in Bristol* (1743) mocked the "once a Month" practice of reading such letters "Wherein are couch'd some shrewd Expressions,/Acquainting of some strange Conversations" (*Progress* 38). The passivity and openness to transformation that Bosquanet and Roe-Rogers describe generated alternative gender scripts and models of agency that became part of the Methodist meeting's testimonies of conversion. The theological focus of these confessional letters and the somatic intensity of their felt experience of divine presence renders a version of the body that appeared to have, as Paul Goring observes, tremendous "textual potential and malleability," but a body that was first and foremost feminine (Goring 6).

Satirists reveled in the connection between Methodism and women. *The Methodists* assures us that the devil used women to help the movement succeed, and the anonymous author of *The Progress of Methodism at Bristol* proclaims that

> Three forth Parts, of what attend 'em,
> Are *Female Sex*, and *John's* to mend 'em;
> For Women are most prone to fall,
> Like *Eve*, their Mother, first of all.   (PROGRESS 20)

The prominence of Methodist women seems to have policed the voices of women elsewhere in eighteenth-century religious life. *The Weekly Miscellany*, a magazine that began in 1732 advocating women's religious influence, changed its course after Methodism appeared, silenced the columns of its fictional women, and became one of the most consistent anti-Methodist papers at the end of the 1730s. Cynthia Cupples argues that Methodism turned mainline Anglican writers like Webster, who published the initially female-friendly *The Weekly Miscellany* under the pseudonym Richard Hooker, to retreat from his celebration of the pious woman in order to protect his publication "from the taint of heterodoxy" (60). Fielding seizes on this anxiety in situating Hamilton's origins in Methodist female community. He supplants the more common soldier or pirate cross-dressing narratives, which Theresa Braunschneider notes are codified in popular literature and ballads, with Methodist "enthusiasm," which provides the conditions of possibility for Hamilton's sexuality as well as the technology of its reproduction in a culture of women (211).

Fielding picks up on the connection between Methodism and women through the general outline of the story and makes digs at Methodist women as failed readers. Like Shamela's library, which jumbles together Whitefield, his enemy Trapp, and pornography, the women drawn in by Hamilton fail to make "proper" distinctions between types of literature and the reading methods appropriate to them, a failure that is part of a broader joke about enthusiasm, sex, and literacy. Hamilton's last wife, also named Molly, responds to Hamilton's evangelism in part because, like other female converts in Fielding and later Smollett, she is only barely literate. Overwhelmed by Hamilton's textual prowess, Molly expresses her surprise at the "loafe" Hamilton expresses in her "litters" and protests that Hamilton's intentions might not be pure: "Sur I wool nut be thee hore of the gratest man in the kuntry" (45). Emily Finlay notes that "kuntry" slides into a pornographic analogy with "cunt," a pattern of sexual/textual slippage Molly shares with Mrs. Slipslop as well as, a few years later, her fellow fictional Methodists Win Jenkins and Tabitha Bramble (Finlay 164). Slipslop calls Joseph "luscious" when she means lusty, and becomes angry when she thinks Joseph is treating her with "ironing" instead of taking her passion seriously. Though the joke is simple at the first level, positing class- and gender-based superiority over these female readers, their Methodist, feminized alternative literacy erupts with desires and sensuous experiences of a material word that evokes a tactile, intimate lived experience.

In addition to its sensuous rhetoric of religious feeling, Methodism also presented women with concrete options for a life separate from the marriage plot. Phyllis Mack notes that for many of the early female leaders of Methodism, the "physical move away from family and toward other like-minded women" was a significant step devotionally and personally (*Heart Religion* 151), one travestied by Fielding when the young "Molly" Hamilton first moves in with Anne Johnson. The passionate friendships of early Methodism included the relationship between Sara Ryan and Mary Bosquanet. Ryan wrote to Bosquanet "as to me my dear enjoy me in God—look for me in God find me in God—love me in God, and live with me in God then shall you die with me into God and we shall live with God together. . . . I am happy very happy" (qtd. in Mack 127). Such arrangements, fostered by early Methodist communities in which believers shared houses and property, were alternatives to heterosexual marriage. For women in particular, the possibility of an adult life outside the context of heterosexual marriage realigned gender expectations around devotional practices. The possibility of a Methodist single life opens up stories that Fielding, as Braunschneider has argued, tried to repackage in a heterosexual "drag act" (212). When Hamilton pleadingly promises her second wife "the pleasures of marriage without the inconveniences," she also presents a version of the antimarriage narrative of Methodism, in which women in particular could have companionship, sociability, and meaningful work instead of marriage, a version of marriage without the "inconveniences," in the words of Hamilton. The "new birth" and the forms of sociability that Methodist communities offered to women pulled up the twin anchors of sex and gender by proposing a viable narrative alternative to heterosexual marriage with its own powerful structure of feeling.

Wesley's public attitude toward marriage, particularly in the 1740s, before his own disastrous marriage, also undermined the primacy of the heterosexual narrative. Wesley advocated the "Single Life" over marriage in his 1743 *Thoughts on Marriage and a Single Life*. He argued Jesus's and Paul's admonitions to become "eunuchs for the kingdom of heaven's sake. He that is able to receive it, let him receive it" were commands (*Thoughts* 6–9). As he explained to his brother Charles in a private letter in September of 1749, he thought he would not marry "Because I should never find such a woman as my father had" (*Oxford Works* 26: 380–82). John Wesley moderated his stance after becoming engaged to Grace Murray in 1749, an engagement which she then broke by marrying another Methodist preacher. John subsequently married a widow, Molly Vazeille, in 1751, claiming that it was a precaution against scandal, but he continued to advocate the single life as the most advantageous state for the believer, eventually separated from Vazeille after a few stormy years of marriage, and reiterated the position in print in his 1785 *A Thought Upon Marriage*. Wesley's public stances against marriage, along with the fact that Whitefield never married, situated Methodism as at odds with the conventional script of heterosexual marriage in the public imagination. It offered concrete alternatives to the marriage plot and a mystical vocabulary of holy intimacy that had been until recently the domain of the convent and monastery, but was now circulating in the Methodist public sphere.

Criminal Conversation and Secret Sins

Much of the erotic charge of early Methodism came through its confessional practices that encouraged the Pamela-esque elaboration of interior states as well as somatic, even sexual tropes to describe spiritual experiences. The early Fetter Lane Society rules insisted on "conversation," and stated that the members were not just encouraged but required to speak "as freely, plainly and concisely as he can, the real state of his heart, with his several temptations and deliverances" (Dreyer 14). As Jeffrey Masten has argued, the sexual as well as textual implications of conversation persisted into the nineteenth century. On the early modern stage, it is freighted with the erotic charges of same-sex friendship, particularly between men, and later in the eighteenth century, the term became legal shorthand for civil prosecutions of infidelity, the criminal conversation, or "*crim. con.*" trial. Intimate conversation and sex are, through this conceptual lineage, euphemistically interchangeable. Notably, Fielding keeps a tight rein on Hamilton, who offers no narration or confession within the picaresque frame of the tale. Hamilton's story is "TAKEN FROM her own MOUTH"; the story is technically hers, but Fielding's narrative intervention interposes satiric distance from the charismatic Hamilton at a structural level to ensure that we can have no conversation with this evangelist of desire.

Talking about one's sins was fundamental to early Methodist culture. Methodist bands, early accountability groups who were charged with asking each other probing questions about their secret desires, incited one another to more sexual discourse in the form of group confession. The regular questions as well as the format of the bands were borrowed from the Moravian practice known as *das Sprechen*, or conversation, in which four or five would meet together and ask each other "as many and as searching questions as may be, concerning their state, sins, and temptations" to determine their fitness to receive communion.[11] At each band meeting, members were to be asked "What known sin have you committed since our last meeting?" "What temptations have you met with?" and

"What have you thought, said, or done, of which you doubt whether it be a sin or not?"[12] On May 12, 1739, *The Weekly Miscellany* printed what was allegedly the catechism used by women's Methodist bands. The questions come to an erotic crescendo:

> Do you desire that in doing this, we should come as close as possible, that we should cut you to the Quick, and search your Heart to the Bottom?
> Is it your desire to be on this and on every occasion entirely open, so as to speak every Thing that is in your Heart without Exception, without Disguise, and without Reserve?
> Are you in Love?
> Do you take more Pleasure in any Body than in God?
> Whom do you love just now, better than any other Person in the World?
> Is not the Person an Idol? Does he not (especially in Public Prayer) steal in between God and your Soul?
> Does any Court you?
> Is there any one whom you suspect to have any such Design?
> Is there any one who shows you more Respect than to other Women?
> Are you not pleased with That?
> How do you like him?
> How do you feel yourself when he comes, when he stays, when he goes away?
> The last ten Questions may be ask'd as often as Occasion offers (HOOKER 2).

The insinuating tone of these questions is amplified by the sense of rites of initiation in the context of the band meeting. These questions are narrative devices inciting members to more sexual discourse, and the confession that they try to elicit is unmistakably sexual. But the broader goal is intimacy, the articulated desire that the inquisitors "should come as close as possible ... and search your Heart to the Bottom" in the interest of knowing the other and helping her or him to salvation. The list, allegedly "copied from one under Mr. W——'s own Hand" made the rounds in other periodical publications and newspapers, including Josiah Tucker's *Life and Particular Proceedings of the Rev. Mr. George Whitefield* and *The Annals of Europe for the Year 1740* (vol. 1), helping to establish the specter of a regular method of sexual conversation among Methodist women in the public imagination.

Methodism's contribution to the Puritan tradition of discursive self-examination was grounded in lay confession, but it blended these verbal practices in its earliest days with Moravian devotional activities such as foot washing and kissing the hands and feet of fellow band members, while the societies were still worshiping together at Fetter Lane.[13] In these acts of intimacy, the boundary between sacred and sexual was porous. The slippage between criminal conversation and the intimacies (conversational and physical) of Methodist band meeting conversation was fodder for Methodism's critics. *The Progress of Methodism at Bristol* hints at the same-sex attraction between women drawn together by confession in the bands. They

> Declare to one another's faces
> Their growing, or declining, Graces ...
> secret some peculiar Crimes
> By them committed, divers times,
> Such as their *Husbands* never knew,
> Nor none but they, with —*they know who*.   (LNS. 357–58, 381–84)

The women become intimates in the shared knowledge of one another's transgressions, but the object of their affections is notably proleptic: "*they know who.*" The construction undermines the power of unknowing husbands with the unspoken knowledge that the women share in their narrative mastery of one another's lives. The confessional process, in both connotation and procedure, mirrored the intimacy of the modern novel, but without the fictional frame.

George Whitefield, the young, charismatic Methodist preacher, crystallized Fielding's general concerns about Methodism as a sexualized conversion rhetoric. Whitefield's confession of his youthful misadventures in *A Short History of God's Dealings with the Rev. Mr. George Whitefield*, written while he was barely twenty-six, left him vulnerable to scandalous interpretations of the soft, feminine, and unstable self he described as being transformed again and again in his "experimental" spiritual journal. *A Short History* was labeled a "Rhapsody of Madness, Spiritual Pride, and little less than Blasphemy" by Joseph Trapp, renamed *A Short Account of the Devil's Dealings with the Rev. G———. W———d.* by the author of the 1740 *The Expounder Expounded*, and called "a perfect Jakes of Uncleanness" by George Lavington, Bishop of Exeter.[14] The hermeneutic practice of "symptomatic reading" in these mocking critiques of Whitefield use sexual explanations familiar to post-Freudian readers to supply the gaps in Whitefield's text. But the readings of Whitefield's autobiography, like the reading of Hamilton that Fielding provides, simultaneously find what they set out to find and, at the same time, fail to explain the desires of these Methodist selves.

Fielding's relationship to Whitefield's *Short History* was not only ideological but commercial. Fielding competed for readers in a marketplace saturated with Methodist journals, autobiographies, sermons, and treatises, many of which shared the confessional and sensational narrative strategies of popular criminal biography that was not sharply distinguished from the early eighteenth-century novelistic world of *Moll Flanders, Colonel Jack*, and even *Pamela*. The popularity of Methodist sermons in particular is cause for Parson Adams's dismay in *Joseph Andrews* when he is informed that the bookseller, overstocked with sermons, is only printing those that "come out with the name of Whitefield or Wesley, or some other such great man," a swipe at the Methodist superstars and Robert Walpole, who all figure in a new fame culture fed by print (Fielding 66). Whitefield published his youthful autobiography in 1740, the same year *Pamela* and *Shamela* appeared, two years after his first *Journals* appeared in print, and six years before Fielding's *The Female Husband*. Fielding turned to Whitefield's *Short History* explicitly in *Shamela, Joseph Andrews*, and implicitly in *Tom Jones* as an example of writing that led young minds astray. He includes it in Shamela's library of questionable reading material. When Squire Booby finds Shamela reading Whitefield's *Short Account*, which she later packs up along with *"Atalantis, Venus in the Cloyster: Or, the Nun in her Smock, God's Dealings with Mr. Whitefield, Orfus and Eurydice . . .* some sermon-books; and two or three plays" (327), he assumes that she is reading Rochester's poems. Tom Keymer has argued compellingly that Fielding links *Pamela* and Whitefield's *A Short Account* to show that "like Pamela, Whitefield scores great worldly success; and like Pamela, he uses the motif of providential direction to deny his own pursuit of it," though the connection also speaks to a somatic immediacy that they both practice in print (Keymer 29). But Fielding also interpolates this energetic preaching style, like Pamela's writing to the moment, into the parodic erotics of *Shamela* and suggests that, as with Whitefield, sexual charisma is part of the mysterious attraction of Hamilton.

Whitefield had burst on to the scene as a "boy preacher" in 1736 at the age of twenty-two, and by 1737 he was attracting enormous crowds at outdoor revivals. The young Whitefield possessed an almost hermaphroditic attractiveness, the combination of masculine and feminine that also proves winning for Mrs. Hamilton, who appeared as "a most beautiful youth" once she begins to pass as a young man. A young Connecticut settler named Nathan Cole, who heard Whitefield preach in 1739 in Middletown, described him as "almost angelical" and "a young, slim, slender youth" (Butler 5) The attractiveness and youth of Whitefield (in spite of his squint), as well as of the Wesley brothers created the impression that their popularity with large numbers of female followers was motivated by more than religious devotion.[15] Whitefield's hermaphroditic appeal is a sign of an unstable self, a self so impressionable as to be unmoored from the poles of masculine and feminine. But this interstitial quality proves wildly attractive, drawing crowds and threatening to make more emotionally responsive converts in his own ambiguous image.

"Enthusiasm Displayed, or the Moorfield's Congregation" (1739) shows a baby-faced Whitefield with his legs exposed, stepping over two women, labeled "Deceit" and "Hypocrisy," who form a temporary pulpit in the open air. "Deceit" has two faces, one listening to Whitefield and one addressing a woman who is giving her a sack of money. "Hypocrisy" takes down a mask and holds a book that says "Sold by Hutton," Whitefield's earliest publisher, who brought out his first sermons, journals, and the first edition of *A Short Account of God's Dealings with the Reverend Mr. George Whitefield*. The languid poses of the women and the folds of their dresses echo in Whitefield's robes and his soft face. Stepping on their bodies, he is both master and dependent, masculine and feminine, with his legs showing like Charlotte Charke in a breeches role. Fielding "superimposed" Charke's life over the Hamilton story, as Jill Campbell has demonstrated in *Natural Masques*, but there is also more than a trace of Whitefield in Fielding's version of Hamilton's adventures.

The figure of Folly also has a crucifix and prayer beads spilling off to her right, devotional items that suggest, with the mask, that Methodism is a front for Roman Catholicism. The rest of the crowd looks on in curiosity at Whitefield and the women who surround him, while the text below warns against "ENTHUSIASM" dressed as simplicity: "The Plot still thickens when ye Play's begun / As Thirty-nine approaches Forty-one / The baleful Consequence our Fears avow / For What was Peters once is Wh-D now." The rhyme compares Whitefield to Hugh Peters, the nonconformist minister who was executed as a regicide in 1660. The connections with regicides and "forty-one," the year of the Irish rebellion and the execution of the Earl of Strafford, suggest that Methodism could revive what Walpole called in 1748 "the folly and cant of the last age" and drag the nation back into a past of civil religious war (Walpole, *Correspondence* 9: 73). The verse below proclaims a political threat, but the visual image suggests that sexual charisma fuels it.

Whitefield promulgated a species of gender confusion in his sermons and published work. In "Christ the Believer's Husband," one of his most famous ser-

Enthusiasm Display'd: Or, the Moor-Fields congregation, G. Bickham, 1739. Courtesy of the Lewis Walpole Library, Yale University

mons, he takes the biblical analogy of the church as the "bride of Christ" and pursues it in unusual detail, positioning the listener as "woman," "wife," and "bride" and repeating his tag line: "our Maker is our Husband" no less than twenty times. As he winds up to the crescendo of the sermon, he proclaims:

> Canst thou not remember, when, after a long struggle with unbelief, Jesus appeared to thee, as altogether lovely, mighty and willing to save? And canst thou not reflect upon a season, when thy own stubborn heart was made to bend; and thou wast made willing to embrace him, as freely offered to thee in the everlasting gospel? And canst thou not, with pleasure unspeakable, reflect on some happy period, some certain point of time, in which a sacred something (perhaps thou couldst not then well tell what) did captivate, and fill thy heart, so that thou could say, in a rapture of holy surprise, and ecstasy of divine love, "My Lord and my God! My beloved is mine, and I am his; I know that my Redeemer liveth"; or, to keep to the words of our text, "My Maker is my husband." (180–81)

Whitefield does not ignore gendered language but rather claims it aggressively, declaring that men and women together "love our blessed bridegroom" (183). His language becomes more distinctly gendered as the sermon goes on, drawing on the Song of Solomon and Proverbs for declarations of marital love and wifely duty in order to commend it to all believers, male and female: "it is impossible of you to think too highly of your heavenly husband, Jesus Christ" (184). This rhetorical gender flexibility has a long history in Christian discourse, but it is redeployed in the narrative of Methodist embodiment, rebirth, and the production of the "new man." The Methodist focus on Christ, and more specifically their preference for speaking of Jesus, embodied the believer's response to God in human form. Whitefield underscores the rhetorical and theological contrast between Latitudinarian sermons that tended to prefer the ethereal vocabulary of "Providence," "Divinity," and "Source" with his embodied Christology in his tag line: "My Maker is my husband." From Fielding's point of view, this spiritual analogy looked like a recipe for gender anarchy.

Whitefield exacerbates the gender confusion of evangelical Christian discourse by persistently describing himself as feminine in *A Short Account*, either by analogy or by action. Whitefield eats, drinks, and desires his way through his *A Short Account*, but he also "weep(s) before the Lord, as Hagar when flying from her mistress Sarah" when he can't get along with his sister-in-law (15). He reads romances. He confesses that his love of acting led him "to dress myself in Girl's clothes, which I had often done, to act a part before the corporation" and not just for the single play that his schoolmaster had written to showcase his thespian gifts (13). His cross-gender identifications are part of a rhetoric of Methodist transformation in which Whitefield merged the theological claim that a Methodist believer ought to be vulnerable to the presence of God, expressed in the metaphor of divine marriage, with his more personal identification with and as women in his *Short Account*. This cross-gender identification blurs tenor and vehicle, conflating Whitefield's rhetorical admonitions to spiritual receptivity with his more emotional and embodied personal experiences of femininity. The striking, even theatrical result was part of Whitefield's proselytizing strategy that sought to arrest his listeners and make them feel *with* him, beyond the conventional boundaries of gender.

A Short Account had plenty to offend readers invested in moral rather than mystical notions of religion. Whitefield's bathetic *in persona Christi* observation that he was born at an inn, like his "dear Savior, who was born in a Manger belonging to an Inn," his multiple admissions to stealing money for fruit and tarts "to satisfy my sensual appetite," and his confession that he was more careful to "adorn my Body" than to care for his soul raised the cry from Trapp and others that this confessional spiritual autobiography was an instruction manual for vice. But it was the infamous "secret sin" he fell into after renewing "Evil communications with my old School fellows . . . the dismal effects of which I have felt, and groaned under ever since" (17) that created the greatest stir and offers the most direct connection to *The Female Husband*. Though the secret sin is never named, Methodism's critics uniformly imagined it to be either masturbation or same-sex activity. Whitefield confessed that he continued in the secret sin and at length got acquainted with "a Set of debauched, abandoned, atheistical Youths. . . . I began to reason as they did, and to ask why God had given me Passions, and not permitted me to gratify them" (20). Whitefield's self description as "atheistical" and subsequent references to his affecting rakishness recall Rochester as prototypical rake-atheist, but they also render Whitefield fluid in his gender identifications. He described his former self as a hedonist following a libertine "experimental religion," interpolating the connection between sodomy and atheism for which Rochester had become shorthand.[16]

Whitefield's critics did not need much prompting to pick up on his cues. *The Expounder Expounded*, which was reprinted as *The Genuine and secret memoirs relating to the life and adventures of that Arch Methodist, Mr. G. W—fi-d* in 1742, carefully arranges its elaboration on the bad habits, sins, thefts, and unspecified moral lapses in the *Short Account* to crescendo with the secret sin. This salacious account of Whitefield's youth uses page numbers from the 1740 edition of Whitefield's own *Short Account*, taking Whitefield out of context in a cut-and-paste proof-texting strategy, a farcical version of puritan Biblical practices, to "expose" the truth of Whitefield's story as sexual rather than spiritual. The author of *The Expounder Expounded* (identified as "R-ph J-ps-n") claims to offer his exposition so that "all true Believers of the *modern* Doctrine, and particularly the *beatified* Sisters of the Foundery in *Moorfields*, will receive much Comfort therefrom" (7):

> Perhaps no Passage that ever dropped from the pen of a *sacred* Writer, hath afforded so much Speculation to the Publick, as the *abominable secret Sin* above mentioned.... One would think, indeed, that Mr. W—d had thrown out this difficult Enigma among his Disciples, that he might exercise their Devotion, and guess at their Progress in the *Light* by their Aptness in discovering it (37–38).

With thinly disguised glee, the author catalogues the possible explanations that have been generated and mockingly rejects each one. The first suggestion, "Defilement of the *Female* Kind" with his mother, makes no sense because his mother (who kept the Bell Inn at Gloucester) "is of unblemished Character" and Whitefield himself known to be notoriously bashful with women (38). Bestiality, in which "Our North-British Saints" are frequently caught is not it (39). Sodomy is briefly entertained and then rejected because "Mr. W—d has never discovered any Propensity to Uncleanness of that Kind," though he suggestively rehearses Whitefield's confession that "the Devil was always uppermost" (39). He settles on the "sin of Onan," which he supposes his male readers will understand, as will his female readers "blessed with a *Boarding-School* Education" (40).

The Expounder Expounded's raucous, outrageous claims translated anxieties about responsiveness, evangelicalism, and sensuality into a proto-sexuality, the onanist, by filling in Whitefield's blanks. The onanist is a primitive sexuality, taking its name from a biblical story (like sodomy) and so referencing a premodern world of sex and its criminalization. But it is also imaginatively prior to sexuality in terms of object choice; the other does not define the agent of this act, which cautionary voices, including John Wesley's, had to describe in terms of permanent damage to the self. Wesley's vociferous antimasturbation tract, *Thoughts on the Sin of Onan, Chiefly Extracted from a Late Writer* (1766), abridged Samuel Tissot's book and followed elliptical strategies like Whitefield's in warning about the "pernicious" habit that "thousands both of men and women groan under" (2), which could leave one emaciated, "effeminate," and incontinent.

The Tar's Triumph, or the Bawdy House Raillery, C. Mosely, sculpt., 1749. © The Trustees of the British Museum. Used by permission

What is "ruined" in these cases is the constitution, a self-unmaking that is the rhetorical opposite of becoming a "new man." The claim that this "snare of the Devil" makes young people "absolute slaves, reason and religion having quite lost their force," using the same point about a loss of agency that Whitefield used to describe his unnamed compulsive behavior (Wesley, *Onan* 11). The connection between onanism and Whitefield's *Short History* is made graphic in a 1749 print "The Tar's Triumph" concerning the sailor's riots in the Strand. Among the contents disgorged are *Onania or the Heinous Sin of Self-Pollution* and "Whitefield's Memoirs," which are thrown together on a bonfire with the furniture, while a cure from Dr. Rock for venereal disease is tacked to the wall, above a bottle and syringe labeled "*Injection.*" Like Shamela, these women keep Whitefield's *Short Account* in their libraries, perhaps to justify their own line of work, or perhaps to titillate with its tale of Whitefield's "secret sin."[17]

The Expounder Expounded circles back to the problem of agency in Whitefield's confession that he "groans under" a mysterious force that is both intrinsic desire and extrinsically supernatural, the force of the "wicked one" who "makes use of Men as Machines, working them up to just what he pleases, when by Intemperance they have chased away the Spirit of God from them!" (*Short Account* 21). Responding to this problem of agency in Whitefield's confession, the author of the *Expounder* goes on to refine his speculation about onanism, which, he claims, is technically correct, but adds that Whitefield's masturbation was a mutual activity, and that "Satan certainly lent his Friend an *helping Hand* towards the Dispatch of the *Sport*, which was some times so vigorously, nay so immoderately carried on, that the poor Patient has been found (page 18) *bleeding* with the Excess" (40). He also claims to have spoken to a bedchamber maid who declared that his sheets were blackened and the bedstead frequently broken down, evidence that Whitefield and the Devil were having sex, though "Satan always made the choice of the *upper* Station" (54). He makes much of the notion of Satan "working [Whitefield] up," intimating that Satan's "advantage" is part of a sexual game:

> There is one very material Circumstance, concerning which the World is much in the Dark, nor is it possible to come at the Truth from Mr. W——s'd own Memoirs, or any other Authorities I have been able to consult; and that is, whether or not my Reverend Author returned the *kindness* of his officious Friend, and —— the Devil in his Turn. Tho' as Charity exacts from us the most favourable construction upon Things doubtful, and as the Gratitude of Mr. W——d was never yet called in Question, I shall conclude that the *Benefit* was *reciprocal*. (41)

This scandalous retort is interesting in its association of spiritual intensity with sexual feeling, which is conventional, and same-sex activity, which is less so. The seducing priest figure of past clerical satire is displaced by the overwhelmed young Whitefield exchanging sexual favors with the devil. The reading, however flippant, interprets Whitefield's feminized rhetorical openness about his spiritual responses, feelings, and fears, as well as the popular image of the Methodist groaning involuntarily during a meeting, into a more materially somatic truth, sex.

The strategy's general outline reaches back into the ancient history of clerical satire, but the particular terms of this attack circulate around authenticity rather than hypocrisy. Because Whitefield is so femininely open to others, willing and even longing to be transformed (by the Wesley brothers, and then by God) he functions as a queer figure. He is feminized in the way Carol Bynum Walker and Luce Irigaray have argued the figure of Christ is, yet he is even further displaced, multigendered, permeable, and mysterious in his materiality, as is Graham Ward's simultaneously poststructuralist and patristic account of the displaced body of Christ.[18] Whitefield is trying to confess something in describing his "secret sin," teetering on the edge of naming it but failing to do so. Fielding's similarly paraleptic strategy regarding "matters not fit to be mentioned" in *The Female Husband* participates, like Whitefield's satirists and Whitefield himself, in attempting to settle the question of the self and its mystical inwardness by making sex the secret, unspeakable, but ultimately material truth of the self. But the strategy cannot fully meet the demand for another truth, a supplement that returns not to the struggle between secular and sacred explanations of the world but to their mysterious intersection. Both *The Expounder Expounded* and *The Female Husband* acknowledge Methodist evangelical excitement generates feelings, acts, and mysterious "matters" not fit to be mentioned, matters which include Fielding's narrative drive to make Hamilton's story meaningful and the proliferation of elliptical talk about Methodism's sensual spirituality.

The Doctor's Wherewithal

The epistemological uncertainty about the new man of Methodism meets medical discourses of folk healing and magical cures when Hamilton becomes a quack doctor. After the sixty-eight-year old widow discovers Hamilton's disguise, the sexual circuit rider takes off for Dartmouth, where "she assumed the title of doctor of physic" and proposed to cure Miss Ivythorn of green sickness, a condition Bonnie Blackwell connects to uterine hysteria, thought to afflict young virgins in need of sex.[19] Hamilton's picaresque stint as a mountebank, like Charlotte Charke's and the actual Hamilton's adventures as quacks and mountebanks, provides her with social and geographic mobility. But it also reiterates the connection between Methodism and questionable medicine. Wesley too provided medical advice, dispensing prescriptions in person from the Foundry, and then moving into print with *A Collection of Receits, for the Use of the Poor* in 1745. He begins with the claim that there are but a few "infallible Medicines," from which he is collecting the least costly and most safe. Hamilton's "infallible nostrum" similarly promises curative certainty, which is too good to be true, yet which captures the public's desire for certainty and the will to believe. Wesley's more famous 1747 *Primitive Physic* remained in print well into the nineteenth century. It was one of the most widely read books in England before 1850 and confirmed his public image as a populist doctor for some, a quack for others (Rousseau 250).

The term primitive signals a pure point of origin that has been recovered for modernity, like the Methodist claim to "primitive Christianity" and the "infallible nostrum" of primitive physic, providing a curative return to a moment imaginatively before culture. This hope of clarity and simplicity in the midst of an overwrought present is a persistent modern longing, in which the superseded past is mystified as a remedy for modern ills.[20]

Wesley's *Primitive Physic* was also implicitly democratic. Like Puritan and American colonial Dissenting ministers, who promoted the use of pills and medicines as an alternative to the ecclesial control of Church of England appointed physicians, Wesley's medical advice was, broadly speaking, "antiprofessional."[21] While in one sense the role of Methodists as physical doctors reached back to earlier models of pastoral care described in Herbert's *The Country Parson* (1674) and Bishop Gilbert Burnet's *Discourse of the Pastoral Care* (1692), which emphasized the importance of some medical education for the country parson, they encouraged "self-dosing" against the emerging notions of professionalism that, notably, led to the rise of the male midwife and the diminution of women's roles in community health care.[22] Wesley proposed self-cures over a physician's intervention, proffering an independence from doctors, but he also emphasized the role of pills and medicines as interventions in the body, about which Fielding was as suspicious as he was of doctors themselves. The doctor who attends Joseph Andrews first neglects him because of his poverty, refuses him food, declares him feverish and near death, then claims credit for his cure due to his prescription, "*that sanative soporiferous draught*" whose virtues "were never to be sufficiently extolled." The medicine, in reality, had "stood untouched in the window ever since its arrival," thus proving that the body will generally cure itself (64). Hamilton's "infallible nostrum" like the "sanative soporiferous draught" Joseph Andrews ignores, supposedly do harm by altering what is otherwise a sound constitution. But Fielding's account of "propense desires" at the beginning of the story, desires that are the function of the contained, natural body in which he wants to believe, is paradoxically vulnerable to various transforming interventions (medical and spiritual) that circulated widely in the public sphere.

Fielding had connected Methodists and medical quackery in the June 17, 1740, issue of *The Champion*, where John Vinegar brings news of a "notorious Quack...Who is meant I know not; but believe it can be no other than the great W—— ... one of the most ignorant, blundering fellows that ever mounted a Stage" (344). "W——," Fielding's Vinegar explains, works like a puffer and disperses "Hirelings and Emissaries" who spread the word of his cures in the Boroughs

94 *Imagining Methodism in Eighteenth-Century Britain*

Dr. Rock's Political Speech, anon., 1743. © The Trustees of the British Museum. Used by permission

(346). "W——," a reference floating between Whitefield and Wesley, claims to cure everything by "Aurum potabile, or liquid Gold" which, Fielding suggests, may be a form of venereal cure that actually infects the patient with the disease. Fielding was not alone in associating Whitefield and Wesley with quackery, and specifically with Dr. Rock, the most famous midcentury quack and vendor of venereal medicines. "Dr. Rock's Political Speech to the Mob in Covent-Garden," originally dated April 2, 1743, shows Dr. Rock in his coach amid a crowd, holding a chalice of medicines in one hand and something M. Dorothy George calls "a long package or instrument" in the other (Stephens 3.1, no. 2598). In the foreground, a slack-jawed man looks up at Rock while the unruly crowd jostles closer to the coach. In the broadside below the print, Rock proclaims that he communicated his "excellent Nostrum" to cure "the *Itch*," an homage to Lord Rochester's exploits as Dr. Bendo. Whitefield and Wesley appear in the second state of the print in August 17, 1743, where they are dropped into the background and elevated above the crowd; Whitefield, cross-eyed and holding his handkerchief, preaches with arms wide and raised, while an only slightly more moderate Wesley preaches to the right with his Bible and in his signature natural hair. The third state of the print includes the subtitle "The GRAND ALLIANCE; Or, A Proposal for uniting the INTEREST and PRACTICE of the two most noted

QUACKS in Christendom." In the letter below, "from famous Dr. Rock to his dear friend the reverend Mr. Geo. Whitfield, A.B.," Rock proposes a partnership to share the mob in the interest of their mutual gain. The assertion that they both succeed because "nothing is so infallible as Mystery" equates them as quacks who know how to "wrap ourselves in Obscurity" in order to abuse a gullible crowd that wants "infallible" cures and is willing to believe anything in order to get them.

The notion of an "infallible nostrum" stands in for Hamilton's phallic supplement, which is both "infallible" in its mechanical reliability and a mystery in the sense that it is the veiled locus of questionable power. The unnamed "vile, wicked, and scandalous" thing found in her trunk, is, from a narrative point of view, evidence that will not submit to the rules of evidence. Phallic in (presumed) form and function, it is an unseen "thing" known in its effects. Like the Methodist experience of the "spirit," the joke that begins his story, this undisclosed scandalous thing both conforms to and refuses the epistemological canons of knowledge on which Fielding wants to ground his notion of gender as a constitutive element of natural law, the "propense inclinations" that will preserve the "continuance of the species." Both the scandal of Methodist conversion and the scandalous thing have observable effects and are thus potentially objects of knowledge, the things that will explain the mystery of Hamilton's success (and the mystery of her own desire), but, like the Methodist "warming of the heart," the wherewithal eludes Fielding's direct "experimental" observation and thus remains an article of faith. This disjunction within its own status as object underscores the ways that gender has been circulating in this story independently of the sexed body. While in Dublin, where she is disguised as a Methodist minister, a bout of laryngitis stalls her missionary work and confines her to print, which confuses her gender more than her appearance does. A forty-year-old widow, who had expressed some interest in Hamilton, rebuffs her love letter as "an Opera song" and expects that once her cold is gone, Hamilton will "sing as well as Farinelli" (36) on the basis of her writing. In Hamilton's case, the sexed body fails to provide the epistemological foundation of a gendered self, rendering it more a matter of belief than knowledge.

Hamilton's last wife Mary, or Molly, a beautiful but poor eighteen-year old who is also "Mary," and thus in some sense Hamilton's double, fully believes that Hamilton is an anatomical male. Her credulity is both comic and heartrending. When Molly tells stories of her wedded bliss to other married women, she "was received as a great fibber, and was at last universally laughed at as such among all," including her own mother, who exclaims "O child, there is no such thing in human nature" (47). Hamilton seems to have bested the anatomical males in Wells, but even when Hamilton's breasts are revealed in a tavern fight, it still does not convince her wife Molly; belief cannot be resolved or banished by physical evidence. Fielding's use of Methodism to interpret Hamilton's story allows Fielding his own space of belief and disbelief about the stability of gender, as well as the ability of Methodism to change people. Whether it was a religious or a sexual experience, the encounter with the Methodist Anne led first to Hamilton's same-sex identity and then to her transformation into a passing male in Fielding's version of the story. Molly's impressionability, an example of what O'Driscoll calls the innocent femme, renders femininity as a case of the more general malleability and tractability of the modern self that undermines a fixed notion of gender. By using Methodism to account for Hamilton's initial transformation, Fielding has himself undermined the notion that gender is grounded in "propense inclinations" for the opposite sex and inadvertently argued that it is an unstable construct, fueled by more amorphous desires. His use of Methodism mocks the movement and, at the same time, takes it seriously as a transformational experience, dancing around the question of what difference belief makes.

As he brings *The Female Husband* to a close, Fielding trips hard over his own speculations and beliefs about the natural law of propense inclinations. Both Molly Price and Mary/Molly Hamilton (who would have legally both been named "Mary Hamilton") are in love. Fielding tells us that "With this girl, hath this wicked woman since her confinement declared, she was really much in love, as it was possible for a man ever to be with one of her own sex" (43). Her "wickedness" fails to counterbalance the declaration of love, a sign of a more "natural," intrinsic goodness, reflected in Fielding's bounce between masculine and feminine pronouns at the end of his tale. If she has been transformed by Methodism into a "new man" through a conversion narrative where gendered pronouns interpolate the believer into the mystery of divine love, then perhaps Hamilton can also be that husband, "really much in love." Their conversation is "tender and delicate," and described without apparent irony by Fielding. Fielding's legal conundrum at the end of the story, as he returns to the court record for closure, is about the status of belief in things unseen like desire, love, and the enthusiastic encounter. Molly returns Hamilton's affection and vows to "attend her husband wherever they conveyed him" once Hamilton is exposed by the family of Miss Ivythorn, wife number two, and Molly Price's mother, who both give evidence against her. Molly supplies the space of innocence and impressionability that Fielding ultimately treats with some tenderness. Hamilton's mercenary motive drops out of Fielding's story at its close, leaving the more ambiguous question of what to do with these two "Mollys" in love.

In the end, Fielding turns out to be the unlikely convert of his own story. Despite his mean handling of Hamilton's case, he has been somewhat captivated by her, as Castle, Campbell, and Blackwell all observe, falling for her infectious enthusiasm against his own propense inclinations. After maintaining an ironic distance on Hamilton's story, milking every pun and overwriting her own tale with his exploitative version, he begins to sympathize with her and with young Molly, transforming Hamilton from monster to martyr in the final moments of the story. Her punishment, to be whipped publicly in four towns, feminizes Hamilton in a way that the exposure of her breast did not: "those persons who have more regard to beauty than to justice, could not refrain from exerting some pity toward her, when they saw so lovely a skin scarified with rod, in such a manner that her back was almost flead," a punishment the historical Hamilton, from whom nothing more is heard, may not have survived (23). In this moment, Fielding "reconverts" Hamilton to her anatomical gender, but it fails to locate Hamilton's meaning. It also comes too late; Fielding himself seems already converted by the spectacle of her suffering. Her "beautiful back" stands in for a normative feminine body, which becomes abject and Christ-like in its final suffering. She is an example of what Graham Ward called the complex and ambivalent maleness of Christ,

> in the way that all things are made ambivalent as their symbolic possibilities are opened up by their liminality. Victor Turner remarks about liminal personae that they become "structurally, if not physically, 'invisible' . . . They are at once no longer classified and not yet classified." The symbols used to represent bodies which are not outside of established categories cross or conflate distinctions—social, racial, or sexual. In what Turner calls their "sacred poverty" of rights and identifications, such bodies become floating signifiers. (G. WARD 170)

Fielding reads her sex through the religious, nongenital Christian trope of the flayed back and, in the process, queers it even further. Her transgressive body becomes a Girardian sacrifice, the wrong victim whose now-mystified body is a replacement-object for some larger systemic problem. His pity for her, after his own cruel burlesque, tips the scales toward sympathy for a figure whose desires have been both given more explanation than the cautionary strand of the tale can bear and, at the same time, have been left a mystery. Fielding, his heart warmed at last, can believe in Hamilton, even if she remains a mystery to him.

The mob as both the spectre of injustice and the expression of communal gender norms haunts the final section of *The Female Husband*, a reflection of real violence against Methodists that spiked dramatically in the 1740s and could not have escaped the notice of Fielding.[23] In one of these cases, rioters attacked a Methodist meeting house in Exeter in broad daylight, beat the minister, stripped some of the women and turned the petticoats over the heads of others. Some of the rioters attempted rape, and others dragged some of the captured members through an open sewer, without the Magistrate or Justice of the Peace reading the Riot Act or attempting to stop the rioters (Wilder 44–51). Fielding is ambivalent about his own mob in *The Female Husband* and its ability to purge, correct, or expose the ambiguous offenses of Hamilton. The mob is the collective, mocking voice that enforces gender norms, but Fielding's sympathy for "Molly" Price-Hamilton, "unjustly" taunted by the mob, collides with their function. Fielding ultimately sides with the vulnerable, Christ-like Hamilton and the devoted Mary who suffers with her. Once she is conveyed to Bridewell, the mob again assembles to insult her, but Fielding remarks that "what was more unjustifiable, was the cruel treatment which the poor innocent wife received from her own sex" (49). They laugh, throw dirt, and "made use of terms of reproach not fit to be commemorated" (48). This closing change of heart transposes Fielding's earlier phrase for Hamilton's prosthesis, the "matter not fit to be mentioned," into the crowd's reproaches, which are "not fit to be commemorated." The shift relocates the problem from Hamilton to the violent crowd, though the problem itself remains persistently elliptical, "not fit" for words.

Silenced and punished in a way that Methodism could not be, Hamilton bears the weight of Fielding's anxieties about selves who are malleable enough to be transformed by belief, and about religious practices powerful enough to relandscape the self. The legal response to her adventures is oddly flat; Hamilton is prosecuted under a clause in the vagrant act, "for having by false and deceitful practices endeavored to impose on some of his Majesty's subjects." Her official crime, the thing that can be named, is impersonation, acting outside of a theater, something strangely fitting for a Methodist from Fielding's point of view, but also a verdict that highlights the questions Fielding has raised about where to locate the self. Three years earlier, in a version of the Lucianic tale of passengers crossing the river Styx, Fielding articulated his sense that Methodism was a prosthetic religion, something exterior to the self. Each passenger crossing into the world beyond must unencumber him or herself of clothing, body parts, or belongings, a vision of the self reduced to a condition of natural authenticity. The Methodist on board must "lay aside that vast Quantity of Religion," which he is only barely able to do (Fielding, *The Champion* 257). This prosthetic notion of religion beyond natural law is at odds with his assumption of a natural self, and as such something that Fielding imagines as a "vast Quantity," something that must be taken off in a final moment of authenticity. Yet Fielding's amorphous, desiring self of "carnal desires" and disorderly yet "natural" appetites demands such a prosthetic religion, something to give shape to the seething shapelessness of desire itself, whether in the form of a governing "virtue and religion" or the dangerous methods of Methodism, which let too much of that desiring self come out. In this context, his definition of "Religion" in number 4 of *The Covent Garden Journal* as "a Word of no Meaning but which serves as a Bugbear to frighten Children with" is a joke that tells on the teller by giving us a glimpse of a polymorphously perverse child-self, prior to the law.[24] Fielding's fascination with Hamilton shows how Methodism, in a moment prior to modern conceptions of sex, gender, and sexuality, yet in the midst of their formulation, could function like a sexuality. Methodism could explain Hamilton's sexuality in the way that it hailed mysterious, even primitive passions from within the self and offered a system of practices that consolidate the self and make her "a new man."

CHAPTER THREE

Words Made Flesh
Fanny Hill and the Language of Passion

From John Cleland's point of view, it must have appeared that the movement called Methodism had overrun his homeland on his return to London in 1740, after eighteen years in Bombay. Between Cleland's homecoming in 1740 and 1749, when the second volume of *Memoirs of a Woman of Pleasure* appeared, the Wesley brothers and George Whitefield had corporately published over three hundred editions of their hymns, tracts, and sermons. They were highly visible in London and the environs, all still young men, and preaching the warming of the heart, repentance, and forgiveness for the toughest cases, particularly prostitutes. Cleland does not mention Methodists by name in his best-known work, *Memoirs of a Woman of Pleasure*, but the novel makes a series of connections between prostitution, sensuality, linguistic immediacy, and Methodism that were current in mid-eighteenth-century culture. The connections to Methodism and Moravianism as species of Christian eroticism shape Cleland's rhetorical strategies and the narrative implications of his pornographic novel. *Memoirs* appeals somatically to the reader in an attempt to warm not the heart, but the sexed body through the power of the word. Like a Methodist sermon, it stakes its procedures on its ability to speak with shockingly affective directness.

Cleland confessed to Lovel Stanhope that Mr. Barvile, the young flagellant who is driven by "wild passionate rapture and enthusiasm" and who wants to be "unmercifully whipped" by Fanny, then to do the same to her, was something he had "fished for in actual life," substituting "a Lay-character, to that of a Divine of the Church of England" in his portrait.[1] While the specific identity of this "Divine" remains a mystery, the young, popular Methodist leaders are good candidates. George Whitefield, John Wesley, and Charles Wesley were all still preaching in Anglican pulpits, and the Wesley brothers were at some pains to emphasize their identity as ordained priests of the Church of England. Enthusiasm, a term identified with the young, clerically coded Mr. Barvile, had also become a functional synonym for Methodism. Furthermore, John Wesley had been tarred with the suggestion that he practiced and encouraged flagellation as a Methodist discipline, and Whitefield's *Short History* opened him to charges of sexual excesses and perversions.[2]

Though *Memoirs* has been given pride of place in the history of pornography, described by Hunt, Trumbach, Wagner, Mudge, and McKeon as distinct from clerical satire and as a commercial end unto itself, Barvile reminds us that clerical satire continues to inform Cleland's novel.[3] Replete with images of the body as machine or engine, *Memoirs* also revels in a religiously coded language of souls, bodies, enthusiasm, and reformation, similar to the sensual language of Methodist sermons, full of holy embraces, espousals, love feasts, and desires.[4] Cleland draws on the language of Christian eroticism in both Methodist and Moravian rhetoric, movements that were still closely related in the early 1740s, for the arc of Fanny's confession and redemption. Both movements articulated an experiential conception of God through an intensely somatic vocabulary of Christian embodiment, including blood, flesh, and pain, read through the suffering body of Christ, language that explodes in the episode with Mr. Barvile the flagellant. The scene, which returns to an older tradition of convent pornography through Moravian and Methodist tropes, illuminates the ways that sacred language is present throughout the novel and party to its pornographic quest for novelty, repetition, and "experimental" knowledge.

Memoirs shares with Methodist discourse an attempt, as William Epstein has argued, to break through the "ornamental" surface of words themselves (106). Cleland's burlesque version of revelation resembles the direct address of Methodist preaching and the Methodist's print appeals that attempted to bring listeners to the point of an experience with divine grace and religious conversion, as Whitefield did in "Christ the Believer's Husband":

> If any of you, amongst whom I am now preaching the Kingdom of God, are Enemies to inward Religion, and explode the Doctrine of inward Feelings, as Enthusiasm, Cant and Nonsense, I shall not be surprised, if your Hearts rise against me whilst I am preaching; for I am about to discourse on true, vital, internal Piety; and an inspired apostle hath told us, "that the natural Man discerneth not the Things of the Spirit, because they are spiritually discerned."
>
> (WHITEFIELD, *FIVE SERMONS* 5)

Those who came to the Whitefield sermon to prove they did not believe, to see the show and remain unshaken, often found themselves overcome, as did Benjamin Franklin, Martin Madan, and thousands of others at field meetings. Fielding parodied this attempt at immediacy in Parson Tickletext's Whitefieldian exclamation "Oh! I feel an emotion even while I am relating this: methinks I see Pamela at this instant, with all the pride of ornament cast off!" (237). Like the illusion of Pamela's writing to the moment, Cleland offers textual events that demand the reader's response through what Frances Ferguson, after J. L. Austin, has called the linguistic "performatives" that link pornography and modern utilitarianism. Fanny laments that her imagined reader must be "cloy'd and tired with the uniformity of expressions" of this kind of subject, which is at bottom "eternally one and the same" since there is "no escaping a repetition of near the same images, the same figures ... *joys, ardours, transports, extasies*" and other terms that necessarily must flatten with overuse (91).[5]

But Fanny also hopes, like Whitefield, to hail the reader into another state by balancing the "gross" subject of the body against the "ridicule of mincing metaphors and affected circumlocutions" (91). In other words, both attempt to go beyond the surface of the body and the surface of words to reach something deeper, something for which a sacred eroticism is both metaphor and content at the very historical moment Bataille and Foucault both speculated that sex becomes the refuge of the sacred in an increasingly disenchanted, secularized world.[6]

Situating *Memoirs* in the light of these implicit and explicit connections with Methodism exposes the linguistic and narrative stakes of a secular account of sex as the new space of the soul, the locus of the deepest truth of the modern self. If sex, as Judith Butler has suggested, is "that through which," then the place it takes Fanny is not only to the mechanical realities of arousal, detailed here to the point of tedium. Fanny participates in a discourse of revelation as a figure of "native purity" whose confessional tale will expose the "stark naked truth" of her sexual adventures and so of herself. But like Whitefield's command to "follow naked the naked Christ," exposing the deepest truths for Fanny reaches the limit of the body as metaphor: what does nakedness show? Striving to get closer and closer to the ineffable returns both Fanny and Whitefield to the body as simultaneously matter and metaphor. Derrida uses a similar collapsing metaphor when he claims that televisual media, like the evangelical appeal, promise an immediacy in which "one can almost put one's finger on the wound" (Derrida 64). *Memoirs* strives to get past the surface of words in the Barvile episode, but it enacts a perverse version of sacramental transformation that makes the word flesh, rending the veil by rending the body. In meeting the pornographic demand for both repetition and novelty, the Barvile scene recreates a passion play that is shocking both in its literalism and its religious structure. The novel temporarily loses the critical distance on what McKeon has called its own "eclectic and ecumenical" figurative style, and Fanny's and Barvile's bodies become real metaphors, temporarily exposed in their sacramental sexuality (667). The sexual danger of the scene is matched by a rhetorical anxiety about how a reader should respond to words are made flesh.

A Magdalen Sinner

The worlds of Methodism and *Memoirs* overlap in their shared interest in prostitution. Because of their social service work in London and their embrace of prostitutes as converts, Methodists were identified with prostitution by association. Wesley's *A Word to a Street-Walker* (1748), one of his many short advice tracts, addressed its hypothetical prostitute with an open question, "Whither are you going? Toward Heaven or Hell?" (1). While the tract raises fears of hell, claiming that "every Moment" the prostitute is in greater spiritual danger, it is theologically Arminian, offering universal redemption that overcomes natural law and its demand for punishment. Wesley assures the prostitute that she is also "the Temple of God" and that she should fly to Christ, who "suffered the Publicans and the Harlots to come unto him," including Magdalen who bathed his feet in her tears (4). Cleland took a similarly sympathetic view of prostitutes in *The Case of the Unfortunate Bosavern Penlez*, where he declared that these women are "fallen angels . . . more deserving of Compassion than Blame" (Cleland, *Penlez* 13). Cleland, sounding more like Wesley addressing the streetwalker than the author of *Memoirs*, bemoans the fate of young prostitutes "given up, at Discretion, to the Lust of every Ruffian who can afford the Price he sets on her" (9).

While Methodists were not the only voices addressing prostitutes sympathetically, they moved away from the more punitive strategies of reform groups like the Societies for the Reformation of Manners, which attempted to prosecute prostitutes in raids, such as those conducted by Sir John Gonson, and toward an acceptance of the sinner if not the sin. This disposition skipped over the self-making modern logic of the penitentiary and instead proposed a range of reformed and semireformed states for the "regenerate" Methodist, saved by grace but not yet perfected. Wesley's direct address to prostitutes, using the first person and the imperative, seems to have had a strong appeal to that segment of the London poor. Some Methodist churches even developed a residential "prostitute problem," where in several cases prostitutes set up semipermanent living quarters in Methodist preaching houses, materializing the idea that Methodism led to prostitution on their own pews.[7]

Methodist work houses and missions were also ideological competitors with the major "public" works projects, like Captain Coram's 1739 Foundling Hospital, for which William Hogarth designed fundraising tickets, certificates, and his portrait of Coram, and the Magdalen Hospital, a large-scale attempt to institutionalize the reform of prostitutes through a combination of housing, education, and work. Public hospitals and charities laid claim to generalized Christian principles in their founding but operated as expressions of a modern secular *civitas*. By comparison, Methodist schools and charities maintained their strongly evangelical and Christian identity, proclaiming a primary interest in saving souls as the warrant for their social activism, while still taking the economic problems of urban homelessness and predatory sex work seriously. Jonas Hanway's case for the 1758 The London Magdalen Hospital, which Mary Peace has called "the cultural high-water mark of the earlier sentimental, Whiggish discourse of improvement" (Peace 125), defined his project against "the absurd notions of the *Methodists*," declaring that the Magdalen Hospital will be governed by rational rather than evangelical Christian principles.[8] But the Methodist's evangelical principles were, by some measures, less judgmental than the scrutiny of the Magdalen Hospital, in which former prostitutes had to wear a uniform signifying their compliance and their participation in a penitential logic of the self. The discourse of individual freedom and rights, which enshrined the value of private property and informed the emerging market ideology in eighteenth-century Britain, situated the poor as a threat to society, as Deborah Valenze has argued, and fostered more punitive attitudes toward poverty and the working poor, which included prostitutes. Methodism short-circuited that logic by insisting not only on charity but universal and immediate salvation. Unlike the Foucaultian panopticism of the Magdalen Hospital, where the penitents submitted voluntarily to be remade by the gaze of the reformer, Methodist reformation was exciting, instantaneous, and trafficked in bodily sensations that flowed freely across sacred and sexual registers. Reform could happen in an instant.

The cultural connection between prostitutes and Methodists grew out of Methodism's rhetoric as well as its domestic missionary focus on sex workers. Whitefield, taking up the plight of the prostitute as a trope for penitence, declared, "if you have been as great a harlot as Mary Magdalen was, when once you are espoused to Christ, you shall be forgiven" ("Christ the Best Husband" 12). The Wesleyan "Magdalen" hymn embraces the Magdalen story, placing Mary Magdalen at the tomb, a woman now forgiven to whom Christ reveals himself. Redeemed by language usually reserved for the Virgin Mary, she becomes both the "favor'd soul" as well as the evangelist who rouses the flagging believers:

> Highly favour'd soul! To her
> > Further still his grace extends,
> Raises the glad messenger,
> > Sends her to his drooping friends. (SELECT HYMNS 27)

The hymn, with seemingly inadvertent eroticism, paints the prostitute as salvific figure who revives her "drooping" fellow Christians. The Magdalen figure, which also appears in a medieval hymn as "felix meretrix" (happy harlot), worked as a stand-in for the general guilt-ridden believer who now "rises the glad messenger."[9] Another Methodist Magdalen hymn, "To-Happy Magdalene," focuses on forgiveness, rest, and redemption, assuring the listener that the burdens of sin and grief will be lifted by Christ, just as those of the first "Happy Magdalen" were:

> Happy Magdalen, to whom
> Christ the Lord vouchsaf'd t'appear
> Newly risen from the Tomb
> Would first be seen by Her. (J. WESLEY, HYMNS FOR THOSE THAT SEEK 14)

"Happy Magdalen" appeared in several Methodist hymnals, including *Hymns for those that Seek and those that have Redemption* (1747) and the multiedition *Select Hymns for Christians of All Denominations* (1761).

Martin Madan, himself a reformed member of one of the Hell-Fire Clubs turned Methodist minister and chaplain of Lock Hospital for penitent prostitutes, became an advocate for sex workers and, eventually, a champion of polygamy. His own Methodist conversion experience took place in spite of his skepticism and intention to mock Wesley. He first encountered Wesley when his club-mates proposed to hear Wesley preach and then to have Madan take off the performance after.

> Madan was deeply struck and on returning to he club and being asked "to take the old Methodist off," he stunned his colleagues with this reply: "No, gentlemen, he has taken me off" (BL, Add. MS 5832, fol. 84). He forsook the bar, his former mode of living, and his erstwhile associates. (POLLARD 58)

Madan's intention to imitate Wesley is reversed as the performative, instantaneous exposure of his own faults. Some years later, in 1763, Madan wrote an account of the life of one of his parishioners, Fanny Sidney, whose story is an example of the popularity of Methodism's more mystical narrative of divine grace as an alternative to a public program of surveillance and punishment. He heralded Fanny as a model of repentance and a young woman whose sins were the result of economic distress rather than the tale of virtue in distress. Fanny first turned to the Magdalen House but eventually found Methodism, which in Madan's account provided the happy ending to the story of her short life.[10]

Part of the relationship of Methodism to prostitution in the public imagination, parallel to the adventuring freedom of Fielding's Mary Hamilton, was the independence from marriage that Methodism represented for some women. As Behn discovered in the equation of "Poetess and Punk," and as Catherine Ingrassia and Laura Rosenthal have demonstrated, wage-earning women still were read as prostitutes in much of the public imagination.[11] Women who worked in the movement as helpers, preachers, or teachers did not necessarily marry, and many found themselves under suspicion as more infamous kinds of "working women." The Orphan House in Georgia, as well as work projects out of the Tabernacle and other London-area missions, residential charities that housed, fed, clothed, and either schooled or employed destitute adults and children were described in paranoid terms as what Cynthia Cupples calls the "orgiastic Methodist workhouse" (49). The concern, however unfounded, illustrates the impact of Methodist institutions as part of a re-networking of urban charitable institutions and the anxieties they prompted, including alternatives to heterosexual marriage for otherwise financially dependent women. *The Weekly Miscellany* of May 1741, a magazine that had previously been sympathetic to narratives of women's spiritual devotion and leadership, claimed that the Methodist home for runaway girls required the girls to greet their male coworkers, "boys as raw as themselves," with "holy kisses." Their spinning profits, the magazine alleged, went to the preachers; the spinning room, which the exposé claimed was only a gateway to sexual labor, had adjoining bedrooms, where "by this means, some poor raw girls, who might have had pretty fortunes, have been drawn away, and their parents have been forced to settle it in a different manner, from what they first intended." Though there was no evidence that the workhouses were ever configured thus or led to such abuses, representations of them as sites of danger were a part of a pattern of discrediting Methodism and the cultural alternative to marriage that it provided.[12]

The spatially paranoid reading of the Methodist workhouse in *The Weekly Miscellany's* account divides into a public, commercial front and a private, sexualized interior, much like Mrs. Cole's house in Cleland's novel.[13] But Mrs. Cole's brothel, in comparison with Fanny's initial exploits at Mrs. Brown's and the specter of streetwalking that lurks at the edges of her story, is a convent of pleasure that rescripts the disciplines of the cloister or the spectre of the workhouse as the freedom of the bourgeois self. Mrs. Cole's provides Fanny with community and safety, imaginatively midway between a convent and a private club. The "outer-parlour, or rather shop" provides an acceptable millinery front for the operation, which is staffed by beautiful and tasteful young girls who "composed the small, and domestic flock, which my governess train'd up with surprising order and management" (Cleland, *Memoirs* 93). The young "flock" of women are "noviciates" admitted into "a little family of love," a reformed convent on modern principles of liberty and sensibility (93). The spacious drawing room, "where a select reveling band usually met," uses the term from Methodist society meetings to describe these "restorers of the liberty of the golden age, and its simplicity of pleasures" (94). Mrs. Cole's idealized brothel promises to return its inhabitants to a lost, salubrious past and give readers a glimpse of a social alternative possible within the present moment. Wesley's reports of Count Zinzendorf's experimental community at Herrnhut likewise described it with a rapture and a sense of return to a prelapsarian communal experience imaginatively prior to the complications of modern life. The "golden age" of simplicity in both cases is a communal setting for the modern self.

Fanny's experience of talk about sex is a salacious version of confession as Methodists practiced it in the form of testimony. Many of these public confessions reiterated the trope of the penitent Magdalen with the stories of real women, as did Sarah Ryan, who happily shared the story of her sexual past. At "about nineteen my person rather agreeable . . . and snares surrounded me on all sides," she had been tricked into bigamous marriages, contracted venereal disease, and then became a Methodist and charity worker. Mary Bosanquet, one of the first female preachers of Methodism, recalled that Ryan "found a kind of holy delight in the practice of rejoicing to be abased . . . and when conversing with strangers she would say 'Suffer me to warn you for I am myself a Jerusalem sinner and have need to be with Magdalene at the masters feet.' "[14] Her confessional disposition became, as Phyllis Mack observes, "an essential part of her new identity as she compulsively told and retold her story" (Mack, *Heart Religion* 147). Like Fanny, Ryan's confessional declaration of the "truth! Stark naked truth" of the self crystallized that self in the confessional pleasures of penitence.

While Mrs. Cole's "secret institution" is home to more action than talk, talk, and particularly confession, is central to the way Fanny and her readers experience sexual pleasure. The men who come there are "professors of pleasure" and who, with the women of the house, initiate Fanny not just into sex but into a condition of verbal intimacy very much like that of a Methodist band. The proceedings begin with group confession among the women at "the assembly-hour," a pornographic version of a band meeting and *das Sprechen*, the group confession favored by Moravians and early Methodists (*Memoirs* 94). Mrs. Cole announces that there will be a "chapter meeting" to receive Fanny. In the subsequent scene Fanny, Louisa, Emily, Harriet, and their "sparks" have their civilized orgy for Fanny's benefit. The sparks, Fanny notes, are moderates, not enthusiasts: "though they occasionally preached pleasure, and lived up to the test, they did not enthusiastically set up for its missionaries, and only indulg'd themselves in the delights of practical instruction of all the pretty women they liked well enough to bestow it upon" (112). These preachers of the religion of sex are not, Fanny insists, enthusiasts, but Barvile is, and what is at stake for Fanny in this encounter is whether an experiment could change her, whether the aesthetic and critical distance she enjoys might collapse, leaving her in the throes of feelings that, once aroused, could not be merely felt but would overtake her.

The conversion narrative, as Foote and other satirists insist, seemed to require and even celebrate sinners and sins, and so fueled suspicions that Methodists were complicit with a sexual underworld. Walpole joked to his absent friend Horace Mann on May 3, 1749, about the growing popularity of Methodism: "The Methodists love your big sinners, as proper subject to work upon—and indeed they have a plentiful harvest" (*Correspondence* 20: 52). Jemima Cawdle of Richard Cumberland's *Henry* finds a "new method of compounding for defaults" through "glowing enthusiasm," and the anonymous author of "A Letter to Mr. Foote . . . ," part of the tract and letter war between Methodists and their detractors that erupted after *The Minor* (1760), made a similar point about the confessional demand of Methodism (Cumberland 39). In reply to Martin Madan's defense of the Methodists in *Christian and Critical Remarks on a Droll, or Interlude, called The Minor* the anonymous author mocked Madan's claim that the Methodists do not deny good works: "I not only imagine, but am certain, that some of them do, if praising bad Works, be denying good.—*Art thou a Sinner?* Good.—*A vile Sinner?* Better still.—*A most wicked Sinner?* Best of all" (11). As Albert M. Lyles observed in *Methodism Mocked*, "This the orthodox believer saw and revolted from in horror. For him Methodism was a device by which one might sin, repent, be converted, sin again, and follow the pattern ad infinitum. The conservative mind thus saw the movement as a real threat to Christianity; if it was not actually antinomianism, it led to it" (Lyles 27).

Satires featuring Methodist whores or madams that are test cases for the liberality of Methodist repentance are sprinkled through the 1740s and 1750s. Foote and Hogarth both co-opted the colorful life of the alcoholic, evangelical madam Mother Needham, who died in 1731 before Methodism became visible, and blended her with the more successful "Mother Douglas," or Jane Douglas, of Covent Garden fame. The Needham/Douglas figure appears in Hogarth's *Harlot's Progress* (1732), which Cleland rewrites (through the lens of Richardson's *Pamela*) as the optimistic libertine story of a woman enlightened and redeemed by sex.[15] Hogarth satirizes Methodist antinomianism through prostitution in scenes like plate 11 of *Industry and Idleness*, in which a Wesley figure is in the cart with Tom Idle as he makes his way to Tyburn, while a Mother Douglas figure, who also appears in *The March to Finchley* and *Enthusiasm Delineated*, swills gin and lifts her eyes in prayer across the crowd.

Images of Methodists as or with prostitutes become even more common after Foote's 1760 *The Minor* and its Methodist brothel. When approached by a potential customer, the Methodist madam Mrs. Cole (a name Foote borrows from Cleland) remarks: "What, I suppose, Mr. Loader, you will be for your old friend the black-ey'd girl, from Rosemary-Lane. Ha, ha. Well, 'tis a merry little tit. A thousand pities she's such a reprobate!—But she'll mend; her time is not yet come; all have their call, as Mr. Squintum says, sooner or later; regeneration is not the work of a day. No, no, no" (41). The Methodist theological loophole of regeneration, the promise of a greater moral perfection not yet available to the believer, keeps her in business. A similar complicity between madams and the

Methodist doctrines of grace and regeneration echoed through Joseph Reed's *The Register Office* (1761), *The Spiritual Minor* (1763), the 1764 version of Johnstone's *Chrysal*, and *The Methodist and the Mimick* (1766). In these satiric afterpieces and farces, modern materialist accounts of sympathy put their stamp on the old pornographic story of the religious hypocrite. As Foote's Lucy explains in *The Minor*, her "enthusiasm" was the "child of melancholy," born of her vulnerability as a young woman alone in London, which has made her ripe for Methodism (79).

Foote's Mrs. Cole capitalizes on the "heated spirits" of young enthusiasts to bring them from the Tabernacle into the sexual marketplace, which Lucy discovers when she, like Clarissa Harlowe, finds herself tricked into a brothel. Mrs. Cole's success depends on the portability of emotions across registers and on a conception of sexual feeling as feeling's penultimate form. Just like Fanny, whose "ardent desires" and longings, once first stirred, are so "ungovernable . . . that I could have pull'd the first of that sex that should present himself, by the sleeve, and offered him the bauble, which I now imagined the loss of would be a gain I could not too soon procure myself" (*Memoirs* 31–32). Religious ecstasy raises passions that will turn sexual in *The Minor* because that is the "cock pit," as Fanny says, of all feeling in a materialist account of the self. Hogarth's thermometers in *Enthusiasm Delineated* and *Credulity, Superstition, and Fanaticism* conceptualize the differences between feelings as a matter of degree, not kind. Samuel Johnson took advantage of a similar affective analogy when, according to William Maxwell, two young women came to consult with Johnson on their inclination to Methodism and he, after dinner, "took one of them upon his knee, and fondled her for half an hour together" (*The Life of Johnson* 323). The more extreme discursive version (glimpsed in the popularity of Lucretius) claimed sex as the primitive truth of the self, while the milder Scottish school of Hume, Hutcheson, and Smith made a broader appeal to sympathetic feeling that found its highest expression in romantic love. Cleland's novel promotes the obviousness of Fanny's pleasures in a plan of "experimental knowledge," attempting to generate them in the reader as well by training their bodies to respond like Fanny's "exemplary instrument" that measures feeling accurately (Jagose 474).[16] The experiment, as Mrs. Cole and Fanny call it, is a dangerous one, because even if "pleasure of one sort or other" is the "universal port of destination" as Fanny assures us, pleasures are "independent of all reasoning" and can have an "unaccountable controul" over the self (144). Wesley's similar account of the power of "spiritual sensations" that form the self, justify the conversion experience, and provide the epistemological proofs of God in "experimental" Christianity depend on the tautology of sensation; feeling is believing, and believing grounds the self.

Clubs, Rites, and Parodic Ritual

The name "Methodist," bestowed at Oxford as a taunt to the members of the Wesleyan "Holy Club" conjured ideas of orgiastic religious practices, secret rites, the more scandalous gentlemen's clubs, and prurient speculations about the Methodist "love feasts" in the minds of some of their less charitable interpreters. These associations inform a variety of topical satires, including *The Methodists, a Humorous Burlesque Poem* (1739), which claimed that the "blessings" of Methodism are all pious lechery; *Merryland* (1741), a political-pornographic fable in which Methodists have recently invaded the country, and *A Plain and Easy Road to the Land of Bliss* (1762), in which the author declares that Methodism delivers bawds, prostitutes, and other criminals from the slavery of conscience. In particular, the notion of the closed meeting and the importance of public confession as part of a reinvention of ancient ritual made for a strong analogy between Methodists and the world of *Memoirs*.

William Epstein, Peter Sabor, and Lewis Clarke Jones have established that Cleland adapted what we know as *Memoirs of a Woman of Pleasure* from a pornographic tale, perhaps provided by Charles Carmichael, perhaps mostly completed in Bombay, and perhaps connected to the Beggar's Benison Society, a Scottish phallic-worship club.[17] The Barvile scene, with its ritualized tropes of flagellation and sacred-erotic mysteries, echoes the alleged activities of the Beggar's Benison club, the Medmenhamite Monks, and the Hell-Fire clubs. These clubs, particularly the Beggar's Benison club, where, on St. Andrew's Day, 1737, "Fanny Hill was read," included libraries of erotic literature used in sexual rites that mixed the sacred and profane.[18] Whatever was read that day in 1737 was not Cleland's completed novel, which would not appear in print for twelve years, but the reference speaks to club practices that may have informed Cleland's *Memoirs*. Cleland's relationship to the circle of clubs with these sexual rites was likely only second order before the publication of *Memoirs*. His uncle Robert Cleland was a member of the Beggar's Benison Society and John Cleland later became a member of the Knights of the Cape, one of the Scottish libertine clubs.[19] His parents kept company in literary and cultural circles that included Gay, Walpole, and Chesterfield, and his own minor associations with Boswell, Garrick, and

Lovel Stanhope (brother to Philip Stanhope, 4th Earl of Chesterfield) placed him in the orbit of generally clubbable men, though not in the inner circle.[20]

The surviving records of club rituals make clear that religious parody was part of the sexual frisson as well as the structure of their identity. The Dilettanti, also guided by Sir Francis Dashwood in their early years, expressed an anticlericalism laced with mockery, as in their 1746/7 resolution "That all Publick pious Charities are private Impious abuses."[21] Among the libertine clubs, erotic fascination is structured by the religiously coded hope of revelation, for which a parodically sacrilized account of sex is both the trope and the test case.[22] A toast by David Anstruther at the annual Beggar's banquet in 1742 proclaimed "because we all want Joys to the front Dormitory, for after saying I believe in God, we end for the night with the Resurrection of the Flesh!" (qtd. in Lord 172). The Beggar's Benison club medals bore the inscription "be fruitful and multiply" above the comically posed naked figures of a man and woman. Beggar's Benison initiates had to read a passage from the Song of Solomon from a specially decorated Bible owned by the club, and their records noted their meetings by the liturgical calendar as "Lammas," "Candlemas," or "St. Andrew's Day." The Medmenham Monks were explicit in their religious references, which Paulson calls a tired parody of Catholic ritual. Knapton's 1742 portrait of Sir Francis Dashwood depicts him as a Franciscan friar celebrating a mock-Eucharist with a chalice of wine inscribed "MATRI SANCTORUM" and leering at a statue of the Venus de' Medici. The portrait hung in the King's Arms tavern in the Dilettanti Club room and became the basis for Hogarth's "Sir Francis Dashwood at his Devotions" (1750), in which the face of the Earl of Sandwich gazes down from within Dashwood's halo.[23]

The parodic, sexualized satire of Christianity in the rituals of the libertine clubs linked sexual and religious enthusiasm. John Wilkes's tell-all *Essay on Woman* claimed that a parody of the Holy Trinity as "cock and balls" and regular mocking references to the Church of England were common among the Monks. William Stapleton, writing to Dashwood, proclaimed his "compliments to all your Brethren" with an obscene joke about their ability to stand during the "litany" (Lord 102). But the Mad Monks also trafficked in the more current phenomenon of Wesleyan enthusiasm (and suspicions that Methodists were closet Roman Catholics), connections that explode in Hogarth's *Enthusiasm Delineated* and *Credulity, Superstition, and Fanaticism* prints, which may have had a Medmenham-inflected origin (*Hogarth's Harlot* 155). The Medmenhamite "Brethren" included Charles Churchill, Robert Lloyd, John Armstrong (an "ob-

Sir Francis Dashwood at His Devotions, William Hogarth, 1760. © The Trustees of the British Museum. Used by permission

server") and John Hall-Stevenson, all of whom had taken aim at the Methodists. Churchill, in "The Ghost" mocked the Methodist participation in the Cock Lane ghost affair; John Hall-Stevenson compared an aviary of birds to Methodist "love feasts, and agapes . . . Methodist night-wakes"; and John Armstrong wrote to John Wilkes that, in comparison to Methodist superstition, the "new order of Franciscans" at Medmenham had found "a good jolly road to Heaven" in their "Religion of Nature" (qtd. in Sainsbury 145). In this set of connections, erotic impulse and religious inspiration are part of the same "natural" religion and are almost indistinguishable from one another.

The Medmenhamites and the Methodists both became the objects of Johnstone's satiric pen in *Chrysal*, an episodic novel about the "adventures of a guinea" that offered glimpses of their behind-doors excesses. Johnstone's parody of Methodist collusion between Mother Brimstone (a Mrs. Cole figure), Doctor Hunch-back (Whitefield), and Momus (Foote) recycled the cast of Foote's *The Minor*, which was itself cobbled together from previous images and source satires, including Cleland's *Memoirs*. These three characters conspire in the brothel's success and in one another's publicity, in spite of their differences. A fight in which Brimstone cuts Hunch-back's head with a glass leaves him making deathbed confessions and both characters covered in blood. The scene ends with songs, "of which Momus's was the most humourous, my master's the grossest, the Matron's the loosest, and the Doctor's the most daringly profane, perhaps to obliterate the remembrance of his late religious qualms" (Johnstone 178). Subsequent volumes to *Chrysal*, which appeared in 1765, added an alleged scene from Medmenham, "the monastery," in which Wilkes let loose a baboon that the Earl of Sandwich believed to be the devil and to whom he confessed, "I never have been half so wicked as I pretended" (141). In both cases, Johnstone mocks moments in which people fail to have critical distance and readerly mastery, and instead lay claim to mystical and supernatural beliefs. In these moments, they are doomed to become comic cautionary tales.

The libertine clubs and the Methodist societies shared another strong analogy in their cultures of initiation and secrecy. While anyone could come to hear Methodist preaching, one had to be admitted to the societies, and then into the smaller groups, called bands, which met privately and heard confession. This declaration of private associations within the movement, which required an actual ticket for admission, signaled a secrecy that was easily mapped into the legendary debauchery of libertine clubs, whether the "Mad Monks," the revelers of Hogarth's *A Midnight Modern Conversation*, or Mrs. Cole's "secret institution" (94). Rumors of clandestine practices and sexual impropriety between Methodist "teachers" and their followers centered on the love feast, an evening meeting, by invitation, modeled on the early Christian practice of the "agape" meal from the third century and borrowed from the Moravians. By all dispassionate accounts it was reserved for prayer, hymn singing, teaching, and refreshments limited to water and a little cake or bread. But the name was enough to fire paranoid imaginations. In 1755, Joseph Boyes, curate of St. Samson's in York, brought charges against William Williamson, vicar and incumbent of a city parish, for attending "the night revels" of a Methodist love feast, a place of bad fame and Reputation and the practices therein are said to be profane and superstitious, great numbers of persons of both sexes being frequently assembled there at very unreasonable hours in the night, the doors for the most part being locked, barred and bolted, in such private assemblies none being admitted without tickets with Popish pictures and devices upon them as of the Virgin Mary, a Crucifix, or a Lamb.[24]

While it is difficult to establish what exactly the Moravians or the Methodists did in their closed meetings, descriptions of the event were tinged with a frisson of sexual excitement. Lavington suggestively claimed that the Moravians revived the "Devotion" of the Brethren, "by celebrating Agapes, or *Love Feasts*, but of what a filthy Nature all their Festivities are, we have already been informed by Mr. Frey" (Lavington, *Moravians* 117), tarring the Methodist by association and implication. Wesley, after a 1753 exposé on the Moravian version of the love feast in *The Gentleman's Magazine* as a near-orgy, claimed that it "informed me of nothing new." His comment was a sign of the deepened rift between the two groups and a suggestion that Wesley knew of and disapproved of Moravian practices that he deemed excessively sensual (Podmore 270).

Looking the Part

The ambiguous history of his source materials for *Memoirs* make Cleland's specific authorial claim to the Barvile episode and its clerical coding even more interesting. Barvile's appearance in plain attire, "far inferior to the ample fortune he was in full possession of," and his bowl cut, which Fanny describes as like those "we are told the Roundheads wore in Oliver's times" (182) parody the visual signifiers of the "new Methodists" and reflect the concerns that the rapid growth of Methodism in the 1740s might lead to another religious revolution in the pattern of Cromwellian Puritanism. While other Dissenter groups such as Presbyterians and Quakers advocated simplicity of dress, Methodism's growing presence in the 1730s and 1740s made it the most visible and current discourse against luxurious display, a devotional position that also encompassed a range of class anxieties about social mobility and unrest. Wesley, who himself sported longer hair carefully coifed, wanted wealthier Methodists to adopt understated wardrobes. In his eighty-eighth sermon, "On Dress," he preached against fine clothing, though he exhorted his followers to show "neatness of apparel" as a sign of godliness (*Abingdon Works* 7). Wesley was especially concerned that his helpers, who represented him in his absence, dress in plain suits, which would project the simple yet careful image he promulgated (Abelove 7). Like Fanny and Pamela, he emphasized the social meaning of a neat, clean, if "rustic" wardrobe, including natural hair as opposed to wigs, as part of a calculated image of spiritual seriousness.

Wesley went so far as to condemn laughter as a spiritual temptation, and declared he would not "voluntarily indulge himself in it" (1: 18–19), something Mr. Barvile seems to have taken to heart in his sternness. The idea that Methodists don't laugh spread quickly. Lavington accused Wesley of putting on "a *sanctified appearance*, by a demure look" and sternly managing his "precise behavior" (*Enthusiasm* 1: 14). The ballad "The Mechanic Inspired, or the Methodist Welcome to Frome," similarly comments on the "holy grimace, and sanctify'd sob" of "pious enthusiasts," while Nathaniel Fletcher asserts that Methodists are ignorant, peevish, and morose.[25] Barvile, with his "air of austerity not to say sternness, very unsuitable even to his shape of face," which "dash'd that character of joy" cuts a dour figure that is the bookend to the ecstatic Methodist overcome by the spirit, a trace of which remains in his "round, plump, flesh-colour'd face" that "gave him greatly the look of Bacchus" (145).

Cleland uses visual rhetoric from Methodist and Moravian devotional literature and sermons to fill out the scene. Moravian spousals in particular, which emphasized white clothing, a communally observed consummation (at least in the sensational account of George Lavington), and sex as a holy mystery pressed on the metaphorical limits of wedding imagery and connected the couple to the body of Christ. The arrival of Fanny in a "thorough white uniform: gown, petticoat, stockings, and satin slippers, like a victim led to the sacrifice" (182) displays the Methodist predilection for bridal imagery with an echo of monastic rites. Combe in *The Love Feast* includes a footnote to explain that Methodist women are especially fond of wearing white and mocks them through the gothic sexual frisson of graveyard school tropes ("When *Death-Watches* alarm the starting *Saint* / And *Screech-Owls* make the *sinless convert* faint"), including the love feasters, clad in white garments, walking with their "lewd Pastors ... to drown a Year's *Hypocrisy* in Wine / And carry on *Impostures* chaste design" (13). Wilkes in Johnstone's *Chrysal* participates parodically in this set of images by putting on "a milk-white robe of the finest *linens*, that flowed loosely round him" (138). The image of the female Methodist clad in white appears in multiple hymns and sermons. Whitefield, preaching to the society of young women at Fetter Lane, pushes the metaphorical quality of the divine marriage to its limits in that context, appealing to the young women to marry Christ now—they do not need their parents consent—and to "espouse" the husband who will never betray them. He invites them to get their wedding gowns:

> and then, my sisters, put on the white raiment, and clean garments, which Christ hath provided for you, the robes of his righteousness; in these garments you shall be beautiful; and in these garments you shall be accepted: you must have the wedding garment on; you must put off all your own good works, for they will be but a means to keep you from Christ; no, you must come as not having your own righteousness, which is of the law, but you must have the righteousness of Christ.
>
> (WHITEFIELD, "CHRIST THE BEST HUSBAND" 18)

Zinzendorf, who also indulged in the bridal imagery, proclaimed "The Saviour's Blood and Righteousness / Our Fin'ry is, our Wedding-Dress" in a sermon quoting a Moravian hymn (55). His disaffected disciple Andrew Frey complained of the extravagance of the Maiden's festivals, pageants in which "These single Sisters were dressed all in white, of the very finest Linnen; a very illusory Emblem of Innocence!" (Frey 48).

These pagan, Puritan, Roman Catholic, and evangelical signifiers swirl around Barvile, culminating in his "mortification of the flesh," a euphemism for religious ascetic "rigors," "discipline," or flagellation. The specific claim that Methodists engaged in self-flagellation dogged Wesley early in his career. In his *The Life of the Rev. John Wesley*, writing in the third person of himself, he admits that he believed his efforts to manifest true faith would be "quickened" by "self mortification and entire obedience," though through conversations with Peter Böhler "he was led to see his error" (*Abingdon Works* 5: 509). Wesley officially denounced the idea of self-flagellation or mortification, but he spoke approvingly of "voluntary instances of mortification" in his journals (2: 5). Methodist leaders had been suspected of too much sternness after the death of William Morgan, a young man at Oxford who died in 1733 amid rumors that the ascetic exercises of the Methodists had killed him (Rack, "The Holy Club"). Lavington stoked if he did not create the rumor that Methodists practiced flagellation by accusing Wesley of "corporal severities or mortification by tormenting the flesh," (31) which Wesley rebutted, but which Pope promulgated in the brief appearance of Whitefield in *The Dunciad*. After the "Harmonic Twang" of his sermon sounds through the city, Pope moves Whitefield toward Bridewell "as morning-pray'r and flagellation end" (2: 270). *The Methodists* picks up on the theme as well, decrying "your Fasts, your Matins, Purgatories / your Floggings, Pardons, other Stories," situating the movement in terms of convent pornography (12).

In Barvile, the sensualist beneath and the severe Protestant without struggle visibly before Fanny's eyes in "a *habitual* state of conflict with and dislike of himself for being enslaved to so peculiar a gust" (145). These references to flagellation painted Methodism as a return to a ritual past, but with a modern pedagogical frisson.[26] Barvile's enthusiasm constitutes a test of Fanny's sympathies that she must pass, something that Fanny and the reader must reject as too violent and unnatural (she compares it to a dose of Spanish Flies; effective, but "more hast than good speed") to establish some boundaries against the range of experimental possibilities for her sexual "religion of nature." The Barvile "experiment," that Wesleyan and scientific keyword, is something that Cleland must paint as a pleasure she undertakes voluntarily, in a state of freedom that is in inverse proportion to Barvile's own compulsion. Before this episode begins, Cleland pauses to affirm the conditions and controls secured by Mrs. Cole's brothel: its secrecy, the assistance of Mrs. Cole herself, and Fanny's own developed "state of ease and affluence enough to look about . . . at leisure" after the death of her keeper, Mr. Norbert (143). Fanny's freedom, which is sociable, sexy, and safe within the terms of Mrs. Cole's house, confirms her as a successful subject who has balanced appetite and taste to create her own modern heaven, as opposed to Barvile's religious, medieval, monastic failures born out of his unregulated enthusiasm.

The Word Made Flesh

The idea of a return to some form of primitive simplicity was something that Wesley and Cleland both indulged; where Wesley's interest was in a primitive piety, Cleland's was linguistic. For both Wesley and Cleland, the "primitive" represented both a return to the past and a way to situate the self authentically in a confusing modernity. Cleland believed it was possible to recapture a lost Celtic past through linguistic inquiry that would reveal the foundations of language and the origins of all meaning in *The way to things by words, and to words by things* (1766) and *Specimen of an etimological vocabulary, or essay by means of the analitic method, to retrieve the antient Celtic* (1768). His linguistic key to all mythologies posited a lost Celtic source language "the more primitive it was, must be the stronger of the energy of nature" (Cleland, *Way to Things* 2). As Carolyn Williams has observed, Cleland's linguistic themes are "a triumph of moderation" in comparison to previous efforts, though like them, he turns to mystical subject matter in the names of Celtic gods (Williams 268). While he defended himself as "no literary nostrum-monger," he wanted to find what he called "primitives," the founding monosyllables that initially formed language (2). Mrs. Jewkes's toast to "the dear Monysyllable" in Fielding's *Shamela* is a reminder that the term "monosyllable" was itself slang for female genitalia, a connection that makes Cleland's interest and his linguistic vocabulary even more loaded. He tried to situate his inquiry between the poles of going not deep enough into the matter and going so deep "as to reduce the language sought for to nothing but the vague of mere minims of speech or sounds of vowels and consonants" (3). Williams argues that the sexual overtones of Cleland's phallic search for order were embedded in his quest for the "great . . . harmony of words and things, so much coherence," which he found in his etymologies of ancient religious terms and concepts. Cleland was bent on revealing the "stark naked truth" of the sources of language itself.

To produce its account of "stark naked truth," Cleland's novel famously eschews vulgar language and depends instead on colorful similes and metaphors that ford through the sublime to the ridiculous. The play between metaphorical and literal meaning that governs the representation logic of the "summits," "fescue," and "engines" of *Memoirs* was also characteristic of the rhetoric of Methodist address. Horace Walpole explained to his friend Horace Mann that Methodist metaphor was always pushing toward a more physical, literal reality:

> For example, you take a metaphor; we will say, our passions are *weeds;* you immediately drop every description of the passions, and adopt everything peculiar to weeds: in five minutes a true Methodist will talk with the greatest compunction of *hoeing*—This catches women of fashion and shopkeepers.[27]

Like Fanny, Methodists seem to get carried away with language. Methodist and Moravian hymns, in their physical, sensual language, share the metaphorical strategies of Fanny's confessional descriptions; both are always on the verge of realizing play that is too deep, the phrase Horace Walpole used to describe the fashionability of Methodism among women, "who play as deep it is much suspected as the matrons of Rome did at the mysteries of the Bona Dea." His complaint about their excessive interest references the Roman fertility goddess whose rites were exclusive to women, rites that were turned into erotic parody by the Medmenham monks.

One telling term that was in a state of linguistic transference between sacred and sexual domains in the vocabularies of the "Mad Monks," Cleland, and Methodists was "ejaculation." The word was a favorite of John Wesley, who referred to "ejaculatory prayer" and marked such prayers in his journals with an "E. J." in the margin. For him, the phrase denoted spontaneous prayer, a form that, according to Lori Branch, shapes ideas about literary originality as well as the nature of sincere devotion.[28] Walpole's "The Parish Register at Twickenham" takes aim at Methodism through Fanny Shirley's rejection of Lord Stanhope after her conversion to Methodism within the small, elite community at Twickenham, "Where Fanny ever blooming fair / Ejaculates the graceful pray'r" (Walpole, *Correspondence* 42: 489). In Walpole's couplet, "ejaculates" denotes evangelical discourse, but he hints at the more sexual meaning that is overtaking the term. In 1758, Lovel Stanhope had sent some erotic books to Sir Frances Dashwood, founder of the Medmenham Abbey, "hoping they will now and then occasion an extraordinary ejaculation to be sent up to Heaven" (qtd. in Suster 104). Wilkes made a similar comment in mock-chastisement of Dashwood for failing to worship Venus sufficiently: "To this object his Lordship's devotion is undoubtedly *sincere*, though, I believe now, not *fervent*, nor do I take him at present to be often *prostrate*, or, indeed, in any way very regular in his *ejaculations*."[29] For the libertine clubs, the use of the word is a parodic term for devotion that includes as a secondary meaning physical, sexual ejaculation. The imported value from the religious domain is that of sincere spontaneity, something that speaks to an inner truth and inspiration. In the libertine use, sincerity is sexual and mechanical, a sacred parody of the expressions of the soul. Notably, with all of the colorful euphemism of *Memoirs*, where Fanny's comic-sublime metaphorization of the body is always on the verge of making the word flesh, the term is reserved for one special occasion, Fanny's sexual reunion with Charles. There, in a state of "delicious enthusiasm" in which Fanny imagines Charles transfusing his heart and spirit in their mystical union, he, "true to nature's laws, in one breath expiring, and ejaculating" makes them at last "one body and soul" (184–85). Cleland's linguistic choices borrow from the evangelical vocabulary for the language of "divine love" that graces Fanny and Charles's salvific reunion, the evidence of her true identity that confirms the validity of her initial "conversion experience" with Charles.

The Spectacle of Feeling

Cleland frames the issue of aesthetic distance at stake in the balance of seeing and feeling in the Barvile scene through Mrs. Cole's spectatorship. Mrs. Cole,

Fanny's "good temporal mother," watches the scene "an eye-witness, from her stand of espial, to the whole of our transactions" (144) as Phoebe and Fanny had watched others before, allowing Fanny to "signal ... my resolution" and "approve my personal courage" (144). Mrs. Cole guarantees Fanny's safety for the sake of her and the reader's pleasure at a moment in the novel that turns from the euphemistic language of velvet, silk, machines, and maypoles to lashes, livid weals, blood, skin, and cuts. Mrs. Cole's watching situates Fanny as a theatrical self, someone who knows she is being read, someone who provides matter for interpretation. Mrs. Cole, the sympathetic spectator, is a secular version of the spectator Adam Smith posits in *The Theory of Moral Sentiments;* she looks on Fanny as "a girl after her own heart" after the event, giving her the reward of having been seen. She embodies a position of aesthetic distance that mirrors our own, a voyeur who witnesses, feels, and participates in the scopophilic circuit without having to be touched. Her stance exemplifies what Taylor calls the modern, Lockean work of "disengaging from my own spontaneous beliefs and syntheses, in order to submit them to scrutiny" (*Sources* 168). The structure of her watching, like Fanny's narration of her experience, keeps her separate from the experiment in which she actively participates.

Persuaded by her sympathy for Barvile and the knowledge that Mrs. Cole is watching, Fanny submits to birching in her turn. Although the birches make her "flesh-cushions ... all sore, raw, and, in fine, terribly clawed off" (187), Barvile stops as soon as he fetches blood, "at sight of which he flung down the rod, flew to me, kiss'd away the starting drops, and sucking the wounds, eas'd a good deal of my pain" (149). The image recalls Gambold's description of the importance of both kissing and blood in Moravian worship: "kissing the son" as well as the wounds of Christ is something that one does in worship, a figure of devotion that slides back and forth across metaphoric and literal registers in the description of the meeting and the exchange of kisses between the congregants (Zinzendorf and Gambold).

A great deal of the midcentury sexual scandal about Methodism had to do with their past associations with the Moravians, sensationalized in Rimius's exposé of the Moravian Brethren, or Herrnhuters, *A Candid Narrative of the Rise and Progress of the Herrnhuters, Commonly Call'd Moravians or Unitas Fratrum* (1753). Walpole owned a copy, which he bound with Frey's *A True and Authentic Account of Andrew Frey* (1753), another tell-all from a former convert. That he put them together and annotated both is an indication of his interest in anti-Moravian and generally anti-evangelical work. Walpole placed large marginal Xs at the most shocking points in *A Candid Narrative*, a mark of interest he also uses elsewhere in his library.[30] Such passages included the claim that the Herrnhuters call the Holy Ghost "the eternal Wife of God"; that their "favourite Wound, the very dear little holy Opening, the precious and thousand times pretty little Side," the side wound of Christ, which they also call "Thou Rocklike Vault on the little Lamb!"; that they have "Strange Ideas concerning the Organs of Generation" (Rimius's note); on the circumcision of Christ; and on the role of the husband as "Vice-Christ" who "whilst he conjugally embraces, towards the Existence of a Child, is to be looked upon as an Office of a Vice-God, and his Wife ought to regard him as acting in the Name of the Creator" as he is "performing his Office."[31] The Moravian emphases on circumcision and holy marriage were echoed in Whitefield's popular and often-reprinted sermons "The Circumcision of the Heart," which trafficked in the bodily intensity of the Jewish practice as Christian metaphor, and "Christ the Best Husband," which made extensive use of marriage as a description of conversion. Rimius's observations were garnered from Nicholas (Count) Zinzendorf's sermons, including *Sixteen discourses on the redemption of man by the death of Christ*, translated into English and published in London in 1740, the same year as Whitefield's *Short Account*, journals from Whitefield and Wesley, and several sermons that emphasized a participatory experience of sacramental life. Zinzendorf announced that, as all Christians are priests of God, "the chief Duty of their Priesthood is to carry the Death and the bloody Sacrifice of their Redeemer continually within their Heart."[32] These images began to pour out in print in the late 1740s in the form of Moravian sermons and confessions, just as Cleland brought *Memoirs* forward.

George Lavington, Bishop of Exeter, was outraged by Moravian and Methodist devotional language for its collapse of sacred and erotic registers. He claimed that it made for "strange Mixtures of Debauchery and Sanctity," in which the threat of literalism becomes a theological problem (Lavington 3: 18). Lavington pulled his sensational and profitable accounts from Rimius's and Frey's tell-all spectaculars; Lavington went into multiple editions with *The Enthusiasm of Methodists and Papists Compar'd*, followed by *The Moravians Compared and Detected*. Of the Moravians, he complains "The *Children of Grace* have a careful *Mother* amongst the *Holy Trinity* and also a dear *Father*, and a faithful *Bridegroom* of their Souls. And these three Things must be understood to be *substantially* or *essentially*, and not in an *allegorical* Manner" (12–13). Lavington fulminated over the Gnostic elements of Moravian theology, which he compares to the Valentinians in its erotic excesses, but for him, the most horrifying consequence of this theology that it makes him into a woman. The problem is grammatical insofar as it is about gendered pronouns used to talk about God, a concern that twenty-first century Christian theologians trying to find less patriarchal devotional language ironically share with Lavington. He frothed that Moravians "have represented the *H. Ghost* as the eternal Wife of God the Father, the Mother of Christ, and of the Faithful" (115); that Christ "is our Husband, in whose Arms and Embraces we are ordained to sleep; we become Women, in his Embraces as a Man" (116); and described erotic scenes of "holy Kissing" between the members of the Trinity and the occasional human (117). Embodiment and feminization are overlapping outrages for Lavington, as are the Methodist and Moravian movements.

While the degree of embodiment in Moravian discourse was ridiculous to Lavington, Zinzendorf and his followers had no problem imagining a female God or even a female Jesus, and refer to "Mamma Jesu" as well as a mothering God in hymns. Rimius quotes at length from one of Zinzendorf's sermons at Zeist that pushes on the gender identifications in the spiritualized sex of a Moravian wedding:

> Member full of Mystery! Which holily gives, and chastely receives, the conjugal Ointments for Jesus's Sake, during the Embraces, invented by the Most Merciful himself, there being then the Seeds of the Church sowed. Mayst thou be blessed and anointed with the Blood that formerly ran from our Husband: mayst thou feel or meet with the great Tenderness at the Side, which is open for the Lamb's Spouse, since the Spear has pushed into it, and which is the Object of married People.[33]

Rimius's and Zinzendorf's cavalcade of tropes, like Cleland's, seem to take on a fleshy life of their own. The languages of revelation through somatic contact with the body parallel those of the Medmenham Monks, as well as *Pandora's Box*, which declares "that these parts [female genitalia] were the true *Pandora's* box, and that this box was neither more nor less than an allegory of the characteristical nature of women" as described by "Pagans" who honored sex with "religious worship" (*The Secret History of Pandora's Box* 51). Though Rimius, like Frey and Lavington, was indulging in an exposé, his account of the Moravian meeting captures the linguistic orgy of pronouns and the unnerving shift from literal bodies, to figurative examples of God, and back again. It was at once a linguistic, theological, and erotic conundrum of self and other.

Perhaps inevitably, watching sex was one of the paranoid claims that Henry Rimius, Andrew Frey, and George Lavington made against the Moravians and Methodists. The Moravians, who argued that male and female genitalia were sanctified through the birth of Christ to a woman and through Christ's own male body, became a lightning rod for criticism of evangelical sensualism. Rimius's book received a page-long review in the *Gentleman's Magazine* in May of 1753, declaring that it proves that Herrnhutism is "not accidentally, but essentially evil." Lavington focused on their erotic marriage rites at Herrnhut, disclosed only to those *"professed Members initiated into the most secret Mysteries of the Society"*:

> Nor are they lawfully Married unless they perform their conjugal Duties in the presence of the Elders . . . Mr. Rimius says, "The Leaders of Herrnhutism are accused of appointing such Ceremonies as suppose them to have entirely given up all Sense of Shame—Ceremonies so horrible that one would be inclined to hope the whole is a Calumny. (LAVINGTON, MORAVIANS 112)

The idea of Moravians having to solemnize their marriages in the "private-public" of the love feast invokes scopophilic pleasures for his readers, who like Mrs. Cole, might be in a position to watch these religious rites reinvented as sacred sexuality, a divine encounter that can be seen. Though Lavington draws the curtain, he does so only because he has no more "particulars of that most glaring Scandal in their Marriage Ceremonies," though he is sure they are "the most filthy and horrible that can be devised" (Lavington, *Moravians* 115). Out of facts, he is still intent on the scene of watching, and encourages his readers to fill in with their own ideas of what they imagine the content of these rites to be.

The image of a tormented Christ finds a parodic echo in Barvile's own "passive fortitude," which amazes Fanny as she views "the skin of his butchered, mangled posteriors, late so white, smooth, and polished" now "a confused cut-work of weals, livid flesh, gashes, and gore, insomuch that when he stood up, he could scarce walk" (185). Fanny for her part plays the sufferer at the hands of Mr. Barvile with Christian fortitude; she "bore everything without crying out" and "did not utter one groan, or angry expostulation" (150), content to be in this arrangement, stopping *in media res* to remind us it is "completely voluntary" and yet that "though she is at full liberty . . . you cannot imagine how much I thought myself bound, by being thus allowed to remain loose" (149). Fanny's purely psychological bondage metaphorizes what Barvile must literalize, but because she can make that translation, she can find a pleasurable yet controlled suspension of agency, what Charles Wesley described as, "in bonds my perfect liberty . . . in grief my joy unspeakable, my life in death, my heaven in hell." Fanny proves she can have access to the intensity of feeling, like a Methodist, but without losing her aesthetic distance or becoming too tied up in her metaphors.[34]

Blood is symbolically overloaded in the Barvile scene, escaping from the aesthetic project of representation at the same time that it marks a visceral physicality. Fanny bleeds during sex initially with Charles, again with Will, and then fakes her virginity with blood-soaked sponges to trick Mr. Norbert. But here, Fanny both watches and participates as "the blood either spun out from or stood in large drops on" his "skin . . . so smooth-stretched over the hard and firm pulp of flesh that filled it." This scene focuses on his body, not hers. Cleland demands that we behold his suffering with Fanny, who was "so mov'd at the piteous site, that I from my heart repented the undertaking" and only "continu'd the discipline" after Barvile begs her. Barvile finds sexual agency in his feminine abjection, while Fanny enters into emotional congress with Barvile through the image of his wounded body. Cleland plays nervously with sacramental meanings and material presence of blood as Barvile's breached flesh violates the metaphoric distance of the novel's euphemized bodies, becoming at once too real and too sacramental.

Fanny's meal with Mr. Barvile, which "would have piqued the sensuality of a cardinal," seems a capstone reference to the love feast and its invocation of a Eucharistic intimacy in name, if not in content. Like the meal Tom Jones and Mrs. Waters share, the sexually laden meaning of consumption evokes debates about Eucharistic theology and transubstantiation that divided Methodist from moderate Anglican theology. As Tillotson had put it in his 1684 *A Discourse Against Transubstantiation:*

> It is very scandalous likewise upon account of the real *barbarousness* of this Sacrament and Rite of our Religion upon supposition of the truth of this Doctrine. Literally to eat the flesh of the Son of Man and to drink his bloud . . . what can any man do more unworthily toward a Friend? How can he possibly use him more barbarously than to feast upon his living flesh and bloud?"

Fielding's objection to the "Nonsense and Enthusiasm" of Methodism, as voiced through Parson Adams in *Joseph Andrews,* aligns with Benjamin Hoadly's *A Plain Account of the Nature and End of the Sacrament of the Lord's-Supper* (1735), which Parson Adams claims was "written with the Pen of an Angel" and to which the Methodist preacher George Whitefield objected vociferously.[35] Hoadly's vision of Christianity "free from the extremes of both superstition and enthusiasm" represented the spirit of a "rational religion."[36] But the Methodist definition of communion as more than "mere memorial" underscored the mystery of embodiment at the heart of Christianity. Their Eucharistic theology refused to define the event as representation and so underscored communion itself as an event, an ethically troubling mystical moment that breaks from the linear temporality of modernity. What must be contained in this vision of Christian religion as law is what Kristeva has called the *jouissance* of spirituality, the ecstatic experience that is both embodied and a gesture beyond embodiment.

After the meal, Fanny reports her pleasure at "such violent yet pleasingly irksome sensations" as the lash marks are "converted into such a prickly heat" (a favorite term in *Venus in the Cloister*) that she can barely contain herself (187). Their mutual suffering is transformed into gratification, yet the discomfiting aspects of this scene linger in its material effects on their bodies. Fanny must stop to tell us, in the midst of this scene, that "in my heart I resolv'd nothing so seriously as never to expose myself again to the like severities" (150). This narrative breach is the obverse of her exclamation on her reunion with Charles: "—oh!—my pen drops from me here in the exstasy now present to my faithful memory! Description too deserts me, and delivers over a task, above its strength of Wing, to the imagination" (183). Writing about Charles is a moment of collapse between somatic experience and literary representation, in which the authenticity of her feeling brings her to the limits of language as she tries to describe "a system incarnate of joy all over" (184). But the caesura in the Barvile narration confirms that, in spite of her temporary enthusiasm, there will be no such collapse, that Fanny remains in narrative control as a reader of her own experience. Later, in a cooler moment, she confesses that this "rare adventure was more to my satisfaction" than expected, but that she was "never to resort again to the violent expedient of lashing nature into more hast than good speed" (152). Like *The Secret History of Pandora's Box*, the sexual truths of *Memoirs* displace former religious mysteries with their material, somatic certainties, but with the trace of pornography's sacred ties still in plain sight. The secrecy of the love feast, the linguistic disposition to euphemism and metaphor, and the visual rhetoric of blood and sympathy in the Barvile scene are reappropriated to the novel's own sexual proselytizing, which includes a hope for something beyond the materiality of the sex act. Fanny knows that this is "just sex," but she also believes that sex should be something more.

Happy Endings

At the end of the novel, Cleland unites Charles and Fanny, the "undeniable proof" of Fanny's initial promise to deliver her testimony as a cautionary tale, describing "those scandalous stages of my life, out of which I emerged at length, to the enjoyment of every blessing in the power of love, health, and fortune to bestow, whilst yet in the flower of youth" (1). Her unlikely tale of redemption speaks the language of Methodist autobiographies and the testimonial frame of a true self remade by evangelical conversion. Her past must be revealed in the interest of others, who can learn from her sacrificial telling as they would from one of the many popular Methodist conversion narratives, but those same narratives undercut the economic logic of sin and punishment with redemption, or free grace. The necessary (verbal) sacrifice of a sordid past proves the saving power of free grace, as does Fanny's story, but it also made for popular, lucrative print narratives. This salvific narrative structure, which can erase the past even as it records it, situates Fanny's pornographic testimony between the old clerical and new commercial terms of the genre.

Mr. Barvile is the trace of a "premodern" fascination embedded in the modern pornographic universe of the eighteenth century, which uses the bad enthusiasm of the convent and the "primitive Christianity" of Methodists and Moravians to buffer the new good religion, "natural" sex. There is, beneath the surface mockery, an urgency to discover meaning in the parodic adaptations of devotional language, an urgency that marks Sade's work as well as *Memoirs*. Sade quizzed the prostitute Jeanne Testard about her religious beliefs then confessed to her he had once shoved communion wafers into a girl's vagina and had sex with her, shouting "if you are God, avenge yourself."[37] While not as stark as Sade's declaration and his erotic experiments, the drive to a sacramental experience of the real finds expression in the lash and the blood of the episode, which is part of a perverse world that Fanny must reject. The religious world is at once primitive and prior to representation, and yet concentrated and proliferated through modern secular accounts of the self and its materiality.

But even once Fanny is "got snug into port" at the end of her story, she still has to confront a narrative problem. At the beginning of her second letter, she wondered how does one keep up the tale without losing the "spirit and energy" that allegedly animated the original encounter? Now she has to figure out how to stop. Lavington chided Wesley over the same problem: "you are able to set

Enthusiasm a-going; but want the Art of stopping it at Pleasure" (3). Fanny breaks out her surplus of metaphors, hurling virtuous sauces, roses, slippers, and flowers as well as dangerous rags, thorns, harpies, fouled feasts, and cankerworms in a linguistic object lesson worthy of Whitefield, in the hopes that she can frame her narrative excesses into the shape of modern virtue in her concluding "tail-piece" of morality (187). Words fly fast and threaten to lose their salt as she tries to tie down her moral, which returns to religious tropes: the "eternally unfading" roses of Virtue, the "incense" she burns to virtue, and the "solemner sacrifice" of vice to virtue.

With Charles's return, Barvile's problematic pleasures take their narrative place as a failed attempt to break through the veil of language to a mystic, primitive truth and help to better clarify good sex with Charles, which is nothing short of heavenly. The French translation of *Memoirs* makes the point visually with an image of Fanny and Charles making love on a celestial cloud as the sun streams from behind them, with the caption "les joies celestes," giving us, literally, a picture of their union as heaven.[38] The marriage settles any questions about her enslavement to "bad" sex practices and affirms that a bourgeois narrative of improvement and profit has always bounded her adventures. Fanny concludes that virtue's pleasures "cannot stand in comparison with those of vice . . . how comparatively inferior its joys are to those which virtue give sanction to" (223). Her "tail piece" of morality winkingly maintains her obvious preference for virtue over "inferior" joys but, like the Methodist conversion narrative, there would be no happy ending without the colorful catalogue of her sins. Redemption is as available to Fanny as it would have been to Wesley's eponymous "Street Walker," but Fanny adapts this rhetoric to secular and modern salvation of the love match with Charles as her religion of choice.

She proves herself a true believer by sending her son off with Charles on a tour of London's brothels in an "experiment" to "inspire him with a fixt, a rational contempt for vice": "The experiment, you will cry, is dangerous. True, on a fool, but are fools worth the least attention to?" (188). The implied definition of a fool is someone who cannot read the lesson of this brothel tour, someone who could not interpret experience in patterns that both should be obvious and that require additional critical reading. In light of her own narrative, her confidence that this test will work grows out of her faith, however blind, in the natural religion of sex, in which the body's desires confirm one's authenticity at a material level that can then be channeled into "health, vigor, fertility, cheerfulness, and every other desirable good in life" (223). Her version of sensation and reflection, like Wesley's adaptation of Locke, requires both raw experience and then reflection. But "true love," like the warming of the heart, remains a self-authenticating event, a truth that needs no translation and as such breaks through the veil of language as an instance of something divinely real and authentic.

Fanny's story, complete with a reversal of the virgin birth in her miraculous ability to avoid pregnancy, concludes with Charles's return, a political-sexual allegory of redemption, where enthusiasm finds its proper place. Their reunion is a moment of transubstantiation: "in a delicious enthusiasm I imagin'd such a transfusion of heart and spirit, as that coaliting [uniting], and making one body and soul with him, I was him, and he, me" (184). Her marriage to Charles, her "idolized youth," her "darling elect," "beloved," and his "scepter-member, which commands all" is at once Restoration, modern fairy tale, and evangelical romance, bursting with religious language as it brings the episodic, confessional narrative to both climax and closure. Charles, in being true "to nature's laws," affirms Fanny's true religion of love over and against "those pleasures that intemperance enslaves them to" (187). Fanny can have her mystic union, which indulges in this religious language, because of Mr. Barvile's sacrifice. His story marks off the domain of enslavement to religious discourse while also bringing to the surface the religious language that, like the cliché of the Methodist brothel, animates a modern secular account of the material mechanics of sex with a sacred flame.

CHAPTER FOUR

Actors and Ghosts
Methodism in the Theater of the Real

On June 28, 1760, Samuel Foote inaugurated a lively round of anti-Methodist satires with *The Minor*, an irreverent afterpiece that mocked Methodism in general and George Whitefield in particular. Foote appeared as himself in the comic prelude, promising his onlookers "one of those itinerant field orators" as "desert" [*sic*] and openly likening these preachers to actors: "I consider these gentlemen in the light of public performers, like myself; and whether we exhibit at Tottenham-court, or the Hay-market, our purpose is the same, and the place is immaterial" (8). Even before *The Minor*, Methodist preachers had been commonly regarded as theatrical, and none more so than Whitefield (Lyles 16–18). Foote's imitation of Whitefield as "Dr. Squintum" (from which even the reckless Foote distanced himself by framing the impersonation as the work of another character) set the stage for the clash of these two large, showy personalities. Whitefield was by every legitimate account sincere in his evangelical work, but his theatrical gestures and vocal techniques made him a test case for mid-eighteenth-century ideas about performance and authenticity. Foote's cynical pitch, that Whitefield is merely an actor who hypocritically objects to theater, masks a more substantive concern that the Methodist meeting, led by charismatic preachers, is a theater of the real, in which something happens, something that is an uncanny illustration of the relationship of performance and belief.

Eighteenth-century theatergoers were trained to acknowledge and appreciate the distance between actor and part. As Peter Holland observes, "The style of acting was not one in which the identification with the part was total; the actor never stopped being the actor" (Holland 60). In this context, actors played with or against type within the framework of shared assumptions about the gap between performer and part that was constitutive of performance. Fielding's Partridge crying out in horror to Garrick's Hamlet *"No farther!"* captured the image of the naïve reader who fails to understand theatrical protocols. But Partridge also captured a longing for a more complete experience of the theater, the hope for an experience of theatrical presence. Even for the sophisticated theatergoer, as Lisa Freeman observes, the problem of representing feeling on stage "only underlines the extent to which the theater complicated and frustrated the desire for authenticity," a desire fed by stagecraft like Garrick's marvelous fright wig (Freeman 36). Methodism came to fruition at a time in theater history when the formal strategies of Quintillian were giving way to the new Garrick school of acting, which was at once natural and mechanical.[1] Within that space, Methodism unsettled the boundary between actor and role, as well as the space between actor and audience in sermons that left congregants deeply moved, even changed, by this theater of the real. Foote's mockery of the Methodists raised further questions about performance as an event; is it playful mastery, in which the actor always remains distinct from the role, or do both observers and performers accept the risk of participation in an event that might change them? Foote, Hogarth, and other critics of Methodist theatricality registered the powerful intersection of presence and performance in the Methodist meeting, and found themselves, through parodic imitation, in dialogue with Methodism's theatrical deep play.

Complicating the desire for theatrical authenticity was the mystification of the theater as an arena of secularized spiritual experience still tied to its ancient Greek and Roman past in religious ritual, a connection underscored by the era's neoclassicism. John Hill went so far as to compare the actor to "the priestess of the Delphic God" who became possessed and uttered oracles in the course of her duties.[2] In a series of essays on acting first published in *The London Magazine* in 1770, James Boswell celebrated the "mysterious power of a good player" that becomes the character he represents and in a certain sense *"is* what we behold"

(469). Boswell confessed his nervous admiration for the good actor's "mysterious power" to "change himself into a different kind of being from what he really is," leaving the boundary between performer and performance temporarily unsecured (468). In his 1760 *The Actor*, Robert Lloyd celebrated Garrick as the model for a kind of acting in which the actor was to feel the emotions on stage, claiming that "No Actor pleases that is not *possess'd*" (4). He idealized an early fourth-century Roman actor, Genest, as someone who accomplished such "acting to the life" by playing a Christian martyr on the stage then becoming one, thus feeling "a Zeal beyond the reach of Art" as his performance became a reality (R. Lloyd 5). Lloyd's claim about possession and his example of Genest play off of the ambiguity between an actor who is possessed of talent and an actor possessed by some spirit, zeal, or mystic force. Both Garrick and Betterton argued that while great acting and dancing were founded on physical, even mechanical prowess, the greatness was itself an infusion of passion, inspiration, and feeling, what Joseph Roach calls the "ineffable mystery" that persisted into twentieth-century theories of acting (226). Good acting in all these accounts is a mystical experience, or at least as much like one as a modern self should experience. These accounts of acting and actors trouble the simple trajectory of a modern theatrical aesthetic as secular by imagining that, at its height, an ancient mysticism erupted through it. As a practice already tied to ritual, event, and primitive religion, it could be socially dangerous in the wrong hands, for instance, the Methodists.

Whitefield met the desire for theatrical possession in the actor that Hill, Boswell, and Lloyd voiced, effacing the line between performance and event. Lord Chesterfield, whose name is synonymous with polite reserve, found himself so compelled by Whitefield's story of a blind old man tottering on the edge of a cliff (representing sin) that, as the preacher reached the climax of his story, he supposedly sprang from his seat shouting "By God, he's over!"[3] The homiletic immediacy of Whitefield and the Wesleys inspired audiences and remedied what Goldsmith (who was elsewhere less complementary to Methodists) saw as the "drowsy" mode of Anglican worship epitomized in Hogarth's *The Sleeping Congregation*. Similarly, Goldsmith, in *The Bee*, observes in "On Eloquence," November 17, 1759, that Methodist preachers lack "common sense" but they affect their hearers deeply, reaching heights that "the ancients represented as lightening" and leaving their hearers in awe (203, 205). But many, including Foote and Hogarth himself, were suspicious of Methodism's theater of the real, in which the critical distance of the observer collapses into the immediacy of the event itself. In his 1760 *Letter from Mr. Foote*, Foote denounced Whitefield's "furious Zeal, which can only become the Tripod of the Delphic Oracle, or the Celebration of the frantic Feasts of *Bacchus*," as an example of a premodern, primitive, and religious theatricality (15). The relationship of theatrical performance to the Methodist meeting underscored the ways that modern Lockean psychology, in both its secular primary mode and the Methodist adaptation of spiritual senses, depended on the "event" of sensation, whether material or spiritual. In the sensory event, an individual consciousness "believes" the senses when it accepts the data and reflects on it to produce ideas. Though Locke's epistemological account of knowledge presents sensation and reflection as the rational and even potentially mechanical procedures of knowledge, the process is predicated on an act of faith—believing the senses. Some belief, some act of faith is a part of any attempt at communication, as is some doubt and anxiety about our own capacity for credulity. Foote, along with Hogarth and a range of other theatrical and graphic satirists, regarded Methodism as something that might overcome modern critical faculties with too much belief. But in situating Methodism as a site of primitive power, they revealed their own fascination with the promise of some mystical presence that defied rational explanation. The "possession" of both minister and congregants was too primitive for British moderns who conceived of themselves as liberated from false illusion and myth; at the same time, it represented the tantalizing promise of transcendence through an event, a performative experience of belief in the "modern" present.

Real Theater

Methodism's appeal to the masses, with its large crowds, charismatic preachers, and outdoor meetings, suggested a parallel if not its alliance with a media culture busy selling theater tickets, stock shares, and miracle cures. Methodist societies, like theaters, actually issued tickets, which had to be validated on a quarterly basis for those who wished to remain members, though anyone could come to hear Methodist preaching. The initial crowds at the popular Methodist "field preaching" events in the Bristol area between March and April of 1739 averaged three thousand per occasion (by John Wesley's estimation). Numbers rose steadily as Wesley and Whitefield shuttled between Bristol and London and became more widely known; Wesley preached to a crowd of ten thousand at Rose Green in May of 1740, while Whitefield gathered seventeen thousand on a single occasion at the same site in July. The range of Whitefield's voice was as remarkable as his popularity and seems to have contributed to it.[4] Between twelve and twenty-four thousand people came to hear Whitefield on Kensington Common in August of 1739, according to the *Gentlemen's Magazine*, and by September, he commanded crowds of thirty thousand.[5]

When compared to the capacity of the London and provincial theaters, the attendance at Methodist field preaching events is even more impressive. The (new) Covent Garden Theatre of 1730 seated around fourteen hundred, while Goodman's Fields was around half that size (Trussler 166). The King Street Theatre in Bristol, at a spacious one hundred and fifteen by forty-eight and a half feet, could hold nine hundred thirty-five spectators; the Orchard Street Theatre in Bath could accommodate roughly four hundred and fifty (Garlick 176–77). Even after the late-century expansions of Drury Lane and Covent Garden, which could eventually accommodate over three thousand each, the total number of spectators that could be at the theater in an evening was dwarfed by the number that could have heard Wesley or Whitefield in a day at the height of the outdoor meeting. The scale of these meetings is a reminder that Methodist membership records are just a fraction of the number in attendance at these outdoor sermons, which provided an unbounded theatrical experience, a setting more like open air theater of the Greek *amphitheatron* than the Roman structure of modern theaters, with their backdrops, proscenia, and scenery. It was a performance without theatrical architecture that created a psychologically open space as well, in which even astute or sophisticated observers had permission to feel the message as an uncontained performance.

These material realities fed the legendary animosity between the theater community and the Methodists, captured in Foote's bitter complaint that "religion turned into a farce is, by the constitution of this country, the only species of drama that may be exhibited for money without permission" (*Letter from Mr. Foote* 2). The Methodist circuit riders, traveling the roads between Bath, Bristol, London, and York, were succeeding while theatrical circuit companies and strolling players were being squeezed after the 1737 Licensing Act, which redirected the careers of such notables as Henry Fielding, Eliza Haywood, and Charlotte Charke by forcing them out of the smaller unlicensed theaters and into prose fiction, autobiography, or fringe ventures like Charke's puppet show. Methodists skirted the restrictions of the Licensing Act and its clerical correlate, the Conventical Act, designed to restrict Dissenting preachers from gathering congregations. Methodists were known to hold their meetings in vacant theaters, some of which had been closed by licensing pressures, an irony not lost on their critics

Illustration from *Memoirs of the Life of the Reverend George Whitefield*, John Groves, J. Lodge sculpt., 1771–72. © The British Library Board

or the displaced actors who once made their living there (Lyles 75). As they gained popularity, Whitefield began building the first of several Methodist meeting houses, using the term "house" from the theatrical vocabulary. The main Methodist "house" was Whitefield's Tabernacle, first constructed in Moorfields in 1741 and then relocated to Tottenham Court Road in 1753. The Tabernacle gave Methodists an architectural identity in London that furthered the theatrical connection; it was a large hall, with multiple portico entrances and seating capacity that rivaled the theaters.[6] John Forster declared that "at the Tabernacle itself, in Tottenham-court-road, his sermons now offered daily and weekly dram-drinking such as none of the theatres could provide; and in the crowds that such stimulants excited were found people of every condition." (Forster 371). The idea that the Methodist meeting was an alternative, even intoxicating, form of theater had broad currency, fed by the visual images of the Tabernacle and the crowds in the fields, the Methodist preaching style, and the successful, independent fundraising of Methodist preachers, most of whom were not affiliated with a regular parish and its tithes. Tate Wilkinson summarized the resentment when he declared that "a Methodist and a player, like a spider and a toad, are natural enemies, each party using his lungs in hopes of a crowded benefit" (Wilkinson 2: 255).

The prickly connection between Methodists and the theater intensified around the conversion of Covent Garden Theatre manager John Rich's wife Priscilla to Methodism in 1744. Priscilla, a former barmaid, actress, and Rich's housekeeper before their marriage, began attending the West Street Chapel, where she came under the influence of Charles Wesley, who soon became a close friend (Glen 351). Priscilla left the stage after a final performance as Anne Boleyn in October of 1744, and she and Rich, the most famous Harlequin of the age, were married on November 25 of the same year. Then, one of Rich's main musicians and composers at Covent Garden, John Frederick Lampe, also became a Methodist and provided many of the tunes and arrangements for Methodist hymnals. Rich was himself suspected of Methodism from thence forward. Smollett's 1748 *Roderick Random* mocked Rich as "Mr. Vandal," who has been "disordered with superstition," and Tate Wilkinson suggested that the Rich conversion was a household-wide (if not theater-wide) matter (Smollett, *Roderick Random* 2: 298–99; Wilkinson, *Memoirs* 3: 34). Rich's antagonism to the movement finds voice in his epilogue to the 1746 production of Theobald's *The Rape of Proserpine, or the Birth and Adventures of Harlequin*, in which he played one of the first in a train of anti-Methodist Harlequins. The production included an additional scene, with the song "Adieu, the Delights of the Stage" composed by "Lun," Rich's Harlequin stage name (Glen 350). In the song, Harlequin throws his coat aside for "the Band and the Gown," and declares that "what the poor Stage tries in Vain / May be done on a Stool in Moorfields," a regular site of Methodist preaching. The stool, or cricket, became a visual trope for Methodist theatricality, a temporary stage that placed them in the domain of street theater, puppet shows, country fairs, and other popular performances.

The lightning-rod figure in most conversations about Methodist theatricality was without doubt the charismatic George Whitefield. Whitefield, described by historian Harry Stout as the "Divine Dramatist," seemed to create a stage wherever he went, with or without a cricket. Writing to Montagu on September 3, 1748, Walpole opined, "Whitfield preaches continually at my Lady Huntingdon's at Chelsea; my Lord Chesterfield, my Lord Bath, my Lady Townshend, my Lady Thanet, and others have been to hear him; what will you lay that next winter he is not run after instead of Garrick" (*Correspondence* 9: 74).[7] The association was reciprocal; according to one anecdote, Garrick declared he would give £100 if he "could only say 'Oh!' like Mr. Whitefield."[8] Even Whitefield's defenders acknowledged his theatricality. At century's end, William Blake described Whitefield as, like himself, a man of passion who did not pretend to holiness. "Foote, in calling Whitefield hypocrite, was himself one; for Whitefield pretended not to be holier than others, but confessed his sins before all the world" (33). Cowper, also in Whitefield's defense, lamented that though he was a blameless, sincere, and loving minister, he was "pilloried on infamy's high stage/And bore the pelting scorn of half an age" (331). Theatrical language, including the "curtain" Cowper promises to draw aside, served equally well to attack and to champion Whitefield.

The theatrical basis of Whitefield's appeal seemed to be located in an aural, persuasive power that was his signature, both in the sense of his originality and its performative iterability. On October 17, 1741, *The Weekly History* reported that a Boston-area opponent of Whitefield thought he heard Whitefield, only to discover it was "one of his own Negroes preaching." Regarding the situation as fit for comic entertainment, he invited friends to come and hear his slave, who "had the very Phrases of Mr. Whitefield," and who preached the following "exhortation" to the assembled mock-congregation:

> I am now come to my Exhortation; and to you my Master after the Flesh: But know I have a Master even Jesus Christ my Saviour, who has said that a Man cannot serve two Masters. Therefore I claim Jesus Christ to be my right Master; and all that come to him he will receive. You know, Master, you have been given to Cursing and Swearing, and Blaspheming in God's holy Name, you have been given to be Drunken, a Whoremonger, Covetous, a Liar, a Cheat, &c. But know that god has pronounced Woe against all such, and has said that such shall never enter the Kingdom of God.[9]

The writer then explains that the man and all his friends were converted by the sermon. As Nancy Ruttenburg observes, it is impossible to determine whether the event actually played out as it was reported, or "whether it represents merely a fantasy of empowerment," but what is clear is that the story maintains Whitefield's oratory as the site of irresistible, mystical power that could turn a critical audience into credulous converts (448).

The implications of Whitefield's theatrical style detonated in the many representations of his preaching. *The Revd. Mr. Whitefield Preaching at Leeds* (1749) illustrates the dislocating effect of the outdoor sermon and its theatrical and sacred resonance. The satiric touches are light; Whitefield, with the ubiquitous handkerchief to dry the tears he cried at most of his sermons, spreads his arms in a theatrical gesture to the attentive crowd. The wealthy couple in the front turn away from the scene with mild bemusement, but other gentry listen along

The Revd. Mr. Whitfield Preaching at Leeds, anon., 1749. Courtesy of the Lewis Walpole Library, Yale University

with the working figures, indicating a mixed "public sphere" hailed into being by Whitefield's preaching. The children, who watch Whitefield from their perch on a ledge behind him, are cherubic, and the crowd is dense but orderly, reflecting the embodied experience of mass culture constituted by Methodist meetings and oratory.

More aggressive graphic satires like anonymous *Harlequin Methodist* took a more critical approach to Whitefield's theatrical preaching. Methodist preachers had been associated with Harlequin as early as the epilogue of Thomas Cooke's 1739 *The Mournful Nuptials*, which referred to "WESLEY . . . and WHITEFIELD *Harlequin*," and the connection only intensified over time, no doubt bolstered by the conversion of Mrs. Rich and other Covent Garden staff.[10] The print shows Harlequin preaching to a motley congregation of old women, rich and poor onlookers, a monk, a woman representing the Countess of Huntingdon, and two kneeling penitents. The black mask, part of the harlequinade, also implies the unavailability of Harlequin's identity; Harlequin is pure performance, pure mutability. Harlequin signifies protean mobility of character, which complements the geographic mobility of the Methodist preacher. Harlequin seems to be preaching on the plaza before Bedlam. This association drew on a twofold connection between Methodists and madness, on which Lyles has remarked, and between the physical proximity of the Methodist meeting houses in London (in particular the Foundry and the Tabernacle) to Bethlehem Hospital.

Performance, appearance, and event collide in the optical illusion that is the print's main visual strategy, which both attests to and derides the power of *Harlequin Methodist*. The print jumbles tropes of observation and participation, visually destabilizing the realms of theatrical and everyday experience. Side boxes, a theater curtain, and chandeliers hang from above. This tromp l'oeil setting connects the theatrical immediacy of Methodist sermons with the commedia dell'arte tradition, in which Harlequin routinely breaks the fourth wall to address the audience directly, often from a makeshift stage at a fair or market. Harlequin Methodist rails from his cricket against the "Old House," the theater, and instead encourages the flock to come "ev'ry Day / To mine: It will soon be the mode." He elides both the difference between Methodist sanctuary and theater with the shorthand "house," and the difference between theatrical and nontheatrical space. Harlequin announces the alliance between the theater and Methodist revivalism in the ballad below. He declares "No players I'll have but are Saints," refers to John Rich's marriage, calls Whitefield "a perfect Comedian," and predicts that the Wesley brothers will "both top their Part / To make

Detail of *Harlequin Methodist*, anon., 1750. © The Trustees of the British Museum. Used by permission

Farce and *Religion* agree." Whitefield appears on crickets routinely in print satire, as he does in *The Raree Show* (1762), and *Dr. Squintum's Exultation* (1763). Hogarth also put Paul on one in his 1751 *Paul Before Felix Burlesqued*, his subscription ticket for the engraving *Paul Before Felix* (1752), connecting Whitefield's claims to apostolic inspiration to the first century evangelist through this visual trope for religion as bad or uncontained theatricality.

Harlequin Methodist splits the audience between the participatory, somatically responsive congregation to whom he preaches, and the smaller audience of smiling ladies and gentlemen who have gathered to the right. The devotional audience, the print suggests, lacks the proper theatrical distance and has thus become part of the theatrical event, while the bemused spectators, even though they are curious about the Methodist spectacle, maintain their physical and emotional autonomy as observers. The result is a hybrid theatrical and "real" space in which Whitefield, performer without boundaries, hails his listeners into his theater of the real. The skeptical spectators in the print mark off the theatrical spectacle of conversion with their own gaze, which interprets the scene as a farce played at the gates of Bedlam, with chandeliers above and the suggestion of sideboxes framing the scene, and invites the reader of the print to take their more detached point of view.

The closing stanza of *Harlequin Methodist* connects Whitefield directly with Garrick, whose first role was Harlequin in *Harlequin Student*, which, John O'Brien has argued, informed his physical acting style (O'Brien 505). Whitefield's connection to the role of Harlequin came through visual satires like this one as well as criticisms of his preaching as overly physical and populist in its appeal. Garrick and Whitefield masterfully used performative and charismatic appeals that seduced their auditors into suspending codes of critical distance, memorialized in Hogarth's energetic 1746 engraving of Garrick as Richard III. In the ballad, Whitefield pitches Garrick the idea that he could join forces with the Methodists by marrying his daughter. Garrick:

> shall have my Right in the house,
> Provided our Faith he'll embrace.
> That when of one Stage he is tired,
> The Methodist Stage he may tread,
> Oh! how he will then be admired,
> For playing in Great Wh——f——d's Stead.

Whitefield, prostituting his imaginary daughter "Rachel" to Garrick, tempts Garrick to "embrace" the faith and replace him in both private and public spheres, with the term "house" now connoting domestic space as well the playhouse. Whitefield too becomes indistinguishable from a theatrical version of himself in the ballad, a charismatic placeholder playing a role that can be filled by another great actor, Garrick, who confirms both the theatricality of the venture and the exceptional status of his performance.

Squintum for Dessert

In what must have seemed like blatant hypocrisy, Methodists, particularly Whitefield, preached against the theaters as sites of spiritual danger, and so the theater wrote back. The best known of the Methodist satires on stage, Foote's *The Minor*, responded to Whitefield's antitheatrical charge against the playhouses, including warnings that actors were "the Devil's children grinning at you" (Wilkinson 3: 13). Whitefield's clerical attack on theaters followed the tradition of Prynne's *Histrio-mastix,* Collier's *Short View of the Immorality and Profaneness of the English Stage,* and even William Law's late-career screed against the stage as the site of "Heathen Festival," evoking the dangers of primitive religious rites. Hume also alluded to antitheatrical messages from the pulpit in his *Natural History of Religion,* where he notes that plays, once a part of ancient religious life, "have been zealously proscribed by the godly in later ages; and the play-house, according to a learned divine, is the porch of hell" (Hume, *Principal Writings on Religion* 190). But Whitefield started the war with Foote when he warned one of his congregations that "However much you all admire Mr. Foote, the devil will one day make a foot-ball of him."[11] In his epilogue to *The Minor,* Foote takes off Whitefield and sarcastically repeats his warning to his congregation: "Let's go see Foote? Ah! Foote's a precious Limb? / *Old Nick* will soon a Football make of him."

The Minor set a new bar for anti-Methodist satire and cemented the imaginative connection between Whitefield and performance. Though *The Minor* initially failed as a one-act show at the Crow Street Theatre in Dublin in January of 1760, Foote enlarged it to three acts later that summer for a successful Haymarket run of over forty performances. The piece was so popular its first year that regular Monday, Wednesday, and Friday performances were added after the eighth night to accommodate the crowds.[12] It was published July 8, 1760, and went through four editions that year. Haymarket performances began daily in August, and after October 25th, the play was appearing alternately at the Drury Lane and Covent Garden theaters, with Foote periodically in the cast. It was staged every year from 1760 until 1780, and enjoyed revivals through 1797. Even Frances Burney's eponymous heroine Evelina goes to see it in London, at Mr. Smith's suggestion, and is "extremely entertained," suggesting that mocking Methodism was, by 1778 at least, genteelly acceptable fun. It used a thin plot about two young lovers in danger of prostitution and bankruptcy respectively to get to its satiric targets: a Methodist madam named Mrs. Cole and her preacher, the Whitefieldian "Dr. Squintum." The eponymous minor Lucy is saved from prostitution by George, who comes to the brothel as a customer but then reforms in the last moments of Act III and castigates Mrs. Cole for "impiously prostituting the most sacred institutions, to the most infernal principles" (Foote 83). George, the profligate son who is actually betrothed to Lucy, is tested for familial loyalty in a theatrical scheme audiences would see again in Sheridan's *The School for Scandal*.

The Minor engaged its audiences with the idea of impersonation to suggest that Methodists, who gloried in a rhetoric of transformation, have chameleon-like, unstable selves. In the first act, Foote played Shift, a character modeled on Tate Wilkinson, an outspoken opponent of the Methodists and Whitefield. Wilkinson, whose father was a minister, admired Foote's talents and was in Winchester acting parts he had first seen Foote perform when *The Minor* appeared.[13] In the second act, Foote became Smirke, a parody of the actor-turned-Methodist Edward Shuter, who continued to share the stage with Foote for the balance of his career. Whitefield had turned out a Tabernacle crowd on a benefit night for Shuter, fueling additional resentment from Foote and justifying accusations of hypocrisy. And in one of his more popular cross-dressed performances as Mrs. Cole, Foote played a madam converted to Methodism who finds no reason to leave her old job because faith and not works is the basis of the "comforts of the new birth." Foote's Mrs. Cole is indebted to Cleland's Mrs. Cole in *Memoirs*, to the historical Mother (Jenny) Douglas, the evangelical madam of Covent Garden, and to Christopher Smart's unlicensed 1750 review, *Mother Midnight's Oratory*, in which Foote also played, alongside several other cross-dressed comedians.

The trope of the Methodist brothel was nothing new in 1760; nor were jokes about the new birth.[14] But Mrs. Cole's inability to see any moral difficulty in her active prostitution of her "girls" and her religious conversion describes a Methodism that is fundamentally theatrical in spite of its appeal to inward states; its strong feelings and affecting performances generate responses that overwrite any substantive or coherent self. Mrs. Cole moves without skipping a beat from talk of her conversion to pimping her girls: "Oh, [Dr. Squintum] is a dear man! But for him I had been a lost sheep; never known the comforts of the new birth; no—There's your old friend, Kitty Carrot, at home still. What, shall we see you this evening! I have kept the green room for you ever since I heard you were in town" (40). Her mention of the green room, meant to be a specific room in the brothel, also evokes the theatrical waiting room. The drag act, perhaps a nod to Whitefield's youthful confession that he used to "dress in girl's clothes" as a child actor, helped to degrade the minister as Foote set up his final impersonation in the epilogue.[15]

The epilogue, in which Foote presented Whitefield "for desert," was the raison d'être of the entire venture. Though Foote only got to take off Whitefield in the epilogue thirty-five times in the initial Haymarket run before the epilogue was banned in performance, he wrote his performance of Whitefield into the text.[16] The epilogue depends on a joke at the expense of Whitefield's squint and fundraising prowess, "gad, I've a thriving traffick in my eye," a dig that associated Whitefield with Wilkes, the other famous "squint" of the age.[17] His Whitefield character promises to bawl "Near the Mad-Mansions of Moorfields" as Foote raves, squints, and warns his audience:

> Think you to meet with side-boxes above?
> Where giggling girls and powdered fops may sit,
> No you will all be cram'd into the pit,
> And crowd the house for satan's benefit.

The epilogue also appeared as a single sheet, entitled "The Epilogue to *The Minor*, or, A Methodist Sermon," which enjoyed an afterlife well beyond the ban on Foote's performance. In his "Observations, GOOD OR BAD, STUPID OR CLEVER, SERIOUS OR JOCULAR, on Squire FOOTE's Dramatic Entertainment, Intitled THE MINOR," Boswell refers to reading the farce and not to seeing it. Boswell's farcically extended title, by bouncing various responses to *The Minor* through the voices of the gathered party, keeps Foote's risk impersonation of Whitefield both at bay and on stage as a topic of discussion.

As Matthew Kinservik has argued, censorship probably benefited *The Minor*.[18] Archbishop Thomas Secker's minimal response to the play ignored the Countess of Huntingdon's pleas to have the play suppressed entirely, and the Duke of Devonshire even restored some of the modest cuts that the Archbishop suggested. Furthermore, the weak editorial changes from the Lord Chamberlain, including "reformation" for "regeneration," and "lost Woman" for "lost sheep," were in performance; the print text retained Foote's original lines.[19] But because the epilogue continued to circulate in print after it was banned from the stage, it still drew attention to Foote's mimicry of Whitefield, baiting the reading and theatergoing audiences with the promised impersonation from Shift's first line in the play's rehearsal frame, "but are you sure he has leave?"[20] Once the censorship scandal made clear that Foote did not have leave, the imagined performance became even more tantalizing from the page.

Foote's defense of *The Minor* as comedy rather than farce plays anxiously with the problem of theater's world-making effects. In the epilogue, he parodies an alleged Whitefield story of a widow and her child fed with a leg of mutton and turnips, which is also a reference to Swift's mock-communion in *Tale of a Tub*, in which Peter passes off a loaf of brown bread as "excellent good mutton" (Swift 117). In Foote's version of the story, the food mystically arrives in the nick of time before starvation, but Foote accuses Whitefield of telling stories that cannot be true, of passing mere comedy off for "literal fact":

> The piece is pretty well known; and after the manner of Aristophanes and Plautus, we will distinguish it from the principal incident, by the name of *Mutton*, a Comedy. As an introduction to this entertainment, we are told by the chorus or prologue, that the persons were then living, that the dialogue really happened between them, and that the catastrophe of the leg of mutton and turnips was a literal fact . . . after the manner of Thespis, the piece was exhibited in a cart upon a common, not a single doubt can, I think, remain. . . . Then, sir, the earnest inclination of your reverend friend always shows to display his abilities in a cart, even though it be with a criminal at Tyburn, I think we may venture, without any impeachment of our understanding, to pronounce him the real restorer of the ancient Thespian Cart Comedy. (LETTER FROM MR. FOOTE 5–6)

The connection that Foote, who was also known as the "English Aristophanes," makes between Methodism and Attic comedy ties the Methodists' "cart comedy" to the primitive power of ancient theater and its religious contexts, in which performance was the occasion for belief. Whitefield restores "ancient Thespian Cart Comedy," providing a window on a lost theatrical world of immediacy. The cart here becomes a sign of boundary-crossing as the Methodist's literal pulpit at fairs and large outdoor gatherings as well as proof of association with criminality, recalling scenes like Hogarth's *The Idle 'Prentice Executed at Tyburn*, plate 11 of *Industry and Idleness*, in which a Methodist attempts to convert the criminal apprentice at the eleventh hour. Foote implies that the comedy of Methodism inverts the moral order, putting faith before works and, in so doing, positing a performative faith over a morally real world of action, liability, and causality.[21] Foote's mocking reference to Whitefield's story of the mutton turns on the quasi-Eucharistic question of whether real food can mystically appear.

The Minor set off a major tract war, with letters allegedly to and from Foote and Whitefield flying through the press, though usually written by other parties. Lawrence Sterne was thrown into this print war via an anonymous pamphlet purporting to be a letter from Whitefield to Sterne. The pamphlet, which was neither by Whitefield nor delivered to Sterne, attacked the Methodists as well as "apostate Sterne," urging him to "throw aside Shakespeare, and take up the word of God" (*A Letter from the Rev. George Whitefield, M.A., To the Rev. Laurence Sterne, M.A.* 20). *The Scheming Triumvirate* (July 1760) grouped Sterne with Whitefield and Foote as masters of a world of mass media and publicity. Sterne hawks *Tristram Shandy* (arguably the biggest literary event of 1760 and another textual experiment in affective immediacy) and Yorick's Sermons while Whitefield preaches to the crowd and Foote sells copies of *The Minor*, promising "I'll cure ye all of Dullness—come to me & Laugh at Care." The print levels the three figures as theatrical hucksters who can draw crowds for their agreed purpose, "to get the Cole," or money. As Harry Stout put it, Whitefield's success made the point that "if religion could be marketed, then, like politics, quackery, and prostitution, it could also be mimicked, demeaned, and condemned" (Stout 248). The print makes the same point, turning his preaching into another scheme perpetrated by a charismatic figure that knew how to manipulate modern media. In this material sense at least, these performances made something happen. The print shows the success of this marketing strategy; of all the bags of money, Whitefield's is the largest.

A pair of hieroglyphic satires, called *The Retort* and *Retort upon Retort*, allegedly an exchange of letters between Foote and Whitefield, substituted objects for obvious words or syllables, beginning, predictably, with a giant foot for Foote. *The Retort* materializes images the way that Whitefield's very metaphorical style did in the pulpit and the way Swift's linguists with their peddler's packs of objects for communication did in *Gulliver's Travels*: it makes words into things. Whitefield calls Foote "a Crack'd pot and not a chosen vessel; thy heart is made of stone." Whitefield himself is represented by his own face, identifiable by the cross-eyed gaze, a visual image that slips between his various designations as Squintum, Preach-field, and Whitefield. The mocking graphic production presses up against the representational function of language and forces the reader to move back and forth from signified to signifier across representational registers. Meaning becomes "real" in the sense that the order of the grapheme erupts into the graphic image. The hieroglyphic, associated with the "acrostick" as a primitive form of wit here underscores the literalism of Whitefield's style that pushes his audience over the edge of their critical distance and into an encounter that is anti-aesthetic.

Bad puns, cheap shots, and literalized language were comic staples for Foote, who proved his own high tolerance for them after a riding accident led to the amputation of his leg in early 1766. For those sympathetic to the Methodist cause, this was providence. Chesterfield declared that heaven had punished him

The Scheming Triumvirate, anon., July 1760. © The Trustees of the British Museum. Used by permission

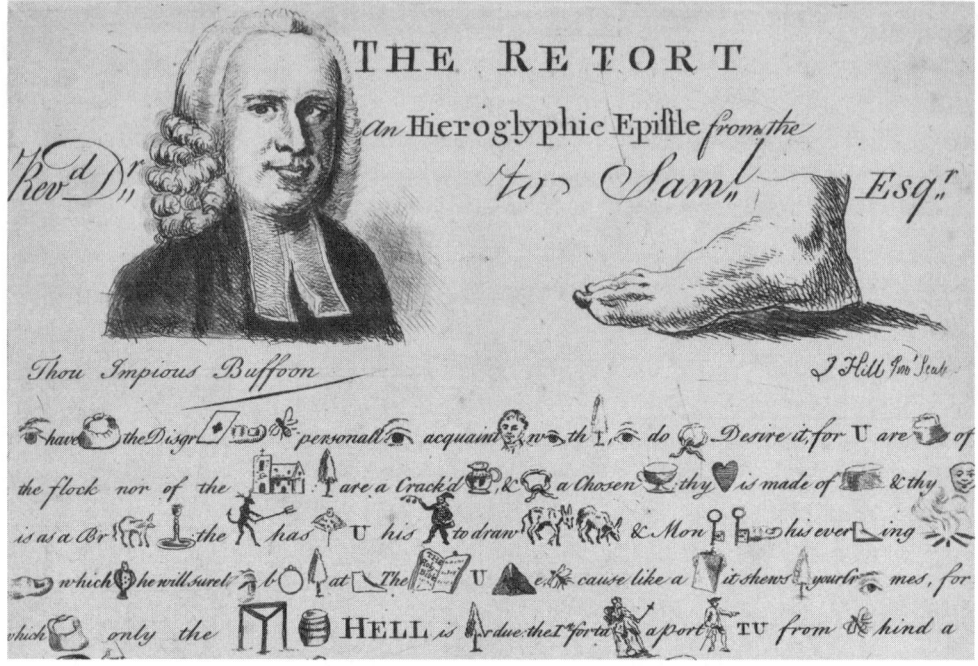

Detail of *The Retort: An Hieroglyphic Epistle from the Rev. Dr. Squintum to Samuel Foote, Esq.*, anon., 1760. © The Trustees of the British Museum. Used by permission

"in the part offending" (*Letters* 3: 1338) while a contributor to *The London Chronicle* quipped:

> What Measure shouldst thou ever keep,
> Friend Sam! Thy fate is such—
> A Foot too little now you are;
> Before a Foote too much. (QTD. IN BELDEN 28)

In reply, Foote began to imitate his enemy and fellow amputee George Faulkner "to the life" and referred to himself as Captain Timbertoe (Genest 5: 113). When he ran out of lame enemies to imitate, Foote presented *The Devil Upon Two Sticks* in May of 1768, a version of a Le Sage story in which the devil, who has been lamed in a fight with the Daemon of Power, advises a young man to become a "mountebank for the mind" and turn Methodist preacher (67).

By breaking the implicit taboo on representing a living clergyman on stage,

Foote opened the floodgates to a series of afterpieces bent on embodying Whitefield in an unattractive light. Among the theatrical echoes were *The Methodists* (1760), which claimed to be a sequel to *The Minor* but which was probably written by Israel Pottinger and never intended to reach the stage.[22] *The Methodists* reprises Foote's cast, but chiefly indulges the pleasure of making Squintum a full-fledged character. Squintum and Cole directly compare the professions of pimping and preaching, and Shift notes that the two "match like a Pair of Tallies: I don't wonder at the Women being so fond of this Fellow, since he is so earnest an Advocate for the sensual Appetites" (15). The farce is squarely focused on the "Methodistical Couple . . . who imagine they have a Right to commit any Crime they please all Day, provided they go to the Tabernacle in the Evening" (59). Joseph Reed's *The Register Office*, which appeared at Drury Lane on April 25, 1761, also had a plot and characters very close to those of *The Minor*, with a madam Mrs. Snarewell and her minister from the Tabernacle Dr. Watchlight. The print copy of the play included Reed's protestation that he had not imitated *The Minor* and, indeed, that his play had been in Foote's possession for three years. The controversy over whether it was an original piece notwithstanding, it was still Reed's most popular venture on the stage, bringing yet another stage Whitefield to life. The play enjoyed long runs in 1767 and 1768, and was acted through the 1770s, though somewhat altered.[23] *The Methodist: a Comedy, being a Continuation and Completion of the Plan of the Minor* (1761) and *The Spiritual Minor* (1763), which revived "Squintum" as a full character but was never intended for live performance, also cashed in on the phenomenon. Squintum declares that "those that have a true faith can never be afraid of anything" (3) while Rakish jokes darkly "I'm something of a methodist myself: I have not the least apprehension of being damn'd, though I indulge myself in the full gratification of all my passions" (30). This explicit statement of the continuity between libertinism and Methodism indicts the movement for giving rein to the passions, appetites, and desires and then excusing them through the doctrine of regeneration.

Among the nondramatic pieces in the wake of *The Minor*, Foote's performance was still a point of reference. *The Methodist and Mimic: A Tale in Hudabristic Verse by Peter Paragraph, Inscribed to Samuel Foote, Esq.* (1766) names Foote and the conflict with Whitefield in the title. The two-volume edition of *Chrysal: or the Adventures of A Guinea* (1764–65) capitalized on the popularity of these anti-Methodist theatrical farces by adding slapstick scenes with Mrs. Brimstone

(Cole), Dr. Hunch-back (Whitefield), and Momus (Foote) who mingle the spiritual language of Methodist new birth and reformation in their discussion of the new young women at Mrs. Brimstone's brothel. Dr. Hunch-back revives the "old point" about the difference between his and Momus's theatricality. Momus insists that he puts "vice and folly out of countenance" by making people laugh at their faults, while Hunch-back paints terrors and horrors that never existed to frighten his congregation. But they agree that "our railing each other in public, answers our own ends" and that they would be fools to stop their own publicity machine. The scene culminates in Mrs. Brimstone throwing a glass of wine at Dr. Hunch-back, causing him to bleed profusely and to make a panicked confession of his hypocrisy. The farce is Eucharistic in its materials—blood, wine, and bread—the elements of the most performative and substantive theological question that Methodism posed back to Anglican Christianity; did anything happen in the Eucharist, or was it a memorial act of mere representation? Momus, Hunch-back, and Brimstone seem to have farcically enacted something between a passion play and communion, between theater and sacrament, that was the occasion for Hunch-back's repentance, however mistaken. These jokes about Methodism returned hysterically to the theological question of what might happen in the religious event.

Real Presence

The most substantive response to Foote's *The Minor* was graphic, not dramatic. William Hogarth pressed on the relationship between performativity and Eucharistic theology in his two prints of the Methodist meeting house. Hogarth's 1761 *Enthusiasm Delineated*, an unpublished print that became the basis for his 1762 *Credulity, Superstition, and Fanaticism*, is, among other things, an elaborate reading of *The Minor* in the context of other anti-Methodist satires. The two prints are part of a series of tendentious jokes about Methodism performed for the public by Hogarth and Foote, beginning in June of 1760 with *The Minor*, followed by *Enthusiasm* in 1761, *Credulity* in 1762, and Foote's *The Orators* later that same year. The most obvious features that Hogarth imports from Foote's farce are the left foreground figure of Mother Cole, who becomes Mary Toft in *Credulity*, the young woman being seduced in the right foreground, and the multiple references to Whitefield, as well as the overall theme that the Methodist meeting house was a place of sexual temptation where a rising tide of enthusiasm explodes into a circus of action. But even knottier questions about representation, theatricality, and presence animate Hogarth's prints, most significantly the question of the nature of communion.

As skeptics and satirists, Hogarth and Foote trafficked in the procedures of demystification and comic exposure, but their shared appreciation of aesthetic representation led them to claim another kind of enthusiasm that mystified art and the artist. Foote used Hogarth as an example of good, aesthetic enthusiasm in contrast to the bad enthusiasm of religion. His *Letter to the Author of Remarks Critical and Christian on The Minor* asserts that the good enthusiasm is "that effort of genius, that glow of fancy, that ethereal fire, which, at particular times, transports the artist beyond the limits of his usual execution, and produces a height of perfection which, in his cooler hour, is astonishing even to himself" (70). He names Hogarth as someone who possesses such "good enthusiasm" in contrast to the anarchic enthusiasm of the Methodists, which is simply a jumble of credulity and sexual excitement, madness without method. Good enthusiasm leads the individual artist to sublime heights; bad enthusiasm is mass hysteria and group insanity, which is just what Hogarth's "good enthusiasm" allows him to display in the prints.

Enthusiasm, like its sequel *Credulity*, takes up the question of the content of religious enthusiasm by depicting the inside of a Methodist meeting house, probably Whitefield's Tabernacle, filled with raving enthusiasts, seductions, and quasi-supernatural events. While Methodism provides the immediate context for the image, *Enthusiasm Delineated* was a more direct assault on Christian belief, with glowing Christ icons, a cartoon below mocking the idea of a visible holy spirit, and biblical puppets around the rostrum.[24] Though the print was not made available to the general public, it seems likely that Foote, as the author of the afterpiece it references and someone on friendly terms with Hogarth, would have been one of few who saw it in this state, with a mock-dedication to Foote's faux-nemesis Archbishop Secker, who had censored *The Minor*.[25] In retaliation for the censorship, according to Walpole, "Foote says he will take out a license to preach, Sam Cant against Tom Cant," a joke based on Thomas Secker's title as "Thomas of Canterbury," signed as "Thomas Cantaur" (Walpole, *Correspondence* 9: 326, 248). Secker's hand-wringing intervention in the licensing of *The Minor* was complicated by his sympathy for the Methodists and his Dissenter origins (Rivers 169). Secker may have carried on a pseudonymous correspondence with John Wesley under the name "John Smith," a correspondence that reflected

Enthusiasm Delineated, William Hogarth, 1761. © The Trustees of the British Museum. Used by permission

"Smith's" sympathy with the project of "laboring to bring all the world to a solid, inward, vital religion," though he questioned Wesley on Christian perfection, inspiration, and contradictions within Wesley's oeuvre.[26] Secker certainly used the language of inward religious feeling in his own public theological writing, including his posthumous *Lectures on the Catechism of the Church of England* (1769). Both Foote and Hogarth regarded Secker as a swing figure, an archbishop who might be soft on enthusiasts.

Hogarth suggests that Methodist mysticism is barely disguised Roman Catholicism. The preacher "Money-Trap" wears the now-familiar Methodist

Harlequin costume as well as the Jesuit tonsure. The text of Whitefield's hymn "Come and Let Us Sweetly Join," the text supporting this theology of love, drapes the pulpit. Hogarth mocks its emphasis on a present experience of divine power in Christian community as a "heav'n to earth come down," in which felt inspiration makes people act:

> Love, Thine image, love impart!
> Stamp it on our face and heart!
> Only love to us be given!
> Lord, we ask no other heaven.

Hogarth puts sexual and religious responses into a single quantifiable scale on the thermometer in the foreground, which rests on "Westley's Sermons" and Glanvile on witches in *Credulity*. In both prints, the thermometer comes out of the Methodist brain, which seems to include male and female genitalia. The thermometer climbs from lukewarm to "love heat" and on to lust, ecstasy, convulsion fits, madness, and raving.[27] Next to the thermometer, two lovers (representations of Lucy from *The Minor* and one of her would-be seducers) embrace, the man with one hand on the woman's neck and the other reaching for her breast.[28] This theater of the real unleashes sexual appetites that destroy traditional piety and delude the masses into experiencing somatic response as spiritual ecstasy.

What Foote parodies as indulgence and hypocrisy in *The Minor*, Hogarth translates into aesthetic chaos, culminating visually and theologically in the eight Christ icons with glowing halos (matching the Harlequin priest's) that are being gnawed by the crowd, mocking transubstantiation or any variety of Eucharistic belief in real presence. Anglican Eucharistic theology declared for both representation and presence, and so found itself divided along those lines in the eighteenth century. The elements stood in for the body and blood of Christ in representational Protestant logic, a view elaborated by Hoadly's *A Plain Account of the Nature and End of the Lord's Supper* (1735). But Whitefield, Wesley, Archbishop Secker, Daniel Brevint, and many other Anglicans subscribed to some version of the doctrine of real presence. Wesley's preface to *Hymns on the Lord's Supper* (1745), extracted from Brevint's *The Christian Sacrament and Sacrifice*, emphasized the deep mystery of the Sacrament, comparing it to the "ancient Passover . . . consisting both of Sacrament and Sacrifice" (4). Methodism's emphasis on the Eucharist sounded Roman Catholic to Hogarth, as it did to the Georgia settler who complained that Wesley suppressed "the Explanation adjoin'd to the Words of Communicating by the Church of *England*, to shew that they mean a Feeding on Christ by Faith, saying no more than *The Body of Christ; The Blood of Christ*."[29] In contrast to Latitudinarian Christianity, Methodism was rhetorically and theologically invested in the body of Christ. After a description of the crucifixion in *Hymns on the Lord's Supper*, Wesley asks the reader to embrace the sacrifice as "still new": "Let us go then to take and eat it . . . the sweet Smell of the Offering still remains, the Blood is still warm, the Wounds still fresh and *the Lamb* still *standing as slain*" (J. Wesley, *Hymns on the Lord's Supper* 7). The christological focus of many Methodist sermons, parodied in Hogarth's "Chroist Blood Blood Blood" song sheet above the thermometer, becomes a class-coded mob chant that accompanies the figures that chew on the Christ icons in the congregation.

Hogarth's carnivalesque representation of Whitefield's Tabernacle captures the intersection of Methodist populism and high-church Anglo-Catholic Christology in a Eucharistic moment of representational credulity. Transubstantiation serves as Hogarth's chief example of his "Intention" as stated below the print: "to give a Lineal representation of the strange Effects of litteral and low conceptions of Sacred Beings as also of the Idolotrous Tendency of Pictures in churches and prints in Religious books &c." His statement resigns any notion of the sacred to a realm beyond representation, where it is safe from "litteral and low" conceptions but also where it can remain, literally, disembodied and unimaginable. He states in his "Apology for Painters" that English religion "forbids, nay doth not require, images for worship or pictures to work up enthusiasm" (89). His hard Protestant line softens with the rhetorical anticlimax: does English religion forbid or just not require images? Is the image an anathema to "true" religion because it does things, "working up" enthusiasm? As anthropologist Birgit Meyer has argued, the materiality of images, prints, photos, and other media practices become part of the "mysterious process through which media make the transcendental tangible in a persuasive manner" (64). The *Enthusiasm* print affirms the power of those images to persuade the masses, and Hogarth, as a visual artist, seems aware that he is engaged in a similar procedure. In this sense, Paulson's and Krysmanksi's arguments that *Enthusiasm* and *Credulity* satirize the world of continental art, collecting, and auction houses are another way to approach the religiousness that is the aim of Hogarth's satire; the image, granted such authority and presence, is always already the fetish, if not the icon.[30]

Hogarth's *Enthusiasm* posed the question whether modern Christianity could retain its Eucharistic mysticism. Hogarth, who did Bishop Hoadly's portrait,

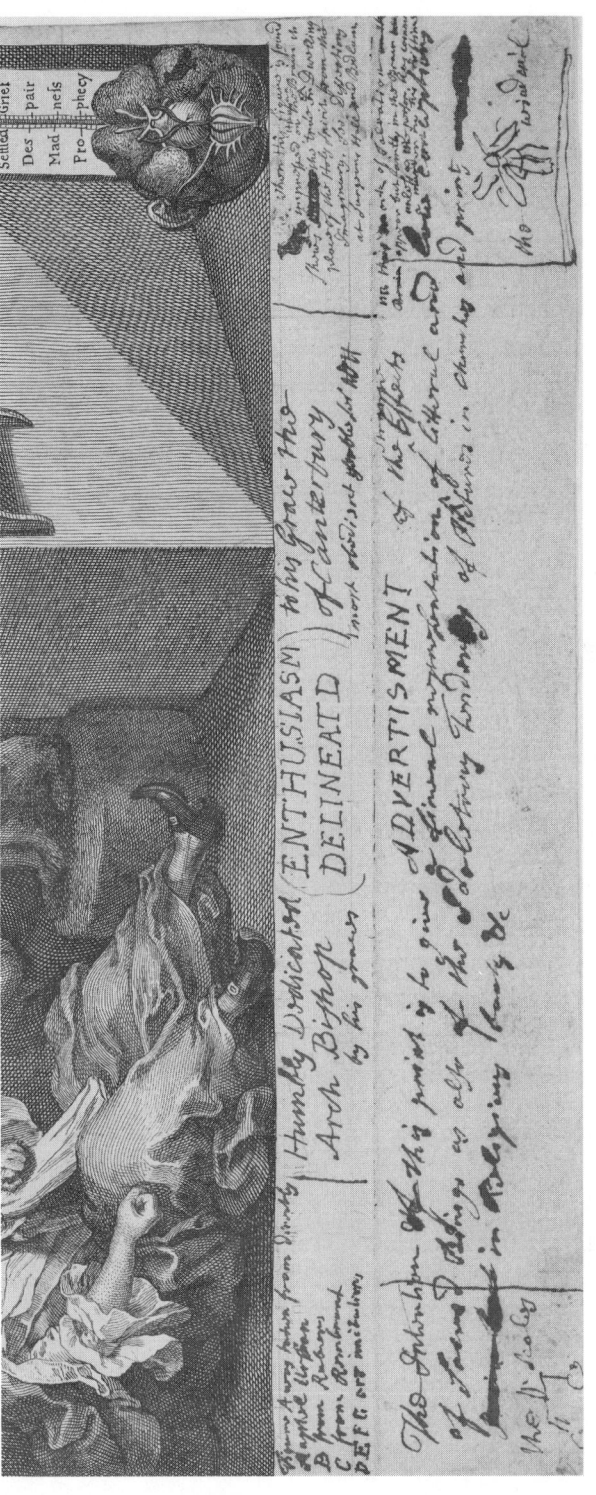

Detail of *Enthusiasm Delineated*, British Museum impression, BM 1858-4-17-582. © The Trustees of the British Museum. Used by permission

clearly sided with Hoadly on a memorial understanding of the Eucharist, but he went even further than the Christ icons suggest. In the bottom corner the print includes Hogarth's pen drawing of a man with a windmill on his head, with "windmill" written to the side.[31] The Steevens's collection of Hogarth prints, housed at Yale's Lewis Walpole Library, includes Ireland's re-engraving of the print with the windmill and the bird from the cartoon, as well as a late-century engraving by Ireland, after Hogarth, with the title *Transubstantiation Satirized*. This is the image that haunts *Enthusiasm* and later *Credulity*. The image first appeared in the background of Hogarth's painting, *The Marriage Contract* (ca. 1733), an early version of plate 1 of *Marriage á la Mode*.[32] In that early painting, the *Transubstantiation Satirized* image is one of the pieces of art on the rake's wall.[33] Hogarth's own history of clerical satire, including *Paul Before Felix Burlesqued* and his extensive practice of what Paulson identifies as "sacred parody," demystified Christian religion and emphasized representation over sacrament, but never so brutally as in *Transubstantiation Satirized*, in which the Virgin Mary drops a glowing Christ child into the hopper of a windmill, where a priest stands below with a paten to collect the newly milled wafers of the "body of Christ."

Hogarth seems to have taken his idea for this image from Bishop Gilbert Burnet's description of an altarpiece in Worms included in his *Travels Through Switzerland, Italy, and Some Parts of Germany*. Burnet writes about the altarpiece, which neither he nor Hogarth saw, with a mix of horror and amusement:

> One would think [it] was invented by the Enemies of Transubstantiation, to make it appear ridiculous. There is a Wind-mill, and the Virgin throws Christ into the Hopper, and he comes out at the Eye of the Mill all in Wafers, which some Priests take up to give to the People. This is so coarse an Emblem, that one would think it too gross even for Laplanders; but a Man that can swallow Transubstantiation it self, will digest this likewise. (BURNET 212)

Transubstantiation, according to Hogarth and Burnet, is indigestible. But Burnet still felt compelled to describe the thing he didn't see, and then Hogarth to paint it, reproducing the offending real altarpiece down to the shape of its frame. This reproduction echoes the theological question behind the image; is there anything like real presence, or is there only representation? The visceral image, troubling both because it makes the body of a child vulnerable and because it literalizes the cannibalistic consumption of the Eucharist, poses the open and lively theological question of how modern Christian Britons were to think about communion. Methodism referenced the stakes of embodiment relentlessly in

Transubstantiation Satirized, William Hogarth, pinxt. Samuel Ireland, 1795. Courtesy the Lewis Walpole Library, Yale University

their hymns, sermons, and devotional tracts about "Christ crucified," the "joy of heav'n to earth come down" of Wesley's "Love Divine," pursuing an embodied Christian mysticism in the midst of the century. Hogarth reproduces the theme of eating, and in particular Burnet's reference to "swallowing" transubstantiation in the rough crowd that ingests the Christ icons, as well as other scattered images of digestion and excretion in both the 1761 and 1762 prints: the man crying his tears into a bottle; Mother Cole drinking a dram; and the Bilston boy vomiting nails, all examples of what Žižek would call the excremental real. Hogarth toys with the Protestant resistance to the image in his satiric account of the Incarnation and the meaning of the body of Christ not as symbolic exchange but, in Žižek's terms, as radical identification "with the excremental Real that is man" (187). By representing the theatrical Methodists in this cavalcade of sacred materiality, Hogarth plunged further into the vexing status of proof, representation, and belief in the modern era.

Holy Ghosts

The Cock Lane ghost affair provided the next trope in the Hogarth/Foote conversation in April of 1762 between Hogarth's *Credulity, Superstition, and Fanaticism* and Foote's *The Orators*. The stories surrounding the "actual" Cock Lane ghost situated the ghost firmly (insofar as one situates a ghost firmly) among the Methodists. In early 1762, newspapers began reporting a ghost discovered in the house of a Methodist, Richard Parsons, knocking on the bed of his young daughter Elizabeth; another Methodist clergyman, John Moore, "decoded" the meaning of her knocking and scratching as yeses and nos. In the public imagination, "Scratching Fanny" or "Fanny Phantom" was a Methodist phenomenon, both because Parsons and Moore were involved, and because she brought in crowds in a manner similar to Methodist preachers: skeptics and true believers alike wanted to test her powers of persuasion and their powers of cognitive distance. Horace Walpole, who came to see this ghost that the Methodists had "adopted," cheekily described it as an "audition" rather than an apparition, since it never actually appeared. But he was curious enough to crowd into the chamber "to which the ghost had adjourned" with some fifty other spectators and to stay amid the "heat and stench" until one thirty in the morning (Walpole, *Correspondence* 10: 6). "Fanny Phantom's" popularity confirmed breadth of fascination with supernatural experience, even when leavened with skepticism, and an awareness of the commercial dimensions of the craze. The way to enjoy this ghost properly, suggested by a raft of plays, prints, and mock-treatises about it, was not so much to believe in the thing itself, but to appreciate her at a spectacular, theatrical, and literary distance. As pure performance (or the anticipation of a performance that was in itself a spectacle), the ghost was, as E. J. Clery has argued, perfectly exploitable by an entertainment economy. "Fanny Phantom" appeared on command and for profit in the following: a revival of Addison's *The Drummer*, Garrick's *The Farmer's Return*, afterpieces like Foote's, Hogarth's revised *Credulity, Superstition, and Fanaticism*, in new treatises like *The Mystery Reveal'd*, and in reprints like Drelincourt's *A Christian Man's Consolation Against the Fears of Death* and Defoe's "The Apparition of Mrs. Veal."[34]

To take the matter seriously at all, Foote and Hogarth suggest, gives superstition empirical heft. But that is exactly what the infamous Cock Lane Ghost commission did. Established by Lord Dartmouth, who was sympathetic to the Methodists, the commission also included Samuel Johnson and John Fielding. *English Credulity, or The Invisible Ghost*, which appeared in February of 1762, mocks the commission's inquiry. As a character in the cartoon, Foote (who had not yet written *The Orators*) comments that he could have used the ghost as a character in his January 1762 *The Liar*, while a group of Methodists exhort one another about the ghost. That John Fielding, who was blind, is featured in the print only adds to the sense that the commission's inquiry into something for which there can be no "ocular proof" is a farce. A Johnsonian figure turns to Foote and declares "now thou infidel, dost thou not believe?," interpolating Foote as the skeptic of all things connected to Methodism. The seated minister issues the warning, "brother don't disturb it," to a man who holds up a pocket watch, challenging the ghost behind the curtain to "knock three times" if it is a gold watch, while a fourth looks under the bed with a candle. Two children rest in bed under the apparition above, which looks like a cross between the Virgin of Guadalupe, the Christ in Rembrandt's *The Hundred Guilder Print*, and the outline of a clergymen raising a mallet in hand, while various women to the right declare their terror in prayerful postures. The main thrust of the satire is that the English are as credulous as Addison suggested they were in the *Spectator* papers, easily persuaded by folk tales and ghost stories. Both in their pure "superstition" (represented by the women around the bed) and their desire for supernatural "proofs" which only lend credibility to the scam (represented by the various men in the cartoon), these people believe in performances they should understand as mere theatrical entertainment. The ghost is something unreal that can only be provisionally and ironically brought into the realm of the visible. Yet

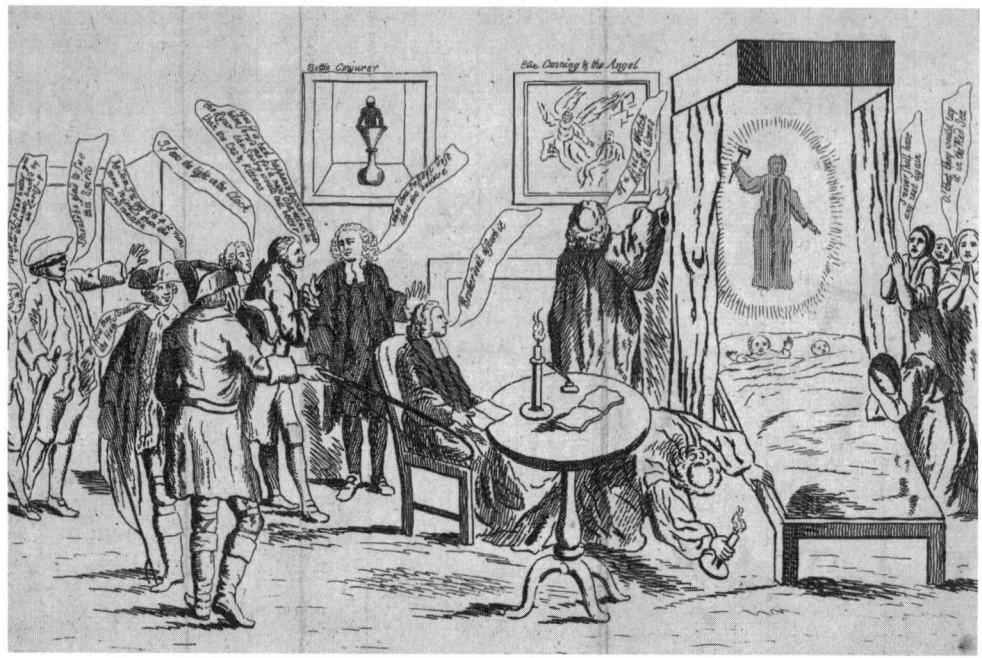

English Credulity, or the Invisible Ghost, anon., 1762. © Trustees of the British Museum. Used by permission

the desire to make it visible, for both the skeptical satirist and the true believer, runs strong.

Behind the scene hang two pictures, "Elizabeth Canning and the Angel" and the "Bottle Cungerer," which, like the image of the ghost, attempt to visualize unseen events that had recently strained or abused credulity. Canning reappeared at her mother's home after nearly a month's absence, claiming she had been robbed, abducted, held captive in an attic with almost no food, but not raped, then escaped and found her way home. A storm of pamphlets tried to establish whether she was a heroic case of virtue defended by angelic protectors, as she claimed, or a con artist selling a story to mask her debauchery. Henry Fielding, one of her defenders, argued that the unwillingness of people to credit her story redoubled the injury she had already received. Instead of skepticism Fielding, somewhat surprisingly, called for belief and sympathy.[35] The other picture of the Bottle Cungerer, or Congerer, was one of the more colorful scams of the mid-century theater world. In January of 1749, announcements for a "Don Jumpedo in the character of Harlequin" promised a performance by a talented dancer and gymnast who would end his show by climbing into a normal-sized wine bottle, which could then be passed around and inspected by the audience. The theater filled with curious ticket holders, who rioted once they realized they had been taken in. At first, audiences suspected Foote, but F. G. Stephens alleges the culprit was probably the Duke of Montagu, Horace Walpole's close friend (Stephens 3.1 no. 3022). Don Jumpedo became shorthand in the subsequent decades for a trick that takes in the public. *The London Chronicle*, quoting Jean Baptiste Suard's Paris review of Sterne's novel, for instance, compared the last two volumes of *Tristram Shandy* to the Don Jumpedo episode, which "carried away their money and left the bottle empty."[36] The figure appears in a number of prints, including *Don Jumpedo in the Character of Harlequin Jumping Down His Own Throat* (1750), an example of the willingness of spectators to believe in the impossible.

The Cock Lane ghost, which has been read productively in a range of symptomatic readings as the sign of what cannot be spoken, is also a direct symptom of conflicting dispositions toward the material nature of reality, presence, and enthusiasm.[37] Churchill's *The Ghost* associates "Fanny's" popularity with the Methodists and their self-promotion:

> A Mystery, so made for gain,
> E'en now in fashion must remain.
> Enthusiasts never will let drop
> What brings such business to their shop,
> And the Great Saint, we WH-TF-LD call,
> Keeps up the HUMBUG SPIRITUAL. (4)

But Churchill, like some other skeptics, was himself obsessed with the ghost, attending the trial over which Lord Mansfield presided, writing *The Ghost*, and attacking Dr. Johnson as "Pomposo" for his part in the inquiry into the credibility of the ghost. These responses are not so much the opposite of Wesley's concern that the waning of belief in ghosts would weaken Christianity as they were its contralateral manifestation. Walpole, Churchill and Hogarth prided themselves on their sophisticated skepticism, but they helped to keep up the Cock Lane ghost mania through their own fascination with the phenomenon of the ghost.

Hogarth used the Cock Lane ghost to reinterpret the sacrilegious symbolic economy of the unreleased *Enthusiasm* print in *Credulity, Supertition, and Fanaticism* (1762). Horace Walpole called *Credulity* "useful and deep satire," and "one

Credulity, Superstition, and Fanaticism, William Hogarth, 1762. © The Trustees of the British Museum. Used by permission

of his most capital works," but also "sublime."[38] Ireland, who said he thought of *Enthusiasm* what Walpole thought of *Credulity*, commented on Hogarth's reasons for making the many changes between the two prints and speculated that "some friend suggested the satire would be mistaken, and that there might be those who would supposed his arrows were aimed at religion."[39] Ireland notes that there are so many variations that he is surprised Hogarth did not start over with a fresh copperplate, but he sidesteps the most striking change; Fanny Phantom displaces the most sacrilegious element of Hogarth's *Enthusiasm*, the glowing Christ icons being eaten by the congregation. Fanny becomes quite literally the cover for *Enthusiasm Delineated*, leaving Christ as the palimpsest beneath her ghostly presence. The crowd chewing on the Christ icons in *Enthusiasm* signifies a faulty apprehension of both the aesthetic principles of representation and religion, a failure linked to theatrical preaching and Harlequin's ridiculous religious puppets. The puppets, which the preacher uses in both prints while gesticulating wildly, transform from biblical figures in *Enthusiasm* to popular ghosts in *Credulity*, encouraging the misrecognition of representation for reality among his rough congregation. Paulson claims that Hogarth's puppets represent bad continental religious art, but they are also theatrical, oversimplified religious messages, performed for a congregation of mixed classes who respond too concretely to representation. Puppets are supposed to make abundantly clear the theatrical distance between reality and performance. But the response of the congregation to the preacher's puppets and their adoration of the Fanny Phantom dolls suggests an irrational, excessive belief in a moment of performance, represented in *Enthusiasm* by the "enthusiastic delusion" of transubstantiation, in which signified collapses into signifier (Ireland 227).

Fanny Phantom's presence in Hogarth's print and Foote's afterpiece masks the theological question at stake of what, if anything, is "made real" in the Eucharist, what Alain Badiou would call the "event" out of joint with the flow of history that is the basis of faith and that marks, as Eagleton suggests, the "contradiction between the West's own need to believe and its chronic incapacity to do so" (Eagleton 141). The violent *Transubstantiation Satirized* is the palimpsest of both *Enthusiasm* and *Credulity*, the buried statement on Christ's "presence" that haunts Hogarth's print and drives his hysterical return to the Eucharist. Hogarth, in seeking to cover his own indigestible skepticism in *Enthusiasm* with a revision that provides some distance from the direct, raw heresy of *Transubstantiation*, returns to the conundrum of performance and belief in his vivid, even manic representation of the Methodist meeting house, where something happens. Hogarth's *Enthusiasm* and *Credulity* conjure the very things they mock: theatrical presence, enthusiastic possession, and the representational crisis of the Eucharist. Hogarth provides a "lineal representation" of religious enthusiasm through his own aesthetic enthusiasm, effacing the difference between the two in the performance under the sign of the Cock Lane ghost.

The next phase of the Foote/Hogarth conversation, Foote's *The Orators*, began as a performance stunt called *A Course of Comic Lectures of English Oratory*, in which Foote presented a mock lecture at noon, as was Sheridan's custom.[40] As it morphed into a theatrical farce, Foote seized on Hogarth's revision for his kitchen-sink satire *The Orators*, which appeared days after Hogarth's print, and used it to organize his farce around the relationship of performance, belief, and Methodism, culminating with the trial of ghostly "Scratching Fanny." Bodkin, the Methodist lay-preacher and tailor, is called as the first witness in Fanny's trial because he has attended her for the "five weeks she did flutter and six weeks she did scratch" (42). On cross-examination, Counsellor establishes that Bodkin is an unreliable witness who is on such friendly terms with ghosts that he has lost his sense of accountability. He has been moved by a "spirit," which he first thought was the "cholic," both to preach and to sleep with a variety of women. Defending himself against the charge of impregnating twelve of them, he asserts "They were barely but nine," to which the Counsellor replies, "Why this was an active spirit" (45). When he is exposed for double-crossing Peter Paragraph in the arrangement to "go halves" with Vamp over the story of Fanny, he declares that he sold the "true scratchings" of Fanny because "What the spirit commanded, that I did." Bodkin is a kind of Methodist automaton, no longer making rational or even conscious decisions, but "possessed" by a spirit that has displaced his individual agency.

Counsellor first suggests that Fanny deserves a jury of her peers, meaning other ghosts, and proposes the ghost puppets from around Hogarth's rostrum in *Credulity* as eligible witnesses in her trial: Sir George Villiers, Julius Caesar, and Mrs. Veal, puppets that were biblical figures in the *Enthusiasm* version (Adam and Eve, Silas with the key to Paul's jail cell, Moses and Aaron). The Serjeant in *The Orators* defeats the proposal for Fanny's jury of her peers with the counterargument that she has forfeited that right by her scratchings and knockings, operations "peculiar to flesh, blood, and body" (39). To materialize, in her case, is to cease to be what she is and to undermine her status as a spirit. The connection to Hogarth's puppets is a reminder of the credulity of general audiences through the uncanny figure of the puppet, the corpse of wood that rises again in performance. Foote would return to the idea of puppets in his 1773 proposal for a "pure, primitive Puppet-Show" at the Haymarket, made of different woods that reflect their authenticity: the patriots are made from boxwood, "a wood that carries an imposing gloss, and may be easily turned" and "weeping willows for Methodist preachers" (Oulton 16). Foote's final offer in *The Orators* to coach any new preachers, lawyers, or actors, claims a critical distance over the evangelical theater of the real, and thus deflates the mystery by exposing the puppetry of its oratorical method. The reality, Foote claims, is mere theater, but that proposition turns out to be complicated by the fascinations of theatricality itself, which made things happen.

Duck Feet

Along with the conversation between Foote's afterpieces and Hogarth's prints, *Transubstantiation Satirized* helps to make sense of several minor but fascinating changes between the two versions of Hogarth's Methodist print. The weeping man of *Enthusiasm* whose tears are being gathered in a bottle by a ghostly Jesus, a reference to a Whitefield prayer for penitents, "O Lord put though their Tears into thy Bottle," disappears and is replaced by an African American man in whose ear a small demon whispers as he sleeps. The barking dog with the Whitefield collar, signifying animal spirits as well as the "howling" of Methodist preachers, becomes a boy spewing nails. The "Methodist brain" at the base of the thermometer, with its strikingly vaginal lower node, is now supported by Glanville on witches and "Westley's Sermons" in *Credulity*. In each of these cases, an image of enthusiastic Christianity becomes a more general representation of folk belief in demons, miraculous events, or witches, though Hogarth does not miss the chance to juxtapose, literally, Wesley's sermons with Glanville's treatise on the supernatural. The small changes in the thermometers reflect a similar motion away from potential sacrilege and toward an indictment of irrationality; in *Enthusiasm*, it proceeds from "prophesy" through sexual stages of "Love Heat," "Lust Hot," and "EXTACY," on the way to "Revelation," while the *Credulity* version goes from the low of suicide to the high of "RAVING."

Reading the dialogue between Foote and Hogarth through *Transubstantiation Satirized* also helps to make sense of one of the quirkier changes in Hogarth's two prints, the disappearance of the duck feet on the weeping cherub of *Enthusiasm*. Paulson and Steevens have observed the duck feet as a whimsical touch on a satire of the "boy preacher" famous for his tears, or another comic deflation of the *putti* in religious art meant to mock Dürer, da Vinci, and other Italian and Dutch masters; Ireland concurs that the "well-fed" figure is probably meant to be Whitefield (Ireland 233). The duck-footed cherub also works as a visual joke about Methodists who were called "quacks in divinity" first by Tristram Land in 1739 and then subsequently by Sterne (as Yorick) and others. The caption to *Enthusiasm* includes another duck-like bird in the large "Methodist Brain" at the base of the thermometer, intended as a satiric representation of the holy spirit as visible and verifiable "when this figure is found imprinted on the brain." The

Detail of *Enthusiasm Delineated*. © The Trustees of the British Museum. Used by permission

series of duck references, like the windmill, the puppets, and the Fanny Phantom/ Christ icons, translate ineffable spiritual concepts into material evidence, the "ocular proof" privileged by Lockean epistemology and the visual demands of empiricism. Though the first intention is to mock Methodist enthusiasm, Hogarth suggests his own longing for presence that, however perversely, connects the duck to Eucharistic theology.

Long before he did either of these prints and before other graphic satires of Methodism appeared, Hogarth had already written about Vaucanson's "Defecating Duck," part of the *Le Mécanisme du fluteur automate* exhibition, which came to the Haymarket in 1741. Hogarth saw the duck during its London tour and commented in his *Analysis of Beauty* on this "little clock-work machine brought from France," which, "being uncovered, appeared a most complicated, confused, and disagreeable object" (62). Vaucanson first exhibited his automata in Paris in 1738; his other inventions included a man who played the flute and a pipe and tabor player. Thanks to an elaborate mechanism hidden in a box, the duck could stretch out its neck, take corn from a hand, and then "digest" and excrete it. The digestion system turned out to be a fraud in that its excretions were separately loaded and the intake corn held in a chamber, but the project was an example of how the design of automata increasingly became, as Jessica Riskin observes, "a matter, not just of representation, but of simulation" (605). The "disagreeable" quality to which Hogarth referred obliquely, its apparent ability to defecate, took the automata project to a new level: the "event" was meant to prove that Vaucanson had achieved living process, or at least simulated it, a proposition that raised further questions about what was real, and what was representation. Hogarth would use the same "event" himself to express his disgust with the church by defecating on a church porch after publishing *The Harlot's Progress* (Paulson, "Putting out the Fire" 96). This act, tendentious under any circumstances, brings Hogarth's "low" deism and interest in the body's materiality into graphic dialogue with the church and Vaucanson's duck. It is a perverse, reductionist, and impious materialism that, in its primitivity, is Hogarth's performative statement about the nature of what Žižek calls the excremental real.

The excremental as the most basic proof of living process pervades the *Enthusiasm* and *Credulity* prints. In *Enthusiasm*, the ghostly Jesus, collecting tears from the sinner, supposed to be sex-murderer Theodore Gardelle, appears to be farting, a satire on the notion of the Holy Spirit as heavenly wind that was fairly common in Methodist sermons.[41] *Dr. Squintum's Exaltation or the Reformation*, in which a winged demon administers an enema in one of Whitefield's ears while another with a trumpet flies poised to catch what comes out and relay it to the crowd, also picks up the theme. A similar image in *The Raree Show* has a flying demon filling Whitefield from the ear with a bellows, suggesting that Whitefield was a "windy" Methodist preacher and his followers "Eolists," also a theme in *The Plain and Easy Road to Bliss* and *The Expounder Expounded*, the latter of which situates Whitefield on a throne "with Wings displayed like another Aeolus, belching out his divine Vapours to the Multitude" (*Plain and Easy* 16). His preaching, which included his theatrical crescendo in tempo and his inevitable tears, raised questions about how mechanical his enthusiasm was, and therefore about how much "spirit" (as opposed to mere hot air) lurked beneath his embodied, vociferous performance. Like the image of Whitefield in *Dr. Squintum's Exaltation or the Reformation*, Hogarth's duck-footed Whitefield and his Eucharist windmill

Detail of *Dr. Squintum's Exaltation or the Reformation*, anon., 1763. © The Trustees of the British Museum. Used by permission

referenced in the caption of *Enthusiasm Delineated* imply that existence is grossly material and demands that the "real" must be manifest in biological terms, not in spiritual notions. The "proof" Whitefield presented in sermon after sermon, his tears, was for Hogarth a faked reality. Like the duck's "disagreeable" ability to defecate, the tears should be the material proof of a deeper truth, an authenticity beyond manufacture. Instead, the tears appeared to Hogarth as another stage device subject to the revelations of theatrical antitheatricality; they are only more wind and crap, signifying nothing.

In the late twentieth century, Vaucanson's duck became a trope for eighteenth-century philosophical questions about the mechanical nature of life as well as what mechanistic physiology and philosophy could not sufficiently explain in Pynchon's *Mason and Dixon*. In the novel, it falls in love with a baker, sails to America, then becomes an invisible blur as it flies furiously along the Mason-Dixon Line, symbolically achieving a kind of spiritual presence at the moment it disappears. In the context of the Whitefield-Methodist phenomenon and the questions about aesthetic distance and real presence that it raised, the duck served as a similar conceptual quilting point, another ghost haunting Hogarth's

Credulity. The specific question of the soulishness of life that Methodism and the duck both raised, a bathetic version of the argument of La Mettrie's *L'Homme Machine*, can only be temporarily closed and imperfectly banished. Like the displaced crying man excreting his tears into a bottle held by Jesus, the missing duck feet are the trace of the uncanny machine that simulated biological process and so raised the question of the possibility of the theater of the real, the performance in which something happens beyond mere representation.

There remains something that Hogarth cannot fully address about Methodism's theater of the real, glimpsed under the sign of the Cock Lane ghost, and the hysterical iconographic substitutions of the *Enthusiasm* and *Credulity* prints, which gave John Keats "a horrid dream" and which made Hogarth's print as compelling as the event it sought to satirize.[42] Though the skeptical Hogarth may be best described by Paulson's label as a "critical deist," his own relationship with "ghosts" adds a final wrinkle to the picture. Hogarth was asked by Arthur Murphy in 1762 to provide a portrait of his old friend Fielding, who was also fascinated with the movement he mocked, as the frontispiece for Murphy's edition of his works. In the story told by Garrick years later, Hogarth struggled with a faulty memory to capture Fielding's face until Garrick, disguised as Fielding's ghost, surprised him one night and commanded "Hogarth! Take thy pencil, and draw my picture!" Hogarth, astonished, obeyed the "ghost," and after the event, questioned his servants about the apparition. Hogarth reported that "fearful of explaining himself too far, lest the idea of ghosts should seize his servants, or he himself might become an object of ridicule," he dropped the subject, but later related the story to Garrick, who confessed to his performance. Hogarth asked Garrick not to speak of this event, "at least during my life," and Garrick honored the request.[43] But Hogarth, inspired by the "apparition" of his old friend, produced the portrait of Fielding in time for the April 26 publication of Murphy's edition, twenty-one days after *Credulity, Superstition, and Fanaticism* and two days before Foote's Cock Lane farce, *The Orators*.

Like Fielding, Hogarth's engagements with Methodism raised aesthetic questions that verged into mysticism. How does an artist or a preacher convey "real" experience, and is the project of representation not premised on some belief in the possibility of immanence that happens in the performance or act of creation, and that transcends the limitations of representation? Hogarth wrote in his *Autobiographical Notes* that he hopes to appeal to modern people who have not been "brought up to the old *religion* of pictures . . . but I own I have hope of succeeding a little with such as dare think for themselves and can believe their own Eyes" (209). Hogarth's modern Kantean credo celebrating viewers who "dare think for themselves" paradoxically takes him back to belief. These viewers must also "believe" their own eyes, a complicated proposition in light of Garrick's persuasive ghost, Fanny Phantom, Whitefield's preaching, and the Worms altarpiece. Hogarth, in the position of the credulous spectator and in need of the "ethereal fire" of creative enthusiasm for his portrait of Fielding, especially with his own health beginning to fail, creates the image only after he has an experience of the theater of the real, courtesy of Garrick's stunt. Garrick's charismatic, compelling performance of Fielding's ghost did, whether Hogarth liked it or not, make something happen.

CHAPTER FIVE

"My Lord, My Love"
The Performance of Public Intimacy and the Methodist Hymn

Methodist hymn singing, more than any other single feature of their worship, exemplified the Methodist assault on Anglican liturgical identity, bringing sonic innovation, emotional intensity, and a participatory aesthetic of worship to the Methodist meeting. Horace Walpole commented wryly to his friend John Chute that he had been "at one opera, Mr. Wesley's. They have boys and girls with charming voices, that sing hymns, in parts, to Scotch ballad tunes; but indeed so long, that one would think they were already in eternity, and knew how much time they had before them" (35: 118). Walpole's comparison of Wesley's church service to an "opera" implies that the Methodists' use of music makes the experience more like an evening at the theater or concert hall than an Anglican service. From both a formal and stylistic perspective, hymns traversed the liturgical boundaries established by the *Book of Common Prayer* and pushed worship to new levels of congregational participation.[1] Methodists and their enemies alike identified the movement with hymn singing: in his preface to the compendious 1780 hymnal Wesley noted that among Methodists, "singing makes so considerable a part of the public service," while *The Gentleman's Magazine,* known for its hostility to Methodism, remarked on the "hymning voice" and "flimsy hymns" of the movement.[2] Pope described the braying of the Dunces in *The Dunciad* as like the "Harmonic twang!" of Methodist preachers. Their preaching, like Methodist singing, is nasal and unmusical: "from lab'ring lungs th'enthusiast blows,/High sound, attempered to the vocal nose" (*Dunciad* 2: 254–55). Chatterton also picked up on the theme of questionable Methodist musicality in "The Methodist" (1770) when he referred to their massive output of "hymns which will sanctify the throat" (*Works* 1: 193). These hymns bore the musical signature of popular and theatrical song, but they also articulated a form of religious desire and longing that worked through and pushed beyond libidinal logic to a performatively shared act of kenosis, or self-emptying. Their embodied language of desire, which harkens back to patristic theologies of incarnation, enables what Graham Ward calls a creative participation in the construction of the self "in and through difference" that opens the individual self to further displacements (172).

The hymns drew their musical texts from a variety of secular and sacred sources, mingling ballad tunes, Celtic music, melodies from church composers like Tallis, and especially theater music, written by Purcell, Handel, Lampe, and other composers connected to the opera houses and theaters. The bricolage of theatrical and ballad tunes made the Methodist hymn, at least to outsiders, a species of holy ballad opera. Musicologists Nicholas Temperley and Sally Drage note that the Methodists took musical textures from the theater and borrowed other popular tunes, practices that gave rise to the "'parody' hymn tune" within the Methodist canon, which played with the mixture of sacred and secular hymn materials (xxvi). Their emotionally intense mixture of Biblical and theatrical language unfolded to aural signatures that hovered between the church and the stage. The sound of a lover pleading with the beloved, where Christ is "my love," borrows the sexual allusiveness of the Moravian tradition and the biblical trope of the sacred romance underscored by music from composers like Covent Garden's Lampe. These more contemporary aural cues made what Richard Rambuss called the "simply conventional" interplay of religion and eroticism in seventeenth-century poetry freshly scandalous in the Methodist hymn, which stirred and deployed the sensuality of Christian embodiment to tunes that were often shockingly modern and theatrical.

Their music confirmed for some that Methodists had made a farce of religion, but their hymns were also cause for concern that Methodists had struck on an operatic, popular, participatory language of emotional intensity that could sway the masses. Wesley provided short music lessons and instructions for sight reading at the beginning of several of the Methodist hymnals, which helped to integrate the working-class Methodists who would not have had formal music instruction with the more affluent Methodists who had. The Methodist movement was identified with the sounds of thousands, even tens of thousands of people, singing together in the Tabernacle, on Kennington Common, and in the fields outside of Bristol, a new experience for both singers and listeners. This shared experience of large group singing was a powerful psychological example of what Catherine Clement has called the collective voice of the "tribe of the chorus," an experience that presses against the boundaries of the individual with sonic immediacy (Clement 20). Singing congregations took the devotional practice of hymn singing from the margins of the church service and made its corporate, public, and often emotional performance the signature feature of their worship.

These singers, who were often in open fields or spaces not designated for worship, enacted a psychological transgression that was also taking place in the textual content of the Methodist hymn. From a historical point of view, the cultural impact of these hymns was substantial. Whether read or sung, they were among the most widely published and read popular works of eighteenth-century poetry. But beyond their immense popularity, the corporate singing of these emotionally and theologically intense hymns about union with God, Christ, and other believers, called for the rupture of the self-possessing individual who remains accountable for his or her emotions. Fueled by an intimate poetic sensibility that asked singers to inhabit a range of gendered subject and object positions, these group declarations of religious devotion struck at the core of the emerging liberal notion of agency, grounded in individual consciousness and self-possession. Donald Davie notes that Charles Wesley accomplished this aim rhetorically in the hymns: "Wesley wants to break down distinctions: principally, the distinction between the devotee and his Saviour; secondly, and consequentially, the distinction between one devotee and the next" (68). Davie's concern is that Wesley goes too far, and he agrees with Martha Winburn England that Wesley is a "vulgar writer," but his point also marks the potential pleasures of the psychological release from the burdens of cognitive isolation that are part of these hymns (57). The grammar of the Methodist hymn, where each instance of the "I" is also an instance of the "we," formulated a collective subject in both sound and sense. Talal Asad and Phyllis Mack have both argued that the combination of docility and empowerment in religious subjectivity marks an in-betweenness that cannot be rationalized in the terms of liberal models of agency, thus troubling the terms of gender and individual selfhood.³ That in-betweenness, which is grammatical and sonic, was the signature of the Methodist hymn. These hymns, composed of sensual, vocative language and performed corporately to popular and theatrical tunes, made good on the threat and the promise of release from a monolithic, isolated notion of the self.

Church Music

Methodism deserves credit for bringing the "human hymn" into the Anglican church, a project that enticed people from the Church of England fold and into the Methodist meeting. As William Vincent opined in *Considerations on Parochial Music* (1787), "for every one who has been drawn from the Established Church by preaching, ten have been induced by music" (Vincent 14). Anglicans and Dissenters alike had written hymns and in some cases preserved Greek and Latin hymns. Canticles like "The Magnificat" had a place in the church of Henry VIII in the popular Vespers service and in its emphasis on Marian worship, where there was also a liturgical place for hymns.⁴ But the "human" or original hymns of Charles Wesley, Isaac Watts, and John Newton were not for use as part of the regular service according to the *Book of Common Prayer*. The development of Anglican liturgy under Queen Elizabeth limited most congregational singing to the psalms and kept vocal music in the domain of professional musicians and choirs. Composers like Thomas Tallis and Henry Aldrich wrote music for choirs, some of which was eventually adapted for hymns in Methodist and other traditions. Hymns were popular in private devotional settings, particularly among Protestants, so Elizabeth's compromise in the *Book of Common Prayer* was to declare that a hymn or song of praise could be allowed before or after common prayers. These most commonly took the form of anthems, related to the Lutheran hymns beloved by Protestants who fled to Frankfurt under Mary, and metrical psalms, particularly the Sternhold and Hopkins's settings (which Wesley later called "scandalous doggerel"), first published in Calvinist Geneva (Temperley and Drage 93).

The place of congregational singing in English worship in the late seventeenth century remained a delicate subject in the eighteenth century, even as sacred choral music flourished. Thomas Secker, Archbishop of Canterbury from 1758 until his death in 1768, encouraged psalm singing and even regular choir practice as a way to enliven the service, in keeping with a liturgically progressive outlook that included sympathy for the Methodists (Gregory 102). Part of the difficulty in establishing the actual practices of worship in parish churches comes from the fact that the term "hymn" in the Anglican tradition meant a few different things: it sometimes refers to metrical psalms; to the "Te Deum," "Sanctus," or other sung pieces of the liturgy; to an anthem by a trained choir; or to the original hymns of Wesley or Watts. Temperley chooses the broader term "psalmody" to describe "sacred music sung in parish churches, Protestant Dissenters meetings, and private devotional gatherings," though this category offers little clarification about the use of Methodist congregational hymns in Anglican services.[5] Generally speaking, Anglican congregational singing, limited to metrical psalms within the *Book of Common Prayer* liturgy, made the difference between orthodox and evangelical Anglicans sonically clear. The psalm's basic musical heritage in plainsong under Gregory VII (Gregorian chant) evened the note values, resulting in monophonic chant rather than measured music with a time signature.[6] Late seventeenth-century psalm tunes were sometimes known as "Anglican chants," and though they represented a move away from penitential psalms to praise psalms within the Church of England, they remained grounded in the plainsong tradition.[7] In contrast to the singing of psalms, congregational singing of "new" seventeenth- and eighteenth-century hymns, sacred poems set to music and often referred to as "human hymns," was strongly associated with Dissent and evangelical groups. For an Anglican traditionalist, they imported elements of private devotional practice (and the stamp of Dissent) into the public service. Gareth Lloyd notes that in 1820, the Bishop of Peterborough condemned their use "because there was no provision for them in the book of common prayer" (75). Even as late as 1925, the *Prayer Book Dictionary* cautiously notes that hymns are "not expressly mentioned in the Prayer Book" and so "their legality cannot be proved" (423). Benjamin Keach, a Baptist preacher of the 1660s, is usually credited with pioneering congregational hymn singing, which would remain associated with Dissent throughout the century, though it was the Methodists who eventually brought it into the mainstream through the scale of their influence (J. R. Watson 110).

The musical contrast between hymns and psalms, whether spoken psalms, the 1654 Psalter, or the new metrical psalms of Nahum Tate and Nicholas Brady's 1696 Psalter, was the aural front line of the eighteenth-century battle over Anglican identity. In Richardson's *Pamela*, Pamela's criticism of her father's psalm singing is one example of the musical stakes of this liturgical debate. Pamela's revision of Psalm 137 as "When sat I sat in Brandon-hall / All watched round about" in order to tell the story of her own "Babylonian captivity" shows her

Biblical literacy and her willingness to translate, as John Pierce has argued, "mythic and archetypal images . . . into the objects of formal realism" (16). But she also notes her father's failure to "observe altogether the method in which they stand" when he sings the 145th psalm in the church prayers, suggesting her discerning if not conservative stance on church music (353). Her objection could have been one of several possibilities. Mr. Andrews could have been "lining" the psalm, which involved a parish clerk singing a line to be repeated by the congregation, thus requiring no music reading ability or prior knowledge of tunes. He might have been using a tune from the Gregorian metrical psalms, which Louis Benson called "droning," displaying an unfashionable degree of traditionalism (Benson 242). Conversely, use of a tune like WINCHESTER, which appears in Playford's revised *Psalms and Hymns in Solemn Music* (1671), or something from Nahum Tate and Nicholas Brady's *A New Version of the Psalms of David* (1696) might have sounded too modern to Pamela, too closely associated with the theatrical world that supplied so many of the Methodist tunes. The fact that she objects to his "method," whatever it might be, keeps Pamela in the territory of Anglican orthodoxy, a defender of the sonic as well as textual care necessary to maintain the forms of the service itself.

These finer points of musical orthodoxy were overshadowed by the concern that Methodist hymns were stealing the flocks of the Anglican church through their extraordinary popularity in Methodist meetings, Methodist hymnals, and non-Methodist periodicals like the *The London Magazine* and *The Ladies' Magazine*, where they were sometimes reprinted (Arnold 83). The musical output of Charles and John Wesley exceeded that of Isaac Watts and dwarfed that of other eighteenth-century figures. Nearly nine thousand hymns are attributed to the Wesleys, who produced them collaboratively, with Charles as primary creative force and John as editor. They appeared at a rapid pace, with roughly one new hymnal or book of hymns and devotional poems each year from 1737 to 1782, each of which appeared in between roughly ten and twenty editions. The circulation of these texts was massive; Lloyd notes that in 1791, over eleven thousand hymnals were housed in the Methodist Book Room awaiting distribution, with several thousand out in shops.[8] Even with that output, the Wesleys were sometimes not credited with hymns they provided, which appeared as anonymous or altered texts (to the fury of John Wesley) or were credited to other hymn writers such as Doddridge, Toplady, or Cowper (Benson 259). On the other hand, the considerable output of the Wesley brothers and the prevalence of hymn singing at Methodist meetings made it easy for readers to group other collections, like

Cennick's *Sacred Hymns for the Children of God in the Last Days of their Pilgrimage* (1741), Allen's *Collection of Hymns for the Use of Those that Seek, and Those that Have Redemption in the Blood of Christ* (1757), and Wallin's *Evangelical Hymns and Songs* (1750) as "Methodist." While varied in quality, these collections shared in an ecumenical border culture of worship that moved in and out of churches, bridging the gaps between private devotion and public worship.

Methodist hymnals, used regularly in worship, band meetings, and for private devotions, translated into book ownership and musical instruction for people who might not otherwise have either. The hymnals were often compact "pocket books"; the 1780 version measured 2½ by 4 inches, though it was 1½ inches thick, which allowed it to be carried easily. The shorter topical hymnals like *Hymns for Times of Trouble* and *Hymns for the Nativity of our Lord* were cheap, between eleven and forty-seven pages, and available unbound for a few pennies, inviting cross-class accessibility. In several of their hymnals, the Wesleys printed basic music and singing lessons for the congregation at large in order to address the fact that many of the people drawn to Methodism had no musical education. Short courses in the "gamut" or sight-reading, "The Grounds for Vocal Music," and Wesley's *Directions for Singing* all express the populist pedagogical thrust of the movement. The essay identifies notes on the treble and bass clefs, reviews time signatures and note values, and offers a short explanation of transposition, along with sight-singing exercises. As Wesley stated in the preface repeated in *Select Hymns: With Tunes Annexed*, which went into ten editions between 1761 and 1790, "I want the people called *Methodists* to sing true, the tunes which are in *common use* among them" (*Select Hymns* A2). The popularity of Methodist hymnals made Wesley's essay one of the leading music lessons available to the eighteenth-century public. The essay reflects John Wesley's commanding style:

> 1. Perfectly understand these Grounds, 2. Get them well by Heart, 3. Learn to sing the Scale and Lessons readily up and down, and 4. To strike the Intervals at once, that is any Note of two Notes between C and C: Particularly the Greater and the Lesser Thirds. (vii)

As he states even more baldly at the beginning of *Sacred Melody*, "Learn *these Tunes* before you learn any others . . . Sing them exactly as they are printed here, without altering or mending them at all," a discipline that makes possible unison singing in very large groups (*Sacred Melody* pref.). In his 1747 "Rules for Preaching," his second instruction was "sing no hymns of your own composing." Wesley wanted to enforce his artistic and spiritual vision of Methodist hymn singing, and he attempted to do so by formulating it as a set of printed rules. But, as law is also the sign of past violation and fear of future transgression, Wesley's prefaces are also a sign that some Methodist congregations were either singing other tunes, or singing very poorly.

The arrangement of the hymnals themselves was not by liturgical season or order of service but by state of mind. These sacred poems, whether read or sung, are meant to be used as affective remedies, not unlike the "receipts" in John Wesley's *Primitive Physic*. Of the many Methodist hymnals, the majority of the collections were organized to address emotional need, such as *Hymns for Times of Trouble* (1744), *Hymns for Petition and Thanksgiving* (1746), and *Hymns for Those that Seek and Those that Have Redemption* (1747). The divisions within the larger hymnals, such as *Hymns and Spiritual Songs* and *Select Hymns with Tunes Annext*, both of which were reprinted widely, preserved the thematic headers in their organization of the hymns. The emotional immediacy of this rubric asked singers to bring their hopes and fears into the public singing of hymns for devotional as well as therapeutic reasons. A 1777 caricature, "Old Orthodox," represents a Wesleyan Methodist, identifiable by his lank hair and thin face with just such a hymnbook. The irony of the title is an oblique reference to the unorthodox Methodist practices in worship, including the use of hymns, played against their claims to be "primitive," hence "orthodox," Christians. His hymnbook, a parody of categories into which Methodists arranged their hymnals, announces "Spiritous hymns to be sung or said, standing or sitting or Lying, Morning or Evening" and trails off, categories still proliferating. The language echoes the world of advertising to the degree that it pitches the hymns as commodities to a consumer who might have uses for them. But the idea of hymns deliberately arranged to the condition of the singer also suggests a degree of engagement with the hymn as an aesthetic object that will have effects on the listener or singer. Indexes of Methodist hymnals make it clear that this is a world of gerunds, and that the singer is expected to participate in the "rejoicing, fighting, praying, watching, working, suffering, groaning" and other activities that constitute the sections of Wesley's compendious *A Collection of Hymns for the Use of the People Called Methodists* (1780). These "human hymns" are poetry meant to be used by people in the act of feeling and being shaped by those feelings.

The appeal of hymn singing reopened questions about sensation and emotion from early modern conversations about music in the context of the broad appeal of the Methodist hymn. Early modern theories about the appeal of music, as Linda Austern has argued, suggested that music might be able to ravish sense

Old Orthodox, anon., 1777. Courtesy of the Lewis Walpole Library, Yale University

and intellect "through its entry by the ear into an unguarded body, within a culture that further equated ravishment and ecstasy with the violence of rape" (Austern 647). Thomas Ravenscroft claimed the "Soveraignty of Musicke in the Affection" as a sensation difficult to rationalize and a potential threat to individual will.[9] Adapting the thesis on the semiautomatic force of music, Isaac Watts declared that singing is directed "by the Light of Nature, in speaking the Praises of God" and, like groaning or sighing, is an outward expression of inward sincerity and spiritual devotion (*Harmony* iv). In a more defensive posture, Addison scoffed at the sublimity of Handel as an example of the foreign "wits to whose tastes we so ambitiously conform ourselves" (Addison 1: 26). Addison's concern makes the appeal of passionate music a potential matter of national defense. More generally, the ancient appeal of sound suggested to critics an antimodern, even subhuman response that further weakened already compromised selves from the lower classes, especially women. William Combe complained that the "fools" who love these hymns "feed on *Sounds*, while *John* enjoys the *Sense*/of thanks return'd in *tributary Pence*" (12). Samuel Foote described the "melodious nasal Twang, produced by an Orchestra of old Women" surrounding Whitefield as he preached (*Letter from Mr. Foote* 6), and the anonymous author of "A Letter to Mr. Foote, Occasioned by the 'Christian and Critical Remarks on his Interlude called *The Minor*'" referred to the "Hummers... Women, hired, as I am told, at so much per Week; to assist in carrying on the great work; not by setting Psalms, but, occasional Groans and Cries" (4). The hymns, which he associated with the collapse and weeping of attendees at the early outdoor meetings, venture into a physical territory that is more sound than sense, a prelinguistic form of communication that appeals to lower instincts and thus to lower classes.

In contrast to these concerns, John Wesley celebrated this primitive power of music in a 1779 essay devoted to that topic, marveling at the ancient Greek accounts of musicians who could inspire love, hate, joy, sorrow, or any other passions they pleased on auditors who were seemingly at their mercy. He contrasts this power with modern music, which he claims has lost its impact because it has turned from the simple, affective focus on melody and lost its way in too much harmony and counterpoint, which appeal to "a quite different faculty of the mind—not to our joy, or hope, or fear, but merely to the ear, to the imagination, or internal sense" (*Oxford* Works 7: 767). His complaint is an extended longing for music connected to "common sense" (meaning a more basic, even basal sensory response) in order to achieve a broad, powerful emotional appeal. He glimpses this power in affecting solo singing, and in

> Scotch or Irish airs. They are composed, not according to art, but nature—they are simple in the highest degree. There is no *harmony* according to the present sense of the word, therein, but there is much *melody*. And this is not only heard, but felt by all those who retain their native taste (OXFORD WORKS 7: 768).

The notion of native taste returns to a notion of innate ideas in the name of patriotism, giving us a Methodist musical take on what Howard Weinbrot has called the poetics of nationalism.[10] For Wesley, the simplicity of melody, something prior to the polyphonic chorale or fugue that evolves out of cathedral music, is the source of emotional power and the focus of the Methodist hymn.

Holy Ballad Opera

The music to which these hymns were first sung was approachable and familiar, even democratic, in a world of sacred music dominated by trained cathedral singers, country parish choirs singing "fuguing tunes," and more sophisticated anthems by composers like Playford. In contrast to the oratorios of cathedral music and the elaborate, contrapuntal fugues of the parish choirs, Methodist hymns are straightforward and manageable for an intentional but not professional singer. They stand between metrical psalms and the glorious, extensive vocal virtuosity of Handel, Bach, and Purcell, which James Peirce called "so curious and difficult, that 'tis beyond the capacity of the common people; and so is not adapted to the edification of the church" (Peirce 3: 100). These sonic differences were part of the debate over what constituted good church music and what was problematic, either as too "Gothic" or too modern. Charles Burney, in spite of his criticisms of the abuses of "Fugue, Canon, & other Gothic Contrivances," confessed in 1782 to William Mason "I sometimes wish the art of Fugue to be cultivated *only* for the use of the Church, where being banished from the Theatres & other public spaces it might under proper restrictions preclude the levity of Secular Melodies" (Burney 340). In the age of Handel, Bach, and Telemann, high church musical taste had arrived, to be distinguished by what it favored as well as what it rejected—simple, ballad-based hymns. This distinction was also about separating out sacred and secular categories of music; the separation seemed to be going poorly, according to Burney, in both theater and church. Wesley's preference for melody over harmony seems to have been part of what made theater songs and "secular melodies," with their solo lines and affective texture, more welcome in the Methodist meeting and more problematic in the Anglican service.

Early Methodist music, including *A Collection of Tunes, Set to Music, as They Are Commonly Sung at the Foundery* (1737), first printed in Charleston by Lewis Timothy, apprentice to Benjamin Franklin, illustrates the blend of familiar, new, German, and English tunes the first Methodist groups used, all with an emphasis on singable, monophonic lines, musically closer to the kind of song Anne Bracegirdle would sing on stage than to the expected psalm or fugue in a church. The collection was the result of an early voyage to South Carolina, during which the Wesleys traveled with a group of Moravians and learned their songs. John

Wesley then translated the Moravian hymnbook *Das Gesang-Burch der Gemein* while in Hernhutt, and Charles Wesley borrowed extensively from German and Lutheran sources, listing four of the forty-three tunes in the Charlestown hymnal as German tunes and another three with German place names, like Herrnhut (printed "Hernhuth"), Marienborn, Leipzig, and Frankfurt. The simplicity of many of these tunes put them in an aural category with ballads if only by contrast to metrical psalms and cathedral music.[11] But because most hymnbooks printed text without music, it is almost certain that some communities, especially rural ones without instruments or many trained musicians, would have used a known tune that met the metrical requirements. Charles Wesley's clean, emphatic verse meshed well with many strophic ballad tunes.

Establishing the precise tunes that were sung in regional and even London congregations in the eighteenth century is difficult if not impossible, but accusations that Methodists used ballad tunes, tavern songs, and theater music followed the movement from its early days. In *The Spiritual Quixote* (1773), the narrator observes that the psalms and hymns of a Methodist meeting led by Whitefield "being chiefly set to popular tunes, had the same effect in recommending their doctrines, as the like cause had formerly in establishing the fame of *The Beggar's Opera*" (236). William Riley's *Parochial Music Corrected* (1762) notes that Methodists in the parishes, while "they have not yet ventured to sing Ballad-Tunes, as at the Tabernacle, Foundry, and elsewhere . . . the Tunes they commonly use are generally too light and airy for Church Music, and consequently have nothing in their composure that may excite a true Spirit of Devotion" (3). The "recycling" of musical settings itself across sacred and secular contexts was not so unusual; Bach, in composing his *Christmas Oratorio* for the church in Leipzig, reused portions of his cantata *Hercules*, transforming the heroic myth of Hercules into an oratorio-opera about the Christ child.[12] Handel's *Esther* was to be an experimental sacred drama, performed as a series of tableaux in the theater, though not without objections.[13] But the particular context of the English ballad opera craze, including (most sensationally) *The Beggar's Opera* (1728) and also such later successes as *The Author's Farce* (1730), *The Grub Street Opera* (1731), and *The Opera of Operas* (1733), made the Methodists' use and reuse of popular tunes conspicuous. Thomas Williams wrote in 1789 that "The method of singing in the congregations, commonly termed methodistical, has been often charged with levity" because of its use of song tunes and "trifling airs," though Williams notes that these were eventually supplanted by "better compositions" (qtd. in Temperley, *Psalmody*). Music that circulates in this way courts the charge of levity in exchange for the return of approachability. Musically, Methodist hymns were bridging sacred and secular categories of sound, and the aural proximity of Methodist hymns to popular tunes was the easiest way for their critics to identify them. Thomas Chatterton wrote that on hearing these "odd" Methodist hymns, "you'd swear twas bawdy songs made godly" (*Poetical Works* 1: 193).

Folk airs that were the source of some of these songs remained associated with the theater and the ballad operas of the 1730s, which held their place in the repertoire as main or afterpieces. The anonymous *A Journal of the Travels of Nathaniel Snip*, the tale of Snip the tailor turned Methodist preacher, informs us that he has given up "prophane Songs, such as *Robin Hood*, the *Taylor's Garland* and the like" in favor of Wesley's "Divine Love Hymns" for which he is "carried before the Chief Magistrate of the Place for a Ballad-Singer and Vagrant" (23, 27). Clearly, the Magistrate can't tell the difference since the songs sound the same to him. *Robin Hood* was both a song and a 1730 ballad opera, a reminder of the various theatrical connections songs might absorb, even if their point of origin was the "Scotch and Irish airs" Wesley praised. Tony Lumpkin's famous song about Methodist preachers who "preach best with a skinfull" in *She Stoops To Conquer*, and anti-Methodist ballads like "Harlequin Methodist" (set to the same tune used for the first air in *The Beggar's Opera*) deploy these connections between ballad, theater song, and Methodist hymn as part of their comic frisson.

Musicologists continue to debate the degree to which Wesleyan hymns were based on folk and tavern tunes. Erik Routley and Dean McIntyre both object to the connection, pointing to the body of complex arrangements by Lampe and Handel on the one hand and to confusion over the term "bar form," a reference to AAB or AABA form hymns.[14] But on at least one occasion, we know that Charles Wesley directly adapted a ballad as a way to communicate with a band of drunken sailors who were disrupting one of his open-air meetings. He took the ballad tune they were singing, "Nancy Dawson," which is similar to "Here we go 'round the Mulberry Bush," and changed their obscene lyrics (the particulars of which are lost) into the hymn "Listed into the Cause of Sin." Wesley turned their tune against their purposes by embracing its earthy associations.[15] The hymn, not one of his best, nonetheless makes his point through musical parody:

> Listed into the Cause of Sin,
>   Why should a Good be Evil?
> Musick, alas! Too long has been
>   Prest to obey the Devil:

The use of "listed" and "prest" associates the abuse of music with press-gangs taking someone (or some tune) forcibly to serve a violent purpose, a reference that would not have been lost on a mostly working-class Methodist gathering. Wesley's second verse spells out his strategy:

> Who on the Part of God will rise,
>   Innocent Sound recover,
> Fly on the Prey, and take the Prize,
>   Plunder the Carnal Lover

Charles Wesley's verse positions the sailors or anyone within his hearing as a potential rescuer of "innocent sound" from the "Carnal Lover," inviting them to become true heroes by helping Wesley pirate popular music for God. Like the Moravian hymn "Chicken blessed/And caressed/Little bee on JESU's breast," which Anstay parodied simply by printing it as is in his 1766 *New Bath Guide*, the homely take on metaphysical mixing could descend into unintentional comedy, the "hoeing and weeding" about which Walpole complained. That Wesley felt comfortable writing the line "plunder the Carnal Lover" while doing it musically indicates a level of engagement with popular culture that mixed registers of sacred and profane and instructed singing congregations to do the same.

The vigorous trochaic launch of "Listed into the Cause" rollicks along in a way that is aurally out of place next to psalms and church anthems. Nicholas Temperley notes several "parody hymns" that come out of the Methodist tradition, hymns which used or barely abridged theatrical melodies. "On all the Earth Thy Spirit Shower," for instance, was first sung to the tune "Virginia," which Temperley identifies as a parody (Temperley and Drage 21). An early setting may have used "True Love" (also known as "Charming Chloe"), a version of which appears in the collection *The Merry Musicians*. The ballad text there reads:

> Charming Chloe, look with Pity
> On your faithful love-sick swain;
> Hear, O hear his doleful Ditty!
> And relieve his mighty Pain
> Find you Musick in his Sighing?
> Can you see him in Distress;
> Wishing, trembling, panting, dying
> Yet afford no kind Redress?
>
>   (*THE MERRY MUSICIAN* 18)

"My Lord, My Love"   185

The hymn, reprinted widely after 1780, takes the concept of longing and applies it to the believer's hope of divine intervention:

> On all the earth thy spirit shower,
> The earth in righteousness renew;
> Thy kingdom come, and hell's o'erpower,
> And to they scepter all subdue.
> Like mighty winds or torrents fierce,
> Let it opposers all o'er-run;
> And every law of sin reverse,
> That faith and love may make all one.   (J. WESLEY, COLLECTION 427)

The comparison of the texts is interesting not so much for the specifics of word substitution but as an example of the regular displacement of erotic love with the believer's longing for an experience of the divine that happened in the hymns.

Of the new music associated with Methodism, John Frederick Lampe's 1746's *Hymns on the Great Festivals, and Other Occasions* is the most significant and the greatest example of their musical ties to the theater. Lampe, a bassoonist and composer for John Rich's Covent Garden Theatre who also played in Handel's orchestras, brought his ear for the mad song to the sometimes frantic longing of the Wesleyan hymn. His conversion to Methodism under the influence of the Wesleys in the 1740s was preceded by a career in ballad opera. He provided the score to Eliza Haywood's collaboration with William Hatchett, *The Opera of Operas* (1733), which adapts Fielding's *The Tragedy of Tragedies* as a burlesque opera. Lampe's involvement with a medley or ballad style of writing, including the "medley overture," such as his overture to *Cupid and Psyche* (1734), hit the popular taste for this kind of music that wove together popular tunes, bits of Handel, and pieces of theater music. This musical bricolage proved useful to him in both Covent Garden and the Methodist meeting houses. He contributed to the fad of "mad songs," including those in *The Dragon of Wantley, The Opera of Operas*, and later *Pyramis and Thisbe*, all of which mock Italian opera, and which stylistically spilled over into his sacred writing.[16] Wesley's "O Love Divine, how sweet thou art," also listed as "Hymn XIX: Desiring to Love" in Lampe's settings of *Hymns on the Great Festivals* (1746) joins the vocative appeal and the language of the mad song with a florid, theatrical musical style to make its point about the experience of divine rapture:

O Love Divine, how sweet thou art.
When shall I find my willing Heart
All taken up by thee?
I thirst, I faint, and die to prove
The greatness of redeeming Love,
The Love of Christ to me,
The Love of Christ to me.   (WORKS 7: 258)

The "I thirst, I faint, and die to prove" echoes tropes from theatrical mad songs, wrenching the language of devotion up to a more desperate pitch. His more ornate pieces, which had the blessing of the Wesleys, are reprinted along with all the tunes from his 1746 collection in *Harmonia Sacra* (1754). Lampe's prominence in the Methodist musical scene and the theatrical influence apparent in his style of writing provided a sonic connection that kept Methodist hymns tied to the world of Gay and Fielding as something like sacred ballad opera.

"Love Divine, All Loves Excelling" one of Wesley's most popular hymns, brings together the effect of words and music as a musical and textual sacred parody of Dryden's "Fairest Isle, All Isles Excelling," the closing aria from Purcell's *King Arthur*. The opera was popular from its 1691 opening through the eighteenth century, with major revivals in 1736, 1763, 1770 (with additional music by Thomas Arne), 1781, and an abbreviated afterpiece in 1784 which still included "Fairest Isle" (Harris 257). When Arne proposed to rewrite Purcell's music in 1770, it was in part because he thought it sounded like "churchmusick," a function perhaps of the Methodist appropriation of Purcell's tunes (Gilman 142). "Love Divine" was first published in 1747 in *Hymns for Those that Seek and Those that Have Redemption in the Blood of Jesus Christ*. As one of the less embellished tunes of what was considered Purcell's more English sound, it was easy enough for congregational adaptation, with trills slightly flattened out, and was printed as such in the 1761, 1770, and 1773 hymnals, with credit to Purcell (though it was also listed as the tune "Winchester"). Wesley's parodic reuse of Dryden's "Fairest Isle" embeds musical connections to the public cultures of nationalism and theater into the individual's intimate experience of God. The song appears in a final masque, in which British history unfolds by mingling royal figures with shepherds and laborers, broadening the thesis of British identity beyond the succession of kings to accommodate the post-1688 realities of the British monarchy, as Jack Armistead has argued.[17] Venus's love song to the nation (in which, notably, she must refer to herself in the third person) becomes

"My Lord, My Love"   187

Hymn XIX Desiring to Love, from *Hymns on the Great Festivals, and Other Occasions*. John Frederick Lampe. London, 1746. © The British Library Board

for Wesley the believer's love song to God. Both strategies depend on the language of romantic or erotic love for their effectiveness, but they must also both relocate the romance narrative into more public forms of love. Dryden's "Venus here will choose her dwelling/ And forsake her Cyprian grove" becomes Wesley's "Fix in us Thy humble dwelling/All thy faithful mercies crown." But where love (Venus) comes to live in England, God as "love Divine" will come to live in the "trembling heart" of the believer. Following the opera's theme of a Britain that takes its national and cultural shape as it displaces pagan ritual with Christianity, the hymn in turn displaces British nationalism with the higher "love Divine." The more intimate residence of God, who will "enter every trembling heart," stirs the erotic subtext, albeit twice removed, through the screen of the Dryden/Purcell original.

"Love Divine" resists the either/or separation between heaven and earth, and between secular and sacred musically, much as Bach did in the *Christmas Oratorio*, celebrating instead "embedded" belief by blending musical and textual forms of meaning into a potent experience of immediacy. Like so many Methodist hymns that traffic in the imperative addressed to God, "Love Divine" is insistent about manifesting God (qua divine love) through tropes of materialized contact, usually the believer's heart. The hymn bridges the gap between heaven and earth created in the scientific and conceptual canons of knowledge, tracing the theology of "joy of heaven to earth come down" for the modern age. In a sense that is different from the experience of a Medieval mystic or even a Renaissance Christian, the presence of God on earth, "come down" is a proposition of rupture, a confusion of epistemological categories and a disruption of the implicit temporality that grounds them. A Deist notion of a creator God who is a point of origin in an unreachable past but not an ongoing entity in human history separates out human history from eternal time and makes history a matter of human agency and activity; conversely, an intervening God delimits that agency and with it, variously conceived enlightenment projects for human progress and autonomy.

The closing verse of "Love Divine," itself a liberal borrowing from Addison, undercuts the autonomous self. Addison opens his hymn "When All Thy Mercies," also known as "Hymn of Gratitude," with an image Wesley plucks for his closing:

> When all thy mercies, O my God,
> My rising soul surveys,
> Transported with the view, I'm lost
> In wonder, love, and praise. (ADDISON 4: 453)

Wesley's brilliant theft turns Addison's individual agent who surveys and is transported to the point of being lost into a collective "we" that disappears at the last moment in abjection, a "new creation" at the hands of God:

> Changed from glory into glory,
> Till in heaven we take our place,
> Till we cast our crowns before thee
> Lost in wonder, love, and praise.

Addison maintains an "I" from which to navigate the religious sublime; Wesley surrenders to the moment of eschatological transformation as the pronoun slips away. The strophic line accents the theological point; the self as agent is purposefully, gleefully "lost," and the line, as Watson observes, is the better for it (J. R. Watson, *English Hymn* 196). Where Addison is at the boundaries of reason in his contemplation of God's mercy, Wesley is in the midst of self-overcoming transformations that have him "lost" in heaven without an "I" as anchor, recouping the sonic passion of the love-based theater tune as the religious sublime. Given the vast population of first person markers in Methodist hymns in general, the translation of Addison's "I" into Wesley's transitioning future-we is a tendentious move that destabilizes the singer's position from individual to collective believer at a moment of sublime encounter. The final two lines provide the sonic anchor of the dental "till" and the plosive "cast," and "crowns," images from the Revelation to St. John that keep the hymn in a Biblical/liturgical orbit. The trochaic pulse strikes each essential word of the last line: lost, wonder, love, and praise. Ultimately, the theological vision that blurs human agent into human object in "Love Divine" is realized by the event of thousands at a time singing these words together.

Lost in Wonder

Hymns of this kind situated a tactile, present, and responsive self between agency and passivity. The hymns asked the singer to describe and enact what Mack calls the "in-betweenness" that marks the religious person's attenuated experience of agency, as opposed to the formulation of triumphalist individual agency in a conception of modernity synonymous with secularization (*Heart Religion* 11). The text of these hymns, which Louis Benson described as "a gathering of individuals conducting their private devotions in public" (250), unleashed the intensity and vulnerability of Donne, Herbert, or Crashaw into public spaces of devotion. Many of the poems in Herbert's *The Temple* were versified as hymns in the Wesleyan Charleston hymnal as well as the 1739 *Hymns and Sacred Poems*. Though the hymns abound in intertextual references to Pope, Milton, Dryden, and Shakespeare, the seventeenth-century devotional poets provide the rhetorical bone structure of Charles Wesley's approach to the Christian story.[18] Rambuss reads the sensual force of these poems, epitomized in Donne's pleas to be broken, imprisoned, enthralled, and ravished by God in his best-known Holy Sonnet, as sites of "excess, transgression, and the heterodoxies of gender and eroticism that can be embraced and inhabited through the mechanisms of devotion" (5). The eroticism of the Moravian and metaphysical traditions feeds into these hymns, an eroticism that helps believers imagine an unbounded devotional self in the experience of worship.

Charles Wesley turned to the unfashionable, even rejected seventeenth-century devotional poets for metaphors and a poetic grammar that modeled a devotional as opposed to autonomous subjectivity. Samuel Johnson famously complained that the seventeenth-century poems he dubbed "metaphysical" are the product of a "perverseness of industry" that violently yokes "the most heterogeneous ideas." Pope's screed against bad verse, *Peri Bathos*, picks up a similar thread about heterogeneity to ground his claims about the proper bounds of verse and damns the mixing on which metaphysical poetry and Methodist hymns depended.[19] Johnson charged that metaphysical poetry ransacks "nature and art . . . for illustrations, comparisons and allusions," resulting in an uncomfortable reading experience in which "the reader commonly thinks his improvement dearly bought" ("Life of Cowley"). The yoking of ideas forces the reader into changes he or she does not want or enjoy, ways of thinking that come at too high a cost to the self. This sense of challenge to the self is precisely what the Methodist hymn marks. In these hymns, the singer moves into a more intimate I/thou grammatical relation to God, usually through an appeal to the embodied Christ, and a more sonically intimate relation to other singers in the context of this shared public intimacy. The "I" of these hymns is not so much Cartesian as it is corporate. It is a feeling, confessional, vulnerable self, always petitioning in the corporate experience of hymn singing. It "can nothing do," is "weakness itself"; it resigns, it waits, it mourns, it longs.[20] The corporate self of the hymns balanced the sensationalist psychology of Locke that forms the self with the triumphant cognitive mastery that gave coherence to the impressionable self. The performative grammar of their formulation of a self that is both subject and object, agent and thrall, opened out the paradox of Lockean psychology, in which the self is both consciously self-consistent and unusually malleable.

The corporate performance of hymn singing shifts the autonomous "I" that marks the site of will and agency toward a position of vulnerability, often figured through the trope of the sacred romance or the marriage of Christ to the church. In "Christ, the true, the Heavenly Vine" (*Hymns and Sacred Poems* 191), a section of the extended hymn called "The Communion of Saints," which comes after "The Love Feast," Christ is the "Husband of Thy Church below" which is betrothed to him, and whom he will possess "Body, Spirit, Soul." The representation of Christ as an earthly husband is self-consciously rhetorical, a way to figure relation:

> Union to the World unknown!
> Join'd to GOD in Spirit One.
> Wait we till the Spouse shall come,
> Till the Lamb shall take us Home,
> For his Heaven the Bride prepare,
> Solemnize our Nuptials there. (190)

The trope of the marriage presses on literal meaning with the promise of "solemnized" nuptials. Using women's voices to lead congregational singing (rather than the standard tenor lead for psalms and anthems) further mixed the gender of the singing "I."[21] That which is "unknown" to the world must be figured in the embodied language of marriage, here opened to men and women as joined brides of Christ, preparing for their wedding night. The innovation here is not the use of mystical Christian language that figures holy love in erotic terms, but the use of it as a public, sung lyric that deploys its gendered tropes amid the sonic textures of theatrical love songs and popular ballads.

The romance narratives that accompany the religious tropes of divine love also lend a temporal urgency to the human/divine relationship. The emotional and grammatical immediacy of hymns like "O Love Divine, What Hast Thou Done?" blurs the line between romantic despair and sacred penitence to advance this point. The hymn's title is a layered reference that uses the vocative in imitation of a German hymn by Johann Heerman in *Lyra Germanica*, "Alas, O Lord, what evil has Thou done," while also picking up, as Watson has noted, on the passage from Luke 23 (Pilate's proclamation "what evil has he done?") and *Hamlet*, "O me, what Hast Thou Done?" (act 3, scene 4).[22] The arrestingly personal question is addressed to God qua "Love Divine" as an individual whose action can be queried, however reverently. The question conveys the sense of an event that cannot be undone, something that unfolded in tragic historical time, yet that is also an ongoing revelation in which the singer participates:

> O Love divine, what hast Thou done:
> Th'immortal God hath died for me!
> The Father's co-eternal Son
> Bore all my sins upon the tree:

Th'immortal God for me hath died!
My Lord, my love, is crucified!

The emotional valence is operatic, sustained by a rising line in $\frac{3}{2}$ that progresses by stately whole notes and saves its motion for the key words "Divine," "died," "Father," and "sins," and the more emotional and difficult flourishes for "for me" and "crucified."[23] The musical emphases connect the singer to the moment of greatest theological importance, the crucifixion. The singer sings to him or herself, reflecting on the personal loss of "my love," while also being part of a group making a public confession of their faith. The immanent, lover-Christ from the mystical tradition blends with more theatrical music, begging the question (as Walpole, Foote, Fielding, and others implied) of what kind of love was being described. As George Haggerty has noted, the line between love as *eros* and love as *philia* is blurry in any culture, to which we can add love as *agape* (Haggerty 14). These hymns thrived in the interstices, tapping into a range of gendered positions for the singer in the search to articulate a higher sense of devotion. The gender flexibility within the grammatical architecture of the Methodist hymn, along with the popular, melodically focused music, pulled the singer through different dispositions for the sake of an event, conversion, that required a self open to its own indeterminacy.

The trope of divine romance leads Charles Wesley into productive ambiguities. "Love Feast," one of the most widely used Methodist hymns, accompanied by a tune of the same name, begins "Come and let us sweetly join, Christ to praise in,/Christ to praise in Hymns Divine." The grammatical uncertainty introduced by enjambment between "sweetly" joining Christ and joining one another is the point of the hymn and the point of the Love Feast itself. The self is corporate, joined to other believers and joined to Christ. The suggestively named practice of the love feast, subject to reams of mockery from outsiders, was on its own terms a sacred parody of a literal "feast" reimagined as a homely Eucharist, with a little bread or cake and water. The love feast transposes the idea of "feasting" into a feast of Christian fellowship and praise. The "feast of love," a provocative image of excess, was to be a feast of mystic communion with other believers and with God and, as such, an antidote to the loneliness of the individual mind. The auditory signifiers backing the emotive hymn texts encouraged the singer to get lost, as it were, in the experience of sweetly joining, to be ecstatic, in the sense of being outside the self.

The stakes of Charles Wesley's emotional immediacy, which drew on the innovations of Isaac Watts, become clearer in close comparison. Wesley's hymns follow Watts's footsteps beyond the boundaries of Psalmody and biblical paraphrase to break open the protections of an observer-singer and demand a present, experimental self whose ego boundaries are compromised. The grammatical hallmark of this strategy is the prepositional phrase "for me," which runs throughout the hymns, keeping the singer the object of God's action. The singer of these hymns, suspended between the "I" and the "me," must balance the individual subject-self hailed into relation to God as a speaking agent, and the individual transformed by the experience of being the object of divine attention, at whom the entire holy drama is directed. The singer-object of these hymns competes with the God-object of praise in the more familiar "to thee" of liturgy and holy song. The grammatical situation of the singer also makes the "thou" of the hymns, directed nominally at God or Christ, the "vocative address" that Davies identifies as characteristic of Wesleyan hymnody, an occasion for destabilizing the "I" by the singer's experiential relation to the divine other of the hymn as well as to fellow singers (68).

Watts's *Hymns and Spiritual Songs* (1707) begins with versions of two biblical Christ hymns, one drawn from the Revelation to St. John and the other from the opening of the gospel of John:

> E're the blue Heav'ns were stretch'd abroad,
> From Everlasting was the Word;
> With God he was; the Word was God
> And must Divinely be ador'd.   (WATTS, HYMNS AND SPIRITUAL SONGS 3)

Watts situates these hymns as Biblical text by running the verse and chapter of the source before the text of each, which underscores his Dissenting biblical orientation and also keeps the hymn itself at a slight distance from the poem or "human hymn" by presenting it as versified scripture. The singer in this case narrates sacred text, which remains relatively stable and distinct from the singer's consciousness. Wesley, though his sources remain biblical, departs further from his original for the sake of drawing the singer into the theological point of the hymn. "Let Earth and Heaven Combine," from *Hymns for the Nativity of Our Lord* (1744) begins with an apocalyptic image of mixed spheres and speaks of "Our God contracted to a Span,/Incomprehensibly made Man" in its first stanza (*Nativity* 7). This compressed account of the Incarnation emphasized the divine within the human in the figure of Jesus, as does Watt's better-known line, "Veiled in flesh the Godhead see" from "Hark, the Herald Angels Sing." As Watts draws on Dryden, who had asked, rhetorically, "Could He His Godhead veil in flesh and blood" in *The Hind and the Panther*, Wesley underscores the incarnation in language similar to Dryden's Roman Catholic apologetic but with a more populist gesture that extends divine incarnation to humanity.[24] Wesley posits the birth as the event that "make(s) us All divine; / And we the Life of GOD shall know, / For GOD is manifest below." The "we" and "All" of the hymn remind the singers of their corporate experience of their own participation in the divine nature. The last line, which Wesley uses to end both the fourth and fifth stanzas, focuses the hymn on the incarnation as event that situates the singer in the action:

> Made perfect first in Love,
> And sanctified by Grace,
> We shall from Earth remove,
> And see his glorious Face;
> His love shall then be fully shew'd,
> And Man shall all be lost in GOD. (8)

As always, the singer enters the world of the hymn as a confessing Christian in history, while also anticipating revelation, a moment that will dissolve the singer, who, with all humanity, "shall all be lost in GOD." As the final line of "Love Divine," "lost in wonder, love, and praise," the end point of this experience is the loss of self as the singer knows it, figured here in apocalyptic time. Whatever grammatical control over sacred content Watts extended to his singer who normally narrates scripture is stripped away in Wesley's active verse, which situates the singer within its frame of action.

The visual trope in Watts, present most famously in "When I Survey the Wondrous Cross," turns even more distressing in Wesley. Watts pursues his visual emphasis on the crucifixion in hymns like "The New Testament in the Blood of Christ," one of twenty-two hymns designated for communion in Watts's collection of 1707 and among the most lurid in his oeuvre:

> Here we behold his Bowels roll
> As kind as when he dy'd;
> And see the Sorrows of his Soul
> Bleed thro' his wounded Side. (186)

The hymn requires the singer to narrate his or her own present-tense observation of the crucifixion, as part of the hymn's corporate "we." As embodied as the image is, Watts makes the singer a witness to the crucifixion, beholding it at an imaginative distance through the Eucharist. Insofar as Watts ventures the first person in this setting, it is plural, which limits the response of the experiential self to that corporate identity. By contrast, Wesley's translation of a Moravian hymn in the Charleston hymnal of 1737, clearly influenced by Watts's prosody, uses observation and the first person as a means to elicit a corporate response from the collective singers. The "I" becomes plural in the singing of the hymn, and though each singer is accountable to respond as an individual, the performative context posits a collective reaction:

> I see thy Garments roll'd in Blood,
> Thy streaming Head, thy Hands, thy Side:
> All hail, thou suffering, conquering God,
> Now Man shall live; for God hath died.
>
> O kill in me this rebel Sin,
> And triumph o'er my willing Breast:
> Restore thy Image Lord, therein
> And lead me to my Father's Rest.   (C. WESLEY, CHARLESTON COLLECTION 26)

Wesley's hymn singer moves from observation to a direct plea to God for direct, violent action through a series of imperatives; like Donne, the singer begs God to kill, triumph, restore, and lead, providing an "experimental" knowledge of the divine that breaks down the individual self.[25] As we/he becomes I/thy, the singer articulates a relational rather than propositional definition of God that opens the door to ongoing experience of the divine as event, a craving for presence, to paraphrase Gumbrecht, that meaning cannot convey.

The Methodist emphasis on crucifixion in the hymns, which Hogarth parodied as "Chroist Blood Blood Blood," returns to the scandal of the cross in the age of liberalism and confronts its optimism about the individualist logic of rights, grounded in having property in oneself. In the version of "O Love Divine, What Hast Thou Done?" printed in *Select Hymns, with Tunes Annexed*, Wesley addresses the eroticized and suffering Christ as the "Love" of the believer:

> [Christ] Is crucified for me and you,
> to bring us rebels back to God.
> Believe, believe the record true,
> ye all are bought with Jesus' blood.
> Pardon for all flows from his side:
> My Lord, my Love, is crucified!

> Behold him, all ye that pass by,
> the bleeding Prince of life and peace!
> Come, sinners, see your Savior die,
> and say, "Was ever grief like his?"
> Come, feel with me his blood applied:
> My Lord, my Love, is crucified! (109)

The sinner, who inflicts this suffering upon Jesus, is involved in the events. The opening present-tense announcement that Christ is crucified "for me and you" leads the singer to implore other sinners to witness the crucifixion and to "feel with me his blood applied." Contact with the body of Christ will come, ostensibly, in the Eucharist, but the hymn figures it first as an imaginative visual experience that comes through belief. In addition to the disconcerting temporality and immediacy of the hymn, its high Christology and Eucharistic focus is also unsettling. Celebrating the crucifixion, particularly in an age with undeniable cultural investments in civil government and the logic of the forensic subject, meant celebrating the fundamental injustice at the heart of the Christian story. The sinners "that pass by" in "My Lord, my Love" become party to the scandal of the cross, which flies in the face of more Leibnitzian, Lockean, or generally Deist hopes of rationalizing Christianity or translating it into a lucid moral system. It is an image of what Žižek and Milbank have called "the monstrosity of Christ," of God not as law but as unjust victim, a concept the hymns do not avoid. The corporate grammar of the hymn presses the singer to disinvest in individualism and embrace a more corporate experience of self that is tied to redemption as well as the possibility of identity with God. The sight of the wounded Christ leads to agency, as in "Savior, the world's and mine":

> Tis done! my God hath died;
> My Love is crucified!
> Break, this stony heart of mine;
> Pour, mine eyes, a ceaseless flood;
> Feel, my soul, the pangs divine;
> Catch, my heart, the issuing blood! (OXFORD WORKS 7: 113)

The visual image of Christ opens the possibility of feeling and fulfillment as the singer becomes involved in the crucifixion through a series of self-directed imperatives: break, pour, feel, and catch. The brutality of the crucifixion and the logic of sacrificial atonement offend a modern sensibility of enlightened self-interest and possessive individualism, but in the hymns, they arouse sympathy, self-examination, and an enlarging of the self beyond its presumed boundaries through Christian redemption.

The depiction of Christ's suffering draws heavily on Moravian hymns and contributes heavily to the rhetorical intensity of these hymns, as Teresa Berger, J. R. Watson, and Donald Davie have each observed. This intensity peaks in *Hymns on the Lord's Supper* (1745) and pivots on the implication of the singer in the event of crucifixion, a position that dislocates the singer from historical time and launches him into an imaginatively tactile relationship that breaks down the boundaries of the body of Christ and, by extension, the singer's subjective autonomy. Some of the more bloody images come from the Moravian fixation on the wounds of Christ and their infamous delight in the "side-hole" of the lamb. For example:

> See trickling fast the Tears and Blood!
> The Blood that purges all our Stains
> It starts in Rivers from his Veins.
> A Fountain gushes from his Side,
> Open'd that All may enter in,
> That All may feel the Death applied. (HYMNS 1745, 19)

A similar moment in "Conference with the little Lamb concerning the very dear Side-Opening," is both graphic and bathetic in rendering the crucifixion as a site of longing.[26] Donald Davie went so far as to call such Wesleyan hymns "carnal," an appropriate term (67). His physical language, describing bodies that melt, agonize, enlarge, inflame, nurse, sweat, and bleed arrests the hearer and breaks the expectations of listeners and singers. But that language is also working through a theological point in unsettling theatrical and visual language; it is a version of a Eucharistic claim about divine presence as an ongoing event that upsets autonomous notions of subjectivity and triumphalist narratives of the self.

The crucifixion is always already present in the nonlinear temporality of the hymns, texts which continually appeal to the singer for a response:

> Still the Wounds are open wide,
> The Blood doth freely flow,
> As when first his sacred Side
> Receiv'd the deadly Blow:

Still, O GOD, the Blood is warm,
Cover'd with the Blood we are;
Find a Part it doth not arm,
And strike the Sinner there!   (LORD'S SUPPER 103–4)

The blood is both a metaphor for forgiveness and an embodied sign that demands a somatic response from the singer, who experiences its warmth and is "cover'd" in it. The Eucharistic theology of the hymn uses the notion of transubstantiation to emphasize the change in the singer. The temporality of this hymn and others like it uses the vocative and imperative to evoke an immediacy that situates the singer in an embodied, immediate experience of sacred presence. If, as Susan Stewart asserts, "the sound of a poem is heard the way a promise is heard," then these hymns are making promises to do something more than ordinary poems, songs, or even psalms (Stewart 104). The singer's plea to be made vulnerable, to have something done to her, partakes of an operatic sensibility that aestheticisizes passivity, though that singer speaks from a position of authority that commands God to find and strike her. The singer gets to experience both (gendered) halves of this equation as a performing worshipper, in a song about the desire to be internally overcome that addresses God in the imperative. The construction is typical of Methodist hymns; in "Holy Lamb who thee receive," the singer exclaims "Jesu, see my panting breast! / See I pant in thee to rest!"[27] The believer is in a visually mutual relationship; he/she sees the "light" and the "Lamb" and is in turn seen by Jesus. The mutuality of experience makes public a speech act that was once reserved for private devotional poetry: the plea to God to erupt into history through the believer, who is both agent in the demand and object of its action.

The critical commonplace about the personal lyric waning in mid-eighteenth-century Britain, like the critical commonplace about the privatization of religious experience, must be weighed against the intimacy of Methodist hymns destined for public performance. Methodist hymns pulled "closet devotions" into a theatrically public space. Devotees sang texts that played with the gendered positions of sacred romance, harmonizing them to theatrical tunes and weaving together the emerging ideologies of modern masculinity and femininity. The use of congregational hymns could not have caught fire as quickly as it did without the infrastructure of Anglican devotional cells, Dissenting congregations, and private worship practices among Anglicans to subtend its success. But it also would not have enjoyed the frisson of being a new form and endured the scorn of so many bishops and satirists if it had not indeed been an unorthodox and groundbreaking practice. The model of gender-mobile, porous subjectivity that is marked by the corporate I/me/my of the Methodist hymn drew on the traditions of Christian mysticism and packed its psychological punch through a sonic mélange of theater, folk song, cathedral, psalm, and opera that defamiliarized old Christian tropes through unexpected musical textures. The Wesleyan plunge into sacramental language, through Herbert, Donne, and Crashaw as well as their borrowings from Milton, Pope, and Addison, makes the narrative of Christianity freshly strange, even perverse. Their eventual reach into the Anglican service of the nineteenth century suggests the appeal of these pieces called "extravagant and unmeaning rhapsodies" by their enemies but considered by George Eliot in *Adam Bede* to be a democratic means for ordinary people to express deep emotion.[28] Eliot's qualified compliment situates Methodism as the language of the underclass and as an expression of something primitive in contrast to an unforgiving modernity. Yet Methodism's self, which does not satisfy the demand for autonomy and agency that liberalism articulates as a requirement of modern consciousness, is part of the eighteenth-century landscape and on display in these popular hymns, in which the singer seems glad to purchase ecstatic, divine presence at the price of an autonomous "I."

CHAPTER SIX

A Usable Past

Reconciliation in *Humphry Clinker* and *The Spiritual Quixote*

O n Friday, October 10, 1766, Horace Walpole wrote to his friend Chute the following description of the Countess of Huntingdon's new Methodist Chapel at Bath:

> The chapel is very neat, with true Gothic windows (yet I am not converted); but I was glad to see that luxury is creeping in upon them before persecution: they have very neat mahogany stands for branches [candelabra], and brackets of the same in taste. At the upper end is a broad haut-pas of four steps, advancing in the middle; at each end of the broadest part are two of *my* eagles with red cushions for the parson and clerk. (*CORRESPONDENCE* 35: 118)

After heaping scorn on the movement so often in his correspondence, Walpole's suggestion that the Methodists are becoming more like midcentury "cultured" Britons, subject to luxury and capable of taste, almost sounds like peacemaking. His observations about the Bath chapel are echoed in *The Historical and Local New Bath Guide*, which announced the chapel displayed "taste and elegance in the interior part."[1] Like his own Strawberry Hill, the Bath chapel is an architectural testament to changing constructions of the past for use within the cultural present. The Calvinist Methodists who built the Bath chapel wanted to recuperate the medieval Gothic style of the cathedral and to redeploy it as, among other things, a sign of historical authenticity from within a self-conscious experience of being modern. Its gothic windows, candelabra, and cushions indicate the chapel's affinity for Anglo-Catholic space over what Paulson calls the "barnlike structures" of Protestant architecture, "monochrome with only clean white walls and sober woodwork," the style that spreads through London after the Great Fire (*Hogarth's Harlot* 13). Walpole finds much to admire in Lady Huntingdon's chapel on Harlequin Row, much he identifies as versions of his own furnishings ("*my* eagles"), so much, in fact, that he jokes parenthetically about not being converted.

In *A Useable Past*, William Bouwsma observes that "Religious symbolism and practice seem to ... concentrate and integrate singularly well what a society is finally 'about'" (Bouwsma 2). Walpole's reading of the Bath chapel suggests that Methodism is participating productively in modern British society through symbols and architectural choices that negotiate their relationship with British religious history as one of continuity. Methodism's greatest appeal was still among the working classes, but it had also managed to speak to figures as diverse as the Countess of Huntingdon, Samuel Johnson, Benjamin Franklin, Sir John Phillips, David Garrick, and Lord Bolingbroke, without necessarily converting them. Methodism, even by Walpole's reluctant admission, had become a part of what modern Britain was about. George Whitefield died in 1771, curtailing the most vicious strains of anti-Methodist writing and leaving the future of Methodism in the domain of John Wesley's managerial genius. The free-floating *idea* of Methodism, that taunt for what was emotionally excessive and psychologically troubling in British religious practice, was beginning to settle into denominationalism. John Wesley, whose 1758 *Reasons Against a Separation from the Church of England* had made a spiritual and practical plea for continuing to regard Methodism as a movement within the Church of England, was reinvited to preach in some Anglican pulpits in the 1770s and was surprised at the number of offers that came his way. After preaching at All Hallows Church in London, he remarked in his journal "How is this? Do I 'yet please men'? Is the offence of the cross ceased? It seems, after being scandalous near fifty years, I am at length growing into an honourable man!" (*Abingdon Works* 23: 41). The establishment of institutional structures also formalized a move from a revival movement within the Anglican church to denominational identity. The Countess of Huntingdon registered her sixty-seven chapels as dissenting places of worship under the Toleration Act, and they became part of her "Connexion" in 1781. This decision, along with the 1784 Deed of Declaration, with which Wesley established a governing infrastructure for the movement after his death, formalized Methodism as a denomination, which in some ways managed the threat it posed to national religious identity by finally separating it out from the Church of England.[2] The softer comic representations of the 1770s reflect on Methodism's appeal across classes and communities within Britain, and in so doing begin to redeem Methodism as a mediating force in British society.

The Expedition of Humphry Clinker (1771) and *The Spiritual Quixote, or The Summer's Ramble of Geoffry Wildgoose* (1773) signal a shift in tone from earlier, more satiric representations of Methodism by their laughable but usable "heart religion." Even though the novels restore traditional class hierarchy, they reflect appreciatively on Methodism's potential to forge connections between people. Similarly, Henry Brooke's Shandian *The Fool of Quality* (1765–1770), with its evangelical vignettes of the life of the Clements and Mr. Fenton's Christian Rousseauian pedagogical plan for his nephew, sought to reconcile a Methodist-style evangelicalism to public morality, charity, and civic sociability. Christopher Anstey continues to make some sport out of Methodists as part of the amusements of Bath, along with "bathing, tumblers, auctions, apes, or players, New fiddlers, Methodists, or dancing bears," but he also suggests they have become one divertissement among many that might tempt "the nymph abroad"; their threat level is now on par with that of apes and auctions.[3] *Clinker* and *Wildgoose* take up the question of Methodism's cultural place in modern Britain in much greater detail through the specific adventures of the title characters. In these novels, Methodism provides an affective supplement to a more materialist account of mind that isolated individual consciousness, as well as a response to the economic materialism of early capitalism. Self-interest or "self-love," in spite of Pope's optimism about its implicit social function, seemed only to be widening the gap between the poor and the rich. These differences were on display in the urban centers of London and Bath, which Matt Bramble calls centers of dissipation and infection, terms he otherwise uses for bodily ailments. Similarly, the transformation of rural life in the modern British capitalist economy, represented in *The Vicar of Wakefield* and *The Village*, was eroding conventional networks of care and economic interdependence without replacing them in kind. Methodist social activism, particularly in the construction of orphanages, poor houses, and charity schools, was a response to the failing system of parish care in an age of urbanization and greater geographic mobility. The Kingswood School for the poor, Whitefield's orphanage in Georgia, The Stranger's Friend Society (which aided the poor who were not attached to a parish), and hundreds of other charitable projects provided relief in London, the countryside, and the colonies to those who would otherwise have been without parish resources (Heitzenrater 122–28, 209). The prison, feeding, and educational commitments of the original Oxford Methodists of the 1730s had, by 1770, developed a national profile and institutional structures for the movement's attempts to intervene in culture of early British capitalism. Methodism in the 1770s was beginning to look more like a social remedy than a social disease.

Smollett and Graves reflect on this shifting perception, which renegotiates Methodism's relationship to British history. The Hudibrastic architecture of the novels provides a comic return to the historical *agon* of the political Puritan revolution but sublimates it into the domestic question of how to bring the British population into a shared sense of community as economic expansion, urbanization, and mobility eroded traditional parish ties. The novels trace an itinerant's path around Great Britain, walking through the topographical and the ideological domains of the nation and synthesizing them through conversation, friendship, and romantic love, all of which can be fostered by Methodism. Instead of a political or psychological threat to the modern British self, here we glimpse a Methodism that mends frayed communities without demanding their conversion. That Methodism, in thirty years of rapid growth, had not become a political movement like old Dissent made it possible for Smollett and Graves to represent Methodism as an affective supplement to British identity, one capable of mediating the nation's relationship to its own religious and political history. In these novels, Methodists unwittingly draw together far-flung communities and help to mend breaches between characters. Like Clinker's literally rent breeches, they show the seams of conflicts over the meaning of religion in the later eighteenth century, but they also provide a sociable patch that unites communities around the somatic, affective values that Methodism shared with the discourse of sensibility. Smollett and Graves may consider Methodism an inferior expression of taste, literacy, or feeling, but they see it as a usable supplement to modern British identity that fosters relationships in a rapidly changing nation.

Smollett and Graves manage the quixotism of Humphry Clinker and Geoffry Wildgoose through the aesthetic confidence of the comic novels themselves. Clinker and Wildgoose still tend to be moved too easily and to read literally. But their aesthetic failures serve as sources of comic pleasure; these novels can accommodate Methodist characters without engaging in the paranoid hostility of Fielding or Foote. The episodic structure of these novels provides the implicit assurance that history goes on, and that even sensational models of the self are more stable than radically malleable. Even though they hold Clinker and Wildgoose at a comic distance, they acknowledge their palliative if not constructive function in modern British society, which can make use of their excesses of enthusiasm. Matt Bramble affirms that his journey with Clinker, about which he has offered so many complaints, has helped to "unclog the wheels of life" (*Clinker* 311), and the narrator of *The Spiritual Quixote* confidently affirms at the close of Wildgoose's Methodist escapades that "Providence frequently makes use of our passions, our errors, and even our youthful follies, to promote our welfare, and conduct us to happiness" (473). Regardless of their particular beliefs, Clinker and Wildgoose are men of feeling who create community. The Bramble family's embrace of Clinker eventually cements their own relations in the discovery that Clinker not only makes relationships but *is* a relation. Wildgoose returns to his native village wiser, chastened, yet still able to bring the lessons of Methodist fervor to bear on community life, replicating their charity and piety in subdued, polite tones. In these novels, it seems possible that Methodists themselves might become pious without enthusiasm.

Coming Around: Smollett and Methodism

It is a critical commonplace held by Sekora, Thorson, Lyles, and others that Smollett extended his career-long assault on Methodism from *Launcelot Greaves* in his most famous novel, *Humphry Clinker*, but Smollett's relationship to Methodism is a more complex affair than this narrative suggests.[4] Early in his career, and in keeping with the more hostile zeitgeist of the 1760s, he positioned Methodism as part of an irrational past from which Great Britain was emerging:

> Imposture and fanaticism still hung upon the skirts of religion. Weak minds were seduced by the delusions of a superstition stiled Methodism, raised upon the affection of superior sanctity, and maintained by pretensions of divine illumination. Many thousands in the lower ranks of life were infected with this species of enthusiasm, by the unwearied endeavours of a few obscure preachers; such as Wh———, and the two W———s, who propagated their doctrines to the most remote corners of the British dominions, and found means to lay the whole kingdom under contribution. (SMOLLETT, *HISTORY* 4: 121–22)

Smollett situates Methodism in his history as a remnant of a past in an era of the "progress of reason" under the clerical leadership of Tillotson, Sherlock, Hoadley, Conybeare, and Warburton (121). In his version of the secularization thesis, Smollett pits the modernity of the 1760s against the cultural primitivity of Methodism which, along with Hutchinsonians (a loose affiliation of Trinitarian Christians skeptical about modern science) and Moravians, "infects" the lower classes and thrives in "remote" parts of the country. Smollett lays anti-Newtonianism at the feet of Hutchinson's followers and accuses the Moravians of sensualism, impurity, and "gross incentives to the work of propagation" (123), leaving Methodism as the more general case of religious delusion, an annoying holdover rather than a live threat. Wesley, after reading some of Smollett's history, wrote in his journal in July of 1770 that "Poor Dr. Smollett! . . . knows nothing about" Methodism, and later chastised him for his impious "manner of speaking against witchcraft" which must be "extremely offensive to every sensible man who cannot give up his Bible (*Abingdon Works* 22: 238).[5] Smollett sees his era as modern in the main, defined against Methodism insofar as he regards it as a form of superstition that seduces "weak minds" and the "lower ranks," thus perpetuating a cognitive-primitive past within the present. Wesley's point that Smollett "knows nothing" about Methodism gestures to another vision of Methodism as progressively oriented around social justice and its own version of the enlightenment project of improvement in its educational and literacy efforts.

Smollett continued to pick at Methodists in his early novels and periodical publications along the lines of conventional anti-Methodist satire, labeling them hypocrites and maniacs. He began the *Critical Review* around the same time that Whitefield's London Tabernacle opened and he referred to Whitefield as "the grimy apostle of Tottenham-Court" (*The Critical Review*, no. 11, January 1761). In his 1760–61 *Launcelot Greaves*, the quixotic Greaves finds himself in a madhouse and is able to identify it as such when he hears a Methodist inmate denouncing good works:

> He that thinks to be saved by works is in a state of utter reprobation—I myself was a prophane weaver, and trusted to the rottenness of works— . . . but now I have got a glimpse of the new light—I feel the operations of grace—I am of the new birth— I abhor good works—I detest all working but the working of the spirit.
>
> (*LAUNCELOT GREAVES* 176)

The lunatic, whose dashes and pauses mimic the "ejaculatory" style of a Methodist preacher, is also a weaver, and like Humphry Clinker the farrier or the cobbler Jeremiah Tugwell of *The Spiritual Quixote*, a barely literate working-class figure. The association of Methodism with the laboring class here is another dig at Methodists who leave their employment to go hear or follow Methodist preachers and thus "detest all working." This weaver is an impressionable self so open to transformation through the somatic experience of the Methodist conversion that he fails to meet the standard of individualism on which modern liberal society depends. His failure, which is here rendered as insanity, helps shore up the hegemony of a middle class whose feelings should not interfere with work.

The more generalized clerical satire in his Lucretian *The Adventures of an Atom* and *Roderick Random* bounces between deism and atheism. In *The Adventures of an Atom*, a political roman à clef satire of the British government set in Japan, which appeared immediately prior to *Clinker*, Smollett's inanimate narrator, the conscious atom who circulates "without a fixed principle of action," observes the amoral violence and motion of an entirely material world that precludes ethical speculation or remedy.[6] Religion of all description falls under the satiric lash, including politics as religion in the worship of the "White Horse," or house of Hanover. Yet Smollett is also cynical about human nature and the possibility of a secular ethical society; like his Lucretian mode in *Count Ferdinand* and *Launcelot Greaves*, *Adventures of an Atom* holds the notion of character development hostage to material, protonaturalistic determinism. The overall effect pushes us away, to watch the chaos of history from a safe distance as spectators. Smollett himself took a similar position of detached fatalism in a 1761 letter to David Garrick: "We are all the playthings of fortune, and that it depends upon something as insignificant and precarious as the tossing up of a halfpenny whether a man rises to affluence and honors, or continues to his dying day struggling with the difficulties and disgraces of life" (Smollett, *Letters* 98).

But Smollett's vision of history was not without lingering hopes of some meaningful form of community based on sympathy. Smollett saw his own moment as an age of degeneracy, marked by "luxury and riot" which alienates people from one another and makes then less capable of sympathy (Smollett, *Complete History* 4: 225). In an extreme example of the historical stakes of sympathetic feeling, Smollett wrote in graphic detail about the death of French regicide Robert Damiens, who remained conscious during his torture with boiling oil, melted lead, and dismemberment. Smollett calls the execution "shameful to humanity" and a violation of sympathetic principles that ought to trump national self-interest with their greater moral purchase. He extends his sympathy with bodies in pain across the human/animal boundary, describing animal vivisection and asking "what benefit has mankind reaped from all this cruelty and torture inflicted on our fellow creatures?" (*Critical Review* 1 (1756): 414).[7] These are moments where Smollett "brings home to our own breast," as Adam Smith put it in *Theory of Moral Sentiments*, making the case for feeling for the other in terms that have implications for the community. Without the possibility of some reforming historical change, Smollett's sympathetic impulse is undercut by the lack of redemptive vision.

Wesley also encouraged the sympathies of his readers and was similarly willing to judge what he saw as the abuses of the social and economic order. Wesley challenged his readers in *Thoughts Upon Slavery* to translate their affective responses into conscious consumer action in the cause of abolition:

> *The blood of thy brother* (for, whether thou wilt believe it or no, such is he in the sign of Him that made him) *crieth against thee from the earth*, from the ship, and from the waters. . . . Thy hands, thy bed, thy furniture, thy house, thy lands are at present stained with blood."
> (THOUGHTS UPON SLAVERY 27)

Wesley asks the sympathetic reader to feel, hear, and see that the other is present, already among "us" through the corrupted economy we share, a system of exchanges similar to the trope of the Bath waters, which symbolizes the corruptions of luxury in its very particles. Wesley grounded his position in the abolition debate of the 1770s in his Arminian belief in universal salvation, which makes all people "brothers" and thus enlarges the domain of human relatedness. Smollett's reflections on torture and animal cruelty, like Wesley's abolitionism as well as his vegetarianism, enlarge codes of sympathy to include a cultural responsibility to feel for the other.[8] What Smollett believes he can do as a writer through the stimulation of sympathetic feeling is limited by the chaos of history in his earlier work, fictional and historical, but in *Clinker*, Smollett shows chaos lurching toward community.

Reading *Humphry Clinker* as the successor in the train of Smollett's representations of Methodists and in the context of his critique of luxury and alienation foregrounds its salvific if messy vision of community, echoed in the novel's epistolarity and the cavalcade of voices that describe the novel's events. The novel mocks the luxury and excesses of Bath but maintains an optimism about modern British community at the structural level, which unites the fragmented epistolary perspectives into a more sympathetic community. The stories of Matt, Jery, Lydia, Tabby, and Win are narratively intertwined, and their perspectives softened and mediated by their interactions. They become, however imperfectly, a family of love. The vigorously comic, Rabelasian landscape of the novel, full of bodies, fluids, and scatological jokes, provides the conditions for communal sympathy. The embodied world of *Clinker*, much like *Tristram Shandy*, engages with discourses of sympathy from both British and Scottish philosophical schools as Gottlieb, Ghoshal-Wallace, and Wetmore have variously argued.[9] The capacity to "bring home" another's feelings and circumstances, to identify somatically (although imperfectly) with the other is the source of affective community for Hume, and an idea appropriated by both Smollett and Wesley (Gottlieb 96). Though Wesley objected to the Hutchesonian version of the Scottish Enlightenment school of sympathy in his sermon "On Conscience," on the grounds that his formulation of "public senses" excluded God, the analogy between Methodist "heart religion" and discourses of sympathy had become plain by the 1770s.

Matt Bramble experiences a secularized warming of the heart at the sight of another's suffering or need when he gives twenty pounds sterling to the ensign's widow at Hot Wells. Matt, whom Jery describes as like "a man without a skin," has a body that is infamously available to the reader through Matt's hypochondriac obsession with his body's own flows and fluids, which perversely destabilize its boundaries and move him beyond the limits of self. He warns Clinker about letting his religious enthusiasm mislead him "till you are plunged into religious frenzy," but that threat parallels the extremes of sensibility to which Matt is also prone. The result of his confrontation with Clinker is another of Matt's mild fits of enthusiasm; when Clinker declares his loyalty, Matt smiles and promises to take care of him. These affective ties, which turn out to be more intimate than either character could have realized, are only revealed through communication that risks the boundary of the self for the sake of the other. Though Matt Bramble must overcome his prejudice about Methodism as an affront to his traditional views on both religion and class order, he acknowledges the effects of Methodism as socially useful. Matt's secular, sociable sympathy and Clinker's "primitive Christianity" work well together as components of a dialogic cure for the chaos, luxury, and alienation of modern life.

The Social Mix of Bath

Smollett looked to Christopher Anstey's *The New Bath Guide*, a rougher satire of religion as it intersected with the tourist culture of Bath, for the templates of his "family of originals" in *Humphry Clinker*. Martin Day goes so far as to call *Humphry Clinker* "a prose rendering" of Anstey's guide; it includes a traveling family and even a character named Tabby who needs to be dosed at Bath (122). *The New Bath Guide: Or, Memoirs of the B-r-d Family* (after 1776, changed to *the B-n-r-d Family*) was reprinted regularly from its 1762 debut until the early nineteenth century. This verse satire was itself inspired by *The New Bath Guide, or Useful Pocket-Companion*, an actual guidebook to the city and its inhabitants, with tables for calculating postage, wages, and the phases of the moon. As Peter Borsay has argued, Bath becomes some of the most significant symbolic territory in the eighteenth-century cultural imagination.[10] Both Anstey and Smollett read Bath as a study in a nation newly awash in luxury goods, including the resources for leisure and tourism, which bring with them a spiritual crisis of meaning. The cures that their characters seek are more than material. In the case of Bath, tourism returned new money to an ancient, even primitive site, the Roman Baths, themselves an effort to "modernize" Celtic, primitive western Britain in the first century AD. The secular, commercial pleasures of Bath were built, quite literally, on a site layered with ancient religions, which seem to animate the "primitive" spirituality that emerges as a cultural force in eighteenth-century Bath.

The New Bath Guide uses ribald comic verse to tell the story of the B-n-r-d family (identified as the "Blunderhead" family in Horace Walpole's personal copy) who come to Bath in search of cures for various vague ailments as well as for entertainment. Beyond the general curiosity about domestic tourism in Anstey's poem, religion is one of the main human foibles on display in its portrait of Bath's tourist culture. Beginning with the fifth edition in 1767, Anstey's *The New Bath Guide* included an illustration of Folly in a cap and bells leading several visitors through a colonnade with strings attached to their noses. One of the party, Miss Prudence, carries a hymnbook, and a ministerial figure, identified alternately as a Moravian minister known as "Rabbi Nicodemus" or a generic Methodist minister, follows the crowd with a hand raised in exclamation.[11] Subsequent editions replaced this image with an engraving entitled "Distemper, Pleasure, Methodism, and Fashion dancing round the bust of Bladud, founder of Bath." The inclusion of Methodism by name reflects the prominence of the

"Distemper, Pleasure, Methodism, and Fashion Dancing around the Bust of Bladud, Founder of Bath," *New Bath Guide*, 1794. © The British Library Board

movement in the Bath–Bristol corridor and its associations with the resort town. In this image, Methodism is represented by one of the dancing tourists celebrating England's pagan past. He is visually equivalent to the other humorous "dancers": distemper, pleasure, and fashion. The illustration, with its Hogarthian textures and heraldry, including a cornucopia, an asses head, and a cupid, looks on the social revelry and mixing of Bath with critical detachment, turning it into a neoclassical parody of primitive worship. According to Geoffry of Monmouth, Bladud, the Athenian-educated father of King Lear, founded Bath after being exiled from court for leprosy around 860 BC.[12] He found a cure for his leprosy in the Bath waters. In the illustration, his bust returns in Augustan style to situate Bath in a classical past, which modern Britons consume as entertainment. Both the "Nicodemus" and the "Bladud" images use Methodism to mock the modern crazes of Bath and, at the same time, to display the modern consumer's cultural mastery of Britain's past as a commodity. In this world, Methodism's primitive Christianity, an echo of the mystical pagan history of the city, is just one consumer choice among many in the buffet of Bath's cures.

Smollett draws much from Anstey: the character of Tabby (in Anstey's version, she is the maid); the use of different voices to narrate the trip; references to individuals as Hogarth sketches (in *Humphry Clinker*, Matt suggests that Hogarth should draw Tabby and Lydia, 135); complaints about adulterated wine and food; and the tension between medical and religious cures. Anstey's satire of Moravians and Methodists has a sharp if conventional sexual edge to it. Prudence seeks a religious "cure" for her discomfort, which Anstey parodies as sexual desire for Nicodemus, who is also known suggestively as Roger:

> Now it hapens in this very House is a Lodger,
> Whose Name's NICODEMUS, but some call him ROGER;
> And ROGER's so good as my Sister to bump
> On a Pillion, as soon as she comes from the Pump;
> He's a pious good man, and an excellent Scholar,
> And I think it is certain no Harm can befall her;
> For ROGER is constantly saying his Pray'rs,
> And singing of spiritual Hymns on the Stairs. (15)

The motives of Roger's piety are on trial as he volunteers "to go out a riding with Prudence behind" and to teach her "Night and Day." He eventually inspires Prudence to have an erotic spiritual encounter:

> For I dream'd an Apparition
>   Came, like ROGER, from Above
> Saying, by Divine Commission
>   I must fill you full of Love.
> Just with ROGER's Head of Hair on,
>   ROGER's Mouth, and pious Smile;
> Sweet, methinks, as Beard of AARON
>   Dropping down with holy Oil.
> I began to fall a kicking,
>   Panted, struggl'd, strove in vain;
> When the Spirit whipt so quick in,
>   I was cur'd of all my Pain.
> First I thought it was the Night-Mare
>   Lay so heavy on my Breast;
> But I found new Joy and Light there,
>   When with Heav'nly Love possest.
> Come again then, Apparition,
>   Finish what thou hast begun;
> ROGER, stay, Thou Soul's Physician,
>   I with thee my Race will run.
> Faith her Chariot has appointed
>   Now we're stretching for the Goal;
> All the Wheels with Grace anointed,
>   Up to Heav'n to drive my Soul. (128–29)

Prudence is an imprudently bad reader who cannot separate spiritual from material feeling, dream from reality. The comic tetrameter signals to the reader that the joke is on Prudence, who misrecognizes somatic, sexual experience as a spiritual encounter. In the 1762 edition, the poem is followed by this short note: "The Editor, for many Reasons, begs to be excused giving the Public the Sequel of this young Lady's Letter; but if the Reader will please to look into the Bishop of *Exeter's* Book, entitled, *The Enthusiasm of Methodists and Papists Compared*, he will find many Instances (particularly of young People) who have been elected in the Manner above" (107). Bishop Lavington derisively claimed that the Moravian and Methodist emphasis on Jesus as a man reduces Christ to "a hearty Carpenter in Heaven." His disgust that the "final Reward" of the believer is "to sleep in the Arms of Jesus Christ, as a *Man*, in his *human* Nature" is laced with psychosexual panic about Methodism's "love divine" and its fluid rhetorics of passion and somatic experience (Lavington, *Moravians* 30). The problem is at once sexual and theological. On the one hand, Lavington's concern about sleeping in the arms of Christ destabilized gender identity for the heterosexual male believer by eroticizing the body of Christ. Methodist satire, including *The Methodists*, Reed's *The Register Office*, and Foote's *The Minor* managed the issue by focusing their attention primarily on female enthusiasts; Clinker's abject, subordinate pose imports some of the gender trouble of the ravished Methodist believer to Smollett's novel. But Lavington also scoffs at the Methodist use of the incarnate Jesus, implying that the *"human* Nature" of Christ is somehow in itself ridiculous. Anstey's citation of Lavington's rant against the Methodists aligns *The New Bath Guide* with a Juvenalian school of anti-Methodist writing as well as with a Latitudinarian theological anxiety about Christian embodiment, which Methodism stoked.

By comparison, the moments of eroticized spiritual language in *Humphry Clinker* are mild. Smollett picks up the joke on "Roger" when Tabitha complains to Dr. Lewis that Roger at Bramble Hall is taking advantage of her dairy: "Roger gets this, and Roger gets that; but I'd have you know, I won't be rogered at this rate by any ragmatical fellow in the kingdom" (73). However shallow her interest in Methodism may be, this Tabby is only being "rogered" in a fiscal sense. The broad joke here targets Tabby's greed, which is in need of reformation, and not her blossoming interest in Methodism. Other characters are more aware of managing the difference between spiritual and sexual feeling and thus avoiding the comic (or pornographic) collapse of the two terms. Lydia differentiates between "that nameless charm which captivates and controuls the inchanted spirit," romantic/erotic love, and "the inward motions, those operations of grace" that others claim to experience at the Tabernacle (127–28). Jery sees that Tabby is trying to convert Mr. Barton to Methodism to establish "a connexion of souls that might be easily improved into a matrimonial union," but this is a transference of spiritual to sexual feeling that both Jery and Tabby comprehend, unlike Prudence, who fails to sort the categories at all.

The character who redeems Methodism in the novel is the unimpeachably pure Clinker. Smollett first establishes Clinker's Methodism by having him preach to the other footmen at St. James, where Matt, with Barton as guide, has taken Jery to observe "all the great men in the kingdom" (91). Instead of civic order, Jery and Matt see a chaotic parade of political disorder and accidental privilege. As they turn from this scene of politics, they literally walk into the congregation that Humphry has assembled, an embodied alternative to this disappointing political version of the public sphere. Clinker, like Sterne's Trim, with "his hat in one hand and a paper in the other, in the act of holding forth to the people," desists immediately when he sees Matt and runs to get the carriage. Clinker submits his religious identity to a premodern class hierarchy, which, paradoxically, allows him to continue a critique of social inequality in Methodist terms. When pressed about his preaching, Clinker tells Matt he hopes to cure working people of swearing by making them understand his disinterestedness. "Make them first sensible that you have nothing in view but their good, then they will listen with patience" (95). When Matt objects that oratory from an undereducated laborer like himself will "leave little or nothing . . . to distinguish their conversation from their betters," Clinker replies that "at the day of judgment, there will be no distinction of persons" (95). Within the temporality of the novel, Humphry's evangelical prophesy comes true; the "distinction of persons" that grounds his own servitude turns into a comic version of the evangelical trope of family when he is revealed as Matt's son. Clinker's potential for radicalism, implicit in his squarely Wesleyan Methodist message, is undercut by traditional obedience, loyalty, and piety, values that provide cover for Clinker's implicitly political statement.

Clinker's appeal to women, his ability to ingratiate himself with Tabby, the revelation of his body in the infamous breeches-splitting scene, and his charismatic preaching, which Matt suggests he can use "to impose on silly women . . . who will contribute lavishly for your support," embody him and render him an object of desire, a feminized commodity of sorts.[13] But unlike Mary/George Hamilton, Mrs. Cole, or Mr. Barvile, Clinker's sexuality doesn't threaten to become roguish. Because he submits so fully to a traditional, even feudal notion of social hierarchy, his enthusiasm can be entertaining and useful by infusing old families with new life. He is also cleared from suspicion about his ulterior motives because he is not a writer in the novel. Eponymous but voiceless, he is artlessly present as a function of his actions and the impressions he makes on others. Those impressions become the fabric of affection that unites the Bramble clan, making the unaccountable interiority of heart religion both sociable and accountable in its effects.

Matt confronts Clinker's theology as a breach of the principles of reason, which he casts in terms of Clinker's relationship to his master. As Jery reports, Matt reproaches Clinker with being deceived by "the new light of grace," which he calls, a deceitful vapour, glimmering through a crack in your upper story—In a word, Mr. Clinker, I will have no light in my family but what pays the king's taxes, unless it be the light of reason, which you don't pretend to follow." "Ah, sir! (cried Humphry) the light of reason, is no more in comparison to the light I mean, than a farthing candle to the sun at noon."

"Very true (said uncle) the one will serve to shew you your way, and the other to dazzle and confound a weak brain—Heark-ye, Clinker, you are either a hypocritical knave, or a wrong-headed enthusiast; and in either case, unfit for my service." (130)

Clinker's naïve, loyal response to Matt's tirade is to conclude that he must be mad and to submit to Matt's traditional authority by allowing him to define, quite literally, the terms of their interaction. Tabby then chides Clinker for not being willing to stand up for Methodism, allowing Smollett to stage Clinker's submission to Matt's authority. Clinker replies that even though "she [Tabby] and lady Griskin sing psalms and hymns like two cherubims" that he is "bound to love and obey your honor," invoking a serf-like relation to Matt (131). Clinker's abject loyalty stabilizes the Bramble family's relationships into an affective version of traditional patriarchy and, through that order, paradoxically authorizes Clinker as a preacher. Though Matt takes exception to the idea of a servant preaching, he soon makes a kinder evaluation that his Methodism is "simplicity warmed with gratitude" based on the effects of Clinker's beliefs (145). His assurance is underwritten by Clinker's deference to his authority. Lydia goes even further and sees "no harm in hearing a pious discourse, even if it came from a footman." Jery follows suit in volume 3; he dismisses Lismahago's "sarcastic remark" about Clinker's Methodism as hypocritical.

Clinker, as part of the cure Matt seeks, is woven into the medical tropology of the novel, what Paul-Gabriel Boucé has called its "therapeutic function" (209). The novel opens with Matt Bramble's protestation to Dr. Lewis that "The pills are good for nothing—I might as well swallow snow-balls to cool my reins." His reference to the self-dosing culture of eighteenth-century popular medicine is exemplified in the phrase "Every Man His Own Doctor," which is included in the titles of at least eight different herbals, medical guides, and recipe books circulating in the eighteenth century, as well as Wesley's tremendously popular *Primitive Physic*.[14] Matt's ambiguous complaint, what Aileen Douglas calls "the apprehensions of disorder," involve a mélange of physical, psychological, and metaphysical symptoms. Clinker is an unstable figure in this democratic medical landscape, a quack who may actually have a useful cure. Matt first mistakes him for a mountebank (Win later says "monkey-bank") and laughs that "he'll make Merry Andrews of us all—" (94). The slip between mountebank and Methodist preacher is both conventional in Methodist satire and a reminder of the more material connections between Methodists and medicine, which echoes in Clinker's basic veterinary training as a farrier's assistant. Clinker proves that he can be an agent of a more material salvation after his second (and urgently necessary) rescue of Matt from drowning when a millhead gives way and a river that the Bramble coach was fording swells to a flood (288). Clinker carries him from the water "as if he had been an infant of six months," helps expel the water from his lungs, then bleeds him "farrier stile," laughing, weeping, and dancing with joy once Matt regains consciousness. The scene unites the material and symbolic economies of the novel and puts Matt and Clinker at their center. It is a baptism that brings Matt into and then through the liquid nightmare of the other that drives his fears with the help of Clinker, who is the remedy and the other that he seeks.

With Methodism mellowing into a more familiar sociability, Smollett was free to recuperate enthusiasm generally as an unsophisticated but functional engine of civic good in both Methodists and Scots, who become the torchbearers of an enthusiasm that channels a native "primitivity" into modern social uses. Jery enjoys Lismahago's "enthusiasm of altercation" in defense of oatmeal, virtuous poverty, and Scotland. Enthusiasm differentiates the "cool" Lowlanders from the "fiery" Highlanders, whose passion "serves only to inflame the zeal of their devotion to strangers, which is truly enthusiastic" (235). Scotland in general becomes a sign of enthusiasm redeemed over time, as the nation "so long reproached with fanaticism and canting, [which] abounds at present with ministers celebrated for their learning, and respectable for their moderation" (216). Matt's reflections on Edinburgh churches, which had "admitted such ornaments as would have incited sedition, even in England, a little more than a century ago," are optimistic about national unity, which depends on the triumph of ecumenism and toleration over orthodoxy (216). The political and religious differences that could still, in 1771, be a cause for paranoia, particularly in the form of Jacobitism, are here reduced to native habits of affect that can fuel national unity within difference. As Evan Gottlieb has argued, Smollett's investments in Scotland's future vis-à-vis the Act of Union lead him to Humean and Smithian theories of sympathy to unite the British population in feeling. Though Gottlieb argues that Smollett is closer to Smith's more cognitively distinct form of sympathy that leaves the "I" autonomous than he is to the near mysticism of Hume's "occult process of the transmission of feelings," a touch of this enthusiasm is good, it seems, for a society (84). Similarly, his sense that the Presbyterian kirk has been reconciled to good sense prefaces his encomiums to the geniuses of Edinburgh: "the two Humes, Roberton, Smith, Wallace, Blair, Ferguson, Wilkie, &c." Matt Bramble is convinced that whatever "fanaticism" might be found in Scotland's past, it was not an inevitable trajectory but a misstep corrected by education, moderation, and good taste. He observes that he would not be surprised ("in a few years") to hear psalms accompanied by organ at the cathedral of Durham (216). His pleasant experience of the churches of the kirk, like Walpole's surprise in the Bath chapel, mends the rift in religious practice between Presbyterians and modern British Anglicans. In this vision, denomination and Dissent are not fixed directions in history or epistemic shifts but parts of an ongoing intranational conversation that remains open.

Smollett maintains an aesthetic high ground over Methodists in his comic mastery of language and, more particularly, literacy, to which Win Jenkins and Tabby Bramble have only incomplete access. They communicate through comically inspired malapropisms that hearken back to a class-coded Methodist "material" form of writing from Mrs. Cole and Shamela, into which the body erupts. Win chides Molly to mind "your vriting and your spilling," complains with Rabelaisian flair of "lying in damp shits at sir Tummas Ballfart's," and urges Molly to "pray without seizing for grease." Methodism is guilty by association in Win's poor English, which capitalizes on what were by then old saws about semiliterate Methodists and their misuse of language in phrases like "the grease of God" and "impfiddles" who mock the "pyebill" (322, 282).

By contrast, Matt's and Jery's letters are peppered with allusions to Horace, Virgil, and Cicero, quotations from Dryden and Shakespeare, and references to continental painting. Jery's and Matt's verbal mastery allows them to play with language and read jokes, providing the self-consciously literary and masculine standard of literacy in the novel in contrast to Win and Tabby's feminized evangelical homonyms and literalisms. Jery's letters take a particular pleasure in playing with cultural references from popular and classical vocabularies (Cropdale looks like "captain Pistol in the play," and Bute is the northern star "Shorn of his beams") as well as his running religious and collegiate joke about his "Jesuitical" education. As a student in Jesus College, Cambridge, Jery is a "Jesuit," a joke that both speaks to his comfortable distance from anti-Catholic anxieties and the ongoing reality of anti-Catholic sentiment that gives the joke its bite. Even more than Matt, who is ashamed of his first name because it "savors of those canting hypocrites, who in Cromwell's time, christened all their children by names taken from scripture" (179), Jery feels free to play with the religious past of England in a series of puns and word games. Notably, Humphry stands outside this linguistic game because he does not write and can thus have no "I." Clinker and Methodism are not a threat to this project, even though they may convert Tabby and Win Jenkins, because Jery's critically self-reflexive "I" tutors the fit reader out of Methodist literalism and into a more playful literacy.

As editors and writers, Smollett and Wesley both were at the center of a public project of taste-making and history, in which they differed in content but not basic approach. Smollett carried out this work in his energetic, often fearless reviewing and writing in *The Critical Review*, *The Briton*, and *The British Magazine*, as well as his *The Present State of All Nations*, multiple *Histories of England*, collections, and translations.[15] For Wesley, collecting and editing was similarly a way of life. Dozens of hymnals, hundreds of sermons, his *Collection of Moral and Sacred Poems*, *The Arminian Magazine*, treatises, tracts, abridgements, his published and private *Journals*, and the monumental *Christian Library* in its fifty volumes are, among other projects, evidence of his drive to catalogue and shape the beliefs and perspectives of the people called Methodists. The unlikely similarities between Wesley and Smollett burst forth in the one moment we see Smollett as a character in the novel. On Sunday, he opens his house to "all unfortunate brothers of the quill" for a lavish dinner on the one day the debtors were free from fear of arrest (117). In this scene, Smollett provides a secular version of the "prison ministry" for which Methodists were famous. His Sunday hospitality includes a "Babel" of accents and voices from shady characters to whom he has supplied money, credit, and his good name, though some of his guests continue to abuse him in print. When Jery presses Dick Ivy for an explanation of Smollett's sacrificial giving, he concludes there is no reasonable motive, that Smollett must be "a most incorrigible fool," and that he did not have the resolution "to resist the importunity of even the most worthless" (125). Smollett's imagined self and his imagined writer's community of hard-luck cases is a vision of remedying the cruelties of the public sphere through his irrational hospitality. Matt expresses the hope that literature and education in general could provide a secular pedagogy of feeling that will transform society, but he is "shocked to find a man have sublime ideas in his head, and nothing but illiberal sentiments in his heart" (100). In practice, it is Humphry and his "simplicity, warmed with a kind of enthusiasm," like the example of Smollett's "foolish" charity, that provides the missing social glue (the role of religion as Durkheim posits it) even though these acts are not in themselves rational. Matt, Wesley, and Smollett (as fictional character and real citizen) each seek some remedy for the heartlessness of the modern economy through compassion connected to material action that print culture can preach but that individuals must choose to practice—feeding, clothing, and paying one another's debts.

History in *Humphry Clinker* literally comes home in the person of Clinker himself, the "love begotten babe" (76) of Bramble's passionate youth. He refers to the "sins of his past," but fathering Clinker turns out to have been his *felix culpa*. Matt's personal history of feeling walks back into his present, answering his unspoken desire for progeny to embody the future for him and redeeming his youthful sexual enthusiasm as the means to community. For Matt Bramble, class in a traditional patriarchal order is already complicated as he has forgone the paternal "Lloyd" for the maternal "Bramble" in order to inherit, a move that also keeps Humphry's mother from finding Matt. But this wrinkle keeps Matt open to the possibility of a broader notion of community in the midst of his conservatism. The revelation of his own fatherhood is a comic echo of the pattern of accidental family in this previously unacquainted "family of originals." Structurally, it upsets the distinctions between self and other, which Matt's passion for propriety tries to control. But it also cements Matt's position as *pater familias*, renewing his family and the promise of community in the mixed logic of the emerging definitions of class.

Clinker's sociable enthusiasm patches fractures in a plot created by multiple refusals of connection: the characters with one another; Matt with his own past; and the future of a public sphere that seems lost amid paroxysms of consumerism, epitomized in the story of the Baynards. Clinker returns Matt's affection to enthusiastic extremes that mirror Matt's own generous outbursts and create a gift economy of ethical obligation, eventually leading to the comic but narratively satisfying discovery of family. Like Wesley's call for universal brotherhood in the context of universal redemption, Matt's experience of sympathy has called up and then annihilated the distinction between self and other, leaving him with a son, a glimpse of paradise (which turns out to be Scotland), and authentic community among the initially alienated Bramble party. Clinker's enthusiasm helps to offset Matt's, providing a useful contrast in degree but not kind that props up and improves Matt's moderate, polite, and secular heart religion. Clinker backs away from his more Whitefieldian street preaching as the novel progresses, but he continues to attend Methodist meetings in Scotland and to evangelize the family, mostly by example. In a parallel movement, Matt observes that Tabby is still a Methodist but that her religious enthusiasm has been tempered by romantic love, the emotion that "is resolved to assert his dominion over all the females of our family." While Matt (and Smollett) cannot brook the extremes of Humean sympathy, just as they cannot embrace Methodism entirely, both find themselves drawn to it as a missing ingredient. Smollett appropriates Methodism's populist gospel in order to relieve the pains of social class and to patch the gaps in his narrative of British history.

Taming the Wild Goose: The Spiritual Quixote's Journey

Richard Graves was, along with Smollett, an inheritor both of Fielding's "comic epic in prose" and its Rabelaisian and Cervantian antecedents. Even more than Smollett, whose resentments of Methodism were matters of temperament and differences of belief, Graves had personal reasons to lash out. Graves was the rector of Claverton, and in 1757 he had the experience of seeing his congregation stolen away from him by a journeyman-shoemaker Methodist who preached and led hymns in a large old house.[16] Graves's own brother also later became a Methodist. But, as Clarence Tracy notes in his preface, *The Spiritual Quixote* is more accurately dubbed a "comic romance," as Graves himself called it, than a satire (xv). One of the several "Quixote" novels of the eighteenth century, it follows the adventures of a young squire, Geoffry Wildgoose, who turns Methodist after reading some old Puritan sermons and sets off to visit the Methodist society at Bristol with his Sancho Panza, Jeremiah Tugwell (Jery), the village cobbler. Armed with this sturdy satiric narrative for addressing delusion, Graves takes on Methodism but produces a gentle, even affectionate portrait of the quixotic Wildgoose, whose adventures both map and unite a nation. The threat of a self transformed or cognitively disordered by Methodism gives way to optimism about the continuity of British culture, which does not just survive but is enriched by Methodism.

Graves reconciles Wildgoose to the past through his personal history of accidental community-making. His name refers both to the idea of an awkward bird and the expression for a pointless search. (Graves may also have had in mind the Celtic trope for the Holy Spirit, as distinct from the more traditional image of the dove.) His early meeting with Miss Townsend, which raises Wildgoose's "compassion" and generates parting sighs from both, returns as a narrative thread that unites the Cervantian story into a socially useful romance. Where Clinker returns as Matt's personal history, Miss Townsend brings Wildgoose into the present of his own life. Wildgoose's evangelistic tour begins with personal pique rather than divine inspiration when he gets his feelings hurt by a joke from the local vicar. Wildgoose is also offended by the vicar's sermon on hypocrisy, which leads him to assume that the vicar knows Wildgoose has been having a dalliance with his mother's maid and preached the sermon to embarrass him. He retreats into a misanthropic funk, during which he reads some sermons written "in the time of Cromwell's usurpation" and a range of nonconformist writing which agreed only "in their inveteracy against the Church of England" (19). His misreading of history is personal rather than political, but it reclaims the interior realm of individual "enthusiasm" for community-building and romantic love. This ancient comic vision of renewal recalculated to fit a late eighteenth-century British context is possible once Wildgoose learns to read his own life as already in harmony with modern Anglican and British identity.

Graves's narrative persona, Christopher Collop, introduces the tale by affirming the value of reading in general and fiction in particular in the education of young people. This comment sets the stage for a reconciliation of religion and literary writing, while acknowledging the historical animus between them. He cites the case of Heliodorus, the third-century Greek novelist who, when faced with the choice of suppressing his novel, *Aethiopica* (*The Ethiopian Story*) or resigning as Bishop, chose to resign. Like Sterne, Graves as a clergyman/novelist has a very personal stake in situating the comic novel as both an aesthetic and a moral project. Collop then mentions the usefulness of *Don Quixote*, *Gil Blas*, *Clarissa* and *Sir Charles Grandison* in the education of young people, but explains,

> The following narrative was intended to expose a species of folly, which has frequently disturbed the tranquility of this nation. The Author indeed by no means considers Ridicule as a proper test of Religious opinions. But they are the practices of their itinerant preachers, rather than the general principles of the people in question, which he thinks exceptionable. And the following work is so far from ridiculing Religion (as perhaps may be objected), that, he flatters himself, it has a direct tendency to prevent Religion becoming ridiculous, by the absurd conduct of such irregular Teachers of it. (GRAVES 3)

The defense is conventional, similar to other defenses of literature's social utility from Dryden, Richardson, Fielding, and Austen. The innovation here is Graves's argument for religious critique that is not Shaftesburian ridicule. Though *The Spiritual Quixote* is full of practical jokes that various parties play on Wildgoose (firecrackers, mud, and more violent attacks), Graves posits a significant difference between skeptical ridicule, which exposes all religious belief to laughter, and his pedagogy of good literacy, which preserves "true" religion from ridicule.

Though he is also comically misguided, Wildgoose, unlike Hudibras, is no revolutionary in a moment of historical crisis. Instead, he is history repeating as farce, re-enacting scenes from Rabelais, Cervantes, and Fielding (including the visit to the Bell Inn) as well as pieces of Methodist history. The responses to his sermons, including offal, dirt, and manure flung at him (though usually hitting Tugwell), are folk-primitive speech acts meant to degrade, like the attacks on actual Methodists at Exeter, Pendleforest, and a number of other locations, where Methodists were dragged through open sewers and doused with blood and offal.[17] But Graves is intent on managing the threat of Methodism without violently rejecting it. Graves gives a short history of religious innovation from the Reformation to the modern "itinerant reformers" who are historically redundant, and who

> have conjured up the powers of darkness in an enlightened age. They are acting in defiance of human laws without any apparent necessity, or any divine commission. They are planting the Gospel in a Christian country: they are combating the shadow of Popery, where the Protestant religion is established; and declaiming against good works, in an age which they usually represent as abounding in every evil work. But there is another species, or rather a slighter degree of Quixotism, which proceeds merely from the mimetic disposition of mankind, and is perhaps more common in the world than is generally imagined; what I mean is, a desire of imitating any great personage, whom we read of in history, in their dress, their manner of life. (40)

The Methodist threat is reduced here to a mistaken relationship to history; they are conjuring things that don't exist "by force of imagination" and so make themselves redundant as they speak of darkness in "an enlightened age" and "plant the Gospel in a Christian country." But Graves acknowledges Wildgoose's attraction to Methodism through the mimetic, theatrical impulse that, he claims, is a function of human nature. He gives that desire and even the pleasures of imitating figures from the past a psychological explanation, a desire to imitate greatness. His implication is that better pedagogy, in the form of advanced literacy to supply both models for imitation (like Sir Charles Grandison, who is written into the novel) and better critical reading strategies, can reinterpret the kind of adventure Wildgoose has, before it becomes a political or historical threat.

Wildgoose falls headlong into the pleasures of imitation, growing his hair long, choosing plain clothes, and setting out on the road as an itinerant. He reads Bunyan and wants to imitate him in his suffering: he "wished for nothing so much as to be persecuted for the sake of his religion" (29). Graves calls all this a "harmless frailty" and "ridiculous affectation," rendering it an aesthetic rather than theological error. Graves can appreciate the way that fantasy can "enlarge our sphere of enjoyment," but the pleasures of reading also assign meaning by "stamping an imaginary value upon the most trifling" objects (40). His examples of this ridiculous affectation are men who chose antiquated fashions in their enthusiasm for the past: a member of the House of Commons who dressed in the early seventeenth-century style of "Vandyke" paintings, a student who insisted on using an oil lamp like Epictetus (and as a consequence ruined one of his tutor's books), and a man who slept in an iron helmet. These anachronistic whimsies are ridiculous ways of participating in the past, but they also betray a touch of what Jameson called "the nostalgia for the present," mobilizing an allegorical vision of the past through which the 1770s can experience itself as modern.[18] Similarly, Methodism mediates the idea of the modern from the position of the present, outlining what modern selves can recuperate from the evangelical past as well as what they must other to define themselves as modern.

In addition to the Puritan past that Wildgoose discovers, Graves, like Smollett, parses "modern" Britain's relationship to both a Gothic and classical past. After attempting to preach at a crowded inn and being doused with water for their efforts, Jery and Wildgoose are saved by the Keeper of Lord Bathurst's Gothic country house, who invites them to stay with him after "having observed that Wildgoose had a watch in his pocket" and thus quietly verified that he is a man of some financial means (112). Like Walpole's Strawberry Hill, "his Lordship" has "built it as old," which a fellow traveler, who turns out to be Miss Townsend's father, worries will "mislead future antiquaries, and introduce great confusion into the English history" (116). Mr. Townsend, a "virtuoso" and historian, wants to be able to read history accurately, to understand what is past and what is present. But his reason is pleasure, not utility; he likes history because it is "agreeable and entertaining. Why has not the imagination or fancy a right to be gratified, as well as the passions or appetites, in a subordinate degree, and under the directions of reason?" (117). His near-paraphrase of Addison on the pleasures of the imagination lays out an imaginative relationship to history that has implicit rather than explicit utility; in gratifying the imagination, history provides an appropriate outlet for the imagination of the individual that both connects the self to the past and separates out the self as modern in relation to that past. Being modern, once again, means being a good critical reader, which is defense enough against the pleasures of a primitive past.

Wildgoose's improper relationship to history is comic rather than threatening, even when he turns iconoclast. During a visit to his old friend Shenstone's home, Wildgoose pulls down the Pan statue and ruins the fountains in his gardens because he fears Shenstone has "set up idols" in his heart and pays "greater regard to Pan and Sylvanus, than to Paul and Silas" (331). Shenstone, an actual poet and legendary gardener, enters the narrative alongside fictional characters like Sir Charles Grandison and provides an aesthetically modern point of view on history that instructs the readers in the virtues of modern critical distance. Graves and Shenstone met as students at Pembroke College, Oxford, in 1732, the year that the term "Methodist" was first used to describe the Oxford Holy Club. Shenstone's appearance in the novel, even without this biographical connection, signifies the triumph of an aesthetic relationship to history over a more agonized historical account of Methodism in the legacy of political upheaval. Graves's novelistic Shenstone, after being initially "provoked" to find his gardens vandalized, responds to Wildgoose's evangelical outburst with laughter. Shenstone masters both classical and Gothic history in his aesthetic choices, having decorated at least one bedroom "in a Gothic taste," and that mastery extends to his own comic detachment in contemplating his guests' reactions to his upset statuary. He leaves it alone, remarking that "the singularity of the adventure would afford his guests as much entertainment, as a greater flash from his cascades, or as viewing his place in more exact order" (331). Wildgoose makes a "scene" that, in the marketplace of scenes and events in the episodic novel, will be judged by the right reader as ridiculous rather than dangerous. His righteous rage has entertainment value, but it can offer no substantive challenge to Shenstone's aesthetic vision.

Graves's novel is full of good readers who model a balance between credulity and skepticism. Mr. Rivers, who became "a sceptic in religion" at university, has since recovered a notion of Christian duty as a gentleman farmer and tenant of Mr. Grandison, Sir Charles Grandison's "near relation" (225, 222). Miss Townsend has read "Dryden's plays, and all the dramatic works of the last age; novels and romances of every kind" as well as "Tillotson's Sermons, the Whole Duty of Man, and the like." Wildgoose objects that Allestree and Tillotson "knew no more of Christianity than Mahomet," missing the point of the nice balance between fictional and devotional reading in her list. Miss Townsend can both engage with a text and separate herself from it, unlike Wildgoose, who takes his place among eighteenth-century Quixotes, among them Fielding's *Don Quixote in England* (1734), Arabella in *The Female Quixote* (1752), Catherine Moreland in *Northanger Abbey* (1817), as well as the multiple translations of Cervantes. The popular Quixote novels and plays of the eighteenth century theatricalize bad reading practices and, in so doing, imply a correct reading methodology that depends on constant cognitive distance, if not skepticism.[19] But the pleasures of the Quixote-figure are in his or her capacity for total involvement with the text and surrender to the everyday, world-making mysticism of believing the words on the page. Lennox's *The Female Quixote* deflates rapidly once Arabella is "cured" of her romantic delusions. Wildgoose, like Don Quixote, indulges the reader in that surrender from a safe critical distance. He lets us see what it must be like to "turn Methodist" but through a comic lens that protects the reader from conversion.

Graves proves generous in his portrait of Wildgoose and his defense of Wesley, who, he is convinced, "had no thoughts, at that time, of separating from the Established Church (the most essential of whose doctrines he has generally adhered to), much less of robbing the community of so many useful mechanics," an assessment that must have partly pleased Wesley (31). Graves's main issue with Methodism, which is related to Smollett's, concerns the potential for social chaos: "if one man may break through the established order of society, another has the same right to do it; which must end at last in utter confusion" (32). Jery Tugwell exemplifies the cultural threat of Methodism as the spread of the "inferior" taste of marginal, working-class readers, which would denigrate the emerging standards of politeness and taste. Jery's preference is for medieval morality plays like "Bel and the Dragon"; books "which dealt in the marvelous and the romantic" like *The Seven Champions of Christendom*; and low humor like *Joe Miller's Jests*, which, Graves later tells us, Whitefield also uses to pepper his sermons (33, 22). Graves's solution is largely literary; both the intertextual form of the novel and the discussions of reading practices within the novel attempt to remedy religious enthusiasm with better literacy. He preaches against the misuse of enthusiasm, "that sort of phrenzy, which we ascribe to enthusiasts in music, poetry, or painting; or in any other art or science; whose imaginations are so entirely possessed by those ideas, as to make them talk and act like madmen, in the sober eye of merely rational people" (20). Wildgoose's enthusiasm by this description is not so much a danger as it is a misapprehension of the proper domain of "phrenzy" in artistic production, a point Foote, Hogarth, and others made in the previous decade; writers, not readers, should be enthusiasts.

Graves saves his ammunition for Whitefield, who was alive while Graves was composing his novel, though dead by the time it appeared. Graves mocks his protestations to humility, reminding the reader that he was "a servitor, and not a fellow" at Oxford. Graves's caricature of Whitefield reflects an older, successful, comfortably bourgeois evangelist whose hypocrisy is mostly a matter of creature comforts and whose fiery zeal has mellowed. Wildgoose meets Whitefield after visiting Whitefield's birthplace, the Bell Inn at Gloucester, which Mrs. Whitefield complains has become a tourist site "pestered with all the trampers that pass the road" since "Squire Fielding, forsooth, in that romancing book of his, pretends that Tom Jones was harboured here" (60). The comic displacement of the inn's fame from Whitefield himself to Fielding's Jones masters Methodism's meaning within the literary sphere. Graves also introduces some critical distance into Wildgoose's actual encounter with Whitefield at Bristol. Whitefield invites Wildgoose to his lodgings, where a rotund Whitefield lolls in a luxurious chair with "a basin of chocolate, and a plate of muffins well buttered before him" (229). His embodied excesses undermine his seriousness of purpose and suggest a Tartuffe-esque figure seeking creature comforts. Furthermore, class, which emerges in the difference between Whitefield's manner and Wildgoose's "more gentleman-like air," is written on their bodies.

Wildgoose's Methodism has a theatrical edge, but it is in his capacity for self-fashioning (amid a lack of self-awareness), and not hypocrisy. Like the Bramble family, whose experience of being a family has, according to McKeon, "something artificial, even theatrical" about it, Wildgoose becomes a Methodist by playing one, which preserves some ironic distance in which the reader and narrator make Wildgoose a source of aesthetic pleasure (*Secret History* 681). Similarly, the crowds at the fairs, markets, and towns where Wildgoose travels seem to encounter him as a sideshow curiosity, a familiar act whose performance they have already seen. Wildgoose, like Clinker, is referred to as a "Merry Andrew," and Wildgoose's preaching throughout the novel is a study in what Lisa Freeman calls antitheatrical theatricalism. He claims that premeditation is not necessary and trusts to "a supernatural power" for his sermons, but he quietly prepares religious similes and metaphors in the style of Whitefield.

Wildgoose's sermons, like Whitefield's, indulge "quaint Hebraisms" and colorful metaphors:

He would tell them, "that God anointed (that is, greased) the wheels of his soul"; and blasphemously makes him act as a surgeon and apothecary, "purging him with hyssop, healing his putrid sores, and binding up his broken bones." Sometimes God is a Grub-street writer; and "writes bitter things against him." (27)

His carnivalesque language blends the literate assurance of a Jery Melford with the humble malapropisms of Win Jenkins into a version of Whitefield's homely and immediate metaphors. He admonishes the runners at a footrace to consider "our spiritual race"; he preaches from the windmill at Bedford not "to be carried about by every *wind* of doctrine"; he urges wrestlers to struggle against the Devil and "to *wrestle* with God in prayer"; and exhorts cudgel-players to *"break the head of that old serpent, the Devil"* (50). His desire to move his audience to an experience of spiritual presence keeps him on the brink of falling into his own literalisms, which he eventually does when a dunking in water "cools" his devotion (112). In adopting "Mr. Whitefield's method of allegorizing," Wildgoose shocks a nursing innkeeper's wife by announcing that he, like her baby, "sweetly leaned on my Savior's bosom; and *sucked out* of the *breasts* of his consolation" as he slept. The woman "a stranger to this pious jargon, stared at him with astonishment" while Tugwell translates Wildgoose's allegorical explanation as "his Worship took a good swinging nap" (114). The comic violence of Wildgoose's verbal style opens language into the material world, but Graves provides readers within the novel who are shocked on our behalf, leaving his own readers free to enjoy the play of Wildgoose's rhetorical immediacy.

Wildgoose eventually cashes in his Quixotic tale (schooled by the Anglican Dr. Greville, much as Charlotte Lennox's Arabella is by the unnamed Johnsonian "Doctor" in *The Female Quixote*) for the romance plot and the life of a gentleman farmer, but not before Graves offers another olive branch to Methodism. Greville, a model clergyman, agrees with Wildgoose that he wishes for "a little more earnest delivery" from the Anglican clergy to rouse "indolent drowsy Christians to a sense of Religion," a plea for reformation of style that echoes Goldsmith's call for an antidote to the "drowsy" politeness of Anglican delivery (1: 480). The underlying attractiveness of infusing Anglican tradition with a touch of Methodist enthusiasm is part of what Paul Goring identifies as the mixture of aversion and desire with which hegemonic eighteenth-century culture encountered Methodist oratory, and a reminder that Methodism eventually proved to be "on, and not beyond, the borders of politeness" (63). Wildgoose, who returns home wiser and lightly chastened by his adventures, brings to his village in the Cotswolds the potential for improvement and "regeneration" through a Methodist past tamed to polite standards.

The Mischief of Methodism (1811) captures the tone of this evolving gentler comic approach to Methodism through its young, bright-eyed Wesleyan minister who boasts that "When I preach at my Chapel you would be astonished to see how full it is. Why do you know the Tradesmen forsake their shops, Lawyers their Clients, and Physicians their sick." His John Bullish fellow clergyman, carbuncled and ample, replies "That's bad! That's bad! I manage things better in my Parish. When I Preach every man minds his own business." The joke here, despite the title, is on the Anglican's disengagement, with the Methodist serving as straight man. Hogarth's *Enthusiasm Delineated* echoes here in the thermometer that hangs on the wall, along with a tendentious set of prints: "A Tale of a Tub," "The Blind Leading the Blind," and "The Four Evangelists," which reiterate the long history of intra-Christian doctrinal dispute in England. But the figures in the foreground, comic "originals" like the characters in *Humphry Clinker*, are dressed identically and are literally at the same table, where they smoke their pipes and take their glasses. To the degree that Methodism is a "mischief" here, it is a familiar one.

The Anglican Greville literally and figuratively walks Wildgoose home in the final scenes of *The Spiritual Quixote*, ending his circuit ride at the estate he will soon inherit. That walk has woven together the lives of his old friend Rivers, reconciled Rivers to his rich relation Mr. Griskin, and laid the groundwork for his own union with Miss Townsend. The cavalcade of places and "originals" as Wildgoose moves through the Cotswolds to Bristol, Stratford-upon-Avon, and points between paints a comic panorama of an English Britain still connected to traditional country life and customs, despite urbanization and economic modernization. In the penultimate chapter "Modern Taste, and that of our Ancestors," Graves reconciles classical tradition to English history through an argument for the traditional English country house, of which Wildgoose is now master. Wildgoose proposes bringing "Miss Townsend thither, to modernize his place," to which Dr. Greville replies:

> For my part, I prefer the plentiful tastes of our ancestors, in whose gardens Flora and Pomona amicably presided, to the barren taste of the present age. Why would you destroy this south wall, covered with peaches and plumbs; and root up these pinks and carnations to make way for some half-starved exotics, or perhaps poisonous shrubs, which nothing but mere fashion can recommend? (469)

The Mischief of Methodism, in *The Caricature Magazine, or Hudabrastic Mirror*, G. M. Woodward, ca. 1811. Courtesy the Lewis Walpole Library, Yale University

The English garden becomes a trope for the nation, with traditions that reconcile pagan and Christian, use and pleasure, past and present. Greville's recommendation of this traditional, agricultural nativism comes, significantly, after he has just conceded to Wildgoose that "he had a very good opinion of Mr. Wesley and Mr. Whitfield, and of their first endeavors to revive the practice of primitive piety and devotion," even if he is more skeptical of the legacy of their followers. Wesley and Whitefield get to count as "native plants" who contributed legitimately to the history of British Christianity. Wildgoose has been well-schooled into seeing the error of his own religious enthusiasm, which has been a failed imitation of these spiritual giants. But he can be reconciled and reunited with his former vicar, Mr. Powell, in the next scene, just as the Anglican tradition, modeled by Greville, can use the oratorical and spiritual energy of Methodism to infuse its own practice without fearing conversion or displacement.

Once the adventure of Methodism is over (contained historically as the "Summer's Ramble"), Wildgoose will now meet, Graves assures us, "with no other adventures than what any man might expect to meet with, who travels through a country that is under a regular Civil Government, and in an age which appears to be under the direction of a general Providence" (472). This was a summer fling, not the arc of history. The telling reference to "Civil Government" returns to the political threat of radicalized Dissent and masters it with the stability of modern Great Britain. The vision is not entirely secular, but it is secularized; the nation is under "Providence," not God, a Latitudinarian compromise distinct from the evangelical vocabulary of the younger Wildgoose.

From her nineteenth-century vantage point, George Eliot observed that Methodism provided a useful, nonthreatening connection between past and present. Eliot waxes lyrical about the way that Methodism's heart religion opened up an inner life as well as a sense of historical continuity for working people. In *Adam Bede*, she describes Methodism as "a faith which was a rudimentary culture, which linked their thoughts with the past, lifted their imagination above the sordid details of their own narrow lives, and suffused their souls with the sense of a pitying, loving, infinite Presence, sweet as summer to the houseless needy" (39). Far from Fielding's concerns about Methodism unleashing queer passions, Eliot reflects a cultural reconciliation with a movement that the novels of Smollett and Graves have glimpsed, a version of Methodism that takes its place imaginatively under a banner of British sensibility in the national "family of originals." As Goring notes, *The Spiritual Quixote* brings together Cervantic and Fieldingesque cultural critique with more sentimental literary textures, a claim that also applies to *Humphry Clinker* (84). The result is a portrait of Methodism's community-making energy compatible with traditional familial relations and comfortably mastered by the polite aesthetic practices of literary reading that the novel models. The specific theological content of Humphry Clinker's beliefs gives way to their affective results, which unite the Bramble-Lloyd clan. For Graves, the quixotic Wildgoose, instead of converting the nation, is himself converted to nationalism. These comic novels reconcile satiric vigor with the language of the warmed heart in a reading practice that trains the reader to critique enthusiastic excess while appreciating the capacity it has for drawing people together and reconciling differences.

For both Smollett and Graves, Methodism is a movement neutralized of politically revolutionary potential while still capable of doing significant cultural and social work. In 1785, fourteen years after Henry Mackenzie published *The Man of Feeling*, he admitted that "in the enthusiasm of sentiment there is much the same danger as in the enthusiasm of religion, of substituting certain impulses and feelings of what may be called a visionary kind, in the place of real practical duties."[20] Both Smollett and Graves avoid the old bromide of Methodist antinomianism and instead connect the domains of enthusiasm and social action, which makes it easier for them to grant the religious movement its legitimate social effects and uses. Methodism is still making something happen in *The Spiritual Quixote* and *Humphry Clinker*, but that something turns out to be community. Mastered in both novels by a literary critical set of strategies that checks its excess, these Methodists energize rather than challenge the emerging *sensus communis* of a modern Britain.

AFTERWORD

1778 and Beyond

Though many more satires would flare, public responses to Methodism mellowed significantly after Whitefield's death in 1771. The exceptional year in the general calm was 1778, when a burst of verse satires poured from the presses. But the terms of these largely forgettable poems seem motivated more by Wesleyan Methodism's growing institutionalization than by its otherness. *Perfection. A Poetical Epistle. Calmly Addressed to the Greatest Hypocrite in England*; *Sketches for Tabernacle-Frames*; and *The Saints, A Satire* all allegedly came from the same pen, probably William Combe's, in 1778. They were followed by *The Love Feast* (1778); *Methodism and Popery Dissected and Compared* (1779); and *The Foundry Budget Opened; or, the Arcanum of Wesleyanism Disclosed* (1780). These disposable satires recycled old themes and trotted out the tropes of the hypocritical minister, the mountebank, and the enthusiast. *Sketches for Tabernacle-Frames* illustrates the general feel of these pieces:

> Where Quack'ry, Pray'r, and Grubstreet Arts, combine
> To furnish out a Tripartite-Divine,
> There dwells an *aged Wight*, well-mask'd with *Grace*,

> Whose lank, monastic, *Sanctuary-Face*
> In solemn Lines betrays his *ghostly Trade;*
> A *pious Mountebank* in *Masquerade*. (1)

Wesley had been identified as all these things: the quack, the zany, the enthusiast, and the publishing phenomenon, this last a reminder of Methodism's influence in the print marketplace as the producer of some of the most widely consumed books of the period. The terms of Combe's rant are familiar, but Wesley is now the "aged Wight," venerable to some and an old joke to others. Elsewhere, he was called "Reynard" the fox, the unscrupulous, preaching trickster. By the end of his career, Wesley seemed to Combe and others to be getting the authority and power they presumed that he wanted, too. Wesley was increasingly functioning like the archbishop of Methodism, including the 1784 declaration of the "Legal Hundred," the first group of officially commissioned Methodist ministers. Even before that act, Combe complains that Wesley dreams of *"Croziers,* and *Keys,* and floating *Mitres* . . . like a *real Bishop"* (13–14). The familiar terms of the attack contain this new thread: Wesley and the Methodists are looking more institutional.

The reasons for the explosion of anti-Methodist writing in 1778 can be traced back to the increased visibility of Methodism in the political sphere. Wesley ventured into the meadow of explicitly political speech with public stances against slavery and his *Calm Address to Our American Colonies* (1775), which plagiarized chunks of Johnson's *Taxation No Tyranny,* and found himself in the crosshairs of his enemies. Wesley's close connections to the American colonies (and Whitefield's connections before him) made him an unofficial person of interest during the American Revolution. And though Wesley remained loyal to the crown, his abolitionism and the magnitude of his influence in the public sphere fueled the concern that he might exercise more political power. 1778 also marked the beginning of Wesley's *The Arminian Magazine* and opening of the London City Road Chapel. With *The Arminian Magazine,* John Wesley, already a publishing industry unto himself, joined the ranks of Fielding, Smollett, Goldsmith, and other literary magazine editors; Combe notes Wesley has set up "his Stock in Trade" to sell his new "Magazine" (11). Like other eighteenth-century magazines, the *Arminian Magazine* provided a digest to organize the array of Methodist publications, a testament to how much printed material the movement was generating.

The architectural presence of Methodism was similarly substantial. Lloyd describes the City Road Chapel as "a visible sign of burgeoning Methodist confidence and stature after forty years of struggle" and "an elegant place of worship and a centre of administration" (189). The City Road Chapel made the visual point that Methodism was to be a continued presence in the post-Whitefield era, a permanent part of the literal British landscape and a viable denomination. The 1781 registration of the Countess of Huntingdon's chapels as Dissenting churches and Wesley's 1784 ordination of two Methodist ministers to serve in America made its denominational status a de facto reality. John Wesley's move to ordain the ministers infuriated Charles Wesley, who was not consulted in the decision.[1] Charles joined the chorus of Methodism's critics when he wrote:

> So easily are Bishops made
> By man's, or woman's whim?
> W——his hands on C——hath laid,
> But who laid hands on him?
>
> ("READER" 430)

Though Methodism would continue to have internal divisions, its scandal in the late 1770s was that it was becoming its own established denomination, eventually taking up the pattern of Dissent. Its evangelical radicalism was in this sense accommodated to the modern state through the denominational split and John Wesley's decision to make his own bishops, as his brother Charles angrily put it. Charles Wesley's decision to be buried in the Anglican yard of St. Marylebone Parish Church in 1788 is a reminder of the intra-Anglican identity that was at stake in Methodism even after its denominational consolidation. By contrast, John Wesley chose to be buried beside the Methodist City Road Chapel in 1791.

In spite of the relative normalization of Methodism late in the century, its association with the evangelical conversion experience would continue to trouble modern sensibilities. When Mary Crawford wants to wound Edmund Bertram after he reproaches her in *Mansfield Park*, she accuses him of delivering an evangelical sermon and suggests that he might be turning Methodist. In 1778, Combe attacks the Pentacostal edge of Methodist conversion practices in his *Sketches*. He wonders, sarcastically:

> What strange *Emotions* shake their *outward Man?*
> Paint 'em, in all their Changes, those who can.
> Delug'd in *Tears* the *Patient* sometimes lies;
> Then, with a Spring, full half his Length he'll rise;

> In whirling Eddies round and round he'll run,
> Like School-boy's Top, or *Flamen* of the Sun
> Throw *Somersets*, vault, caper, and curvet,
> Like Herds, when in their Tails the *Breeze* is set;
> Or madd'ning Mares, by Lust, or *Oestron*, stung
> Or *Bacchanals*, when frantic Peals are rung
> On rattling Cymbals, stirring ev'ry Nerve
> To *Rage*, in Honour of the *God* they serve.
> Seiz'd with *spasmodic Pangs* of the *New-Birth*
> These *Saints*, like baited Bulls, tear up the Earth. (26)

Methodism still exemplifies the loss of rational self that is sacred to secularity, the reasoning *cogito* that must remain autonomous, implicitly masculine, detached, cool. Combes imagines the barely human convert alternating between a bull, a mare, and a bacchic reveler, primitive figures with uncontrollable animal bodies. Combes implies that this enthusiastic Methodist does not qualify as a self at all, and is a destructive force that will "tear up the Earth" and by implication the community of the nation. He goes on to follow a pair of converts who, within six weeks, have become professed hypocrites, and closes with a rallying cry for *"Satire"* to "chase th' *Imposter* to the Tomb" where "His *flinty Front ✝* my *Stigma* shou'd retain" (35). As Combes posits satire as the cure, he also reaches into the sacramental symbolic economy—the stigma, the sign of the cross, and the mark of Cain.[2] His attack on religious enthusiasm ironically hinges on his own appeal to the incantatory, magical power that Robert Elliott traces in early satire: the invective and curse as the defenders of a reasonable, secular society, on which Methodism remained a stain.[3]

If, as Hans Gumbrecht put it, the principle "that all knowledge about the world should be knowledge produced by humans" establishes the hermeneutic field in the eighteenth century as the "dominant outline for human self-reference," it is an uneven idea that comes with its own counter-reformation in Methodist heart religion (Gumbrecht 34–35). The story about what Methodism, the most consolidated expression of modern evangelicalism, did to the modern self, and the question of whether its converts could be said to be modern selves, continues to put the historical narrative of secular modernity on the line. As the success of the 2011 musical *The Book of Mormon* suggests, satiric attacks on religious beliefs and religion as a primitive threat to a more literate and critical modern self can reveal the ways that ostensibly secular subjects remain fascinated with the prospect of belief itself. But contemporary literary criticism has its own investments in restaging the opposition between a religious past and a secular modernity. Lori Branch has framed the contemporary critical situation thus:

> In an ideology-replicating maneuver ... our discipline produces scholarship that precludes the religiousness of the past (or present) from calling its own ideology of secularism into account. This seems, to me, worth pointing out, and a task worth taking up in mainstream English criticism. And both historical and theoretical frameworks in the humanities provide powerful tools for the endeavor. From Derrida and Caputo to Lyotard and Žižek, a host of literary theorists after philosophy's linguistic turn points us precisely toward this accounting, toward recognizing how *belief*, or choice and action within uncertainty, is indicative of what we might call the linguistic condition, of the production of all knowledge, and indeed, of all personal relation. In this sense, secularity—as a space free of faith—is a fantasy.
>
> (BRANCH, "METANOIA" 4)

Literary studies, according to Branch, has had a greater stake in the project of reading past religion and is now faced with the uncomfortable task of parsing the implications of this narrative for its own future practices.

The problem of how literary and cultural studies can or cannot talk about religion is not merely recorded in but created by the idea of a clear distinction between secular and religious domains. Michael Kauffman, Jürgen Habermas, and John Caputo have argued that the idea of such a distinction is itself subject to historical construction and is neither essential, static, nor self-evident.[4] Literary studies as a discipline has depended on the secularization narrative to help make sense of what it is we do. In the Arnoldian version of a natural progression of enlightened inquiry, literature functionally replaces religion as the means of transmitting moral and spiritual values to modern people. Even the critiques of Arnoldian literariness, including those from George Marsden, Robert Scholes, Gerald Graff, and Bruce Robbins, still depend on the binary secular/religious in their own rise and fall narratives of biblical proportions.[5] As Kauffman explains, "these narratives of secularization, including the Arnoldian replacement version, do not rely on an a priori categorical difference between the religious and the secular as much as they create one in the act of narration. . . . Anyone constructing a narrative of secularization (even if finally to refute it) needs to evaluate certain ideas, truth claims, or values that may seem more or less transcendent, more or less spiritual, more or less 'religious.'" (617). In strikingly similar terms,

Foucault suggested that, pace Bataille, the eroticization of language since the eighteenth century has filled the void left "since Sade and the death of God," implying though stopping short of stating that the discourse of sexuality itself builds on a longing for a lost God (Foucault 70). The discursive construction of a modern distinction between secular and religious is itself shot through with theological imperatives and religious longing, even as the binary continues to exert tremendous influence on the way we read history.

Recent historical and philosophical work by John Sheehan, Charles Taylor, John Caputo, Ann Pellegrini, Webb Keane and others indicates that the secularization thesis is under pressure as forms of "postsecular" critical inquiry have begun to ask questions about how we might read religion in rather than out of history. The conversation about religion, literature, and culture has been more robust in seventeenth-century studies, eighteenth-century American studies, and British Romanticism in the work of scholars such as Harry Stout, Regina Schwartz, Stanley Fish, Jon Mee, Colin Jager, Shaun Irlham, Richard Brantley, and Sharon Achinstein. In other words, it has been carried on primarily around eighteenth-century British studies rather than within it. That eighteenth-century Britain has been until recently an aporia in the conversation about religion is critically revealing and suggests the doubling effect that investments in a secular eighteenth century as the era of enlightenment(s) has on the kinds of questions scholars and critics bring to their work. John Caputo and William Scanlon frame this critical moment as one in which philosophers, theologians, and critics are able to push past "the constraints of this old, methodologically constricted, less enlightened, strait and narrow Enlightenment, which found it necessary to cast 'reason' and 'religion' in mortal opposition" and in which an axiomatic secularism "has enjoyed pride of place" (Caputo and Scanlon 2). If the old "straight and narrow" Enlightenment has been under some pressure in the last fifty years, the methodologies for talking about religion as constitutive of the eighteenth-century British self are still emerging and only beginning to shape the way we tell the story of the period. Examples of how scholars within eighteenth-century British studies are reconceptualizing this narrative and finding ways to talk about religion as such in literary history include the recent work of Lori Branch, Jennifer Snead, Kevin Seidel, Dan White, Adam Potkay, and Neil Saccamano.[6] My contribution to this conversation has been to illuminate, through the archive of eighteenth-century British representations of Methodism, how the idea of modernity is intertwined with the articulation of what kinds of religious beliefs are too excessive or too uncritical for a modern self.

The cultural features of the early twenty-first century, which include the spread of religious fundamentalisms in postmodernity, the emergence of religious progressives concerned about international human rights and environmental justice, and a "theological turn" in philosophy and critical theory, provide points of resonance that may help us take a fresh look at the eighteenth century as a field of ongoing contests over the domains of religious and aesthetic meaning. The place of religion within modernity is among the most urgent and knotty of our ongoing late enlightenment conversations; whatever modernity means, it has not led to the disappearance of religion, which leaves its great political project, Western liberalism, with serious questions to answer. Is the religious devotee, whose experiences of divine presence cannot be submitted to external proofs, a viable self, or a failure to be a modern critical reader who holds knowledge (particularly spiritual or religious knowledge) at a sufficient interpretive distance? And how does Western liberalism avoid the assumption that nonsecular cultures await the "cure" of political modernity? These questions have, implicitly, defined the terms of a secular subjectivity in both a political and a cognitive sense. Religion as we now know it has gathered focus from the separation out of religion from a secular public sphere, as well as the separation of religion as an institution from private belief. But reading the modern self as necessarily secular invokes the secularization thesis in ways that distort cultural history, which includes the popular experience of religion. It also undercuts the urgent political project of dialogue between religious and secular global citizens, a dialogue that must somehow move beyond the recalcitrant religious and ideological fundamentalisms of a worldview that pits secularism against religion in a deadly contest.[7]

Imagining Methodism in Eighteenth-Century Britain has attempted to redress some of the blind spots of a defensively secular account of eighteenth-century culture by showing how significant the idea of Methodism was to modern British identity, and how investments in "experimental religion" are woven into the project of what it means to be a self. Insofar as the story of Methodism resembles post- or late-modern experience of religion, it can remind us that the foreign country that is the eighteenth century continues to offer up archeological traces of the history of the self as well as glimpses of different ways of knowing, feeling, and believing. If the image of the sexual or theatrical Methodist resonates with televangelist culture or global Pentacostalism, perhaps so too will possibilities for reconciling secular and religious views around what Bruno Latour has called "matters of concern," matters that call for the attention of communities which are not so easily divided into secular and religious selves.[8]

Notes

INTRODUCTION: Longing to Believe

1. Richardson, *Sir Charles Grandison* 6: 22.
2. Mack, *Heart Religion*; Hempton, *The Religion of the People* and *Methodism*; Noll, *The Rise of Evangelicalism*; Ward, *Early Evangelicalism*; Heitzenrater, *Wesley and the People Called Methodists*; and Rack, *Reasonable Enthusiast*.
3. Lyles and Shepherd gather together a wide range of satires and literary responses to Methodism. My work builds on theirs in that I turn my attention to attempting to understand what Methodism means culturally in these works. See Lyles, *Methodism Mocked* and Shepherd, *Methodism and the Literature of the Eighteenth Century*.
4. See Shaw, *Miracles in Enlightenment England*.
5. Locke, *An Essay concerning Human Understanding* 2: 27, 345. Locke uses the example of Socrates to illustrate his point that "personal Identity" consists in an identity of consciousness, which means that sleepwalkers should not be responsible for their actions. Locke then complicates this forensic question by pointing out that the law, "with a Justice suitable to their way of Knowledge," must punish drunken people and sleepwalkers because it is impossible to distinguish with certainty a real from a counterfeit case. See 2: 27, 341–45.
6. The quotation comes from Asad, *Formations* 1. For a more extended discussion of the postsecular, see De Vries, *Philosophy and the Turn to Religion*; Derrida, "Above All"; and Habermas, "Notes on a Post-Secular Society."
7. Taylor's argument calls for a more precise definition of secularism not as a narrative of historical progress or the contest between scientific and religious views, but as a condition in which a religious worldview is no longer axiomatic. For a useful history of the term evangelical and an explanation of the eighteenth-century provenance of the core commitments of modern evangelicalism, see Noll, *The Rise of Evangelicalism*.
8. See Barker-Benfield, *The Culture of Sensibility*; Nussbaum, *The Autobiographical Subject*; and Mack, *Heart Religion*. The phrase "reasonable enthusiast" as a description of Wesley is Henry Rack's.
9. Salvaggio uses the terms classical and enlightened to describe ideas about order and hierarchy that have a deep history in the Western tradition but that find "their most precise expression" in the eighteenth century. See Salvaggio, *Enlightened Absence*.
10. Kramnick's argument is specifically about eighteenth-century models of mind, as opposed to "subjectivity, privacy, interiority, selfhood, the individual, autonomy, the human, or even (save for Locke) consciousness." I extrapolate his point about mind and agency with caution in the context of this argument about modern selves and Methodism. See Kramnick, "Empiricism, Cognitive Science, and the Novel" 264.

11. Leigh Eric Schmidt has discussed the priority of the visual over the aural, paradoxically, in Whitefield's preaching as part of "the decline of listening in the face of the ascendant power of vision in modern culture" in Schmidt, *Hearing Things* 15.

12. The letter to Home was dated December 2, 1737, reprinted in Hume, *New Letters of David Hume*, qtd. in Branch 118.

13. The phrases "primitive Christianity" and "warming of the heart" were phrases used throughout sermons, published journals, and appeals to their followers by both of the Wesley brothers and George Whitefield from the very early days of the movement.

14. See Kramnick, "Rochester and the History of Sexuality" and Freeman, *Character's Theater*.

15. For a good summary of Methodist stages of belief, see Rivers, *Reason, Grace, and Sentiment* 234.

16. Eagleton in this phrase is speaking of Dawkins's *The God Delusion*. He chastises both Richard Dawkins and Christopher Hitchens for an "ideology of progress, for which the past is so much puerile stuff to be banished to the primeval forests of prehistory. . . . A self-preening Enlightenment reason was largely blind to the nature of religious faith. . . . Because it could find in that faith nothing but laughable superstition and childish irrationality, it proved incapable of overcoming it." See Eagleton, *Reason, Faith, and Revolution* 90.

17. Derrida, "Autoimmunity: Real and Symbolic Suicides" 114, qtd. in Saccamano, "Inheriting Enlightenment" 421. Derrida's critique of Enlightenment critique, Saccamano argues, leads him to acknowledge the trace of religion in the allegedly secular values of universality, humanism, and tolerance that philosophy offers as an alternative to religion.

18. See, for example, Goldsmith's *History of England* (1764) and his *Abridgement*, both in Oliver Goldsmith, *The Collected Works of Oliver Goldsmith*. Smollett's *Complete History of England* (1757–8), and E. P. Thompson's *The Making of the English Working Class* (1963).

19. Valenze, *Prophetic Sons and Daughters* 3. Valenze references Halévy and Thompson; Christopher Hill's *The World Turned Upside Down* similarly identifies religious revivalism with political reaction. Hill, like E. P. Thompson, came from a Methodist background but translated the legacy of radical Protestantism into Marxist historiography. For more on Hill's personal background as a Yorkshire Methodist, see Corfield, "'We Are All One in the Eyes of the Lord.'"

20. For a remarkable discussion of how the concept of enlightenment as both demystification and liberation draws on Christian narrative, see Saccamano, "Inheriting Enlightenment."

21. See especially Jakobsen with Pellegrini, *Dreaming Secularism*; Bouwsma, *A Useable Past*; Taylor, *A Secular Age*; Keane, *Christian Moderns*; Caputo, *On Religion*.

22. Thomas Jefferson to James Smith, 1822, qtd. in Hempton, *Methodist* 48, and Jefferson, *The Writings of Thomas Jefferson* 15: 404.

23. Hans Frei notes that the particularly English approach of eighteenth-century biblical hermeneutics inaugurated an historicism that was framed by scientific procedures of evidence, that helps explain the storm of religious controversy that surrounded the publication of Darwin's *Origin of the Species*, a storm that has persisted into the twenty-first century. See Frei, *The Eclipse of Biblical Narrative*.

24. A more extended discussion of this set of assumptions takes place in Mack, *Heart Religion*; Gregory, "The Other Confessional History"; and David Gary Shaw, "Modernity

Between Us and Them: The Place of Religion within History," *History and Theory* 45 (Dec. 2006): 1–9.

25. Examples are indeed numerous. A contributor to *The Centinel* of September 17, 1757, identified only as "Mercator," also complains that his house, which was "once a picture to look at, is now never clean. If I seem to be uneasy at it, the immediate answer is 'what signifies an *earthly* mansion? Fix your mind on an heavenly one'" (231–32). The idea of women who leave off housekeeping is particularly widespread.

26. Qtd. in Mee, *Romanticism, Enthusiasm, and Regulation* 46.

27. The Lewis Walpole Library catalogue originally dated this print as 1751, but the presence of Wilkes, who did not come to public prominence until the early 1760s, suggests that this date may warrant revision. An earlier state of the print may have existed without Wilkes, who was likely added into the foreground later.

28. Stuart Sherman discusses the effect of timekeeping on the literary construction of time in the age of the modern clock in Sherman, *Telling Time*.

29. Ure, qtd. in E. P. Thompson 362.

30. Phyllis Mack notes that Thompson's own familial and educational ties to Methodism, as the grandson of a Methodist minister who was sent to a Methodist school, may help explain the zeal of his denunciations of the movement for terrifying children with the threat of hell and the psychosexual perversion that he calls "a pollution of the sources of spontaneity" (372). The comment bears a less precise relationship to the laboring-class experience of childhood in the eighteenth century. Tolar Burton, summarizing the work of Cruickshank, Rule, Speed, Spufford, Tuttle, and others, makes clear that Wesley's Methodist school at Kingswood and his appeals for children's literacy are models of progressive thinking and gentleness next to the brutal realities of urban orphans, the "climbing boys," memorialized in Blake's *Songs of Innocence and Experience*, who swept chimneys, and children crippled by work in textile manufacturing and other industries. These conditions framed the last of Jonas Hanway's great reform campaigns, and the orphans who were the most vulnerable of these children were some of Wesley's pupils at Kingswood and the Methodist Sunday School movement (Burton, *Spiritual Literacy in John Wesley's Methodism* 267–69).

31. Nancy Armstrong, *The Rise of Domestic Woman*; Michael McKeon, *The Secret History of Domesticity*; Raymond Williams, *Culture and Society*; and *The Long Revolution* are just a few of the studies that have been directly and indirectly shaped by Thompson's work.

32. See Snead, "Print, Predestination, and the Public Sphere" 95. Snead works from multiple recent critiques of Habermas's formulation of a secular, print-oriented public sphere, including Ruttenburg, *Democratic Personality*.

33. McKeon, *The Secret History of Domesticity*, claims that Protestantism provides the logic of secularization, though he also claims its reforming aim is "not to secularize but to re-sanctify" by separating out religion from its cultural matrix, thus "purifying" it "from a universal precondition of existence to the personal and private experience of the individual" (33–34). For a critical discussion of the continuities between Methodist hymnody and Roman Catholic theology, see Berger, *Theology in Hymns?*

34. Rivers, *Reason* and "Dissenting and Methodist Books of Practical Divinity." Margaret Doody, Paula Backscheider, and Donald Davie have all drawn attention to the importance of the eighteenth-century hymn in eighteenth-century poetry.

35. The imprint of Watt's argument that secularization births the novel shapes subsequent accounts by G. A. Starr, John Richetti, Michael McKeon, Nancy Armstrong, and

William Warner, though Snead also notes critiques of epistemic secularization in the work of Barker-Benfield, Weinbrot, and Hunter. For examples of this narrative, see Watt, *The Rise of the Novel;* Thompson, *The Making of the English Working Class;* Armstrong, *Desire and Domestic Fiction;* and McKeon, *The Secret History of Domesticity.* For examples of challenges to it in the 1990s, Snead notes Hunter, *Before Novels;* Weinbrot, *Britannia's Issue;* and Barker-Benfield, *The Culture of Sensibility.*

36. Anderson, "Mr. Barvile's Enthusiasm." Early satires of Methodists remained preoccupied with sexuality in more conventional terms, but as the group became more identifiably distinct from some Puritan predecessors, the locus of the satire shifted from sexuality to theatricality.

CHAPTER ONE: Historicizing Methodism

1. For more on Charles Wesley's shaping influence on Methodism as well as his differences from his older brother, see Gareth Lloyd, *Charles Wesley and the Struggle for Methodist Identity.*

2. For an extended discussion of enthusiasm's general role in enlightenment England, see Taves, *Fits, Trances, & Visions.*

3. For this point, I am indebted to the 2008 Lewis Walpole Library lecture by Leo Damrosch, "Feeling Free in the Enlightenment."

4. Chalmers posits this basic question in "Facing Up to the Problem of Consciousness." Jonathan Kramnick has taken it up in the context of the late seventeenth-century revival of interest in Lucretius and the question of "how can matter think" in "Living with Lucretius."

5. Lady Betty Bruce Boswell, *Observations upon Effectuall Calling.* Lady Betty was also reading Poiret, another of the French mystics influential on the early career of John Wesley.

6. The controversy sparked by Foote's *The Minor* led to a broader debate about the place and nature of Methodism. The anonymous "Letter to Mr. Foote" was critical of the movement in general.

7. I am grateful to Thomas J. Heffernan for his help in tracing the recurring claim to "primitive" Christianity in reform movements.

8. Tecusan, *The Fragments of the Methodists.*

9. See Rousseau, "John Wesley's *Primitive Physic.*" For a fascinating discussion of the relationship between femininity, diet, devotional material, and spirituality, see also Guerrini, "The Hungry Soul."

10. All references to the service for communion are taken from "The Order for the Administration of Holy Communion, or the Lord's Supper," *Book of Common Prayer,* London, 1720.

11. For more on the considerable number of Protestant claims to miracles in the seventeenth and eighteenth centuries, see Shaw, *Miracles in Enlightenment England.*

12. See Bonhoeffer, *The Cost of Discipleship.*

13. See Nash, "Benevolent Readers."

14. The quotation is from Terence's *Eunuchus,* and reads "nihilo plus agas quam si des operam ut cum ratione infanias." Shaftesbury begins his quotation from Terence midsentence: "[If you should propose to make uncertain things certain by means of reason,] you would accomplish nothing more than if you should put effort into going mad by means

of reason." My thanks to Betsy Sutherland and Joshua Schoenfield for their help with this translation.

15. Oglethorpe's soldiers were instrumental in making Savannah uncomfortable for the Methodists by their incessant taunting of Whitefield. For more on the tense relationship between Norris and the Methodists, see Stevens, *A History of Georgia* 355.

16. Wesley wrote about the sincerity and frankness of affection in the Herrnhut community in letters to his mother Susanna and his brother Charles. This exclamation, which is a quotation from Julian the Apostate, comes from a letter to Susanna dated July 6, 1738, MS 153, Pitts Theological Library, Emory University and *Works* 1: 557.

17. Horace Walpole's personal copy of Frey's exposé was bound with Rimius's *A Candid Narrative of the Rise and Progress of the Herrnhuters*, which complains of the erotic excesses of their hymns, "blood and wounds" theology, and their marriage ceremonies. See also Podmore, *The Moravian Church in England*.

18. Craig Atwood argues that the Moravian program of sacralizing sex was a way to "control the centripetal force of individual sexuality that could destroy a communal society" (28). Atwood, "Sleeping in the Arms of Christ."

19. McKeon, building on the work of Starr, Armstrong, and Hunter, makes the connection between Puritan self-scrutiny and salvation as means of identifying an internal authority that is authentic and subjective. "Theological developments like these may be related to the way in which the word 'conscience,' until the seventeenth century an inclusive term ill-distinguished from 'consciousness,' by the beginning of the eighteenth century was acquiring its modern, distinctively internal reference." McKeon, *Secret History* 35–36.

20. In a letter to Joseph Hoole, a neighboring clergyman, dated October 12, 1716, Susanna offers a critique of Locke's notion of "personal identity" as self-consciousness, and Hoole's gloss, that personal identity exists in the capacity for self-consciousness. The letter exists in a copy in manuscript, with notes indicating it was sent to Mr. Wesley as well as their daughter Sophia, evidence that her philosophical debates were circulating in the family and close community. Her reply to Hoole seizes on the point that "capacity" really means power:

> Power is always a relative term and does not necessarily suppose some being that hath or sustains or to whom that power belongs or in whom it is placed. For of power abstracted from all relation we can have no idea. (85)

Susanna Wesley's relational definition of identity and agency in Locke's model of consciousness provides the terms for a feminist critique of Lockean civil subjectivity, which suffers from the over-authorization of some self-possessing individuals at the expense of others (namely, servants and wives). Though Susanna does not name women in her critique, she moves from a relational conception of power to a metaphysical proposition that "spiritual immaterial beings," or souls, must have some "substratum" of the divine real to give them meaning and consistency. The proof, a repudiation of the secular account of subjectivity, stresses relation over identity, a strategy she also pursues in *A Religious Conference*, where she distinguishes moral argument from other logical forms of argument that can be demonstrated "by visible signs like a proposition in mathematics. Nor does their force usually consist in one single evidence, but in the united strength of several considerations." Her claims are distillations of arguments from Pascal and Malebranche that situate knowledge in a series of power relations.

21. For a more sustained discussion of the anti-miraculous arguments of the late seventeenth and early eighteenth centuries, see Champion, *The Pillars of Priestcraft Shaken*.

22. The anonymous author of this pamphlet was likely Richard Hardy, Vicar of Knoulton in Nottinghamshire. See Lyles, *Methodism Mocked* 48.

23. Philip Gibson was called a "lunatic" by a witness for the defense, an early version of an insanity defense, because he used to sing to himself that he would be hanged. He was sentenced to be hanged in 1751. See Rabin, "Searching for the Self."

24. *Plain and Easy Road* ... 51. See also Forster, *Historical and Biographical Essays*. An early nineteenth-century historian who fashioned a narrative out of historical records left by Sir James Stephen, Tate Wilkinson, private and published letters, and other historical accounts, Forster provides a blended if second-hand account of their stories. He was first and foremost an historian of the stage, and his account of Whitefield is background to an essay on Foote's life and times.

25. Badiou, *Saint Paul* 2. Like Weber and Thompson, Badiou also sees in Christian history the facilitation of capitalism and claims that the communitarian language of Paul is actually the ground work for "monetary abstraction," instrumental in establishing a logic of universalism that will configure, pace Marx's prediction, the world as a market (7, 9).

26. For more on the relationship between oratory and modern politeness, see Goring, *The Rhetoric of Sensibility*.

27. For more on Wesley's appropriation of different professional and cultural languages, see George Lawton, *John Wesley's English* and Noppen, *Transforming Words*.

28. *Eloisa to Abelard* 209–14, as qtd. in "Earnest Appeal," *Oxford Works* 11: 46.

29. Steiner, *Real Presences*. Steiner's argument for an immanent dimension of "presence" in the work of art is similar to claims made by Jean-Luc Nancy and Hans Gumbrecht. See especially Gumbrecht, *Production of Presence*.

30. See Hempton, *Methodism*.

31. For an extensive rhetorical analysis of John Wesley's style, see Lawton, *John Wesley's English*.

32. My argument here is indebted to Saccamano's "Inheriting Enlightenment," which concludes that "a critique or deconstruction of Enlightenment critique, then, marks the historical, ideological, and hegemonic traces of religion in what the Enlightenment opposes to religion—universality, humanism, tolerance, mediation, to mention only these few. And it does so in keeping faith with an unconditionality that exceeds the limited norms and general rules of the ethical. Yet despite his reading of ethics as irresponsible to the unconditional demand for justice or democracy, Derrida continues to insist on the necessity of law, right, and norms in international politics." It is in this sense that Saccamano speaks of "keeping faith with reason in Derrida" (42).

33. See Hume, "Letters of David Hume" 1: 12–17.

34. Tierney-Hynes, "Hume, Romance, and the Unruly Imagination" 646. Tierney-Hynes argues that Hume uses gender to indicate the dangerous inferiority of literature, especially novels and romances, to philosophy and history.

35. Lawton, *John Wesley's English* 26. Lawton shows Wesley's writing to be richly rhetorical, with an expansive vocabulary that drew from the languages of trade, medicine, navigation, farming, classical literature, and domestic life, yet single-mindedly focused on his evangelical mission of saving souls.

36. Whitefield writes to an unidentified "Rev. Mr. M" on July 18, 1739. He used

"follow naked the naked Christ" in multiple letters (to men and women) as well as in the sermon "Persecution Every Christian's Lot." See *Works* 1: 52, 56, 99, and 125, and 6: 355.

CHAPTER TWO: The New Man

1. Ward, working through patristic theology and poststructuralist criticism, argues that the body of Jesus is "brought within a complex network of sexualized symbolic relations" though allegorical displacements that are central to the "ontological scandal" at the heart of Christianity. See G. Ward, "The Displaced Body of Jesus Christ."

2. See Armstrong, *Desire and Domestic Fiction*; Haggerty, *Men in Love*; Lanser, "Sapphic Picaresque"; and McKeon, "Historicizing Patriarchy."

3. For more on the argument that *The Female Husband* plays out the formation of sexuality, at the intersection of ideologies of sex and gender, see Braunschneider, "Acting the Lover."

4. See Lanser, "Sapphic Picaresque"; O'Driscoll, "The Lesbian and the Passionless Woman"; and Braunschneider, "Acting the Lover."

5. The 1903 edition, edited by James P. Browne, cuts the punch line to read "I fear not, for they are powerful men. —But pray my lord." See Fielding, "Miss Lucy in Town" 14.

6. Abelove, *The Evangelist of Desire* 66–67. See also John Wesley, *The Journal of the Rev. John Wesley, A.M.* 4: 320 and Jackson, ed., *The Lives of the Early Methodist Preachers* 1: 153.

7. Outler, ed., *Works* 19 (April 18–26, 1739): 50–51.

8. See Rack, *Reasonable Enthusiast*.

9. Mack had previously argued the associations between evangelicalism, spiritual experience, and women in modernity in Mack, *Visionary Women*.

10. Quoted in Mack, *Heart Religion* 130–34.

11. See Podmore, *The Moravian Church in England* 31–32.

12. The list of questions appeared in "Rules of the Band Societies," *Abingdon Works* 9: 78.

13. See Podmore, *The Moravian Church in England*.

14. Trapp, *The Nature, Folly, Sin, and Danger of Being Righteous Overmuch* 59. The Bishop of Exeter (George Lavington) was a long-time opponent of Methodism and linked it with Roman Catholicism in his anonymous *The Enthusiasm of Methodists and Papists Compar'd* 13, in which he also criticized Whitefield's *Short Account*.

15. See Chilcote, *John Wesley and the Women Preachers of Early Methodism*.

16. For more on this connection, see McFarlane, *The Sodomite in Fiction and Satire*.

17. Fielding served as the magistrate during these riots and upheld the letter of the law under the Riot Act when he had a young man, Bosavern Penlez, executed for looting. Fielding's legal attempt to impose order on these unruly bodies turned out to be politically complex and raised a public outcry for grace and mercy for Penlez and the prostitutes. John Cleland wrote *The Case of the Unfortunate Bosavern Penlez* in defense of Penlez.

18. Walker's *Fragmentation and Redemption* (158–60) and Irigaray's *Speculum of the Other Woman* (199–200) are two examples of the coincidence of argument between pre- and postmodern accounts of Christian embodiment and its embrace of permeability. Graham Ward's arresting "The Displaced Body of Jesus Christ," through a theology of displacement, claims both a "multi-gendered" body of Christ and, by extension, a multi-gendered, transcorporeal account of bodies and sex within the Christian church, an argument with significant implications for queer theology.

19. Blackwell identifies traditions of Dutch painting that emphasize erotic connections between physicians and "greensick girls," as well as other medical details in names such as "Baytree" that link Hamilton to the sexual threat of the doctor. See Blackwell, "An Infallible Nostrum" 59.

20. Beyond what we might broadly term the universalizing impulse of empiricism, the twenty-first-century popularity of magazines like *Real Simple* and the raw foods movement capitalize on desires for simplicity amid a culture of complications, a desire that speaks of itself as a spiritual longing with potential spiritual rewards.

21. See Rogal, "Pills for the Poor." I am also grateful to Stephen Latham, Director of the Interdisciplinary Center for Bioethics at Yale, for his insights about colonial medicine and the eighteenth-century social meaning of pills.

22. For a differing perspective that situates Wesley's interest in health care in a strain of eighteenth-century Anglicanism that proposed bridges between the fields of theology, science, and medicine, even as they were becoming more distinct from one another, see Haas, "John Wesley's Views on Science and Christianity."

23. See Shoemaker, *The London Mob* 112. In September of 1740, Charles Wesley helped to quell a riot of colliers in Kingswood, near Bristol, but he and other Methodist preachers were more commonly the objects of anti-Methodist mob violence. In May of 1740, William Seward was killed by a mob in Wales, and in May of 1743, Charles Wesley was beaten and assaulted, along with David Taylor, at Walsal and then Thorpe, where mobs dragged them to the ground and threw stones at them. Similar insults and attempts to make the Methodists abject by throwing them in filthy pits "full of noisome Things and stagnated Water," flooding their meeting rooms by using fire engines and pond water, and throwing "another young Man into a Mud-pit three Times successively" were reported in some twenty-six affidavits filed against their tormentors. See Whitefield, *A Brief Account* 6 and Wilder, *The Methodist Riots* 64.

24. Quoted in Paulson, *The Beautiful, Novel, and Strange* 127.

CHAPTER THREE: Words Made Flesh

1. PRO SP 36/111/158v, "Cleland to Stanhope," Nov. 13, 1749, qtd. in Epstein, *John Cleland* 76.

2. When William Morgan, one of Wesley's young comrades at Oxford, died, rumors abounded that the rigors of the "methodist" group, possibly including flagellation, had killed him. See Heitzenrater, *Wesley and the People Called Methodists* 45–47.

3. McKeon, *Secret History* 660. On the subject of the rise of a modern category of pornography, which exists for sexual and economic reasons, apart from the tradition of clerical satire, see Hunt, ed., *The Invention of Pornography;* Trumbach, "Erotic Fantasy and Male Libertinism"; Wagner, *Eros Revived;* Mudge, "How to Do the History of Pornography."

4. For a summary of the research and arguments about mechanism and *Memoirs*, see Braudy, "*Fanny Hill* and Materialism"; Lonsdale, "New Attributions to John Cleland"; and Turner, "'Illustrious Depravity' and the Erotic Sublime."

5. Though she does not include Cleland's work in her study, Ferguson argues that pornography is "one of the principle examples of essentially utilitarian social structures that aim to manifest the differential value of actions to individuals and that raise questions about the justice of social recognition." See Ferguson, *Pornography, the Theory*.

6. For a discussion of the intersection of religious and queer studies, as well as an assessment of Foucault's and Bataille's claims about sex colonizing the domain of religion, see Jordan, "Religion Trouble."

7. See Abelove, *The Evangelist of Desire* 73. Methodist reports of the problem are recorded in *Minutes of the Methodist Conference* (London, 1862) 1: 126.

8. Hanway wrote several treatises about the Magdalen House, including *Thoughts on the Plan for a Magdalen-House for Repentant Prostitutes* (1758). He called the Methodists' notions "absurd" in the long title of his *Letters written occasionally on the customs of foreign nations in regard to harlots: the lawless commerce of the sexes: the repentance of prostitutes: the great humanity and beneficial effects of the Magdalene charity in London: and the absurd notions of the Methodists: with prayers and meditations on the most interesting circumstances and events of life* (1761).

9. The "Hymn for Lauds on the feasts of Holy Women" speaks of two Magdalen stories, the anointing of Christ and the witness to the resurrection. See East, "Educating Heloise" 114.

10. Later, in 1780, Madan would be widely discredited as a voice in religious debates after his publication of *Thelyphthora; or, a Treatise on Female Ruin*, a defense of polygamy on the grounds that it would reduce prostitution. His late-century controversial thesis was one of the many ways the connection between Methodism and prostitution continued to thrive even as majority attitudes toward Methodism mellowed into acceptance.

11. See Ingrassia, *Authorship, Commerce, and Gender* and Rosenthal, *Infamous Commerce*.

12. For more on the interconnection of women's public profile and Methodist satire, see McInelly, "I Had Rather Be Obscure. But I Dare Not."

13. For more on the architectural and imaginative meanings of public and private space in *Memoirs*, see McKeon, *Secret History* 660–72.

14. My references to Sarah Ryan's work come from Mack's *Heart Religion* and her archival work at the John Rylands Memorial Library in Manchester. Subsequent references to Ryan cite Mack's page numbers. MS from the Fletcher-Tooth collection, Methodist Archive, Manchester (John Rylands Memorial Library) Fl 2/2/7–10 and FL 24/3/3/, as quoted in Mack, *Heart Religion* 146–47.

15. Paulson argues at much greater length for sacred parody in the works of Hogarth, citing *Paul Before Felix Burlesqued*, *Enthusiasm Delineated*, and *Transubstantiation Satirized* among other prints. *A Harlot's Progress* is a more complex case, but Paulson maintains that its parody of sacred images by Dürer is part of a substantive rather than decorative plan of allusion and demystification. See Paulson, *Hogarth's Harlot*.

16. Jody Greene argues that the issue of taste is central to *Memoirs*, which sets out to account for a variety of tastes and then teach readers how to favor the best kinds of taste. Anna Marie Jagose uses Greene's argument to show how the novel engages in a similar kind of normative training with regard to heterosexuality.

17. Epstein, *John Cleland*; Sabor, "From Sexual Liberation to Gender Trouble"; Jones, *The Clubs of the Georgian Rakes*.

18. See Epstein, *John Cleland* 69–71 and Lord, *The Hell-Fire Clubs*. According to Lord, the Beggar's Benison legend was tied to a story of James Stuart wandering in exile, who received this blessing from, depending on the account, an old woman or a beautiful young woman: "May your purse never be empty and your prick never fail you."

19. Evelyn Lord notes Cleland's involvement with the Knights of the Cape originated

in 1764. Cleland's nickname (or "cape name") was "Cat-Hole." See Lord, *The Hell-Fire Clubs* 180.

20. Boswell's nickname "Icaro Tarsense" or "Icaro of Tarsus" was given to him by the College of Arcadia, a pastoral-classicist academy that revived the Olympic games, admitted women, and served as a model for Dashwood-organized Dilettanti, which preceded the Medmenham Monks. Garrick was a member of the Dilettanti, which, like the Arcadians, was distinct from the "Mad Monks of Medmenham" and distinguished itself as a community for cultivating interest in the arts and classical culture. See Pottle, "Boswell as Icarus."

21. *Minutes and Reports*, February 7, 1746/47, quoted in Redford, *Dilettanti* 8.

22. Paulson grants that this mockery betrays a fascination, a "secret sympathy with the travestied" that informs sacred parody in Hogarth's work and that traffics more generally in feelings across sacred and sexual registers. Paulson, *Hogarth* 257.

23. Knapton's 1743 portrait of fellow Dilettante the Viscount of Galway dressed as a cardinal electing a pope (a reference to Dashwood's impromptu mimicry of Cardinal Ottoboni in Rome during a papal election) while the head of Pan looks on was a companion piece. See Redford, *Dilettanti* 34–5.

24. Quoted in Hempton, *Religion of the People* 156. Boyes accused Williamson of a range of other offenses and violations of the Thirty-Nine Articles. Williamson eventually won his case.

25. Bowden, *Poems on Various Subjects*. Bowden also published the same ballad as "The Methodists welcome to Pewsey: A new ballad, to the tune of, the cordelier and thief, or, Abbot of Canterbury" in 1765. See also Fletcher, *A Methodist Dissected* 2.

26. Fanny's description of his condemnation "to have his pleasure lashed into him, as boys have their learning," is a sly reference to Richard Busby, head of Westminster School, from which Cleland was expelled in 1723 after only two years. Busby makes an appearance in the 1742 *Dunciad in Four Books* as sadistic persecutor of schoolboys with a birch garland, "Dropping with Infant's blood, and Mother's tears," an image Kristina Straub has read insightfully as homoerotic. The religious signifiers of Mr. Barvile's sexual ritual connect the scene more closely to attitudes toward the modern body as well as the body of Christ.

27. *Correspondence* 21: 81. The Walpole editors note that "Apparently the only Methodist book in the SH records was Whitefield's Sermons, 1739 (Hazen. *Cat. Of HW's Lib.*, no. 1427)," but there are several titles in the Hazen catalogue under Wesley and Whitefield, among others, in addition to the anti-Methodist tracts.

28. See Branch, *Rituals of Spontaneity*.

29. Quoted in Paulson, *Hogarth's Harlot* 154.

30. Hazen's catalogue indicates that the markings are Walpole's.

31. Reference pages in Walpole's copy of Rimius are to pages 41, 44, 47, 55, 60, 62, and 64 respectively. The marks drop out in his copy as the material becomes less titillating.

32. Zinzendorf, *Sermons* 41. Later in the same text, again quoting a hymn within one of his sermons, Zinzendorf presents one of many images of the bleeding Christ: "Thy pierc'd, they through-bor'd Side,/Thy Sweat in thy deep Need,/Secure and keep thy Bride/Till they Day shall shine,/Bleeding King of Thine!" (56).

33. The quotation continues: "A Kiss of Peace (is given) and a Greeting to all our dear Bones and Ribs, upon the Breast, where our little Children take their Nourishment from,

and the Body of the Sister, incorporated with the Chaste: (The Saviour, I suppose, is meant here) Item, the 2d, 3d, and 4th Versese of the 2114th Humn, where the Ideas agree with such an Address. *Deine heil'de erfie Wunde,* &c. May they (vis, Saviour's) first holy Wound anoint me for the conjugal Business upon that Member of my Body, which is for the Beenefit of my Wife; and the Purple red Oil flow upon my Priest's Hole, and make it rightly fitted for the Procurator-Business; that I may embrace my precious Rib with the same Tenderness, thou didst embrace thy Wife, when it went out of thy Side." Rimius, *A Candid Narrative of the Rise and Progress of the Herrnhuters* 54n.

34. The lines are from the Wesleyan hymn "Thou Hidden Source of Calm Repose."

35. Paulson expands on the connection of ideas between Hoadly, Fielding, and Hogarth. Hoadly was allied with Woolston and Toland through his claims of the importance of "sincerity rather than creed," the definition of the Eucharist as a "frequent cheerful Meeting" at which people "in the Presence of one another, and in the service of the supreme Being, make Promises of being good, friendly and benevolent to each other." See Paulson, *Hogarth's Harlot* 173.

36. The view that Christianity could be rationalized included versions of earlier heresies, such as Socinian (a fifteenth-century proto-Unitarian doctrine rejecting Trinitarianism) and Arianism (the fourth-century anti-Trinitarian heresy that led to the first council of Nicea and the Nicene Creed), both of which tended to be grouped under the header of Deism.

37. This story is drawn from the court and police records in Schaeffer, *The Marquis De Sade* 56–63. See also Lori Branch's thoughtful situation of Sade's claim in the context of moral philosophy, utilitarianism, and sexuality in ch. 3, "True Enthusiasm," in *Rituals of Spontaneity.*

38. The image is reproduced in Hunt, ed., *Invention of Pornography.*

CHAPTER FOUR: Actors and Ghosts

1. For a useful summary of the changes in acting styles and philosophies, see Joseph Roach, *The Player's Passion.*

2. Quoted in Wahrman, *The Making of the Modern Self* 173.

3. Quoted in Belden, *The Dramatic Work of Samuel Foote* 83.

4. For speculation about the literal and figurative range of his voice, see Ruttenburg, "George Whitefield, Spectacular Conversion, and the Rise of Democratic Personality."

5. *Gentlemen's Magazine* (1739) 9: 417; Heitzenrater, *Wesley and the People Called Methodists* 100.

6. The sketch of Whitefield's Tabernacle compares visually to the image of The Old Theatre, Drury Lane, in *Smith's Antiquities of London* (1794).

7. Chesterfield was much impressed by Whitefield's preaching. See Seymour, *Life and Times of Selina Countess of Huntingdon* 194, and *Papers of the Earl of Marchmont,* ed. Sir George Henry Rose (1831) 2: 377.

8. Quoted in Shepherd, *Methodism and the Literature of the Eighteenth Century* 193. Garrick did contribute £500 to the building of Whitefield's Tabernacle, though he was no conventional Methodist supporter and parodied them on stage in his 1749 *Lethe.*

9. Quoted in Ruttenburg, "George Whitefield, Spectacular Conversion, and the Rise of Democratic Personality" 448.

10. *The Mournful Nuptials* was printed in 1739 with the epilogue, though it was not

acted until 1741. Cooke includes an explanatory note about Methodism on the grounds that "it is almost impossible that the names of these men should be known many years hence."

11. Belden, *The Dramatic Work of Samuel Foote* 83. Somerville, who praises Whitefield as "dignified by solemnity of manner and elegance of diction," is reluctant to blame him, but Foote's paraphrase of the insult indicates that Whitefield initiated the bad pun (66).

12. In early August, a published statement appeared declaring that "Mr. Foote's License from the Lord Chamberlain for the New Theatre in the Haymarket, expiring the last Day of this Month, and Vast Numbers of People not being able to gain Admittance, on the three usual Days of Performance, Mr. Foote is encouraged to open the Theatre every Night." Quoted in Belden, *The Dramatic Work of Samuel Foote* 85.

13. Wilkinson later took over Foote's roles in regional productions, including those in Portsmouth, and even put together medleys in which he advertised that he was playing Foote playing certain characters, such as Mrs. Cole. The playbills in the Lewis Walpole Library collection of theater ephemera shows Wilkinson actively marketing himself as a regional version of Foote. Wilkinson would later write a memoir, primarily about his life in the theater, *Memoirs of His Own Life*.

14. Charles Macklin in his 1746 *A Will and No Will, or, a Bone for the Lawyers* featured a similar Methodist in drag, Widow Bumper, who seeks comfort in the arms of Dr. Preachfield because she was "afraid of Spirits, Ghosts, Witches and Fairies." The Widow Bumper finds a different kind of new birth: two of her fifteen children have arrived since the death of her husband, and another is on the way (24).

15. By 1760, Smart had been confined to an insane asylum for his evangelical outbursts, providing a curious loop of connections through Foote's stage dames and religious revival that leads from performance to reality.

16. The ban on the epilogue took effect when the show transferred to Drury Lane.

17. For more on this connection, see West, "Wilkes's Squint."

18. As Kinservik explains, the epilogue was officially censored by order of the Lord Chamberlain when the play moved to Drury Lane, but it remained part of subsequent print editions. Kinservik argues that the flap about censoring *The Minor* masks the complicity of the Duke of Devonshire (the Lord Chamberlain), Thomas Secker (the Archbishop of Canterbury), and Foote, demonstrating that *The Minor* actually benefited from the censorship process. Devonshire was relieved that he "got off" from pressure from the Archbishop to ban it, and for his part Secker refused to amend the play lest it appear in a version as corrected by the Archbishop of Canterbury. Garrick, *The Private Correspondence of David Garrick* 1: 120.

19. See *The London Chronicle*, November 22–25, 1760, viii, 507.

20. The epilogue is present in the 1760, 1761, 1764, 1767, 1771, 1781, 1787, 1789, 1792, and 1798 editions. The epilogue was printed separately in 1760 and 1790.

21. For a sophisticated study of the question of liability in the context of the eighteenth-century novel, see Macpherson, *Harm's Way*.

22. This was also the case for his later political ballad-opera *The Duenna*, which recycled material from Sheridan's *Duenna* and added a Wesley, "John Cantwell."

23. Reed's complaint squares with the anonymous *An Additional Scene to the Comedy of The Minor* (1761), which mocked Foote's comic hubris ("I have the town under my thumb;—I can take 'em thus and twirl them about like a top") as well as his cheap character assassinations. John Genest, *Some Account of the English Stage*. Genest observes: "noth-

ing is said which could justify the Licenser in striking out the character—he ought to have been ashamed of himself for objecting to Mrs. Snarewell after having licensed Mrs. Cole."

24. Krysmanski, *Hogarth's* Enthusiasm Delineated.

25. For more on the connections between Foote and Hogarth, see Krysmanski, *Hidden Parts* 147 and Norton, *Mother Clap's Molly House*, ch. 11, "The Age of Scandal." Ronald Paulson also notes that the pro-Pitt Lord Hardwicke secured Secker the deanship at St. Paul's and, later, the Archbishoprick of Canterbury. For Hogarth, according to Paulson, this made Secker a Pitt appointee, an additional source for his hostility. *Hogarth* 3: 262.

26. The question whether John Smith was indeed Thomas Secker is unresolved. Henry Rack believes the attribution to be erroneous, but the Wesley College archives at Bristol, which holds the correspondence, claims that Smith was indeed Secker, as did Alexander Gordon, author of the previous DNB entry on John Wesley. See Rack, "John Wesley."

27. Terry Castle has discussed the sexualized thermometer and the enlightenment fascination with measuring emotion and anthropomorphizing technology. See Castle, *The Female Thermometer*.

28. Bernd Krysmanski presses even further on the pornographic extremes of the image, noting (as Terry Castle has) the phallic thermometers, but also the optical illusion of the priest's penis draped over the rostrum, the Christ icon "engaging" with Mrs. Cole, who is also a version of a swooning Virgin Mary. He suggests that the latter image may be a parody of George Whitefield's "Christ the Best Husband." See *Hidden Parts* 370.

29. The colonists' complaint also included Wesley's appointment of "Deaconesses" and a general tendency to "Popery and Slavery" that threatened the Georgia colony ideologically, as Spanish settlements to the south threatened it in more directly political terms. The complaint was reprinted as an appendix to *The Progress of Methodism in Bristol*.

30. See Paulson, *Hogarth's Harlot*, and Krysmanski, *Hogarth's* Enthusiasm Delineated.

31. The Joly-Fairfax Murray impression of the print housed in San Francisco, which is almost identical to the British Museum copy, also includes a sketch of the Virgin Mary placing the infant Christ into the hopper of the windmill. Ireland reproduced both of the small pen drawings when he re-engraved the image that is in the Steevens folio of Hogarth's at the Lewis Walpole Library. See also Krysmanski, *Hogarth's* Enthusiasm Delineated.

32. The painting, which was damaged in a cleaning, currently hangs in the Ashmolean Museum. My thanks to Ronald Paulson for his advice on the interpolation of this image from Hogarth's painting.

33. The British Museum's *Catalogue of Political and Personal Satires* (ed. Stephens) discusses the piece in entry 2156.

34. For a summary of the publications concerning the Cock Lane ghost and their relationship to the rise of the literary management of terror, see Clery, *The Rise of Supernatural Fiction, 1762–1800*.

35. For an extended discussion of how Fielding's legal writing shaped his notions of narrative proof, see Lamb, "Exemplarity and Excess in Fielding's Fiction."

36. Quoted Howes, *Yorick and the Critics* 18.

37. For examples of such readings, see Clery, *The Rise of Supernatural Fiction, 1762–1800*. I use the phrase "symptomatic reading" in the sense that Best and Marcus use it in their recent lead article for a special issue of *Representations* on "the way we read now." See Best and Marcus, "Surface Reading."

38. Walpole, *Anecdotes of Painting in England* 4: 72. "Sublime" is a problematic designation for an artist who was at pains to separate himself from Reynold's notion of the sublime artist. Paulson and Krysmanski have both argued persuasively that both versions of Hogarth's print demonstrate his resistance to Burkean ideas about the sublime and about painting.

39. Ireland 236. Ireland preferred *Enthusiasm Delineated*, which he identified also as "First Thought for the Medley" to *Credulity*, writing, "I think of the *First Thought*, what Mr. Walpole, in his *Anecdotes*, asserts of the *second*,—that *for useful and deep satire it is the most sublime of all his works*. It forms one great whole; and the skill with which he has appropriated the absurd symbols of painters, and combined the idolatrous emblems of popery with the mummery of modern enthusiasts, presents a *trait* of his genius hitherto unknown—displays the powers of his mind on subjects new to his pencil, and shews an extent of information, and depth of thought, that is not to be found in any of his other works" (236).

40. Sheridan lamented the necessary failures of written language as an attempt "to do that with the pen, which can only be performed by the tongue" and advocated the necessity of oratory, like an extemporaneous Whitefield sermon or a Garrick performance, to convey meaning beyond what language itself can bear (xii). Foote used a virtuosic lineup of comic actors (including Quin, Bannister, Booth, Young, and of course, Foote himself) to satirize Sheridan's efforts to teach oratory to the general public. The *Course of Comic Lectures* was a mixed bag of an attack on Sheridan's courses, the debating societies, lawyers, Foote's Irish foe George Faulkner ("Peter Paragraph"), Methodists, and the Cock Lane ghost.

41. Krysmanski identifies the weeping penitent as Gardelle. He suggests that Gardelle farts, but the cloud of wind comes from behind the Jesus figure. Paulson notes that Gardelle was carted by Hogarth's home on his way to his execution, and that Hogarth watched the scene with interest. See Krysmanski, *Hidden Parts* 374–77, and Paulson, *Hogarth* 3: 321.

42. Keats, *The Letters of John Keats* 465. The letter is dated Feb. 14, 16, 1820, from Hampstead Heath, to James Rice.

43. See Paulson, *Hogarth* 3: 367. Garrick supposedly told La Place, Fielding's French translator, years later in Paris. There were competing versions of the story, all focusing on Hogarth's mental block in remembering his friend's face, but Garrick's version theatrically connects the great skeptic with a more personal experience of ghosts.

CHAPTER FIVE: "My Lord, My Love"

1. See Harford, Stevenson, and Tyrer, ed., *The Prayer Book Dictionary*.
2. Wesley, *Works* 74.
3. Mack notes that Asad's example of the professional actor provides a way for a secular person to apprehend a religious person's experience of agency. It is also a useful way to think about the complex experience of agency involved in singing these hymns. Like an actor, the hymn singer is always mediating between scripted text, self expression, and the disempowering of oneself for the sake of another. See Mack, "Religion, Feminism, and the Problem of Agency" 12 and Asad, "Agency and Pain."
4. See Peter Wilton, "Hymn." I am especially grateful to Dr. Frank P. Tirro for his

instruction on church music and the history of the hymn from its medieval to its Renaissance uses.

5. Temperley and Drage, *Eighteenth-Century Psalmody* xxiii. Temperley explains that he confines the term hymn "strictly in the eighteenth-century sense of a strophic metrical text of 'human' authorship, as distinct from the divine inspiration widely attributed to the psalms," a distinction he admits is far from absolute. Temperley's very useful definition frames my interest in the question of where these songs were sung and by whom as a crucial piece of the story behind their meaning when sung in public in large groups.

6. While psalm form has a long history of complication and then simplification, its musical roots returned the form again and again to simplicity grounded in plainsong. I have necessarily simplified the arguments of Nicholas Temperley, the most authoritative musicologist on this history. See *The Music of the English Parish Church* (Cambridge, 1979).

7. Nicholas Temperley, "If any of you be mery let hym synge psalms" 92.

8. Lloyd, *Charles Wesley and the Struggle for Methodist Identity* 75. Lloyd quotes from a MS inventory of books belonging to John Wesley from the Wesleyan Conference collection.

9. Thomas Ravenscroft, *A Briefe Discourse of the True (but Neglected) Use of Charact'ring the Degree* (London, 1614) A3, qtd. in Austern 621.

10. Weinbrot argues in *Britannia's Issue* that the development of a British literary tradition was deeply tied to emerging discourses of nationalism. See especially chapter five, "Dryden's 'Essay of Dramatic Poesie': The Poetics of Nationalism."

11. See *Grove Music Online*, "The Methodist Church."

12. Rathey, "Lecture: Bach's Christmas Oratorio." My gratitude to Professor Markus Rathey of the Yale School of Music and the Institute of Sacred Music for his instruction on the subject of Bach's use of musical parody.

13. According to Dean Winton, Bishop Gibson initially refused permission to perform it on the grounds that it was sacrilegious for scripture to be performed by actors and musicians, so Handel presented the sacred drama as oratorio without costume or actions. The musical boundary-breaking across stage and cathedral led an anonymous critic to declare in *See and Seem Blind* "this Sacred *Drama* a mere Consort," with Handel "plac'd in a Pulpit, I suppose they call that their Oratory," indicating an unsettling sense of mixed forms. Winton, *Handel's Dramatic Oratorios and Masques*. See also the discussion of Handel and oratorio in Burrows, *The Cambridge Companion to Handel*.

14. References to ballads and "Scotch ballads" in the popular press confirm that some groups of singers were using such tunes. For more on the controversy, see Routley, *The Musical Wesleys* 35–38 and Dean McIntyre, "Did the Wesleys Really Use Drinking Song Tunes for Their Hymns?" *General Board of Discipleship* website, www.gbod.org/worship/default.asp?act=reader&item_id=2639&loc_id=17,627,628.

15. This episode and the text of the hymn are reported by Brian Wren. See Wren, *Praying Twice* 9.

16. See the *Grove Music Online*, "Ballad Opera" and "John Frederick Lampe."

17. For more on *King Arthur* and the shaping of history, see the 2010 special issue of *Restoration: Studies in English Literary Culture: 1660–1700* 34: 1–2 and Armistead, "Dryden's *King Arthur* and the Literary Tradition."

18. Examples include "None is like Jeshuron's God," hymn 395 in the 1780 collection, which echoes *The Rape of the Lock, Paradise Lost*, and the *Odyssey*, in "Jesus is thy *sevenfold*

shield [italics added],/Jesus is thy flaming sword." "Come Sinners to the Gospel Feast" returns to *The Rape of the Lock* again as singers urge one another "His conqu'ring love consent to feel/Yield to his love's resistless power." John Wesley also paraphrased Pope's *Essay on Poetry* for the introduction to his 1753 *Hymns and Spiritual Songs*, in which he declared their hymns had "no doggerel, no botches, nothing put in to patch up the rhyme, no feeble expletives." For more on the richly allusive qualities of the hymns, see *The Works of John Wesley*, vol. 7, ed. by Franz Hilderbrandt and Oliver A. Beckerlegge, with James Dale, Oxford UP.

19. He described the bad poet as a "Grotesque Painter" who "is to mingle Bits of the most various, or discordant kinds . . . and connect them with a great deal of *Flourishing*, by *heads or Tails*, as it shall please his Imagination, and contribute to his principal End, which is to glare by strong Oppositions of Colours, and surprise by Contrariety of Images" (93, Dublin 1728).

20. These images repeat throughout the hymns, but particular cases occur in hymns 122 ("Too strong I was to conquer sin"); 123 ("Wherewith, O God, shall I draw near"); 126 ("Thou God unsearchable, unknown"); and 128 (Jesu, the sinner's friend, to thee"). Wesley, *Works*.

21. The practice was begun by George Whitefield. See Temperley and Crawford, "Psalmody (Ii)."

22. Teresa Berger also notes that the line is a reference to Ignatius of Antioch to Romans. See Berger, *Theology in Hymns?* 107.

23. Hymn no. 113, *Harmonia Sacra* 76. The tune listed is "Welch."

24. J. R. Watson makes the observation of this connection with Dryden in Watson, *An Annotated Anthology of Hymns*.

25. "Divorce me, untie, or break that knot again,/Take me to you, imprison me, for I/Except you enthrall me, never shall be free,/ Nor ever chaste, except you ravish me."

26. For more on the eroticism of Moravian hymns, see Atwood, "Sleeping in the Arms of Christ."

27. In the 1740 hymnal, Wesley indicates this hymn is from the German. See Wesley, *Works* 7: 500.

28. *Letter to the Rev. Mr. M——Re B——K-R, Concerning the Methodists* 16.

CHAPTER SIX: A Usable Past

1. Bryan Little, *The Buildings of Bath* 47, 1947, pl. 51. The chapel is described in *The Historical and Local New Bath Guide*, 1801, 51–52, as displaying "taste and elegance in the interior part. The ground floor is intersected by a light iron railing into several divisions, each well furnished with seats covered in red cloth; a handsome gallery runs round, supported by fluted pillars, every two of which form an arch with the side of the gallery. The communion table is placed in a circular recess at one end, with a fine toned organ directly over it; at the other end, two steps higher than the floor, there are two reading desks, each supported by a spread eagle, behind these the throne rises six steps higher still, with another reading desk, borne by a spread eagle also, that stands on its summit. These ornaments unite to make the whole to have a pleasing effect on the eye of the beholder."

2. The Deed of Declaration (ratified on March 9, 1784) established the "Legal Hundred" (the hundred preachers designated by Wesley) to govern the conference. After Wesley's death in 1791, the break with the Anglican church became even more defined.

For more on Methodist history, see, among others, Vickers, *A Dictionary of Methodism in Britain and Ireland*; Hempton, *Religion of the People*; Hempton, *Methodism*; and Ward, *Early Evangelicalism*.

3. *London Chronicle* February 27, 1777. Anstey goes on to mention the "learned dog," a popular sideshow in the mid-eighteenth century and perhaps a source of Samuel Johnson's alleged comment comparing a female preacher to a dog walking on its hind legs. My thanks to Gordon Turnbull for bringing this reference and its context to my attention.

4. See Thorson's introduction to Smollett, *Humphry Clinker* and Sekora, *Luxury*.

5. Smollett's editorial contribution to the thirty-five volume *Works of Voltaire* (1761–81) made him familiar with Voltaire's declarations against Christian intolerance and fanaticism, in which the vision of an enlightened, tolerant public space is undercut by religious violence and orthodoxy.

6. *Atom* shows us intolerance and fanaticism, but lacks such an enlightened public sphere.

7. His piece is a reply to Robert Whytt's *Essay on the Vital and Other Involuntary Motions in Animals*. Though not a vegetarian, as Wesley was, he even complains about the smell of a neighbor cooking veal in butter sauce (which is "almost as disagreeable" as working on his *Universal History*).

8. Notably, Smollett, the beneficiary of income from a Caribbean plantation in his wife's dowry, avoided a public stand on slavery.

9. For a more sustained conversation on Smollett and sympathy, see Gottlieb, "Fools of Prejudice"; Wallace, "'About Savages and the Awfulness of America'"; and Wetmore, "Sympathy Machines."

10. For more on the architectural and cultural history of Bath, see Borsay, "Myth, Memory, and Place"; Borsay, *The Image of Georgian Bath, 1700–2000*; Forsyth, *Bath*; and Brooke, *The History of Lady Julia Mandeville*.

11. The identification of Rabbi Nicodemus is in the British Museum entry for the illustration no. 4167.

12. See Clark, "Bladud of Bath."

13. For a more extended discussion of the relationship of the novel's representation of luxury economy and gender, see Weed, "Sentimental Misogyny and Medicine in *Humphry Clinker*."

14. For example, see Sully, *Sully's Domestic Physician: Or Every Man His Own Doctor*; Archer, *Every Man His Own Doctor: Compleated with an Herbal*; T. Johnson, *Every Man His Own Doctor: Or the Family Physician*; Tennent, *Every Man His Own Doctor: Or, the Poor Planter's Physician*; Robinson, *Every Man His Own Doctor: Or the Sick Man's Triumph over Death and the Grave*; Johnson, *For the Public Benefit Johnson's Domestic Physician: Or, Every Man His Own Doctor*; *Nature the Great Physician: Or, Every Man His Own Doctor*; and Lover of Mankind, *Nature the Best Physician: Or, Every Man His Own Doctor*.

15. Smollett wrote three distinct histories: *The Compleat History of England from the Descent of Julius Caesar, to the Treaty of Aix la Chapelle* (1757); the five-volume *A Continuation of the Compleat History* (1763–65); and the eight-volume *The Present State of All Nations* (1768). In addition, he also edited the seven-volume *A Compendium of Authentic and Diverting Voyages* (1757).

16. The preacher evidently brought with him "a large congregation" to which he added out of Graves's flock (24). For more on the source of the novel in this incident, see Hill, *The Literary Career of Richard Graves*.

17. For an account of the range of mob violence against Methodists, see Wilder, *The Methodist Riots*.

18. My adaptation of Jameson's point about nostalgia film comes from Jameson, *Postmodernism, or, the Cultural Logic of Late Capitalism* 286–89.

19. For more on the British Quixote novel in the eighteenth century, see Gordon, *The Practice of Quixotism*.

20. See MacKenzie, *The Lounger*.

AFTERWORD: 1778 and Beyond

1. For more on the events surrounding the "collapse" of John Wesley's efforts to keep Methodism a parachurch movement at the end of his career, see Noll, *The Rise of Evangelicalism* 203–10.

2. The graphic representation of the cross is an echo of *Tristram Shandy* as well that returns to the Roman Catholic/Methodist association.

3. Elliott argues in *The Power of Satire* that, in spite of the conservative or even curative pose of the satirist, the power of the word he or she invokes appeals to their sacredness in small acts of verbal magic. See esp. 276–79.

4. See Habermas, *An Awareness of What Is Missing*; Kauffman, "The Religious, the Secular, and Literary Studies"; and Caputo and Scanlon, *God, the Gift, and Postmodernism*.

5. Kauffman's argument situates Marsden's *The Soul of the American University* (1994), Scholes's *The Rise and Fall of English Studies* (1998), Graff's *Professing Literature* (1987), and Robbins's *Secular Vocations* (1993) in dialogue with the Arnoldian transmission thesis. Notably, the titles and the "rise and decline" trajectory of their arguments engage with religious language and biblical narratives of the fall. See Kauffman, "The Religious, the Secular, and Literary Studies."

6. Branch, *Rituals of Spontaneity*; Snead, "Religion and Eighteenth-Century Literature"; Saccamano, "Inheriting Enlightenment"; Potkay, *The Story of Joy*; White, *Early Romanticism and Religious Dissent*; and Seidel, "Beyond the Religious and the Secular in the History of the Novel."

7. For a series of views on this question, see Habermas, *An Awareness of What Is Missing*.

8. Latour, "Why Has Critique Run out of Steam?"

Bibliography

Abelove, Henry. *The Evangelist of Desire: John Wesley and the Methodists*. Stanford: Stanford UP, 1990.
Acosta, Ana. "Voices of Dissent and the Public Sphere in Hackney, Stoke Newington, and Newington Green." *Eighteenth-Century Life* 27.1 (2003): 1–27.
Addison, Joseph. "The Spectator." Ed. Donald F. Bond. Oxford: Clarendon P, 1965.
Anderson, Misty G. "Mr. Barvile's Enthusiasm." *Launching Fanny Hill: Essays on the Novel and Its Influences*. Ed. Patsy Fowler and Alan Jackson. Brooklyn: AMS Press, 2003. 199–220.
Anstey, Christopher. *The New Bath Guide: Or, Memoirs of the B-r-d family. In a Series of Poetical Epistles*. 5th ed. London, 1767.
Archer, John. *Every Man His Own Doctor: Compleated with an Herbal*. London, 1673.
Armistead, Jack. "Dryden's *King Arthur* and the Literary Tradition: A Way of Seeing." *Studies in Philology* 85.1 (1988): 53–72.
Armstrong, Nancy. *Desire and Domestic Fiction: A Political History of the Novel*. New York: Oxford UP, 1987.
Arnold, Richard. *The English Hymn: Studies in a Genre*. New York: P. Lang, 1995.
Asad, Talal. "Agency and Pain: An Exploration." *Culture and Religion* 1.1 (2000): 29–60.
———. *Formations of the Secular: Christianity, Islam, Modernity*. Stanford: Stanford UP, 2003.
Atwood, Craig. "Sleeping in the Arms of Christ: Sanctifying Sexuality in the Eighteenth-Century Moravian Church." *Journal of the History of Sexuality* 8.1 (1997): 25–51.
Austen, Jane. *Northanger Abbey*. Ed. Barbara Benedict and Deidre Le Faye. Cambridge: Cambridge UP, 2007.
Austern, Linda Phyllis. "'For, Love's a Good Musician': Performance, Audition, and Erotic Disorders in Early Modern Europe." *The Musical Quarterly* 82.3/4 (1998): 614–53.
Badiou, Alain. *Saint Paul: The Foundation of Universalism*. Cultural Memory in the Present. Stanford: Stanford UP, 2003.
Barker-Benfield, G. J. *The Culture of Sensibility: Sex and Society in Eighteenth-Century Britain*. Chicago: U Chicago P, 1996.
Barry, Jonathan, and Kenneth Morgan. *Reformation and Revival in Eighteenth-Century Bristol*. Vol. 45. Stroud: Bristol Record Society, 1994.
Battestin, Martin C., with Ruthe R. Battestin. *Henry Fielding: A Life*. London: Routledge, 1989.
Belden, Mary Megie. *The Dramatic Work of Samuel Foote*. Hamden: Archon Books, 1969.

Benson, Louis F. *The English Hymn: Its Development and Use in Worship*. London: Hodder & Stoughton, 1915.
Berger, Teresa. *Theology in Hymns? A Study of the Relationship of Doxology and Theology according to a Collection of Hymns for the Use of the People Called Methodists (1780)*. Nashville: Kingswood Books, 1995.
Best, Stephen, and Sharon Marcus. "Surface Reading: An Introduction." *Representations* 108.1 (Fall 2009): 1–21.
Blackwell, Bonnie. "'An Infallible Nostrum': Female Husbands and Greensick Girls in Eighteenth-Century England." *Literature and Medicine* 21.1 (2002): 56–77.
Blake, William. *William Blake*. Ed. Michael Mason. Oxford: Oxford UP, 1988.
Bonhoeffer, Dietrich. *The Cost of Discipleship*. New York: Simon and Schuster, rpt. 1995.
Borsay, Peter. *The Image of Georgian Bath, 1700–2000: Towns, Heritage, and History*. Oxford: Oxford UP, 2000.
———. "Myth, Memory, and Place: Monmouth and Bath 1750–1900." *Journal of Social History* 39.3 (2006): 867–89.
Boswell, James. *The Life of Johnson*. Ed. David Womersley. London: Penguin, 2008.
———. "On the Profession of a Player." *The London Magazine*, 1770.
———. *On the Profession of a Player*. London: Elkin Mathews and Marrot, 1929.
Boswell, Lady Betty Bruce. *Observations upon Effectuall Calling*. Boswell Family Papers, New Haven, 1925.
Boucé, Paul-Gabriel. *The Novels of Tobias Smollett*. London: Longman, 1976.
Bouwsma, William J. *A Useable Past: Essays in European Cultural History*. Berkeley: U California P, 1990.
Bowden, Samuel. *Poems on Various Subjects*. London, 1754.
Branch, Lori. *Rituals of Spontaneity: Sentiment and Secularism from Free Prayer to Wordsworth*. Waco: Baylor UP, 2006.
Brantley, Richard E. *Locke, Wesley, and the Method of English Romanticism*. Gainesville: UP of Florida, 1984.
Braudy, Leo. "*Fanny Hill* and Materialism." *Eighteenth-Century Studies* 4 (1970): 21–40.
Braunschneider, Theresa. "Acting the Lover: Gender and Desire in Narratives of Passing Women." *Eighteenth Century: Theory and Interpretation* 45.3 (2004): 211–29.
Brooke, Frances. *The History of Lady Julia Mandeville*. London: Rivington, 1820.
Burnet, Bishop Gilbert. *Bishop Burnet's Travels through Switzerland, Italy, Some Parts of Germany, &c. . . . To Which Is Added, an Appendix, Containing Some Remarks on Switzerland and Italy, Writ by a Person of Quality*. Dublin, 1725.
Burney, Charles. *Letters of Dr. Charles Burney*. Ed. Alvaro Ribeiro. Vol. 1. Oxford: Clarendon P, 1991.
Burrows, Donald. *The Cambridge Companion to Handel*. Cambridge: Cambridge UP, 1997.
Burton, Vicki Tolar. *Spiritual Literacy in John Wesley's Methodism*. Waco: Baylor UP, 2008.
Butler, Jon, Grant Wacker, and Randall Balmer. *Religion in American Life: A Short History*. New York: Oxford UP, 2007.
Butler, Judith. *Bodies That Matter: On the Discursive Limits of "Sex."* New York: Routledge, 1993.
Bynum, Caroline Walker. *Fragmentation and Redemption: Essays on Gender and the Human Body in Medieval Religion*. New York: Zone Books, 1992.
Campbell, Jill. *Natural Masques: Gender and Identity in Fielding's Plays and Novels*. Stanford: Stanford UP, 1995.

Caputo, John D. *On Religion*. Thinking in Action. London: Routledge, 2001.
Caputo, John D., and Michael J. Scanlon. *God, the Gift, and Postmodernism*. Bloomington: Indiana UP, 1999.
Carroll, John, ed. *Selected Letters of Samuel Richardson*. Oxford: Clarendon P, 1964.
Castle, Terry. *The Female Thermometer: Eighteenth-Century Culture and the Invention of the Uncanny*. New York: Oxford UP, 1995.
Cavendish, Margaret. *Philosophical Letters*. London, 1664.
Chalmers, David. "Facing up to the Problem of Consciousness." *Journal of Consciousness Studies* 2 (1995): 200–19.
Champion, J. A. I. *The Pillars of Priestcraft Shaken: The Church of England and Its Enemies 1600–1730*. Cambridge: Cambridge UP, 1992.
Chatterton, Thomas. *The Poetical Works of Thomas Chatterton*. New York: AMS, 1968.
Chilcote, Paul Wesley. *John Wesley and the Women Preachers of Early Methodism*. Duke University, 1984.
Churchill, Charles. *The Ghost*. London, 1762.
Clark, John. "Bladud of Bath: The Archeology of a Legend." *Folklore* 105 (1994): 39–50.
Cleland, John. *The Case of the Unfortunate Bosavern Penlez*. London, 1749.
———. *Memoirs of a Woman of Pleasure*. Ed. Peter Sabor. Oxford: Oxford UP, 1985.
———. *The Way to Things by Words, and to Words by Things*. London, 1766.
Clément, Catherine. "Through Voices, History." *Siren Songs: Representations of Gender and Sexuality in Opera*. Ed. Mary Ann Smart. Princeton: Princeton UP, 2000. 17–28.
Clery, E. J. *The Rise of Supernatural Fiction, 1762–1800*. Cambridge Studies in Romanticism. Ed. Marilyn Butler. Cambridge: Cambridge UP, 1995.
Combe, William. *Sketches for Tabernacle Frames*. London, 1778.
Cooke, Thomas. *The Mournful Nuptials*. London, 1739.
Corfield, Penelope J. "'We Are All One in the Eyes of the Lord': Christopher Hill and the Historical Meanings of Radical Religion." *History Workshop Journal* 58 (2004): 110–27.
Cowper, William. *The Poems of William Cowper*. Oxford English Texts. Ed. John D. Baird and Charles Ryskamp. Oxford: Clarendon P, 1980.
Cumberland, Richard. *Henry*. Vol. 1. 4 vols. London, 1795.
Cupples, Cynthia. "Pious Ladies and Methodist Madams: Sex and Gender in Anti-Methodist Writings of Eighteenth-Century England." *Critical Matrix* 5 (1990): 30–60.
Damrosch, Leo. "Feeling Free in the Enlightenment: Diderot versus Rousseau, or, Philosophy versus Lived Experience." New Haven: Yale Lewis Walpole Library Lecture, 2008.
Davie, Donald. *The Eighteenth-Century Hymn in England*. Cambridge: Cambridge UP, 1993.
Davies, Rupert E., E. Gordon Rupp, and A. Raymond George. *A History of the Methodist Church in Great Britain*. 4 vols. London: Epworth P, 1965.
Day, Martin S. "Anstey and Anapestic Satire in the Late Eighteenth Century." *ELH* 15.2 (1948): 122–46.
Derrida, Jacques. "Above All, No Journalists!" *Religion and Media*. Ed. Hent de Vries and Samuel Weber. Stanford: Stanford UP, 2001.
De Vries, Hent. *Philosophy and the Turn to Religion*. Baltimore: Johns Hopkins UP, 1999.
Downes, John. *Methodism Examined and Exposed: Or, the Clergy's Duty of Guarding Their Flocks against False Teachers*. London, 1759.
Dreyer, Frederick A. *The Genesis of Methodism*. Bethlehem, NJ: Lehigh UP, 1999.
During, Simon. *Exit Capitalism: Literary Culture, Theory, and Post-Secular Modernity*. New York: Routledge, 2010.

Dyson, John B. *Methodism in the Isle of Wight: Its Origin and Progress Down to the Present Time*. Ventnor, Isle of Wight: George M. Burt, 1865.
Eagleton, Terry. *Reason, Faith, and Revolution: Reflections on the God Debate*. New Haven: Yale UP, 2009.
East, W. G. "Educating Heloise." *Medieval Monastic Education*. Ed. George Ferzoco and Carolyn Muessig. Leicester: Leicester UP, 2000.
Eliot, George. *Adam Bede*. Ed. Stephen Gill. New York: Penguin, 1980.
Elliott, Robert C. *The Power of Satire: Magic, Ritual, Art*. Princeton: Princeton UP, 1960.
England, Martha Winburn, with John Hanbury Angus Sparrow. *Hymns Unbidden: Donne, Herbert, Blake, Emily Dickinson, and the Hymnographers*. New York: New York Public Library, 1966.
Epstein, William H. *John Cleland: Images of a Life*. New York: Columbia UP, 1974.
Ferguson, Frances. *Pornography, the Theory: What Utilitarianism Did to Action*. Chicago: U Chicago P, 2004.
Ferguson, Ronald. *Chasing the Wild Goose: The Story of the Iona Community*. Glasgow: Wild Goose Publications, 1998.
Fielding, Henry. *The Champion*. Vol. 2. London, 1743.
———. "The Female Husband." *The Journal of a Voyage to Lisbon, Shamela, and Occasional Writings*. Ed. Martin C. Battestin. The Wesleyan Edition of the Works of Henry Fielding. Oxford: Clarendon P, 2008.
———. "Miss Lucy in Town." *The Works of Henry Fielding*. Vol. 2. Ed. James P. Browne. London, 1903.
Finlay, Emily. "'So Lovely a Skin Scarified with Rods': Modern Notions in Fielding's *The Female Husband*." *antiTHESIS* 17 (2007): 154–70.
Fletcher, Nathaniel. *A Methodist Dissected: Or, a Description of Their Errors. By Nath. Fletcher*. York: Printed by Caesar Ward, 1749.
Foote, Samuel. *A Letter from Mr. Foote: To the Reverend Author of the Remarks, Critical and Christian, on the Minor*. London, 1760.
———. *The Plays of Samuel Foote*. *Eighteenth-Century English Drama*. Ed. Douglas Howard and Paula R. Backscheider. 3 vols. New York: Garland, 1983.
Forster, John. *Historical and Biographical Essays*. London: J. Murray, 1858.
Forsyth, Michael. *Bath*. Pevsner Architectural Guides. New Haven: Yale UP, 2003.
Foucault, Michel. *Religion and Culture*. Ed. Jeremy R. Carrette. Manchester: Manchester UP, 1999.
Free, John. *A Sermon Preached before the University at St. Mary's in Oxford, on Whitsunday, 1758*. 2nd ed. London, 1758.
Freeman, Lisa A. *Character's Theater: Genre and Identity on the Eighteenth-Century English Stage*. Philadelphia: U of Pennsylvania P, 2002.
Frei, Hans W. *The Eclipse of Biblical Narrative: A Study in Eighteenth and Nineteenth Century Hermeneutics*. New Haven: Yale UP, 1974.
Frey, Andrew. *A True and Authentic Account of Andrew Frey*. London: J. Robinson et al., 1753.
Garlick, Görel. *Theatre Outside London, 1660–1775*. *The Cambridge History of British Theatre*. Ed. Peter Thomson. Vol. 2. 3 vols. Cambridge: Cambridge UP, 2004.
Garrick, David. *The Private Correspondence of David Garrick*. Ed. James Boaden. 2 vols. London, 1831–2.

Genest, John. *Some Account of the English Stage from the Restoration in 1660 to 1830*. Bristol: Thoemmes P, 1997.

———. *Some Account of the English Stage from the Restoration in 1660 to 1830*. Bath: Printed by H. E. Carrington, 1832.

Gibson, Edmund. "Observations upon the Conduct and Behaviour of a Certain Sect Usually Distinguished by the Name of Methodists." London, 1740. http://galenet.galegroup.com/servlet/ECCO?c=1&stp=Author&ste=11&af=BN&ae=T041877&tiPG=1&dd=0&dc=flc&docNum=CW120568993&vrsn=1.0&srchtp=a&d4=0.33&n=10&SU=0LRF&locID=29002. Full text online.

Gilman, Todd. "David Garrick's *Masque of King Arthur* with Thomas Arne's Score (1770)." *Restoration: Studies in English Literary Culture, 1660–1700* 34.1–2 (2010): 139–62.

Girard, René. *Violence and the Sacred*. Trans. Patrick Gregory. Baltimore: Johns Hopkins UP, 1977.

Glen, Robert. "'Adieu the Delights of the Stage': An Anti-Methodist Song of 1746." *Notes and Queries* 244 (1999): 350–56.

Goldsmith, Oliver. *The Collected Works of Oliver Goldsmith*. Ed. A. Friedman. 5 vols. Oxford: Clarendon P, 1966.

Gordon, Scott Paul. *The Practice of Quixotism: Postmodern Theory and Eighteenth-Century Women's Writing*. New York: Palgrave Macmillan, 2006.

Goring, Paul. *The Rhetoric of Sensibility in Eighteenth-Century Culture*. Cambridge: Cambridge UP, 2005.

Gottlieb, Evan. "'Fools of Prejudice': Sympathy and National Identity in the Scottish Enlightenment and *Humphry Clinker*." *Eighteenth-Century Fiction* 18.1 (2005): 81–106.

Graves, Richard. *The Spiritual Quixote, or the Summer's Ramble of Mr. Geoffrey Wildgoose: A Comic Romance*. Oxford English Novels. Ed. Clarence Rupert Tracy. London: Oxford UP, 1967.

Gregory, Brad S. "The Other Confessional History: On Secular Bias in the Study of Religion," *History and Theory* 45 (Dec. 2006): 132–49.

Gregory, Jeremy. "The Prayer Book and the Parish Church: From the Restoration to the Oxford Movement." *The Oxford Guide to the Book of Common Prayer: A Worldwide Survey*. Ed. Charles C. Hefling and Cynthia L. Shattuck. New York: Oxford UP, 2006. 93–115.

Gumbrecht, Hans Ulrich. *Production of Presence: What Meaning Cannot Convey*. Stanford: Stanford UP, 2004.

Haas, J. W. "John Wesley's Views on Science and Christianity: An Examination of the Charge of Anti-Science." *Church History* 63.3 (1994): 378–92.

Habermas, Jürgen. *An Awareness of What Is Missing: Faith and Reason in a Post-Secular Age*. Trans. Ciaran Cronin. Ed. Michael Reder and Josef Schmidt. Cambridge: Polity, 2010.

———. "Notes on a Post-Secular Society." *New Perspectives Quarterly* 25.4 (2008): 17–29.

Haggerty, George E. *Men in Love: Masculinity and Sexuality in the Eighteenth Century*. New York: Columbia UP, 1999.

Halperin, David M. *How to Do the History of Homosexuality*. Chicago: U of Chicago P, 2002.

Hanway, Jonas. *Letters Written Occasionally on The Customs of Foreign Nations in Regard to Harlots; The Lawless Commerce of the Sexes; The Repentance of Prostitutes; The Great

Humanity and Beneficial Effects of the Magdalene Charity in London; And the Absurd Notions of the Methodists: With Prayers and Meditations on the Most Interesting Circumstances and Events of Life. London, 1761.

———. *Thoughts on the Plan for a Magdalen-House for Repentant Prostitutes, with the Several Reasons for Such an Establishment . . . And the Great Advantages Which Must Necessarily Arise from the Good Conduct of This Institution . . . Addressed to the Promoters of This Charity.* 2nd ed. London: Sold by J. and R. Dodsley [etc.], 1759.

Harford, George, Morley Stevenson, and J. W. Tyrer, ed. *The Prayer Book Dictionary.* London: Pitman & Sons, 1925.

Harris, Ellen T. "*King Arthur's* Journey into the Eighteenth Century." *Purcell Studies.* Ed. Curtis Price. Cambridge: Cambridge UP, 1995. 257–98.

Heitzenrater, Richard P. *Wesley and the People Called Methodists.* Nashville: Abingdon P, 1995.

Hempton, David. "Evangelicalism and Reform, c. 1780–1832." *Evangelical Faith and Public Zeal: Evangelicals and Society in Britain, 1780–1980.* Ed. John Wolffe. London: SPCK, 1995.

———. *Methodism and Politics in British Society, 1750–1850.* Stanford: Stanford UP, 1984.

———. *Methodism: Empire of the Spirit.* New Haven: Yale UP, 2005.

———. *The Religion of the People: Methodism and Popular Religion c. 1750–1900.* London: Routledge, 1996.

Hill, Charles Jarvis. *The Literary Career of Richard Graves.* Northampton: Smith College, 1935.

Hoadly, Benjamin. *Sixteen Sermons Formerly Printed, Now Collected into One Volume.* London, 1754.

Hogarth, William. *The Analysis of Beauty.* Ed. Ronald Paulson. New Haven: Yale UP, 1997.

Holland, Peter. *The Ornament of Action: Text and Performance in Restoration Comedy.* Cambridge: Cambridge UP, 1979.

Hooker, Richard. "A Method of Confession Drawn Up for the Use of the Women Methodists." *Weekly Miscellany,* 1739.

Howes, Alan B. *Yorick and the Critics: Sterne's Reputation in England, 1760–1868.* New Haven: Yale UP, 1958.

Hume, David. *Letters of David Hume.* Ed. J. Y. T. Greig. Oxford: Clarendon P, 1932. Vol. 1.

———. *Principal Writings on Religion.* Oxford World's Classics. Ed. J. C. A. Gaskin. Oxford: Oxford UP, 1998.

Hunt, Lynn Avery, ed. *The Invention of Pornography: Obscenity and the Origins of Modernity, 1500–1800.* New York: Zone Books, 1993.

Hunter, J. Paul. *Before Novels: The Cultural Contexts of Eighteenth-Century English Fiction.* New York: W. W. Norton, 1990.

Ingrassia, Catherine. *Authorship, Commerce, and Gender in Early Eighteenth-Century England: A Culture of Paper Credit.* Cambridge: Cambridge UP, 1998.

Ireland, John. *Hogarth Illustrated, from His Own Manuscripts.* Vol. 3. London, 1812.

Irigaray, Luce. *Speculum of the Other Woman.* Trans. Gillian C. Gill. New York: Cornell UP, 1985.

Jackson, Thomas, ed. *The Lives of the Early Methodist Preachers, Chiefly Written by Themselves.* 3 vols. London, 1838.

Jagose, Annamarie. "'Critical Ecstasy': Orgasm and Sensibility in *Memoirs of a Woman of Pleasure*." *Signs: Journal of Women in Culture and Society* 32.2 (2007): 459–82.

Jakobsen, Janet R., with Ann Pellegrini. "Dreaming Secularism." *Social Text* 18.3, Duke UP, 2000.
Jameson, Fredric. *Postmodernism, or, the Cultural Logic of Late Capitalism*. Durham, NC: Duke UP, 1991.
Jefferson, Thomas. *The Writings of Thomas Jefferson*. Ed. Albert Ellery Bergh. Washington, DC: Thomas Jefferson Memorial Association, 1907.
Johnson. *For the Public Benefit Johnson's Domestic Physician: Or, Every Man His Own Doctor.* London, 1735.
Johnson, Samuel. *Yale Edition of the Works of Samuel Johnson*. Ed. W. J. Bate, John M. Bullitt, L. F. Powell. Vol. 2. New Haven: Yale UP, 1963.
Johnson, Thomas. *Every Man His Own Doctor: Or the Family Physician*. Salisbury, NC, 1798.
Johnstone, Charles. *Chrysal: Or, the Adventures of a Guinea. Library of Early Novelists*. Vol. 13. Ed. Ernest Albert Baker. New York: E. P. Dutton, 1907 [1760].
Jones, Louis Clark. *The Clubs of the Georgian Rakes*. New York: Columbia UP, 1942.
Jordan, Mark. "Religion Trouble." *GLQ: A Journal of Lesbian and Gay Studies* 13.4 (2007): 563–75.
J-ps-n, R-ph. *The Expounder Expounded*. London: Printed for the author and sold by W. and T. Payne, 1740.
Kaufman, Michael W. "The Religious, the Secular, and Literary Studies: Rethinking the Secularization Narrative in Histories of the Profession." *New Literary History* 38.4 (2007): 607–27.
Keane, Webb. *Christian Moderns: Freedom and Fetish in the Mission Encounter.* Berkeley: U of California P, 2007.
Keats, John. *The Letters of John Keats*. Ed. Maurice Buxton Forman. London: Oxford UP, 1947.
Keymer, Tom. *Richardson's Clarissa and the Eighteenth-Century Reader*. Cambridge: Cambridge UP, 2004.
Kinservik, Matthew. *Disciplining Satire: The Censorship of Satiric Comedy on the Eighteenth-Century London Stage*. Lewisburg: Bucknell UP, 2002.
Kramnick, Jonathan. "Empiricism, Cognitive Science, and the Novel." *The Eighteenth Century: Theory and Interpretation* 48.3 (2007): 263–85.
———. "Living with Lucretius." *Vital Matters: Eighteenth-Century Views of Conception, Life, and Death*. Ed. Helen Deutch and Mary Terrell. Ann Arbor: U Michigan P, 2009. 3–27.
———. "Rochester and the History of Sexuality." *ELH* 69.2 (2002): 277–301.
Kristeva, Julia. *Intimate Revolt: The Powers and Limits of Psychoanalysis*. Trans. Jeanine Herman. European Perspectives. New York: Columbia UP, 2002.
Krysmanski, Bernd W. *Hogarth's* Enthusiasm Delineated: *Nachahmung als Kritik am Kennertum: Eine Werkanalyse*. Vol. 2. 2 vols. Hildesheim: Georg Olms Verlag, 1996.
———. *Hogarth's Hidden Parts: Satiric Allusion, Erotic Wit, Blasphemous Bawdiness and Dark Humour in Eighteenth-Century English Art*. Hildesheim: Georg Olms Verlag, 2010.
Lamb, Jonathan. "Exemplarity and Excess in Fielding's Fiction." *Eighteenth-Century Fiction* 1.3 (1989): 187–207.
Lanser, Susan S. "Sapphic Picaresque, Sexual Difference and the Challenges of Homo-Adventuring." *Textual Practice* 15.2 (2001): 251–68.
Latour, Bruno. "Why Has Critique Run Out of Steam? From Matters of Fact to Matters of Concern." *Critical Inquiry* 30.2 (2004): 225–48.

Lavington, George. *The Enthusiasm of Methodists and Papists, Compar'd.* London: Printed for J. and P. Knapton, 1749.
———. *The Moravians Compared and Detected.* London: Printed for J. and P. Knapton, 1755.
Lawton, George. *John Wesley's English: A Study of His Literary Style.* London: George Allen & Unwin, 1962.
A Letter from the Rev. George Whitefield, M.A., to the Rev. Laurence Sterne, M.A. London, 1760.
Letter to the Rev. Mr. M———Re B———K-R, concerning the Methodists. Dublin, 1752.
Lloyd, Gareth. *Charles Wesley and the Struggle for Methodist Identity.* Oxford: Oxford UP, 2007.
Lloyd, Robert. *The Actor: A Poetical Epistle to Bonnell Thornton, Esq.* London: Printed for R. and J. Dodsley, Pall-Mall, 1760.
Locke, John. *An Essay concerning Human Understanding.* Ed. Peter H. Nidditch. Oxford: Clarendon P, 1975.
Lonsdale, Roger. "New Attributions to John Cleland." *Review of English Studies* 30 (1979): 268–90.
Lord, Evelyn. *The Hell-Fire Clubs.* New Haven: Yale UP, 2008.
Lyles, Albert M. *Methodism Mocked: The Satiric Reaction to Methodism in the Eighteenth Century.* London: Epworth P, 1960.
Mack, Phyllis. *Heart Religion in the British Enlightenment: Gender and Emotion in Early Methodism.* Cambridge: Cambridge UP, 2008.
———. "Religion, Feminism, and the Problem of Agency: Reflections on Eighteenth-Century Quakerism." *Signs: Journal of Women in Culture and Society* 29.1 (2003): 149–78.
———. *Visionary Women: Ecstatic Prophecy in Seventeenth-Century England.* Berkeley: U of California P, 1992.
MacKenzie, Henry. *The Lounger.* June 18, 1785.
Macpherson, Sandra. *Harm's Way: Tragic Responsibility and the Novel Form.* Baltimore: Johns Hopkins UP, 2010.
Mankind, Lover of. *Nature the Best Physician: Or, Every Man His Own Doctor.* London, 1772.
Masten, Jeffrey. *Textual Intercourse: Collaboration, Authorship, and Sexualities in Renaissance Drama.* Cambridge: Cambridge UP, 1997.
McFarlane, Cameron. *The Sodomite in Fiction and Satire, 1660–1750.* New York: Columbia UP, 1997.
McInelly, Brett C. "'I Had Rather Be Obscure. But I Dare Not': Women and Methodism in the Eighteenth Century." *Everyday Revolutions: Eighteenth-Century Women Transforming Public and Private.* Ed. Diane E. Boyd and Marta Kvande. Cranbury, NJ: Associated University Presses, 2008. 135–58.
McIntyre, Dean, "Did the Wesleys Really Use Drinking Song Tunes for Their Hymns?" General Board of Discipleship website, http://www.gbod.org/worship/default.asp?act=reader&item_id=2639&loc_id=17,627,628.
McKeon, Michael. "Historicizing Patriarchy: The Emergence of Gender Difference in England, 1660–1760." *Eighteenth-Century Studies* 28.3 (1995): 295–322.
———. *The Secret History of Domesticity: Public, Private, and the Division of Knowledge.* Baltimore: Johns Hopkins UP, 2005.

Mee, Jon. *Romanticism, Enthusiasm, and Regulation: Poetics and the Policing of Culture in the Romantic Period.* Oxford: Oxford UP, 2003.
The Merry Musician: Or, a Cure for the Spleen; Being a Collection of the Most Diverting Songs and Pleasant Ballads, Set to Music. Vol. 3. London, 1731.
The Methodists, an Humorous Burlesque Poem: Address'd to the Rev. Mr. Whitefield and His Followers. London: Printed for John Brett, 1739.
Mudge, Bradford. "How to Do the History of Pornography: Romantic Sexuality and Its Field of Vision." *Historicizing Romantic Sexuality.* Ed. Richard C. Sha. Romantic Circles Praxis Series. Baltimore: U of Maryland, 2006.
Nash, Richard. "Benevolent Readers: Burnet's Exposition and Eighteenth-Century Interpretation of the Thirty-Nine Articles." *Eighteenth-Century Studies* 25.3 (1992): 353–60.
Nature the Great Physician: Or, Every Man His Own Doctor. London, 1744.
Noll, Mark A. *The Rise of Evangelicalism: The Age of Edwards, Whitefield, and the Wesleys.* History of Evangelicalism 5.1. Downers Grove, IL: InterVarsity P, 2003.
Noppen, J. P. van. *Transforming Words: The Early Methodist Revival from a Discourse Perspective* 5.3. Bern: Peter Lang, 1999.
Norton, Rictor. *Mother Clap's Molly House: The Gay Subculture in England, 1700–1830.* London: GMP, 1992.
Nussbaum, Felicity. *The Autobiographical Subject: Gender and Ideology in Eighteenth-Century England.* Baltimore: Johns Hopkins UP, 1989.
O'Brien, John. "Harlequin Britain: Eighteenth-Century Pantomime and the Cultural Location of Entertainment(s)." *Theatre Journal* 50.4 (1998): 489–510.
O'Driscoll, Sally. "The Lesbian and the Passionless Woman: Femininity and Sexuality in Eighteenth-Century England." *The Eighteenth Century: Theory and Interpretation* 44.2–3 (2003): 103–31.
Oulton, Walley Chamberlain. *The History of the Theatres of London.* London: Martin and Bain, 1796.
Paulson, Ronald. *The Beautiful, Novel, and Strange.* Baltimore: Johns Hopkins UP, 1996.
———. *Hogarth: His Life, Art, and Times.* Vols. 1–3. New Haven: Yale UP, 1971.
———. *Hogarth's Harlot: Sacred Parody in Enlightenment England.* Baltimore: Johns Hopkins UP, 2003.
———. "Putting out the Fire in Her Imperial Majesty's Apartment: Opposition Politics, Anticlericalism, and Aesthetics." *ELH* 63.1 (1996): 79–107.
Peace, Mary. "The Magdalen Hospital and the Fortunes of Whiggish Sentimentality in Mid-Eighteenth-Century Britain: 'Well-Grounded' Exemplarity vs. 'Romantic' Exceptionality." *Eighteenth Century: Theory and Interpretation* 48.2 (2007): 125–48.
Peirce, James. *A Vindication of the Dissenters.* London, 1717.
Pierce, John. "Pamela's Textual Authority." *Passion and Virtue in the Novels of Samuel Richardson.* Ed. David Blewett. Toronto: U of Toronto P, 2001. 8–26.
A Plain and Easy Road to the Land of Bliss a Turnpike Set Up by Mr. Orator—: On Which a Man May Travel More Miles in One Day, Than on Any Other Highway in Forty Years. London: Printed for W. Nicoll and W. Tesseyman. York, 1762.
Podmore, Colin. *The Moravian Church in England, 1728–1760.* Oxford Historical Monographs. Oxford: Clarendon P, 1998.
Pollard, Arthur. "Martin Madan." *Oxford Dictionary of National Biography.* Oxford: Oxford UP, 2004.
Potkay, Adam. *The Fate of Eloquence in the Age of Hume.* Ithaca: Cornell UP, 1994.

———. *The Story of Joy: From the Bible to Late Romanticism*. New York: Cambridge UP, 2007.

Pottle, Frederick A. "Boswell as Icarus." *Restoration and Eighteenth-Century Literature*. Ed. C. Camden. Chicago: U Chicago P, 1963. 389–406.

The Progress of Methodism in Bristol. Bristol, 1743.

Puff, Helmut. *Sodomy in Reformation Germany and Switzerland, 1400–1600*. Chicago: U Chicago P, 2003.

Rabin, Dana. "Searching for the Self in Eighteenth-Century English Criminal Trials, 1730–1800." *Eighteenth-Century Life* 27.1 (2003): 85–106.

Rack, Henry D. "The Holy Club." *Oxford Dictionary of National Biography*. Oxford: Oxford UP, 2007.

———. "John Wesley." *Oxford Dictionary of National Biography*. Oxford: Oxford UP, 2009.

———. *Reasonable Enthusiast: John Wesley and the Rise of Methodism*. London: Epworth P, 1989.

Rambuss, Richard. *Closet Devotions*. Durham: Duke UP, 1998.

Rathey, Markus. "Lecture: Bach's Christmas Oratorio." New Haven: Yale U, Dec. 6, 2008.

Redford, Bruce. *Dilettanti: The Antic and the Antique in Eighteenth-Century England*. Los Angeles: J. Paul Getty Museum, 2008.

Richardson, Samuel. *Pamela; or, Virtue Rewarded*. Ed. Peter Sabor, with Margaret A. Doody. New York: Penguin, 1980; 2003.

———. *Sir Charles Grandison*. 1753–4. Ed. Jocelyn Harris. Oxford: Oxford UP, 1986.

Riley, William. *Parochial Music Corrected*. London, 1762.

Rimius, Henry. *A Candid Narrative of the Rise and Progress of the Herrnhuters, Commonly Call'd Moravians or Unitas Fratrum*. London: A. Linde, J. Robinson, et al., 1753.

Riskin, Jessica. "The Defecating Duck, or, the Ambiguous Origins of Artificial Life." *Critical Inquiry* 29 (Summer 2003): 599–633.

Rivers, Isabel. "Dissenting and Methodist Books of Practical Divinity." *Books and Their Readers in Eighteenth-Century England*. Ed. Isabel Rivers. New York: St. Martin's P, 1982.

———. *Reason, Grace, and Sentiment: A Study of the Language of Religion and Ethics in England, 1660–1780*. Cambridge: Cambridge UP, 1991.

Roach, Joseph. *The Player's Passion: Studies in the Science of Acting*. Michigan: U Michigan P, 1993.

Robinson, Lewis. *Every Patient His Own Doctor: Or the Sick Man's Triumph over Death and the Grave*. London, 1785.

Rogal, Samuel J. "Pills for the Poor: John Wesley's *Primitive Physick*." *Yale Journal of Biology and Medicine* 51 (1978): 81–90.

Rosenthal, Laura. *Infamous Commerce: Prostitution in Eighteenth-Century British Literature and Culture*. Ithaca: Cornell UP, 2006.

Rousseau, G. S. "John Wesley's Primitive Physic," *Harvard Library Bulletin* 16 (1968): 242–56.

Routley, Erik. *The Musical Wesleys*. New York: Oxford UP, 1968.

Ruttenburg, Nancy. *Democratic Personality: Popular Voice and the Trial of American Authorship*. Stanford: Stanford UP, 1998.

———. "George Whitefield, Spectacular Conversion, and the Rise of Democratic Personality." *American Literary History* 5.3 (1993): 429–58.

Sabor, Peter. "From Sexual Liberation to Gender Trouble: Reading *Memoirs of a Woman of Pleasure* from the 1960s to the 1990s." *Eighteenth-Century Studies* 33.4 (2000): 561–78.

Saccamano, Neil. "Inheriting Enlightenment, or Keeping Faith with Reason in Derrida." *Eighteenth-Century Studies* 40.3 (2007): 405–24.

Sainsbury, John. *John Wilkes: The Lives of a Libertine*. Aldershot: Ashgate, 2006.

Salvaggio, Ruth. *Enlightened Absence: Neoclassical Configurations of the Feminine*. Chicago: U Illinois P, 1988.

Schaeffer, Neil. *The Marquis de Sade: A Life*. Cambridge, MA: Harvard UP, 2000.

Schmidt, Leigh Eric. *Hearing Things: Religion, Illusion, and the American Enlightenment*. Cambridge: Harvard UP, 2000.

Schwartz, Regina Mara. *Sacramental Poetics at the Dawn of Secularism: When God Left the World*. Stanford: Stanford UP, 2008.

The Secret History of Pandora's Box. London, 1742.

Seidel, Kevin. "Beyond the Religious and the Secular in the History of the Novel." *New Literary History* 38.4 (2007): 637–47.

Sekora, John. *Luxury: The Concept in Western Thought, Eden to Smollett*. Baltimore: Johns Hopkins UP, 1977.

Shaw, David Gary. "Modernity between Us and Them: The Place of Religion within History." *History and Theory* 45 (Dec. 2006): 1–9.

Shaw, Jane. *Miracles in Enlightenment England*. New Haven: Yale UP, 2006.

Sheehan, Jonathan. "Enlightenment, Religion, and the Enigma of Secularization: A Review Essay." *The American Historical Review* 108.4 (2003): 1061–80.

Shepherd, T. B. *Methodism and the Literature of the Eighteenth Century*. New York: Haskell House, 1966.

Sheridan, Thomas. *A Course of Lectures on Elocution*. London, 1762.

Sherman, Stuart. *Telling Time: Clocks, Diaries, and English Diurnal Form, 1660–1785*. Chicago: U Chicago P, 1996.

Shoemaker, Robert Brink. *The London Mob: Violence and Disorder in Eighteenth-Century England*. London: Hambledon and London, 2004.

Smollett, Tobias. *The Adventures of Roderick Random*. 2 vols. London, 1748.

———. *Complete History of England*. London, 1757–8.

———. *Continuation of the Complete History of England. By T. Smollett, M.D.* Vol. 4. 4 vols. London, 1768.

———. *The Critical Review*. London.

———. *Humphry Clinker: An Authoritative Text, Contemporary Responses, Criticism*. Ed. James L. Thorson. New York: Norton, 1983.

———. *The Letters of Tobias Smollett*. Ed. Lewis M. Knapp. Oxford: Clarendon P, 1970.

———. *The Life and Adventures of Sir Launcelot Greaves*. Ed. Robert Folkenflik and Barbara Laning Fitzpatrick. Athens, GA: U of Georgia P, 2002.

Snead, Jennifer. "Print, Predestination, and the Public Sphere: Transatlantic Evangelical Periodicals, 1740–1745." *Early American Literature* 45.1 (2010): 93–118.

———. "Religion and Eighteenth-Century Literature." *Literature Compass* 5.4 (2008): 707–20.

Somerville, Thomas. *My Own Life and Times, 1741–1814*. Edinburgh: Edmonston and Douglas, 1861.

Southey, Robert. *The Life of Wesley: The Rise and Progress of Methodism*. London: Frederick Warne, 1889.

Stebbing, Henry. *An Earnest and Affectionate Address to the People Called Methodists.* London, 1745.
Steiner, George. *Real Presences: Is There Anything in What We Say?* London: Faber, 1989.
Stephens, Frederick George. *Catalogue of Political and Personal Satires.* 11 vols. London: British Museum Publications, 1978.
Stevens, William Bacon. *A History of Georgia: From Its First Discovery by Europeans to the Adoption of the Present Constitution.* New York: Appleton, 1847.
Stewart, Susan. *Poetry and the Fate of the Senses.* Chicago: U Chicago P, 2002.
Stout, Harry S. *The Divine Dramatist: George Whitefield and the Rise of Modern Evangelicalism.* Library of Religious Biography. Grand Rapids: W. B. Eerdmans, 1991.
Sully. *Sully's Domestic Physician: Or Every Man His Own Doctor.* London, 1783.
Suster, Gerald. *The Hell-Fire Friars.* London: Robson Books, 2000.
Swift, Jonathan. *Jonathan Swift: Major Works.* Ed. Angus Ross and David Woolley. Oxford: Oxford UP, 2003.
Taves, Ann. *Fits, Trances, & Visions: Experiencing Religion and Explaining Experience from Wesley to James.* Princeton: Princeton UP, 1999.
Taylor, Charles. *A Secular Age.* Cambridge, MA: Harvard UP, 2007.
———. *Sources of the Self: The Making of the Modern Identity.* Cambridge: Cambridge UP, 1989.
Tecusan, Manuela. *The Fragments of the Methodists: Methodism Outside Soranus.* Leiden: Brill, 2004.
Temperley, Nicholas. "'If Any of You Be Mery Let Hym Synge Psalms': The Culture of Psalms in Church and Home." *Noyses, Sounds, and Sweet Aires: Music in Early Modern England.* Ed. Jessie Anne Owens. Washington, DC: The Folger Shakespeare Library, 2005.
———. *The Music of the English Parish Church.* Cambridge: Cambridge UP, 1979.
Temperley, Nicholas, and Richard Crawford. "Psalmody (Ii)." *Grove Music Online.*
Temperley, Nicholas, and Sally Drage. *Eighteenth-Century Psalmody.* London: Stainer and Bell, 2007.
Tennent, John. *Every Man His Own Doctor: Or, the Poor Planter's Physician.* Williamsburg: William Parks, 1734.
Thompson, E. P. *The Making of the English Working Class.* New York: Vintage, 1963.
Thompson, Helen. "'In Idea, a Thousand Nameless Joys': Secondary Qualities in Arnauld, Locke and Haywood's Lasselia." *The Eighteenth Century: Theory and Interpretation* 48.3 (2007): 225–43.
Tierney-Hynes, Rebecca. "Hume, Romance, and the Unruly Imagination." *SEL: Studies in English Literature, 1500–1900* 47.3 (2007): 641–58.
Tillotson, John. *Sermons on Several Sujects.* London, 1702.
Trapp, Joseph. *The Nature, Folly, Sin, and Danger, of Being Righteous Over-Much with a Particular View to the Doctrines and Practices of Certain Modern Enthusiasts: Being the Substance of Four Discourses . . . By Joseph Trapp, D.D.* London: Printed for S. Austen; L. Gilliver and J. Clarke; sold by T. Cooper, 1739.
Trumbach, Randolph. "Erotic Fantasy and Male Libertinism in Enlightenment England." *The Invention of Pornography: Obscenity and the Origins of Modernity.* Ed. Lynn Avery Hunt. New York: Zone, 1993. 253–82.
Trussler, Simon. *The Cambridge Illustrated History of British Theatre.* Cambridge: Cambridge UP, 1994.

Turner, James Grantham. "'Illustrious Depravity' and the Erotic Sublime." *The Age of Johnson* 2 (1989): 1–38.
Tyerman, Luke. *The Life of the Rev. George Whitefield*. 2 vols. London: Hodder & Stoughton, 1876.
Valenze, Deborah. "Charity, Custom, and Humanity: Changing Attitudes toward the Poor in Eighteenth-Century England." *Revival and Religion since 1700: Essays for John Walsh*. Ed. John Walsh, Jane Garnett, and Colin Matthew. London: Hambledon P, 1993. 59–78.
———. *Prophetic Sons and Daughters: Female Preaching and Popular Religion in Industrial England*. Princeton: Princeton UP, 1985.
Vickers, John A. *A Dictionary of Methodism in Britain and Ireland*. London: Epworth P, 2000.
Vincent, William. *Considerations on Parochial Music*. London, 1787.
Wagner, Peter. *Eros Revived: Erotica of the Enlightenment in England and America*. London: Secker & Warburg, 1988.
Wahrman, Dror. *The Making of the Modern Self: Identity and Culture in Eighteenth-Century England*. New Haven: Yale UP, 2004.
Wallace, Tara Ghoshal. "'About Savages and the Awfulness of America': Colonial Corruptions in *Humphry Clinker*." *Eighteenth-Century Fiction* 18.2 (2005–6): 229–50.
Walpole, Horace. *Anecdotes of Painting in England*. Vol. 4. 4 vols. Twickenham: Strawberry-Hill, 1780.
———. *The Yale Edition of Horace Walpole's Correspondence*. Ed. W. S. Lewis. 48 vols. New Haven: Yale UP, 1937–1983.
Walsh, John. "Religious Societies: Methodist and Evangelical, 1738–1800." *Voluntary Religion*. Ed. William J. and Diana Wood Sheils. Vol. 23. Studies in Church History. Oxford: Oxford UP, 1986. 279–302.
Ward, Graham. "The Displaced Body of Jesus Christ." *Radical Orthodoxy*. Ed. John Milbank, Catherine Pinstock, and Graham Ward. New York: Routledge, 1999. 163–81.
Ward, W. Reginald. *Early Evangelicalism: A Global Intellectual History, 1670–1789*. Cambridge: Cambridge UP, 2006.
Watson, J. R. *An Annotated Anthology of Hymns*. Oxford: Oxford UP, 2002.
———. *The English Hymn*. Oxford: Clarendon P, 1997.
Watson, Richard. *The Life of the Rev. John Wesley, A.M.* New York: B. Waugh and T. Mason, 1836.
Watt, Ian. *The Rise of the Novel: Studies in Defoe, Richardson, and Fielding*. Berkeley: U of California P, 1957.
Watts, Isaac. *The Harmony of All the Religions Which God Ever Prescribed*. London, 1742.
———. *Hymns and Spiritual Songs*. London, 1707.
Weed, David. "Sentimental Misogyny and Medicine in *Humphry Clinker*." *SEL: Studies in English Literature, 1500–1900* 37.3 (1997): 615–36.
Weinbrot, Howard. *Britannia's Issue: The Rise of British Literature from Dryden to Ossian*. Cambridge: Cambridge UP, 1993.
Wesley, Charles. *Charles Wesley: A Reader*. Ed. John R. Tyson. Oxford: Oxford UP, 2000.
———. *Collection of Psalms and Hymns*. Charleston, SC: Lewis Timothy, ca. 1737.
Wesley, Charles, and John Wesley. *Hymns and Sacred Poems*. London: Strahan, 1739.
Wesley, John. *A Collection of Hymns, for the Use of the People Called Methodists*. London, 1780.

———. *Hymns for Those That Seek and Those That Have Redemption in the Blood of Jesus Christ*. Bristol: Felix Farley, 1747.
———. "Hymns on the Lord's Supper." Bristol: Felix Farley, 1745.
———. *Hymns on the Nativity of Our Lord*. London, 1744.
———. *The Journal of the Rev. John Wesley, A.M.* Ed. Nehemiah Curnock. 8 vols. London, 1909–1916.
———. *On Perfection*. London, ca. 1740.
———. *Sacred Melody, or a Choice Collection of Psalm and Hymn Tunes, with a Short Introduction*. Bristol, 1773.
———. *Select Hymns: With Tunes Annext; Designed Chiefly for Use by the People Called Methodists*. Bristol: William Pine, 1770.
———. *Thoughts on Marriage and a Single Life*. Bristol, 1743.
———. *Thoughts upon Slavery*. London: R. Hawes, 1774.
———. *A Word of Advice to Saints and Sinners*. London, 1746.
———. *A Word to a Street-Walker*. Bristol, 1748.
———. *The Works of John Wesley*. Oxford Edition of the Works of John Wesley. Ed. Frank Baker. Oxford: Clarendon P, 1975.
———. *The Works of John Wesley*. Ed. Albert Cook Outler. Nashville: Abingdon P, 1987.
Wesley, Susanna Annesley, and Charles Wallace. *Susanna Wesley: The Complete Writings*. New York: Oxford UP, 1997.
West, Shearer. "Wilkes's Squint: Synecdochic Physiognomy and Political Identity in Eighteenth-Century Print Culture." *Eighteenth-Century Studies* 33.1 (1999): 65–84.
Wetmore, Alex. "Sympathy Machines: Men of Feeling and the Automaton." *Eighteenth-Century Studies* 43.1 (2009): 37–54.
Wheeler, Sondra. "Prosperity and Its Discontents." *Reflections: Yale Divinity School* 97.1 (2010): 47–51.
White, Daniel E. *Early Romanticism and Religious Dissent*. Cambridge: Cambridge UP, 2006.
Whitefield, George. *A Brief Account of the Occasion, Process, and Issue of a Late Trial at the Assize Held at Gloucester, March 3, 1743*. 2nd ed., 1744.
———. "Christ the Best Husband or an Earnest Invitation to Young Women to Come and See Christ. A Sermon Preached to a Society of Young Women, in Fetter-Lane." London, 1740. Printed for C. Whitefield. 28p. http://galenet.galegroup.com/servlet/ECCO?c=1&stp=Author&ste=11&af=BN&ae=T069893&tiPG=1&dd=0&dc=flc&docNum=CW119407825&vrsn=1.0&srchtp=a&d4=0.33&n=10&SU=0LRF&locID=29002. Full text online.
———. *Five Sermons on the Following Subjects: I. Christ the Believer's Husband. Ii. The Gospel Supper. Iii. Blind Bartimeus. Iv. Walking with God. V. The Resurrection of Lazarus*. Microform. Philadelphia: B. Franklin, 1746.
———. "A Short Account of God's Dealings with the Reverend Mr. George Whitefield." London: W. Strahan, 1740.
———. *The Works of the Reverend George Whitefield*. 7 vols. London: Edward and Charles Dilly, 1771.
Whitehead, John. *The Life of the Rev. John Wesley, A.M.* Baltimore: Dobbin and Murphy, 1807.
Wilder, Franklin. *The Methodist Riots: The Testings of Charles Wesley*. Great Neck: Todd & Honeywell, 1981.

Wilkinson, Tate. *Memoirs of His Own Life*. 4 Vols. York, 1790.
Williams, Carolyn. "'The Way to Things by Words': John Cleland, the Name of the Father, and Speculative Etymology." *Yearbook of English Studies* 28 (1998): 250–75.
Williams, Raymond. *Culture and Society*. New York: Columbia UP, 1983.
Wilton, Peter. "Hymn." *Oxford Music Online*. Ed. Alison Latham, http://www.oxfordmusiconline.com/subscriber/article/opr/t114/e3366, 2007.
Winter, Cornelius. *Memoirs of the Life and Character of the Late Rev. Cornelius Winter*. Ed. William Jay. New York: Samuel Whiting & Co., 1811.
Winton, Dean. *Handel's Dramatic Oratorios and Masques*. London: Oxford UP, 1959.
Wolffe, John. *God and Greater Britain: Religion and National Life in Britain and Ireland, 1843–1945*. London: Routledge, 1994.
Wren, Brian. *Praying Twice: The Music and Words of Congregational Song*. Louisville: Westminster John Knox P, 2000.
Zinzendorf, Nicolaus Ludwig. *Seven Sermons on the Godhead of the Lamb: Or the Divinity of Jesus Christ*. London, 1742.
Zinzendorf, Nicolaus Ludwig, and John Gambold. *Maxims, Theological Ideas and Sentences: Out of the Present Ordinary of the Brethren's Churches; His [I.E. Zinzendorf's] Dissertations and Discourses from the Year 1738 Till 1747*. London: Sold by F. Beecroft, 1751.
Žižek, Slavoj. *The Parallax View*. Cambridge, MA: MIT Press, 2006.
Žižek, Slavoj, and John Millbank. *The Monstrosity of Christ: Paradox or Dialectic?* Ed. Creston Davis. Cambridge, MA: MIT Press.

Index

Abelove, Henry, 75, 116, 245n6, 247n7
actors, 62, 64; Methodists similar to, 130–33; and puppets, 164; Whitefield like Garrick, 141–42. *See also* Garrick, David; Shuter, Edward; Whitefield, George: theatricality of
Addison, Joseph, 6, 45, 159; on foreign taste, 179–80; hymns of, 188–89, 199; Graves paraphrases, 223
Anstey, Christopher, 184, 255n3; *New Bath Guide*, 202, 209–13
apparition, 74, 158, 202, 209, 211. *See also* Cock Lane ghost; ghosts; Phantom, Fanny
Arminian Magazine, 218, 233
Asad, Talal, 13–15, 239n6, 252n3
Austen, Jane, 14, 221, 225, 234

Badiou, Alain, 58–59, 163, 244n25
ballad opera, 183, 185, 250n22, 253n16
Bath: as a spa, 208–11, 255n10; Methodist chapel in, 200–202, 217; theaters in, 134
Belden, Mary Megie, 148
Blackwell, Bonnie, 92, 97, 246n19
Bladud, 209–11
Book of Mormon, 235
Bosquanet, Mary, 77–78, 80
Boswell, James, 38, 111, 131–32, 144
Boswell, Lady Betty Brucem, 39, 242n5
Bouwsma, William, 16, 201, 240n21
Branch, Lori, 44–45, 53, 120, 236–37, 240n12, 248n28, 256n6
Bristol: and Bath, 211; Methodist associations of, 71, 75–78, 83, 220, 226, 228; outdoor preaching in, 133–34, 173; Charles Wesley's church in, 35
Burnet, Bishop Gilbert, 10, 44, 156–57
Burney, Charles, 181

Burney, Frances, 28, 142
Butler, Judith, 102

Caputo, John, 16, 236–37, 240n21, 256n4
Castle, Terry, 74, 97, 251n27
Christ: blood of, 43–45, 68, 194; body of, 26, 43–45, 71, 91–92, 97, 116, 154–58, 196–98, 212–13, 245; child, 182; crucified, 44–46, 54–58, 158, 195–96; desire for, 71, 172; divinity of, 34; gospel of, 12; as husband, 190–95; icons of, 151, 153–39, 163–66, 251; incarnation of, 30; love of, 186–87; monstrosity of, 45, 196; naked, 68, 103; union with, 78; wounds of, 121–24, 196
Christianity: Anglican, 150; embodied, 30, 109; enthusiastic, 165; eroticism and, 100–101; evangelical, 11, 38, 49, 126; event and, 58; experimental, 28, 111; formal, 44; Latitudinarian, 154; Methodism and, 38, 41–42; modernity and, 15–16, 52, 154; mysticism and, 2–3, 15–16, 30, 43, 46, 55, 71, 169, 199, 217; primitive, 3–4, 35, 41–42, 54, 93, 127, 224, 240, 242; reasonable, 30, 49, 126, 196; satire of, 112, 161; state forms of, 51–52
Churchill, Charles, 112–13, 161
Church of England: continuity with Methodism, 5, 35, 43, 201–2; *Essay on Woman* and, 112; "free grace" and, 54; liturgy of, 154; medicine and, 93; *Memoirs of a Woman of Pleasure* and, 101; Methodism as threat to, 45, 48, 66, 174; music and, 175; Secker and, 152; toleration and, 51
class, 2; attitudes toward Christ and, 45, 154; Fielding and, 79; *Humphry Clinker* and, 201–2, 208, 214, 217–20; hymns and, 173, 177, 184; later Methodism and, 201–8; lit-

class (cont.)
   eracy and, 60; Methodism as challenge to traditional, 47, 59, 115; Methodism used to explain, 17–18, 22, 32; *Spiritual Quixote* and, 206, 219, 225–26. *See also* hymns; Methodism; Thompson, E. P.
Cleland, John: closure and, 128–29, 135–36; clubs, 111–12; language and, 119–21; *Memoirs of a Woman of Pleasure*, 91, 100–103, 107–12, 114–29; *The Minor* and, 143; Moravian imagery, 115–18, 122–26; and Bosnavern Penlez, 100–103, 245n17; on prostitution, 103–4, 115; Sade and, 127; Westminster School and, 248n26
clerical satire: atheism and, 206; conventions of, 29, 56, 71; Hogarth and, 156; hypocrisy in, 91; pornography and, 101, 115, 246n3
Clery, E. J., 159, 251n34, 251n37
clubs, libertine, 40, 112, 114, 120
Cock Lane ghost, 2, 53, 113, 158–61, 163, 169, 251n34. *See also* apparition; ghosts; Phantom, Fanny
Combes, William, 116, 233, 235
communion: as event, 126–27; Hogarth and, 150–58; hymns for, 154, 190, 194, 197–98; Love Feast and, 192; as memorial, 10, 126; mock, 144–45; preparation for, 43, 81; service of, 242n10. *See also* Eucharist; Lord's Supper
community: appeals to, 8–9; Herrnhut, 46–47, 107, 243n16; lack of Methodist, 56, 111; Methodist, 2, 13, 71, 231; national, 32–33, 202–21, 235; as religious term, 5; secularism and, 10, 50–51; sermon on, 208, 243n16; women and, 79, 107; writers and, 218
consciousness: access to another's, 64; belief and, 36–37, 133; emotional, 25; false, 17; hard problem of, 36, 242n4; individualism and, 173, 193–99, 202, 239n5, 239n10; Methodist Lockean, 12–13, 28–29, 50–59; as related to conscience, 2–7, 243n19; Susanna Wesley on, 243n20
Covent Garden, 109, 134, 136, 139, 142–43, 185
credulity: the Cock Lane ghost and, 159–62; Hogarth and, 110–12, 150–56; as necessary to communication, 37, 133; puppets and, 164; readers and, 224; in *The Female Husband*, 95; as threat to reason, 9–10

Damiens, Robert, 206–7
Dashwood, Sir Frances, 112–13
Derrida, Jacques: on belief, 236, 239n6, 240n17, 244n32; Enlightenment and, 14, 64; on immediacy, 103
Dilettanti, 112, 248n20
disenchantment, 14–16, 64
Dissent, 7, 46, 50–51, 175, 217, 234
divine: eroticism and, 7, 62, 71 116–17, 120–23; hymns and, 183–99; presence and, 3–4, 23, 28, 49–50, 101, 153; the self and, 57–58, 78; temporality and, 9, 49, 185; Susanna Wesley on, 243n20
domesticity, 22–23
Dr. Squintum's Exaltation, 18, 140, 167–68
Drury Lane, 134, 142, 149, 249n6, 250n18
Dryden, John, 186–89, 217, 221, 224
duck, 166–69; Vaucanson, 166–67

Eagleton, Terry, 11, 14, 163, 240n16
Eliot, George, 199, 230
embodiment: femininity and, 88; hymns and, 172, 190–99; language and, 26–28, 30, 172, 191; religious, 42–46, 87, 126, 158; Whitefield and, 167
Enlightenment, 4–6, 14–15, 63–64, 237. *See also* Scottish Enlightenment
enthusiasm: artists and, 37, 60–62, 67, 151, 170, 225–27; bad, 127, 151; failure of progress, 37, 43–51, 61, 223; good, 151; Hogarth on, 150–58, 161–70; illiteracy and, 225–27; Lavington on, 67, 116, 122–24, 212–13; Locke and, 7–11, 51–53; and Methodist Eucharistic theology, 125–26, 154–58, 162–63; Methodists labeled as, 49–50; as opposite of Enlightenment, 64; as sexual desire, 71–79, 85–87, 97, 101–2, 109–12, 118–20, 126–29; sociability and, 204–8, 214–21, 228–31; Wesley speaks against, 49–50. *See also* Lavington, George; Locke, John; Methodism
Epstein, William H., 246n1, 247n17
Eucharist, 10–11; as event, 150, 153, 163; high Christology and, 30, 35; Hogarth and,

150–59, 167, 249n35; in hymns, 195–96; Love Feast and, 192; modernity and, 42–43; parodic, 112–14; Roman Catholicism and, 46, 153; transubstantiation and, 27, 43, 125, 129, 154–58, 198. *See also* communion; Lord's Supper

event: crucifixion as, 44, 197; Eucharist as, 30, 126, 150–58, 163; performance as, 131–33, 139–41; reading as, 68; religious conversion as, 4–5, 28–29 49–51, 192–95; sensation as, 36–37, 129; sermons as, 9, 62–63; as sign of the real, 167–69; temporal rupture and, 58–60, 191–92

faith: class and, 230; language and, 63–64; salvation by, 54–56; secularism and, 13–16; sensation and, 36–37, 43–45, 133; works vs., 143–45, 154, 163

fanaticism, 16–18; enlightenment vs., 64; history and, 204, 216–17; Voltaire on, 255n5

feminine, 7, 53, 72, 78, 83–85, 87

Ferguson, Frances, 102, 246n5

Fielding, Henry, 5, 7, 66, 125, 134, 169–70, 185–86, 220–22, 230, 233; *Amelia*, 74, 75; *Don Quixote in England*, 225; *The Female Husband*, 28–32, 70–85, 92–102, 106; *Joseph Andrews*, 74, 84, 125; *Miss Lucy in Town*, 74–75; *Shamela*, 63, 74, 84, 119; *Tom Jones*, 74–75, 84, 131, 226; *Tragedy of Tragedies*, 185

flagellation, 111, 117–18

Foote, Samuel, 2, 133–34, 242n6; *The Minor*, 28, 37, 55, 108–10, 114, 130, 141–53, 180; *The Orators*, 150, 158–59, 163–64, 169

Foucault, Michel, 30, 102, 237, 247n6

Freeman, Lisa, 68, 131, 240n14

Frey, Andrew, 47, 115, 117, 121–24, 243n17. *See also* Moravians

Garrick, David, 9, 64, 111, 131–32, 136, 141, 159, 169

Gay, John, 111, 186; *Beggar's Opera*, 182–83

gender: Fielding and, 95–99; in hymns, 189–91; for Methodist women, 80; modern, 7, 22; permeability of, 71–77; pronouns in Methodist discourse, 123, 174–75; Whitefield, fluidity of, 85–88, 91. *See also* feminine; queer; sex/gender system; sexuality

ghosts, 9, 54, 70, 74, 123, 158–61, 164, 167, 169–70, 212. *See also* apparition; Cock Lane ghost; Phantom, Fanny

Gibson, Edmund, 47–49, 55–56

Goldsmith, Oliver, 31, 132, 227, 233

Gothic, 15, 116, 181; architecture and, 200–201, 223

Gottlieb, Evan, 208, 216, 255n9

Graves, Richard, 2, 255n16; *Spiritual Quixote*, 32, 182, 200, 202–4, 206, 220–30

Gumbrecht, Hans Ulrich, 27, 235, 244n29

Habermas, Jürgen, 6, 16, 236, 239n6, 241n32, 256n4

Haggerty, George, 71, 192, 245n2

Hamilton, Mary/George, 70–84, 92–99

Handel, G. F., 172, 179, 181–83, 185, 253n13

Hanway, Jonas, 104, 241n30, 247n8

Harlequin Methodist, 136, 139–41, 160, 183

Heitzenrater, Richard, 2, 39, 203, 239n2, 246n2, 249n5

Hempton, David, 2, 16–17, 22, 34, 62, 77, 239n2, 240n22, 248n24, 255n2

Herrnhuters, 121–22, 243n17, 249n33

heterosexuality, 73–75, 80–81, 106, 213, 247n16

Hoadly, Benjamin, 9–10, 27, 35, 38, 153, 156, 249n35

Hogarth, William, 18, 32, 37, 104, 112–14, 131–33, 140–41, 145, 150–70, 247n15, 248n22, 249n35, 251n25, 251n31, 252nn38–39, 252n41, 252n43; *Credulity*, 9, 54, 110–12, 133, 150, 153, 156, 161–69; *Enthusiasm Delineated*, 109–10, 150–52, 155, 163, 168; *Paul Before Felix*, 140; *Transubstantiation Satirized*, 156–57, 165, 247n15

homosexuality, 73. *See also* gender; queer; sex/gender

Hume, David, 11, 37, 64–65, 110, 142, 208, 217, 240n12, 244n34

Hunter, J. Paul, 242n35, 243n19

hymns, 18, 27, 30–31, 34, 46, 64, 100, 105, 123, 153–54, 158, 171–78, 180–98; ballads and, 18, 60, 79, 116, 139, 141, 182–83; congregational singing and, 31–32, 171, 173, 175, 177–80, 182–83, 189–99, 211; harmony and, 119, 179–81, 221; hymnals and,

hymns (cont.)
27, 31, 177–78, 186, 218; melody and, 172, 180–81; Methodist hymnals and, 105, 136, 173, 176–78; metrical psalms and, 174–75, 181–82; Moravian hymns, 119; music, 31, 171–72, 174–76, 178–82, 184–86, 192, 225; psalms and, 174–76, 180, 182, 184, 191, 199, 217; songs, and, 52, 71, 87, 112, 114, 136, 174, 177, 181, 183, 186, 198; Wesleyan, 183, 185, 197

Ingrassia, Catherine, 106, 247n11
inspiration: aesthetic, 29, 59–63, 120, 132; religious, 51, 53, 58, 76, 113, 152–53
Ireland, John, 156–57, 162–63, 165, 251n31, 252n39

Jagose, Annamarie, 110, 247n16
Jakobsen, Janet, 16, 240n21
Johnson, Anne, 70, 75, 80
Johnson, Samuel, 31, 49, 110, 159, 161, 190, 201, 233
Jumpedo, Don, 160–61
justification, 13, 38, 54–55

Keane, Webb, 16, 42, 237
Keats, John, 169, 252n42
Kinservik, Matthew, 144, 250n18
knowledge: epistemological canons of, 95; experimental, 101, 110; Lockean conception of, 36–37, 52, 133; produced by humans, 235–36; spiritual, 59, 238; traditional vs. modern, 24–26
Kramnick, Jonathan, 7, 12, 29, 239n10, 240n14
Kristeva, Julia, 16, 30, 126
Krysmanski, Bernd, 251nn24–25, 251n28, 251n31, 252n38

Lampe, J. F., 136, 172, 183, 185–86
Lanser, Susan, 71–73, 245n2
Latham, Stephen, 246n21
Lavington, George, 4–5, 7, 35, 39, 47, 50, 55, 65–67, 83, 115–17, 122–24, 127, 213, 245n14
Locke, John, 4–5, 7, 11–12, 26, 36, 52–53, 56–57, 61, 129, 133, 190, 239n10, 243n20
Lockean self, 5, 28, 54

London, 39, 68, 100, 103–4, 110, 122, 133–35, 142, 187, 201–3
Lord's Supper, 43, 153–54, 197–98, 242n10. *See also* communion; Eucharist
Lyles, Albert, 109, 130, 135, 139, 204, 239n3, 244n22

Mack, Phyllis, 2, 5, 7, 16, 25, 36, 57, 77–80, 108, 173, 239n2, 239n8, 240n24, 241n30, 245n9, 247n14, 252n3
Mackenzie, Henry, 231
Magdalen Hospital, 104–5
marriage, 80, 106–7, 122, 124, 128–29, 136, 156, 190–91
McKeon, Michael, 23–25, 72, 101, 103, 245n2; *Secret History of Domesticity*, 5, 23–24, 49, 123, 126, 226, 241n31, 241n33, 241n35, 243n19, 246n3, 247n13
Methodism: as a denomination, 201–4, 232–33; agency and, 4, 7, 29–30, 36, 56–57, 78, 90–91, 125, 173, 188–90, 196, 199; Antinomianism, 18, 35–36, 42–48, 55–59, 75, 109; Arminianism and, 48–49, 78, 103, 207, 233; band meetings of, 36, 51, 62, 71, 81–83, 107–8, 114; confession and, 36, 46, 51, 71, 78, 81–84, 88–89, 101–2, 107–11, 119–22, 129, 190–92; conversion experience of, 2, 4, 29, 59, 73, 78, 95, 128, 206; crucifixion and, 10–11, 42–46, 154, 186, 192–98; early history of, 1–6, 9–10, 19–21, 28, 34–60; education and, 22–23, 51, 60–61, 104, 217–18; Eucharistic theology of, 10–11, 26–27, 30, 35, 42–46, 55–56, 112–14, 125–26, 145, 150–63, 166–69, 192–98, 249n25; as experimental religion, 3, 10, 13, 28–29, 44, 51–53, 72, 77, 83, 88, 95, 101, 110–11, 195, 238; free grace and, 21–22, 48, 54–59, 127; Garrick and, 9, 64, 131–41, 201, 249n8; ghosts and, 2, 9, 53–54, 113, 158–65; as "heart religion," 2–4, 23–28, 33, 36–38, 56–60, 201, 208, 214, 219–20, 230, 235, 240n13; as Holy Club, 111; literacy, 1–2, 5, 9, 21, 60–67, 79, 203–4, 206, 217–18, 227, 235; literature and, 27–28, 60–69, 120, 126, 146, 221–26, 230; love feasts and, 18, 101, 111–15, 124–26, 190–92; medicine, 92–94, 216, 244n35, 246n22; metaphor, 22, 55, 88, 102–3,

116–28, 146, 190, 197–99, 232; miracles and, 9–11, 42–43, 53; origins of name, 35, 38–43; Oxford and, 7, 28–29, 38–40, 43, 60, 68, 75, 111, 117, 203, 224–26; popularity of, 2–3, 12, 25–26, 42, 50–51, 75–76, 101–2, 169, 172–74; prostitution and, 100–111, 142–50, 247n10; relation to Calvinism, 21–24, 30, 48, 201; represented in farce, 2, 110, 134, 140–41, 144, 149–50, 159, 164, 172, 222; riots, 90, 97–98, 245n17, 246n23, 256n17; Roman Catholicism and, 112; same-sex desire and, 71–75, 81–83, 88, 96; self-improvement and, 2–3, 18, 23, 68; sermons, 10, 31, 62–63, 84, 100–101, 139, 154, 167; spiritual senses and, 7, 26, 36–37, 52–54, 110, 133; taste and, 60–61, 118, 180, 200, 203, 225; theaters and, 31–32, 56, 60–62, 98, 130–45, 150–53, 160–72, 181–89; Wesleyan, 17, 20, 24, 27, 32, 59, 105, 111, 118, 178, 214, 232; women and, 7–8, 16–18, 45–48, 53, 57, 73–87, 106, 116–19, 123, 139, 159, 180, 191, 214, 241n25, 243n20; work and, 17–23, 80, 104, 106, 206. *See also* enthusiasm; Moravians; Wesley, Charles; Wesley, John; Whitefield, George

Methodism Examined, 65, 211

Methodism Mocked, 35, 109, 244n22

miracles, 9, 42–43, 53, 64, 205

Mischief of Methodism, 228–29

modernity: belief within, 26–28; inspiration in, 60; Methodism as boundary of, 2–4, 28, 36; narratives of, 6, 11–17; "primitive" simplicity and, 42, 93; as secular, 16, 21–24

Modern Reformers, 18–19

Moravians, 46–48; as anti-modern, 205; at Bath, 209–13; Peter Bohler and, 55; confessional practices of, 81–83, 108; eroticism of, 100–102, 114–24, 127, 172, 190; hymns of, 181–84, 195–97. *See also* Hernnhuters; Lavington, George; Zinzendorf, Nicholaus

Mountebank, 92, 216, 232

Mudge, Bradford, 101, 246n3

novels: comic, 207–8, 221; epistolary, 63–64; Methodists and, 7, 23, 66, 83; pornographic, 100–103; rise of, 27

Nussbaum, Felicity, 6, 239n8

O'Brien, John, 141

O'Driscoll, Sally, 72–73, 96, 245n4

Oxford, 38–39, 41, 43, 52, 111, 117, 180, 196, 224, 226; Methodists, 40, 68, 203

Paul (saint), 58–59, 140, 224, 244n25

Paulson, Ronald, 112, 154, 156, 165, 167, 201, 246–49, 251–52

performance: Cock Lane ghost as, 159–60, 163–64; event, 169–70; harlequin, 139–41; hymns and, 173, 190, 198; Methodist preachers and, 56, 106, 130–34; modern self and, 29, 37; as overwhelming, 64–65, 132; performers, 32, 131–32, 141; in *The Spiritual Quixote*, 226; Whitefield and, 141–46; in writing, 68

Phantom, Fanny, 158–59, 162–63, 166, 170. *See also* apparition; Cock Lane ghost; ghosts

Pope, Alexander, 21, 189–90, 199; *Dunciad*, 61, 117, 172, 248n26

Progress of Methodism in Bristol, 48, 76, 78, 83, 251n29

puppets, 136, 163–64, 166

Purcell, Henry, 172, 181, 186, 188

Quakers, 29–30, 48, 115

queer, 10, 72–75, 91, 230; homosexuality, 73

Quixote, 33, 66, 182, 221, 225. *See also* Graves, Richard: *Spiritual Quixote*

Rack, Henry, 2, 35–36, 76, 117, 239n8, 251n26

Rambuss, Richard, 10, 172, 189

redemption: as economic metaphor, 21, 55; *Fanny Hill*, 127–29; in Methodist hymns, 177–78, 186, 196; prostitution and, 101–5; revelation and, 14, 16

religion: enthusiasm and, 77, 112, 151, 163, 220, 225, 230, 235; experimental, 3, 10, 28, 44, 51, 72, 77, 88, 238; modern, 23–24, 26; somatic experience and, 24, 26, 37, 46, 71, 77, 198; state, 51

Restoration, 29, 47, 129

Retort Upon Retort, 146, 148

Rich, John, 136, 139

Rich, Priscilla, 136, 139

Richardson, Samuel, 5, 34, 116; *Pamela*, 27, 35, 63–68, 81–84, 102, 109, 175–76; *Sir Charles Grandison*, 1, 221–22, 224

Rimius, Henry, 122–24, 243n17, 248n31, 249n33
rioters, 40, 98
Roach, Joseph, 132, 249n1
Rock, Dr., 90, 94–95
Rosenthal, Laura, 106, 247n11
Ruttenburg, Nancy, 137, 241n32, 249n4

Sabor, Peter, 111, 247n17
Saccamano, Neil, 63–64, 237, 240n17, 240n20, 244n32, 256n256
sacrament, 66, 125, 150, 153–56; sacramental language, 10, 199. *See also* communion; Eucharist; Lord's Supper
Salvaggio, Ruth, 7, 239n9
Scottish Enlightenment, 12, 110, 208, 216, 219–20. *See also* Enlightenment
Secker, Thomas: Archbishop of Canterbury, 144, 151–53, 174, 250n18, 251nn25–26
secularism, 6–16, 236–39; as distinct from secularization, 11–16, 23–26; Michael McKeon and, 23–24; as progress, 26–28; E. P. Thompson and, 22–23. *See also* Jakobsen, Janet; Taylor, Charles
self: boundaries of, 3, 6, 31, 35, 57, 60, 68, 88, 131–32, 173, 189–93, 208; definition of, 2–13; identity and, 11–13, 29–30; malleability of, 96; Methodism and, 26–33, 36–40, 51–59, 71–73, 77, 235–38; modern aesthetics and, 60, 68; sex as truth of, 101–3; sexual identity and, 71–73; subjectivity and, 12–13, 22, 197; theater and, 132
sex/gender system, 30, 72; homosexuality, 73. *See also* feminine; gender; queer; sexuality
sexuality, 2, 237; homosexuality, 73; in *Humphry Clinker*, 214; libertine, 114; and Methodism, 29–30, 70–75, 79–81, 89, 91–92, 96–99; sacramentalism and, 102–3, 107–10, 125–29. *See also* feminine; queer
Shenstone, William, 224
Shepherd, T. B., 2, 38, 186, 239n3, 249n8
Sheridan, Thomas, 143, 164, 250n22, 252n40
Shuter, Edward, 62, 143
"Sir Francis Dashwood at His Devotions," 112–13
skepticism, 2, 6, 11, 36, 106, 151, 158–59, 161, 224–25
Smith, Adam, 18, 110, 152, 207, 217

Smollett, Tobias, 2, 56, 223; *Adventures of an Atom*, 206; *Critical Review*, 205, 207, 218; and Richard Graves, 2, 203, 230–31; *Humphry Clinker*, 2, 28, 32, 38, 202–9, 211, 213–15, 228, 231; *Launcelot Greaves*, 204–6
Snead, Jennifer, 23, 27, 237, 241n32, 242n35, 256n6
sociability, 26, 33, 80, 216
Socrates, 5, 239n5
sodomy, 71, 75, 88–89; homosexuality, 73. *See also* queer
soul: feminine self and, 78–82; *Humphry Clinker* and, 212–13; in hymns, 191; materialism and, 169; *Memoirs of a Woman of Pleasure* and, 101–2, 120–22, 129; sensible, 49–52; sex and, 30; Whitefield and, 64, 88
Southey, Robert, 20, 22
spirit, 49–50, 52, 58, 95, 102, 116, 120, 126, 129, 132, 164, 167, 191, 205
Straub, Kristina, 248n26
sublime, 37, 67, 119, 162, 189, 252n39
Swift, Jonathan, 144–46
sympathy: culture of, 76; Fielding's, 97–98; materialist accounts of, 110, 121, 126; for Methodists, 151–52, 160, 174; Smollett and, 32, 206–8, 216, 219, 255n9

"Tar's Triumph," 90
Taylor, Charles, 5, 14, 26, 121, 239n7, 240n21
Temperley, Nicholas, 174–75, 184, 253nn5–7, 254n21
theology, eucharistic, 10–11, 125–26, 150, 166, 198. *See also* Eucharist; Methodism
Thompson, E. P., 17, 22, 240n19, 241nn30–31, 242n35, 244n25
tracts, 27–28, 36, 38, 53, 100, 103, 109, 218
Trumbach, Randolph, 101, 246n3
Turnbull, Gordon, 255n3

Valenze, Deborah, 15, 104, 240n19
Vaucanson, 166–67; duck, 166–69
vulnerability, 4, 12, 44–45, 110, 189–90

Wahrman, Dror, 12–14, 249n2
Wallace, Tara Ghoshal, 208, 255n9
Walpole, Horace, 4–5, 35, 43, 56, 85, 108, 111, 119–21, 136, 151, 158, 161, 200–201

Ward, Graham, 71, 92, 97, 172, 245n18
Watts, Isaac, 174–76, 179, 193–95
Weber, Max, 17–18, 20–22, 24, 244n25
Weinbrot, Howard, 180, 242n35, 253n10
Wesley, Charles: Anglicanism of, 35, 101, 234; Covent Garden, 136, 185; early Methodism and, 1, 39, 76; *Hymns and Sacred Poems*, 12, 189–99; hymns of, 10, 12, 125, 171–74, 182–99; Moravians, 197–99; at Oxford, 28, 75
Wesley, John: ambivalence about women preaching, 77–79; attractiveness of, 84, 115; Calvinism and, 17, 22–24; Church of England and, 5, 35, 51, 101, 225; early Methodism and, 1–3, 28–30, 34–46, 75; *Earnest Appeal to Men of Reason and Religion*, 54, 61; hymnals of, 178–81; interpretation of Locke, 36–38, 51–58, 77, 128–29; journals of, 46, 49, 63, 120, 122; on laughter, 116; on marriage, 80–81; on masturbation, 89–90; medicine and, 92–95, 215; Moravians, 46–48, 55–56, 115; music and, 171–73, 176–82; mysticism of, 2–3, 32, 44–46, 53–55, 158, 161; at Oxford, 28, 38–43, 60, 68, 75, 111, 117; in pictorial satire, 109, 139, 165, 178–79, 228; politics of, 43, 50, 233; preaching of, 31, 52–53, 76–77, 132–34; *Primitive Physic*, 42, 92–93, 178, 215, 242n9; on prostitution, 103–6, 128; as publishing phenomenon, 36, 61, 67, 84, 100, 218–19, 233; as "reasonable enthusiast," 6–7, 35–36, 49–50; on slavery, 207; somatic theology of, 7–9, 25–27, 60–67, 71, 110–11, 208; suspected of self-flagellation, 111, 117–18; vegetarianism of, 207, 255n7; Weber on, 17–21; Whitefield and, 21–22, 58–61; works of, 21, 25, 28, 31, 34–35, 39, 41–46, 50–57, 76, 80, 115, 117, 180, 196, 201, 205, 244n28, 245n12. *See also* Christianity: primitive; Methodism; Moravians; religion: experimental; Zinzendorf, Nicholaus
Wesley, Susanna, 21, 52, 77–78, 243n16, 243n20
Wetmore, Colin, 208, 255n9
Wheeler, Sondra, 21
Whitefield, George: as a quack doctor, 94–96; Calvinism of, 21; "Christ the Best Husband," 105, 117–22; death of, 201, 232; enthusiasm of, 58–59, 151–54; improvisational style of, 22, 62–63; marriage metaphors, 116–17; Methodist Connexion of, 17, 48–49, 201–2; at Oxford, 28; Paul and, 58–59, 140; poverty of, 88, 226; sermons of, 8–10, 59–65, 74–75, 248; sexualization of, 83–91, 101–3; *A Short Account of God's Dealings*, 63, 74, 76, 83–85, 87–91, 122, 245; as Squintum, 109, 130, 141–43, 146, 148–49; Tabernacle of, 56, 106, 110, 135, 139, 151–54, 173, 182, 213, 249n6; theatricality of, 59, 62–63, 130–50, 165–69
Whitefield Preaching at Leeds, 137–38
Wilkes, John, 18, 112–14, 116, 120, 144, 241n27, 250n17
Wilkinson, Tate, 135–36, 142–43, 250n13
Williams, Carolyn, 118–19
witches, 54, 153, 165, 205, 250n14
women, 7–8, 16, 76–80, 82–83, 85, 87–90, 100, 105–9, 111–12, 119, 123–24, 159, 180, 214. *See also* feminine; gender; Methodism: women and

Zinzendorf, Nicholaus, 46–47, 61, 117, 121–23, 248n32. *See also* Herrnhuters; Moravians
Žižek, Slavoj, 148, 196, 236